D1568886

Masha Greenbaum

THE JEWS
OF LITHUANIA

A HISTORY OF A REMARKABLE COMMUNITY
1316 · 1945

gefen גפן
publishing house בית הוצאה לאור
JERUSALEM ◆ NEW YORK

www.israelbooks.com

Copyright © Masha Greenbaum
Jerusalem 1995/5755

Cover Photos: Oil paintings by Samuel Wodnitzky.

Typesetting: Marzel A.S. - Jerusalem

Cover Design: Rachel Amir

ISBN 965 229 132 3

Edition   19 18 17 16 15 14 13 12 11 10

Gefen Publishing House, Ltd.   Gefen Books
6 Hatzvi St.   600 Broadway
Jerusalem 94386, Israel   Lynbrook, NY 11563, USA
972-2-538-0247   516-593-1234
orders@gefenpublishing.com   orders@gefenpublishing.com

www.israelbooks.com

Printed in Israel   *Send for our free catalogue*

Contents

PREFACE

This work is dedicated to the memory of over two hundred and twenty thousand Lithuanian Jews, men, women and children who perished at the hands of the Nazis and their Lithuanian collaborators; among them my father, Sholem Halevi Ralsky, my grandmother, Ethel Tartak Flink and numerous other members of my family.

May this book serve as a source of inspiration to all Lithuanian Jews and their descendants – including my own grandchildren, Shiri, Danishai, Jonathan, Nava, David, Yitzchak, Sima, Nili, Tova, Judith and Daniella – for the further study of their proud heritage.

I wish to express my deep gratitude to my husband Avraham, without whose encouragement, help and advice this book would never have been written.

A special word of thanks is also due to my editor, Naftali Greenwood.

MASHA GREENBAUM

GRAND DUCHÉ
DE LITHUANIE
divisé par Palatinats.
Par le Sr Robert de Vaugondy
Fils de Mr Robert Géog. du Roi
avec Privilège.
1749.

ROYAUME DE PRUSSE

POLOGNE

HAUTE

RUSSIE POLONOISE

Chapter 1

THE POLITICAL CULTURE TAKES SHAPE

Migrations and Monarchies in a Distant Diaspora

Lithuania, a wedge of land in the northeast of Europe on the crossroads between Russia and the western section of the continent, is bound by Latvia in the north, White Russia (Belorussia, today Belarus) in the east, Poland in the south, and Germany and the Baltic Sea in the west. Together with its sister states, Latvia and Estonia to the north, it forms part of the geographic region known as the Baltic.

Between Prussia and Livonia, a former province of Russia now divided between Latvia and Estonia, is the cradle of the Lithuanian people, with its rivers, the Nemunas and Neris-Vilija, its many mountains, and its forests and swamps, bordering on the Baltic Sea. The earliest known use of the name "Lithuania propria" for this province was in 1009 C.E.; sixteenth-century Polish historian John Dluzgosz quotes the German "Annales Quedlinburgenses" of that year as using this term and noting the local inhabitants' prowess in agriculture and "amber, wax, flax, honey, salt, [and] fish."

The Lithuanian language is a pleasant and valuable anomaly in the linguistic world. The Eastern Balts spoke an ancient version of Lithuanian, which can be traced to the tongue spoken today. Philologists consider Lithuanian one of the oldest living languages in the world and the one most akin in substance and spirit to Sanskrit. Indeed, a nineteenth-century

1

Lithuanian traveler named Poskevicius[1] claimed to have found in India an isolated tribe that spoke a language similar to Old Lithuanian. The Lithuanian tongue also contains enough Latin to fascinate etymologists.[2]

The Lithuanians are Balts, one of several nations bearing that name, including the Prussians. Their forebears were Eastern Indo-European and Prussian tribal peoples that gradually merged into nations. In their earliest chronicles, the Lithuanians were called Samogitians (Zemaitija) or Aistians. Cornelius Tacitus (50-120 C.E.) referred to the inhabitants of Lithuania by the latter name and lauded their agricultural and other skills (livestock, wax, furs, salt, etc.).[3]

Recorded history had little to say about Lithuania until the ninth century C.E., when one begins to encounter the region in conventional historiography, i.e., chronicles of war. Lithuania's enemies were two. To its east were the Slavs of Russ' (later Muskovy), who launched military expeditions against their Aistian neighbors from the ninth century on. To its west, on the German border, were the knights of the Teutonic Order, who warred with the Aistians and other pagan tribes for the ostensible purpose of converting these heathens to Christianity. Their real goals were booty, land, and prisoners – and, incidentally, religion.

Politically united under its dukes, nobles, and landowners, Lithuania developed as an agrarian country, as Tacitus noted, and has remained one, predominantly, to this day.

The First Jews in Lithuania

How and why Jews first reached Lithuania is a matter of informed hypothesis. Historian Abraham Elijahu Harkavi maintains that they came from Babylonia and elsewhere in the Near East in the ninth and tenth centuries C.E., after the decline of the Jewish communities there. Harkavi also believes that Jews reached Lithuania from the shortlived but flourishing Jewish state of the Khazars, who were among the founders of Kiev in 865. The Khazars lost their kingdom in 969[4] to the Russian princes, who introduced the Russian Orthodox Church, a denomination influenced by the Christianity of Byzantium, and a faith to which they had recently converted. Thus inspired, the Russians expelled the Jews (and the Karaites – see below), who moved en masse to the then-Lithuanian towns of Gardinas (Grodno), Minsk, Pinsk, and other fortress cities. Other Jews reached the country by diverse means – as individuals, in groups of merchants, and as prisoners-of-war in the ongoing conflicts between the Russian Slavs, the Tartars, and the Aistian-Lithuanian tribes.

Since the Lithuanian tribes fought among each other as well, the Jews found a country that had disintegrated into a collection of large estates entrusted to dukes and other nobles. The Royal Court and the government were unable to meet the new needs of these estates and left the untitled populace defenseless. The result was feudalism. The most important aspect of this system with respect to the Jews was its rigid class structure. The untitled included weak freemen, serfs, and small landowners, all born into their respective stations, all destined to remain there. At the bottom of the hierarchy was the serf – one step removed from slavery, the property of a lord, to whom he paid tribute and owed allegiance, from whom he received a minimum of protection and tolerated abuse up to legal limits. This was the modality of life in most of Europe through the Middle Ages, with variations among countries and noblemen.

Unlike most Lithuanians, who, irrespective of tribal affiliation, were serfs bound to the ducal estates, the newly arrived Jews belonged to a class of their own: the international merchant class. The emerging powerful rulers of Lithuania – nobles, lords, magnates[5] – warmly welcomed them, viewing them as a positive element that would colonize, build, and organize the country.

Thus, at a time when much of Europe seethed with anti-Jewish hostility, Lithuania endowed the nascent Jewish population with special privileges. They were given the status of *Servi Camarae Regis*, servants of the Royal Chamber, a special status offered only to Jews in those provinces of Medieval Christendom that favored them. It implied royal protection, allegiance to the king, and payment of taxes directly to the royal treasury. Thus it enabled Jewish communities to develop without the fetters of feudalism.

By the early thirteenth century, fragmented Lithuania had formed a governing body of sorts and entered into a treaty with neighboring Wolhynia. The Wolhynia Chronicle (1219 and thereafter) mentions 20 Lithuanian dukes who participated in the arrangement at this time; in later years we find 48-50 "magnates" signing peace and economic treaties with other countries. Since these generations coincide with the formative phases both of modern Lithuania and of Lithuanian Jewry, the story of the latter is told below with reference to the former.

The "Begats" of Lithuania and Lithuanian Jewry

Mindaugas

The most prominent of the 20 dukes mentioned in the Wolhynia Chronicle was **Mindaugas**. According to the Chronicle, Mindaugas eliminated or expelled his more ambitious relatives, united the Lithuanian tribes, and became the sole ruler-king of Lithuania in 1236. Mindaugas and his wife Martha, together with a large group of nobles, accepted Christianity and were converted by Pope Innocent IV, but later reverted to the paganism that had prevailed theretofore after the pagans defeated the Teutonic knights in the Battle of Shiauliai in 1260. (Hostilities with the Teutonic knights, and Lithuanian oscillation between paganism and Christianity, would persist for another 200 years.) The Jews, despite their status in the royal structure, are not known to have played a role in these developments.

Gediminas (1316-1341)

If Mindaugas was the unifier of Lithuania, the empire builder of the country was **King Gediminas**. It was a considerable empire, especially in view of the modest Lithuania of the present time: it included Belorussia (White Russia) and parts of the Ukraine, and it stretched from the Baltic Sea to the Black Sea.

Narbutt and Bialinsky mention the presence of organized Jewish communities in various parts of Lithuania by the middle of the fourteenth century[6]. Some historians even trace the history of the Jews in Lithuania to the reign of Gediminas, dismissing hypotheses of an earlier Jewish presence. Lithuanian historian Yanulaitis[7] explains that at this time, "Jews from Germany and France came to Lithuania fleeing the Crusades, blood libels, and other false accusations[8]". For almost 200 years, Jews had refrained from settling in the German-Lithuanian border zone because of the war between the Lithuanian and Germanic tribes, the latter with the eternal need for *Drang nach Osten* ("land and loot").

A salient feature of Gediminas's rule was his dialogue with Christendom. The Lithuanian king corresponded with Pope John XXII (by the initiative of Rome), the Archbishop of Riga, the Dominicans and Franciscans of Saxony, and the Hanseatic League (a defense alliance of German towns and cities). In his inquiries, Gediminas expressed an interest in Christianizing Lithuania but complained about the Teutonic knights, accusing them of wishing to occupy his country and obstruct his communication with the West. In one letter, stressing his religious tolerance and his belief in freedom of worship, he noted that a cathedral had already been built in Vilnius (by merchants, artisans, and colonists who helped Gediminas expand the country, and by Catholic missionaries who operated in Lithuania under terms of freedom of worship).

Again, however, Gediminas is best known as the empire builder of Lithuania. From Vilnius, where he had established his capital after moving from nearby Troki in 1323, he enlarged the country through expeditions to the south, the north, and the east, and through marriage arrangements with Polish and Russian-Slavic princes, mostly involving the sons of kings. Like other conquerors, he solicited foreign assistance and found it readily available. Thus an influx of German migrants – Jews and others – colonized, cultivated, populated and, in essence, economically controlled the vast territories of his newly enlarged kingdom.

Gediminas then extended an open invitation to all peoples to come and settle in his land, luring them with privileges such as tax exemptions, freedom of worship, and religious tolerance. He urged artisans, merchants, and traders to ply their vocations throughout Lithuania. To tillers of the soil, he promised land. Jews, Karaites, Russians, Tartars, and Germans heeded his call, among them merchants and burghers from the border cities. Jews from the Near East (Babylonia, Persia, Bukhara, etc.) moved up through southern Russia and joined those from Germany. Soon there were organized Jewish communities in many important towns, such as Brisk, Gardinas, Lutzk, Troki, Kaunas-Wilijampole, and Vilnius.[9]

Jews in Lithuania enjoyed a considerable degree of official religious tolerance and goodwill. They were spared the devastation and upheaval wrought by the Crusaders upon their counterparts elsewhere in Europe, and were not blamed for the Black Plagues of 1348 and 1350. Their good treatment may have been due to the fact that the Lithuanians were still pagans and, as such, were uninfluenced by their western Christian neighbors. In fact, Lithuania was the last European country to embrace Christianity, rejecting the faith until the late fourteenth or early fifteenth century. This story follows.

Wladislaw II – Yagiello (1377-1392)

The new faith swept the country as a result of the marriage in 1386 of Gediminas' grandson, Yagiello, to Princess Hedwig-Yadviga[10] of Poland and Hungary. The newlywed king, now Wladislaw II, adopted his wife's faith and introduced it to his people. Shortly afterwards, the influence of the fanatical Catholic clergy that controlled Poland at the time began to infiltrate the Lithuanian milieu.

Yadviga's entourage promoted the religious development of Poland and Lithuania. She tried to unite the Occidental and Oriental Churches, reorganizing and enlarging the theological faculty of the University of Cracow. She also promoted missionary activities. Yadviga set up a special college for young Lithuanians at the University of Prague. The Church schism of 1378 had no effect on Catholic activity in Poland and Lithuania. The Poles recognized Pope Urban VI, who godfathered the conversion of the new king and his people. Yadviga introduced Polish governing, educational, and religious institutions in Lithuania. The Polish-Lithuanian union immensely enlarged the Corona Regni Poloniae with Lithuania and border towns. As if to symbolize the "Polandization" of Lithuania, the couple settled in Cracow. The Polish domination of Lithuania – the larger but less populous country of the union – was under way. Just the same, Lithuania maintained its identity, its populace constantly resisting Polish ways and opposing the union itself.

The Polish-Lithuanian union inevitably caused Jewish life and status in Lithuania to change. In the formal, legal, and social spheres, the basic concepts of servi-camerae prevailed. However, the Lithuanian Jews lost the privileges they had enjoyed under Gediminas and suffered much the same intolerance as did their brethren in other lands. Here too, however, Lithuania remained distinct, accepting the Polish Church laws but interpreting and applying them differently.

Vytautas the Great (1392-1430)

Yagiello's plan to rule Lithuania from Poland was unrealistic, even though the Lithuanians were granted a charter that assured them various liberties, freedom, and autonomy. In 1392, a pact known as the Treaty of Ostrow reconfirmed all these guarantees. The Lithuanians, however, rejected this accord as inadequate. In 1401, Yagiello's cousin, Prince Vytautas, who maintained his castle near Kaunas, took action to secure Lithuanian autonomy and equality once and for all. He demanded and received an iron-clad legal guarantee. This was the so-called Union Treaty, signed in Vilnius. The principles of the union remained unchanged: Lithuania was to have a Grand Duke who would function with the consent of representatives of both countries. Henceforth, the two states would interrelate under terms of political alliance. As for Vytautas, the former Prince became Grand Duke (alternately, King) of the Grand Duchy of Lithuania. His first action was to declare Lithuanian autonomy permanent, for which he was called (first by his countrymen, subsequently by historians) Vytautas the Great. Vytautas the Great chose the city of Lutzk as his capital,[11] and reigned there until his death in 1430.[12]

The reign of Vytautas witnessed the advent of a new and interesting player in the saga of Lithuanian Jewry: the Karaites. This breakaway Jewish sect, founded in Babylonia at the beginning of the eighth century CE, is distinguished mainly for its acceptance of Scripture (Heb. *miqra*, hence the sect's name) as the sole source of religious law, to the exclusion of rabbinical tradition. Having rejected the Rabbanites, as they called the Jews, the Karaites developed a non-Biblical oral code of their own, the *sevel ha-yerusha* or Yoke of Inheritance.[13] Although their vernacular was Tartar, they continued to study Bible and the Hebrew language intensively. In the Middle Ages, they also retained their distinctive dress and culinary habits, which originated in the Middle East, Byzantium, Turkey, and the Crimea.

According to Karaite tradition, Vytautas brought a large contingent of Tartar prisoners to Lithuania, including a number of Karaite families, after defeating the Tartars in 1392. Tradition aside, Vytautas is known to have settled Tartars, Jews, and Karaites in Vilnius that year. The first Karaite communities coalesced in Troki or Trakai (near Vilnius), Lutzk, and Halicz; the sect later branched to other Lithuanian towns including Panevezys, Birz, and Suwalk. Vytautas called the Karaites, Judaei Troceuses, "Jews of Troki," and most Lithuanian documents referred to them as Jews. The Karaites, for their part, regarded themselves as nothing of the sort, and insisted on receiving their own charters from Vytautas and subsequent Lithuanian monarchs. The first document, based on the Magdeburg rights, was issued in 1441.

Thus the Jewish and Karaite communities of Lithuania developed side-by-side. In Vilnius, a "Jewish neighborhood" took shape in the vicinity of Lukishky Square. The Karaites numbered 483 families including 330 in

Troki, which became the Karaite spiritual center for communities from
Poland to the Crimea. Religious differences aside, the Karaites dwelled in
relative harmony with the "Rabbanites" for centuries; they even shared
several of their religious facilities, such as the *shohet* (ritual slaughterer),
special foods, certain religious books, and yeshivot. Accordingly, their history
is part of this narrative.

Seeking to create a middle class, Vytautas preferred Jews over the Polish
and German minorities within his kingdom. He felt comfortable with them,
and he considered them politically trustworthy. He gave them political, social,
and civil rights, and even intervened on their behalf so they might travel for
business purposes to otherwise forbidden areas, e.g., Danzig and Moscow.

Vytautas' court received many visitors from afar. One of them was
Ghillebert de Lannoy, an emissary of King Henry V of France, who visited
Lithuania in 1414 and commented on the multinational character of the
country. He wrote that in Troki, near Vilnius, he had encountered Germans,
Lithuanians, and a large number of Jews, who spoke Yiddish and a Tartar
dialect. Members of all the other nationalities spoke their own languages:
Russian, Polish, Swedish, Belorussian.

Vytautas officially endorsed the existence of the Jewish communities in
the Grand Duchy on June 24, 1388, when he granted a charter to the Jews of
Troki and Brisk, and a year later to the Jews of Grodno. His charter was based
on that given to the Jews in Poland by King Boleslav the Pious in 1264. This
charter spelled out the Jews' legal rights and provided opportunities for
economic progress. It exempted synagogues and Jewish cemeteries from
taxation and made provision for Jews' personal and religious security. It
assured freedom of transit and trade, to the extent of allowing Jews to mint
coins of the realm. Special regulations related to money-lending against
pledges of landed property. Whereas most Catholic countries denied Jews the
right to own land, Lithuania granted property rights by means of licenses
purchased from the Grand Ducal Council. Jews were allowed to trade in liquor
and peddle merchandise in the street, marketplace, and shops, like any
Christian citizen. They were empowered to deal in all commodities, including
bread and corn. They were permitted to work as artisans or craftsmen. They
could dwell wherever they wished. To safeguard Jewish businesses, the
charter stipulated that if a Christian was tardy in payment of interest to the
Jew, he would have to pay twice the sum due. Jews were absolved from having
to repay pledges on the Sabbath and Jewish festivals. They were exempt from

the jurisdiction and authority of the Church and the municipal courts of law, which were hostile to the Jews. They were placed under the protection of the king (grand duke) of Lithuania and, later, of the nobles.[14] By orders of the Pope, the Charter proscribed the blood libel.

The Charter contained an ordinance against false accusations: the testimony of a Christian against a Jew had to be corroborated by a Jewish witness. If a Christian injured a Jew, he would have to pay damages and medical expenses, as well as a fine to the State Treasury.[15] If a Christian killed a Jew, he faced penalties including confiscation by the State of all his property and possessions. For throwing stones at a synagogue, cemetery, house, or other Jewish-owned property, Christians were liable to fines. This last part of the Charter is most illuminating in view of the next 700 years of Jewish life in Europe.[16]

Russian historian Sergei Bershadsky summarized the importance of this document by asserting that "The Charter laid the foundations for a system of Jewish autonomy." Indeed, it formed the basis of the political, legal, economic, and social structure under which Jews dwelled in Lithuania between the fourteenth and the eighteenth centuries.[17]

Vytautas' reign was a golden era in the ongoing territorial tug-of-war. His armies checked an attempted Mongol invasion. His true claim to fame and popularity, however, was his victory over the Teutonic knights in the Battle of Tannenburg. This triumph marked the beginning of the decline of the Teutonic orders, which had caused the Lithuanian tribes so much suffering over the centuries. Vytautas' spoils included prisoners-of-war from the Crimea, among whom were Jews and Karaites who had lived among the Slavs. The Jewish captives were redeemed by Jews already settled in Lithuania; most remained and brought their families to organize new settlements in the large, sparsely populated country.

While Jewish sources shed little light on the origins of Lithuanian Jewry, Karaite tradition states that the first Karaite community in Lithuania was founded in Troki, where Karaites, Jews, and others lived side by side for many centuries. (There are Karaites in Troki to this day.) Like the Jews, they sent their sons to yeshivot in the south of France (e.g., that of Rabbenu Tam) and Constantinople-Istanbul in Turkey, in order to benefit from the erudition of renowned rabbis.

Lithuanian Jewry flourished under Vytautas as it never had before. Jewish migrants poured in from principalities near and far – Bohemia, Germany,

France, Spain, Italy, the Crimea – in search of trade possibilities or a convenient place to settle. Prosperity embraced them all. Vytautas' commitment to religious tolerance, pursuant to the tradition started by Gediminas, was not limited to the Jews. He granted the Hussites, a rebellious and persecuted German Christian sect, a haven in Lithuania. For this reason, the waning but still-vital Teutonic Order distrusted Lithuanian Christianity and considered Lithuania a pagan state at this time. Only in 1422, with the peace of Melno, did the Order give up militarism in favor of diplomacy. It was then, too, that a proper border was drawn between Lithuania and "Order" Germany; it lasted until 1914.

In its own progress toward maturity, Lithuania took one step forward and one step back in Vytautas' final years. *Gubernyas* (counties) were set up in Lithuania. One year before his death in 1430, Vytautas reconfirmed the Union with Poland. His death triggered a civil war – one side supporting the union with Poland, the other seeking its dissolution and the formation of a completely separate state.

Casimir the Great (1444-1492)

As Lithuania reeled under the effects of the civil strife, the rival parties agreed to appoint Prince Casimir, son of King Yagiello, as the grand duke. Casimir was all of 13 years old and knew nothing of the language and customs of the country. His religious mentor, Bishop Olesnicki, president of the regency council, was hostile toward all non-Catholics, including, of course, the Jews. However, after the death in battle of King Ladislas of Poland in 1444, the Poles themselves invited Casimir to become their king. This brought about a renewal of the union with the Grand Duchy of Lithuania, and Casimir was installed as the monarch of both countries. The new monarch settled in Cracow.

Casimir's first priority was the aggrandizement of the dynasty.[18] In 1453, over Bishop Olesnicki's objections,[19] Casimir reconfirmed Vytautas' Jewish charter: "We take the Jews under our protection, in our own interest and in the interest of the State, so they may feel safe." Also strongly opposed to his move was the Polish Church, which was influenced by the presence in Poland at the time of John of Capistrano, the "Scourge of the Jews." Capistrano blamed the Jews for the epidemic of 1464 as well as for defeats inflicted on Poland by the Russian army. Casimir was unable to withstand the pressure. Under coercion, he signed the Statute of Nieszawa, which nullified the Jews' privileges. "They are contrary to Divine Law and the law of the land," he explained.

Having signed the Statute of Nieszawa, the king promptly disregarded it by allowing Jews (local and recently arrived) to lease cultivated and uncultivated lands in Lithuania.[20] Casimir also allowed them to trade freely and awarded them a concession to collect tolls at the frontier and the city gates.[21] The king hired Jews as financiers, allowed them to be tax farmers, and appointed them as customs inspectors. They even acquired special privileges such as an exemption from taxes to the Crown and the community. Over time, a small number of Jews evolved into a rich and elitist group, sending their children abroad for study and imitating the nobility in their ways of life. The clergy, the burghers, and the petty nobility did not conceal their hostility and envy. Casimir responded by reconfirming all the rights and privileges that his predecessor had given the Jews and the Karaites.

The Jews spoke three languages at this time: Yiddish, Belorussian, and a Tartar dialect. While Kiev was the center of learning and culture for both Jews and Karaites, important Lithuanian Jewish centers began to take shape in Lutzk and Troki.

We now find the first mention of a Jewish personality in Lithuania: Rabbi Moishe Hagoleh ("The Exile") ben Jacob, son of Moishe of Kiev, born in Shadov in Zamut county in 1448, died in 1529. He prospered in Zamut; his family business was considered the wealthiest between "Spain and Zamut." He was also the first Jewish author and publisher in Lithuania, his works including Otsar Nehmad and Shoshan Sodot – Talmudic commentaries and topical ordinances for his time. Several notable Jews lived in Kaunas, including Daniel of Troki and his son Ze'ev, a tax farmer in the vicinity of the border towns; Moishe of Troki, a businessman; and Sadka-Saadia and Zadok, both of them tax farmers. Early Lithuanian Jewry was composed of Ashkenazi and Sephardi elements. Although the former was the dominant, the communities were not separate and no evidence of discord has come to light.

During Casimir's reign, the Council of Nobles, representing the growing landowner class, became prominent and vastly powerful. The nobles exploited to the hilt the authority that the absentee barons, who spent most of their time in the West or in Poland, had invested in them. One of the Council members, the Noble Jonas Gostautas of Vilnius and Troki, actually ruled the Grand Duchy of Lithuania in the name of the king, and his council was the de facto government of the country. The aims of this body were two: greater independence from the Polish Sejm (alternately: Diet), the country's gestational parliament, and retention of territories disputed between the Lithuanians and Poles.[22] The efflorescence of the landowners also reduced the peasant class to serfdom, despite Casimir's efforts to alleviate their suffering.

In the meantime, Casimir added much territory to the kingdom, thus acquiring new Jewish communities. He promoted the cause of centralization and was averse to meddling with or changing ancient laws. He favored Lithuania to the detriment of Poland and did not allow Poland to annex Lithuanian land, regarding this as both unjust and politically inexpedient. He allowed an influx of secular influences from Germany and Italy, even as enlisting the clergy into the service of the State. Casimir supported the gentry (the petty nobility, the army, and other groups) against the magnates; he was strong enough to clip the magnates' wings and criticize their incompetence when the occasion demanded it. He announced the first free elections for the Sejm in the important city of Piotrkow. Before the elections could take place, however, he died in Grodno in 1492, after 48 years on the throne, on his way to the Diet of Radom. The Jews of Poland and Lithuania greatly mourned his death.[23]

Alexander Yagiello, Supremus Dux of Lithuaniae (1492-1506)

Casimir was succeeded by two of his sons: John Albert as King of Poland and Alexander Yagiello as the Grand Duke of Lithuania. Both had been pupils of the Polish historian Jan Dluzgosz, known for his hatred of the Jews. Under Dluzgosz' influence, John reconfirmed the Statute of Nieszawa and placed Polish Jewry under the thumb of the Church. Alexander, like Casimir, disregarded the Statute. He was a man who enjoyed life, good food, and the company of women. He considered himself a humanist and was regarded as the first modern king of Lithuania to be influenced by Western culture and the Italian Renaissance.

Under Alexander, Lithuanian separatism from Poland gained momentum as the magnates and nobles attempted to limit monarchic authority. Yielding to their pressure, Alexander gave legal status to the Grand Ducal Council, whose membership was limited to bishops, princes (some titled, others related to the king), Lithuanian magnates, and high-ranking state officials. These acquired enormous political power, not to mention control of the national budget and exchequer. A similar de facto takeover occurred across the border in Poland, where Alexander's brother reigned.[24]

Lithuania came under grave external pressure at this time. Ivan III ("the Terrible"), King of Muscovy, declared war on the Grand Duchy, ostensibly for reasons of religious differences and mistreatment of adherents of the Russian Orthodox Church in Lithuania. Thirst for booty was a more convincing reason. Indeed, after annexing strips of Lithuanian land, Ivan accepted Alexander's entreaties – the Lithuanian Grand Duke hated war – and negotiated a peace treaty in 1494. To ensure a real and lasting peace, Alexander married Helena, Ivan's daughter, in February 1495, on the understanding that she would be free to practice her Russian Orthodox religion in Vilnius, and that she would be considered the wife of the king but not the queen of a Catholic country. Ivan, ever the expansionist, continued to attack Lithuania with short respites. His reasoning: as the noble defender of the true Church, he could hardly do less, despite the treaty and his daughter's marriage.

Meanwhile, Alexander was occupied with a second front against the Tartars, who invaded from the south under Khan Sheikh Ahmed and ravaged the Lithuanian countryside.

Upon the death of John Albert in 1501, the Diet in Piotrkow elevated Alexander to the Polish throne. The two countries drew closer together than ever before, this time with the approval of the Lithuanian magnates. New contracts were signed and stipulations made for a common defense. A common currency was introduced and a unified Diet established for both countries. Polish law was now the law of both lands. Again, Lithuania implemented these agreements selectively. However, Alexander surrounded himself with Polish advisors and officials, and for the first time Polish was spoken and written in the royal court and used in official correspondence in Vilnius.

Increasingly, Alexander fell under the influence of the Catholic Church and its priests. He appointed Cardinal Frederici as Regent for Lithuania, built Latin churches around the country, and proselytized for the Catholic rite even in the Ruthenian countries. Church officials, aided by Alexander's wife and local magnates, pressed for measures against the Jews. Unlike his predecessors, Alexander complied, expelling the Jews and the Karaites from Lithuania in April 1495, and confiscating their property. Historian Simon Dubnow lists three specific reasons for the expulsion:

—Catholic influence and pressure following the expulsion of the Jews from Spain in 1492 and Portugal in 1495;

—the influence of Alexander's wife, Princess Helena of Muscovy, daughter of Ivan III;

—the magnates' desire to be rid of their Jewish creditors.

Those who converted to Christianity were allowed to remain in Lithuania and retain their wealth. Several affluent Jewish families chose this option; one of the converts was Abraham, one of the Josephowitz brothers, who had received the title Baron-Hauptman of Kaunas and Smolensk and the further title of Noble of the Grand Duchy.[25]

Fifteenth-century Lithuania, however, was not a country that could afford to expel its financier and merchant class. Specifically, the Lithuanian nobility and the state exchequer, drained by the wars with Muscovy and Turkey, needed the Jews. In 1503, Alexander invited them (and the Karaites) to return, restored their property, ordered their debtors to repay their loans, and reinstated and reinforced all the privileges granted them by his father Casimir.

In Poland, he appointed Abraham Bohemas as Senior and Judge of all the Jews in Poland and Lithuania. In Lithuania itself, a new life dawned for both the urban and the rural communities. Many Jews relocated to riverside towns, where business was good. Quite a few Jews leased land; some became recognized tax farmers. The highest echelon of tax farmers was the *mitna-kontura*, i.e., those with autonomy vis-a-vis the central authorities; those of lesser status were called *mitniki*, "dependents." Jewish officials were stationed near city gates to collect entrance tolls; the term for them was *prikamarki*.

After much delay, Alexander incorporated the discarded Vytautas Jewish Charter into the Polish code of law. Officially, this was a radical change of attitude; practically, it was not. The Charter was confirmed and ratified at the Mielnik Union on October 25, 1500, by which time the king and the magnates were resigned to the inevitability of readmitting the expelled Lithuanian Jews. Legislation to this effect was already being prepared. (The Polish Jews, of course, had not been expelled.)

Alexander's wars against the Russians and the Tartars continued. The Lithuanian and Polish aristocracy and gentry forced him to accept further restrictions on his powers until, by the end of his reign, he was little more than a figurehead. Alexander became paralyzed and died heirless in 1506. In his last will and testament, he named his brother Sigismund (subsequently Sigismund I) as his successor, stressing the hereditary right of the descendants of Gediminas to the throne of the Grand Duchy of Lithuania.

Sigismund I (1506-1548)

King Sigismund I was well received by the Lithuanian-Polish Sejm (alternately: Diet), which promptly endorsed his coronation. This reaffirmed the Polish-Lithuanian alliance and gave it a new lease on life.

The reign of Sigismund I began with an influx of Jews from all over Europe, especially Spain, Portugal, Bohemia-Moravia, and Germany. The burghers of Vilnius, fearful of the economic competition, petitioned Sigismund for a special anti-Jewish charter. Although considered a liberal ruler, the Grand Duke acceded to their request in 1528. The ensuing charter, *De non tolerandis Judaeis*, barred Jews from residence and trade in Vilnius. (The ban was subsequently extended to Kaunas.) In that very year, however, Sigismund appointed Joshua Paskowitz, a Jew, as collector of taxes on wax and salt for the city of Vilnius. He also employed several Jews from Vilnius and Brisk as tax farmers.[26]

Sigismund I, like his predecessors, needed the Jews of his country for their capital, knowledge, and loyalty. For almost eight years, Sigismund I fought an ongoing war with Basil III of Muscovy, who, like him, professed to be the defender of the true faith and the country's Russian Orthodox population. Thus he appointed Jews to important economic positions. One example is Aaron Najumowitz, whom he awarded the wax and salt brokerage of Kaunas even though Jews were allowed to live only in nearby Wilijampole-Slobodka. Michael Rabikowitz was the supplier of various goods to the Court, and other Jewish brokers handled Lithuanian exports to Prussia. The Hebrew term for these brokers, *shama'im*, appears in Jewish, Polish and Lithuanian documents of the time.

The country and the Jewish communities coalesced in tandem. Gazetting of laws in the Grand Duchy began in 1510, when magnates of the Radziwill family established the first printing press in Lithuania.[27] One of the gazetted documents was a statement ratified by the Polish Sejm in 1529, reconfirming the special status and rights of the Jews. The Jews had their own courts, where *Doctores et Seniores Judaeorum* administered justice.[28] They also chose their spiritual leaders. There were, however, two known cases of government-appointed rabbis. The first took place in 1531 in Brisk, when

Mendel Frank was appointed chief rabbi and assistant to Michael Jozephowitz (or Josephowitz), one of the King's tax farmers. The second appointment, by Queen Bona in Grodno in 1549, involved a member of the rich and famous Yudowitz family. Although the Jewish community rejected both appointments, it was powerless to take remedial action.

The king's beneficence toward the Jews met with resistance from two quarters: the Sejm and the powerful local Church establishment, both influenced by the Inquisition. The parliament, meeting in Piotrkow in 1538, applied several Inquisition stipulations in Lithuania (Poland had begun to enforce them earlier). One denied Jews various privileges and barred them from positions and occupations that they had held for over a century. Another required Jews to wear special hats or a colored patch on their clothing. Sigismund, by contrast, continued to value Jews and Jewish out-converts for their loyalty. Since they had no political aspirations, he seemed to trust them more than his own people. The three Josephowitz brothers – the apostate Abraham, and two practicing Jews named Michael and Isaac – are a case in point. Sigismund appointed Abraham to the position of *lazensky podskarbi* (finance minister) of the Duchy of Lithuania. Michael became Court Banker and Master and Judge of all the Jewish Communities. In 1514, the king gave Michael Josephowitz the title of baron for life at a ceremony in Cracow; never had a Jew who had not converted to Christianity been so honored in the Commonwealth. The third brother, Isaac, ran the family enterprise, composed of inns, fish ponds, salt mines, and real estate. When the partnership was dissolved after forty• years, the brothers' declared assets included gold, precious stones, jewelry, fish ponds, inns, houses, and large sums of money owed to their company.

The following ruling from the time is indicative of the Jews' station in Lithuanian society and law: the murderer of a burgher was required to remit 12 *shoks* to the exchequer; the murderer of a nobleman or a Jew carried a fine of 100 *shoks*.[29]

The situation of the Jews in Lithuania was superior to that of fellow Jews in Poland or any part of Western Europe. As the German Reformation consolidated, Jews came under attack from Luther and his followers and were subsequently expelled from various localities. In Spain and Portugal, city after city was scourged by the Inquisition, which saved backtracking conversos' souls by the *auto-de-fe*. Italy confined Jews first to certain cities and then to clearly defined, enclosed areas within these cities. Thus the country that fathered the Renaissance also gave birth to the term "ghetto."

It is no wonder, then, that the Jews in Lithuania – and even in Poland – felt safer and more secure than their brethren elsewhere in Europe, who, accordingly, continued to gravitate to the Baltic country.

Sigismund II Augustus (1548-1572) and the Union of Lublin

Sigismund I was succeeded by his son, Sigismund II Augustus. The new monarch had been groomed for the throne: co-regent in Lithuania together with his father since 1529, acting Grand Duke of Lithuania since 1544 (four years before his father's death), husband of Elizabeth of Habsburg until her death in 1546. He then married Barbara Radvila, sister of Lithuanian magnate Nicholas Radvila-Radziwill (alternately: Radziwil). His second marriage affected more than his domestic life: it subjected Sigismund II to the influence of the Lithuanian nobility and, especially, the powerful Radvila families. The Radvilas were Lithuanian patriots, distrustful of the Poles and the Polish-dominated Lithuanian church hierarchy. Thus, although Lithuania was officially Catholic, the new Grand Duke developed a strong commitment to freedom of worship. The major beneficiaries were Christian denominations that German immigrants had brought to Lithuania in the wake of the Reformation and Calvinism.[30] Coronated as King of Poland and Lithuania in Cracow in 1548, Sigismund II spent two years resisting the Polish Sejm's demand that he divorce his Lithuanian wife. Only in 1550 did the parliament accept Barbara as Queen of Poland and Lithuania. Parliamentary affairs aside, there was little love lost between the two peoples and their magnates.

Three factors shaped Lithuania, including its Jewish communities, under Sigismund Augustus: the ongoing hostilities with Muscovy; the Lithuania-Poland union known as the Union of Lublin, however unwillingly the Lithuanians accepted it; and the agrarian reform of 1557.

a. The Duchy of Moscow (Muscovy) had been encroaching on Polish and Lithuanian border principalities since the middle of the fifteenth century. In the middle of the sixteenth century, the increasingly powerful and ambitious Dukes of Moscow proclaimed themselves Czars of all the Russias and began to push toward the Baltic Sea. All of Lithuania was at risk; war was inevitable.

The czars (Ivan IV in the time of Sigismund Augustus) ostensibly pursued this conflict in defense of the Russian Orthodox Church and the

Orthodox minority in Lithuania. Lithuania obtained a truce in 1562 by promising the Orthodox Church greater freedoms; the respite held for only ten years, whereupon war broke out again.

Sigismund Augustus appealed to Poland for help. The Poles, although closely allied with Lithuania, were not sympathetic; considering the Lithuanian-Russian war an exclusively Lithuanian problem, they offered less help with each entreaty. Sweden and Denmark filled the breach sporadically. In 1571, Lithuania obtained another truce, this time ceding territories to Russia. The country was on its way to the modest contours for which it is known today.

b. In 1569, Lithuania and Poland agreed to merge under a common government and legislation. This arrangement, known as the Union of Lublin, would play a decisive role in the development of both countries and, no less, of the Jews of Lithuania. Lithuanian Jewry now became one of many national minorities within an expanded state. Each minority sought to defend rights and privileges that the separate countries had granted it. The German immigrants and the burghers had their Magdeburg Laws, which the Sejm had recognized and periodically reconfirmed. Together with the Polish petty nobility, as part of the *schlachta*, they had long fought to limit Jewish rights in commerce and restrict their admission to the artisan guilds. Their attitude was informed by two factors: socioeconomic and antisemitic. In the first respect, the decades preceding the Union of Lublin were noted for a shrinking economic pie. In the second respect, anti-Jewish actions were encouraged by the Church and reflected in the Sejm. Sometimes they spilled into the streets in what were called "little pogroms," often resulting in ritual-murder accusations. (The Karaites of Troki were exempt, having asserted their non-Jewish status.)

After the Union of Lublin, the petty nobility, including that of Poland, underwent a change of heart. The Jews were now recognized as important actors in the new economic system; they were hired as tax collectors and estate managers – privileges for which they would subsequently pay dearly.

c. In the meantime, Lithuanian feudalism had begun to crumble. In 1557, in need of new sources of revenue, Sigismund Augustus introduced land reform in the grand ducal estates – first in the western part of the country, then in the east. The land was surveyed and parcelled; insofar as magistrates and nobles were unable to provide documentary "evidence" of ownership, it was apportioned to peasant families. The new landowners were taxed for their farmsteads and ordered to render services to the Lord of the Manor. The next reform overhauled the management of the forests. As timber, tar, and other forest products were exported to England and Germany, the owners were taxed by the Crown. In 1567, two Jewish agents, Jacob b. Yugilo and Reuben b. Aaron, remitted such a tax on behalf of all the Jews in Lithuania. The same year appears on the oldest known document pertaining to the Jewish community of Memel-Klaipeda and its tax remittances; many Jews in this town were middlemen in business transactions between Germany and Lithuania. The artifact also mentions the date of their expulsion from Memel-Klaipeda by one Herzog Albrecht; not until 1643 were they allowed to return.

All told, however, it was a time of continued benevolence for the Jews of Lithuania. Sigismund Augustus employed Jewish physicians in his court and, in 1549, reconfirmed the Jewish Charter. Like his father, Sigismund II valued the Jews for their economic contribution. Unlike his father, he also regarded them as a permanent source of income, imposing a Jewish head-tax of one zloty per individual of any age or gender. (The community elders were in charge of collection.) Nevertheless, Jews were exempt from military service, and their community institutions were given new powers. The authority of the rabbinical courts (*batey din*, sing. *beyt din*) derived directly from the Crown. From 1551 onwards, Sigismund Augustus enlarged the activities and scope of the Kahal, the Jewish community council. Anxious to streamline tax collection, Sigismund's government outlawed the auctioning of official positions in the *Kahal* (e.g., rabbi, judge) and sponsored free elections in the councils so the Jews might select their own leaders. The king often sided with the Jews in business affairs and, in 1550, asked Czar Ivan IV to allow Lithuanian Jewish merchants to trade in Russia, a request that Ivan rejected. Jews moved freely between Poland and Lithuania on the basis of permits issued by the *kahal*.

Insofar as Jews relocated within the union, Lithuania was the preferred destination. In 1551, the families of Simon Doktorowitz and Israel b. Joseph moved from Cracow to Vilnius, where they opened five shops and engaged in moneychanging. In 1560 the Felix and Borodavka families, also of Cracow, secured a moneychanging concession for the whole of Vilnius. The first synagogue in Vilnius was built in 1573 by permission of the king; previously, Jews had prayed in private homes. The first Karaite synagogue was built in Troki three years later, by which time the breakaway sect also had a *Talmud Torah* (boys' religious school) and communal institutions including police.

The Polish Church and the parliament took issue with Sigismund Augustus' treatment of the Jews. The Church blamed the Jews (and other nonbelievers) for epidemics that struck Lithuania in 1550 and 1569-1571. In 1562 and 1565, anti-Jewish parties in the Sejm reconfirmed the 1539 Piotrkow restrictions. The king treated these measures with the benign neglect that we have encountered before. He rejected all accusations against the Jews and held ritual-murder charges in special contempt.

Sigismund Augustus' stature in Lithuania was such that the machinations of the Church had no effect on relations between Jewish and Gentile Lithuanians.[31] However, the Church, in concert with antisemitic members of the Sejm, continued to influence the Crown and society at large. In 1566, the Sejm enacted the so-called Second Statute of Lithuania, which expanded the anti-Jewish provisions of the First Statute instituted in Piotrkow in 1538. Among other prohibitions, Jews were not allowed to wear "Christian" clothing, ostentatious attire, or jewelry. Jews were forbidden to own Christian serfs or hire Christian servants. Again, Lithuania treated some of these strictures with disregard.

* * *

Sigismund Augustus, the last Yagiellonian of a 200-year dynasty, in essence a humanist, was characterized by tolerance far in advance of his time. He was a great collector of books, many of them printed in Poland. In his time, many Lithuanians, influenced by the Bible, made pilgrimages to Rome and Jerusalem. He toyed with the idea of a Lithuanian republic, as expounded by his friend John Zamoyski,[32] vice-chancellor of the University of Cracow and a renowned scholar. It would take the form of a Commonwealth which, although based upon ideals of liberty and equality, would be limited to the gentry, along the lines of a classical Greek city. The republic concept and humanistic individualism were integrated into the post-Lublin Polish constitution and made this document unique in modern Europe. However, Sigismund's republic was never implemented; nor was the concept expanded to include commoners, ordinary Polish citizens, and non-Catholic religious groups. Nevertheless, the minorities benefited from this constitution. With the ascendency of every new ruler, these groups had to wage their struggle for privileges anew. They were often helped by the nobles or the Crown itself. By virtue of their vital role in the massive overland trade that developed between the Ottoman Empire and Christian Europe, abetted by contacts with their brethren in the Ottoman Empire, the Jews assumed and retained a special position among the minorities of Lithuania. Their importance was such that the nobles protected them against the Church and the burghers – when this suited their needs and interests.

Henry of Valois (1573-1574)

Sigismund Augustus died childless and heirless in 1572, plunging the domestic and foreign affairs of Lithuania into anarchy. The Union of Lublin had not been consolidated and, in fact, was grossly unpopular in Lithuania. There was no recognized central authority. Civil war was imminent; it was averted only by the convening of a national assembly in Warsaw for the purpose of electing a king.

The monarch-designate was a pretender to the Polish-Lithuanian throne: Prince Henry of Valois, Duke of Anjou. Henry indeed ascended to the Polish throne in 1573. A fanatical Catholic who had taken part in the massacre of St. Bartholomew in Paris on August 23, 1572, he nevertheless granted complete religious liberty to all non-Catholic denominations shortly after coming to power in early 1573, and he proclaimed religious freedom throughout his domain at the Warsaw Confederation later that year. The Jews were emphatically included: on May 6, 1574, Henry of Valois reconfirmed the Jewish privileges of the Statute of 1529, as well as exclusive minting rights that Sigismund Augustus, in 1569, had conceded to Abraham Dlugatz, Isaac Baradovsky, David Lipman, and Joseph b. Salomon. Henry's liberalism had an ulterior motive: his struggle with Ivan the Terrible of Russia for the throne of Poland. He needed all the allies he could muster. Indeed, Henry was greatly helped in his struggle by Salomon Ashkenazi, a Turkish Jewish diplomat.

After ruling Poland-Lithuania for only 13 months, Henry of Valois, having decided that France and the French were more civilized than the provincial and primitive Poles and Lithuanians, fled the country to become King Henry III of France.

Stephen Istvan Bathory (1575-1586)

The next elected King of Poland-Lithuania was Prince Stephen Istvan Bathory of Transylvania, brother-in-law of Sigismund Augustus. Assuming the monarchy in 1575, Stephen, like his predecessor Henry of Valois, looked to the Jewish communities for help in his need to stabilize the country and solve its financial and economic problems.

Polish history considers Stephen Bathory one of the country's greatest kings in both foreign and domestic policy. He set eyes on the Danzig River area, aware of the importance of this watercourse in giving Poland access to the sea. In his successful campaigns against Muscovy, he captured the river area and cleansed the Baltic area of Russian forces and influence, a condition that lasted many years. Nevertheless, Stephen had a powerful local enemy: the Lithuanian gentry, which resented its exclusion from the election process. Convening its own Diet in Gardinas, the gentry protested Bathory's use of the title Grand Duke of Lithuania and presented the king with a *pacta convecta*[33] demanding that he return to the Lithuanian treasury all the estates that Sigismund Augustus had given to his sister Anne, Bathory's wife. The gentry also stipulated that the national Sejm convene alternately in Poland and Lithuania, instead of Warsaw only, and that all high-ranking positions in Lithuania be reserved for Lithuanians. Only after Stephen accepted all the terms did the Lithuanians endorse him as their Grand Duke.

Stephen was a reform-minded monarch by the standards of the time. He reformed the judicial system and upgraded the schools of Vilnius by summoning renowned Jesuit educators to the Lithuanian capital. Equally at home in Poland and the Ukraine, Stephen bestowed concessions and privileges on two of his most important minorities, the Ukrainian Cossacks and the Jews. In fact, the Jews came away more favored than ever. In his eagerness to promote Jewish merchants, he even curtailed the trading rights of some 30,000 Scots peddlers who were active in Poland and Lithuania.

Sigismund III (1587-1632)

Stephen Bathory died in Grodno in 1586 while preparing for a military expedition against Turkey. The Lithuanians mourned him greatly, since, although King of Poland as well as Lithuania, he had given them greater freedom within the Union than they had enjoyed theretofore. He had indeed served the Grand Duchy well, promoting Lithuanian agriculture and improving the peasants' circumstances. (By contrast, Europeans termed Poland "the peasants' hell.") It was Stephen Bathory, too, who had exposed Lithuania to the influence of Western culture.

With Stephen Bathory's death, a vague interregnum ensued. There exists a legend among the Jews that one Saul Wahl, an agent of Lithuanian Prince Radziwill, was elected King of Poland and Lithuania and that his reign lasted but one day. Be this as it may, Sigismund III, son of King John of Sweden and cousin of Sigismund II Augustus, became the first Vasa king of Poland in 1587. He was awarded the title of Grand Duke of Lithuania two years later, after he had acknowledged the Third Lithuanian Statute. He also accepted three Lithuanian conditions: (1) Livonia, together with those parts of Lithuania annexed by Poland at the Diet of Lublin, would be integrated into Lithuania proper; (2) the Diet would endorse and honor the truce between Lithuania and Muscovy; and (3) the Third Lithuanian Statute, revised by Vice Chancellor Leon Sapiega, would be accepted without modifications. This statute, which contained nothing of specific importance to the Jews, remained the basic Lithuanian code of law until 1840.

Stephen Bathory's legacy to Sigismund Vasa included the internal civil strife in Poland. John Zamoyski, then leader of the *schlachta* supported Sigismund III's candidacy for the throne, whereas Samuel Zborowski, head of the magnate class, supported Maximilian, a Habsburg. This was not unusual at the time; foreign powers often intervened to promote favored candidates in order to further their own interests.

The dispute between the magnates and the *schlachta* raged even during the new monarch's coronation. It was said that Zamoyski turned down a 200,000 ducat bribe from the Habsburgs to support Maximilian. Sigismund Vasa won the election but lost the fight, becoming increasingly dependent on the gentry's goodwill. Forced to accede to most of their demands, he whet their hunger for power, and their thirst for revenues. The Diet/Sejm fell victim to a self-inflicted paralytic illness known as the *Liberum veto*. Under the *Liberum veto*, incredibly, even one of the several hundred delegates to the Sejm, in either house, had the right to negate and revoke any parliamentary act by simply calling out "Veto!" New legislation was out of the question; parliamentary work stagnated. The magnates and the lower nobility defended this concept as the last resort of free men who wished to defend their freedom. It was, in fact, based on selfish class interest. Its abuse by the nobles, who used it to curtail the king's political, military, and financial power, led the country to disaster.

Sigismund Vasa moved his court from Cracow to Warsaw. In 1592, before he had succeeded in consolidating his court in that city, he learned of his father's death. This made him the King of Sweden as well as ruler of the Lithuanian-Polish Commonwealth.

Although born to a Protestant father in a Protestant country, Sigismund Vasa became a devout and loyal Catholic and, under his mother's influence, a disciple of the Jesuits — so much so that he eventually became known as King of the Jesuits. Totally committed to the Catholic cause, he introduced a new atmosphere of religious fanaticism and gave the Jesuits *carte blanche* to proselytize by means of sermons, processions, and prayer gatherings. It was a sign of the new spirit in the land that in May 1592, a mob led by Jesuit-inspired burghers attacked Jewish homes and property in Vilnius, including the synagogue. The culprits were found; the Lithuanian Supreme Court sentenced them to prison terms and 13,500 *shoks* in damages to the Jewish community. In the absence of any power capable of enforcing these decisions, however, the accused disregarded the verdict and eluded imprisonment. The jittery Jewish establishment petitioned the new king to reconfirm the Charter of the Jewish Communities of Lithuania. Their appeal had the backing of the Lithuanian nobles class, and it was accepted in 1593.

It was under these circumstances that Sigismund Vasa arrived in Protestant Sweden in 1592 to be crowned as its king. It took him two years to secure this status; he first had to promise unconditionally to uphold the decrees and principles of the Swedish Church as confirmed by the Upsala Resolution. His Swedish crown secure, he placed the Swedish administration in the hands of his uncle, Duke Charles IX, and returned to Cracow.

Turning his attention to Lithuania, Sigismund Vasa continued to abet the growing Jesuit influence. In 1596, with the support of Pope Clement VII, he created the Uniate Church for Greek and Russian Orthodox believers who were willing to acknowledge the supremacy of the Pope in Rome but wished to retain their Eastern ritual and Slavonic liturgy.[34] In 1600, he appointed Father Peter Skarga as the first Jesuit rector of the University of Vilnius and the official Court preacher. Throughout this period, Sigismund helped the Jesuits in their struggle to counteract the Renaissance and humanist ideas that prevailed in Poland and Lithuania at the time. He also furthered their efforts to punish heretics (above all the Jews), suppress Protestant denominations, and strengthen the Catholic Church in Lithuania, whose members still retained many old pagan customs.

In the meantime, Charles IX of Sweden – a proud Lutheran who considered his nephew's rule not only a conflict of interest but, especially, a conflict of conscience – gradually attained political power and had himself appointed the official regent of the country. This is not to imply that the war between Sweden and Poland that broke out in 1601 was purely a royal family feud. Vital interests were at stake: the Baltic coasts and their harbors were as important to Sweden as the Channel ports were to England.[35] Sweden also sought to secure markets for its copper and attract German capital for its trading ventures. The ensuing hostilities became known as the Thirty-Year War.

In his first battles with the Polish army, Charles IX was so successful that the Rikstag coronated him in Sigismund Vasa's place. Sigismund Vasa, defeated, retreated to Poland and regrouped. The next round, instigated by Sigismund in 1605, was fought not to fulfill Sigismund's pretensions to the Swedish throne but to protect the Lithuanian-Polish Commonwealth. Sigismund was victorious this time, earning the congratulations of the Pope, the Emperor of Austria, and even the Turkish Sultan.

On its eastern and western fronts, the Commonwealth had been recording victories against the Ottoman armies and the Teutonic Order, respectively, since the second half of the sixteenth century. This greatly expanded the territory ruled by Poland and Lithuania, including much of the fertile territory in the Ukraine and Belorussia.

Jews became active and valued partners of the nobility in the task of developing the new regions; they were even allowed, under certain conditions, to own some of the lands they developed. Both circumstances – partnership with the nobility and the novelty of land ownership – gave the Jews much pride. Many Jews still engaged in lending, tax-collection, peddling, and brokerage. Many others, however, were active in agriculture, crafts, and diverse trades such as dyeing, forestry and timber, livestock (horses and cattle), and, especially, import-export. They were considered specialists in economic administration, with emphasis on the aforementioned *arenda* system of leasing mills and taverns. They were granted brewing and distilling rights, and were allowed to purchase dairy concessions from manors and villages. Jewish communities spread across the newly settled countryside.

Despite their shared and complementary goals, it must not be inferred that the Jews had become the nobles' equals. They had become middlemen who carried out the orders of the magnates and the nobility vis-a-vis the Ukrainian peasantry. As such, they became buffers, for which, especially in the case of the highhanded Polish nobility, they eventually paid the price.

On their estates, the noblemen began to establish and develop new private townlets (*shtetlakh*, sing. *shtetl*). In the early seventeenth century, between 770 and 900 such townships were founded in the Grand Duchy. Jews are known to have constituted 20 percent of the urban population at that time.[36] They earned their livelihood in every way that the law and their privileges allowed them.

At this time, the country's political instabilities triggered another round of turmoil. In 1605, Sigismund Vasa, with the counsel of Father Skarga, persuaded the Sejm to modify the *Liberum veto* principle in order to increase his power at the expense of the gentry. When, as a result, revolt broke out in Poland in 1606, the Lithuanians joined the rebels in defense of their traditional liberties. (The Jewish community discreetly sided with the rebels but played no important role.) In their struggle to restrict the powers of the king, whom they regarded as an absolute monarch, they insisted that Sigismund Vasa sign a liberal contractual agreement – the *Pacta Convecta* – setting forth relations between, and the respective obligations of, the king-elect and society at large. (This arrangement was similar to the Italian *promessi* as constituted in Venice.)

It took until 1609, when a general amnesty for all the rebels was proclaimed, for the revolt to ebb. The weakened Crown had been shown that the gentry would not easily surrender the prerogatives and privileges that it had acquired in almost three centuries of organic evolution.[37]

Reasonably secure at home but still at odds with Sweden, Sigismund Vasa now tussled with Muscovy. The struggle began when Boris Godunov, brother-in-law of Czar Theodore, proclaimed himself ruler of Russia after Theodores' death. Sigismund Vasa, who had still not relinquished his claims to the Swedish throne, now evinced a sudden wish to become the new Czar and invaded Muscovy in 1616 for this purpose. In 1617, when it became apparent that his expedition had failed, the Commonwealth and Muscovy arranged a truce. The Tartars, in the southern extreme of the Commonwealth, exploited the war to loot, plunder, destroy, and take captives. Meanwhile, Sigismund engaged the Turks in strife, even though the Turkish army, under

Sultan Othman II, was well prepared to face the Polish and Lithuanian forces. Then Gustavus Adolphus, the champion of monolithic Lutheranism who ascended to the Swedish throne in 1628 after the death of Charles IX, attacked his cousin, Sigismund Vasa, in order to safeguard the Protestant character of Sweden.

The Commonwealth, now in turmoil on all fronts except the German (where business and other treaties maintained peace) went on a war economy. The armies were self-supporting as long as they did well, since the enormous cost of the wars was borne by "contributions" – cash, raw materials, and industrial and agricultural products – from the occupied areas. Now, however, in the face of military disaster and dissatisfaction within the Commonwealth itself, the system broke down. Sigismund, desperately short of cash, entreated the Jews for help through his business agents in Lithuania, the affluent Jewish brothers Eliezer and Samuel b. Moshe, originally from Frankfurt am Main, now of Vilnius. Indeed, the brothers helped arrange private and government loans.

Jesuit influence notwithstanding, the Jewish Charter Privilegium was again reaffirmed in 1629, almost as a *quid pro quo*. Jewish privileges actually expanded: Jews were now allowed to practice any trade without belonging to the exclusively Christian guilds. Jews could be summoned only to the Fortress or Royal Courts, thus circumventing the lower courts and their general anti-Jewish bias. The Jews were taxed as were the burghers but were exempt from any surtaxes by virtue of the poll tax to which they were liable.[38] Sigismund Vasa also allowed the Jews to enlarge their cemeteries, slaughterhouses, and bath-houses, and this, in turn, strengthened the communities internally.[39] Three years later, in May 1632, Sigismund issued an injunction forbidding violence against Jews and interference with their trading and crafts. He advised the burghers that in the event of any quarrels with the Jews, they should seek arbitration rather than burden the courts with litigation. In his formal endorsement of the Charter, the king showed partiality towards the Jews in all their dealings with him.

Sigismund Vasa still was unhappy with his limited powers as King of the Lithuanian-Polish Commonwealth. So, as if to flex his muscles, he marched on Sweden and Russia in 1631. These were the first campaigns in which Jews were prominent as royal financiers. Non-believers though the Jews were, the monarch considered them more trustworthy than his own magnates and nobles.

Wladislaw IV (1632-1648)

Wladislaw IV Vasa (alternately: Wladislaw), son of Sigismund III, was very popular while still a prince in Lithuania and Poland. Known to be interested in public opinion and the welfare of the people, he was unanimously elected King after his father's death by the Fourth Diet with the participation and approval of the Lithuanian representatives. Jewish delegations attended his coronation, at which time the Jewish Charters were reconfirmed.

Wladislaw IV labored to abate the country's religious tensions and upheld equality and freedom of worship for all denominations. In other respects, however, his reign was a turbulent period for the Commonwealth. It began with an invasion by Czar Michael, the first of the Romanovs, before the new king could consolidate his regime. Michael's goal was to seize long-coveted territories in the eastern and southeastern sections of the Commonwealth. A well-organized army of Poles and Lithuanians, under Lithuanian command, repelled the Russian troops in 1634 and forced the Czar to accept a truce under which Moscow had to pay an indemnity of 250,000 rubles. The truce lasted for about twenty years and was known, like its many successors, as "the everlasting peace."

Pleased with this success, Wladislaw was eager for further battle. His first gambit was an attempt to regain the Swedish throne. Before taking up arms, he proposed marriage to Maria Eleonora, widow of Gustavus Adolphus. The lady turned him down, and the Swedes dismissed his pretensions altogether. With this, Wladislaw declared war on Sweden in 1635. The Lithuanians supported him in this struggle; the Poles did not. In 1637, as his campaign limped on, the Danes surprised him with an attack that historian C. Barnett likens to Pearl Harbor. The Royal Court survived the blow.

The home front was restless, too. From the very beginning, Wladislaw Vasa had had difficulties with the Commonwealth Diet or Sejm (parliament) and Senate (governing body). The Diet, meeting two years in Warsaw, Lublin, Cracow, or Piotrkow, rejected most of his plans for advancement and progress simply by use of the sweeping veto power. As for religious affairs, Catholics and Protestants met in Thorn to resolve their differences but adjourned without results. The Uniate Church, founded by Wladislaw's father Sigismund Vasa to facilitate the Catholicization of the Cossacks, struggled with the Old Orthodox Church for hegemony in Lithuania.

Jewish Society Finds Its Slot

As noted, certain trades were reserved for the Jews by royal decree. Jews in Lithuania also dominated the occupation for which they were known throughout Medieval Europe: moneylending, or, to the critics, usury. They gravitated to this trade by circumstance: the Church forbade Christians to lend at interest,[40] and Medieval Europe desperately needed a banking system, albeit primitive. Thus, by virtue of expertise and responsible conduct, talented Jews turned the handling of money into an important source of livelihood that provided a much-needed service for all of society, especially the royal houses. They also developed barter trade with the estates and among the peasants and serfs.

The undeveloped Ukraine, for example, had no commerce or barter system. Even the large estates did not have managers. The nobility enticed Jews to act for them as administrators, bailiffs, and managers of their harvests, mills, distilleries, and inns. To increase their income, the petty nobility forced the peasants to buy and drink their beer, and this made the Jewish innkeepers responsible for the distribution and sale of this commodity. It was also the Jews' responsibility to collect money from the serfs and peasants after they had brought in the harvest and were about to enjoy their produce. Aware of the extent to which the nobility needed their skills, the Jews felt relatively safe and protected. In historical perspective, they were wrong.

The king himself greatly needed the services of the Jews. Accordingly, he reconfirmed their Charter in 1644 and empowered the Relazioni (Appeals) Court, composed of himself and his ministers, to protect Jews from all assailants, including the burghers and the clergy.[41] Wladislaw IV then enacted an ordinance (1644-1645) dealing with trade, work, domicile and taxation of the Jewish community. It gave them rights to deal on behalf of the nobles in skins, clothes, linen, furs, silver, gold, mead, flax, animal fat,[42] and spices.

Concurrently, Wladislaw IV restricted the Jews' rights in other areas. They were allowed to purchase cattle for their own needs only, although they were permitted to sell meat to all comers including Christians. They could sell alcoholic beverages to all Jews under any terms, but to Christians only wholesale and in the cities. When working for Christians, they were restricted to specialized trades for which no guilds existed, e.g., jewelry, fur, and glass; for fellow Jews they could perform any type of work. In Vilnius, the Jews succeeded in obtaining a special charter that spelled out further prerogatives in crafts, guilds, and small industry. In due course, they succeeded in extending these privileges to all of Lithuania.

Liberal or not, the new regulations also "ghettoized" the Jews, forbidding them to rent or buy houses outside their defined area of residence. The explanation given was that the ghetto would protect Jews from looting and attacks, especially by disciples of the Jesuits, who were not subject to municipal jurisdiction. Real-estate conflicts had to be adjudicated in a special land court. Jews had to pay a small municipality tax, which doubled in wartime. Wladislaw's ordinance, like similar documents, concluded by asking municipalities to protect the Jewish population.

Wladislaw was willing to expand the Jewish role further. Now that relations with Muscovy were favorable, he pursued business interests in Russia and wanted "his" Jews to represent him and actually appointed such an agent, one Aaron Markowitz. The Czar agreed to host any Polish or Lithuanian merchant but not a Jewish one; Russians, he explained, were not allowed to do business with Jews.

At this time, trouble was brewing in the Ukraine, which was then controlled by the Polish-Lithuanian Commonwealth. Both Wladislaw and the magnates in the Ukraine disregarded certain warning signals and allowed the ferment to erupt into violence, for which the Jews paid dearly.

The immediate perpetrators were the Ukrainian Cossacks, a subnationality that had been impoverished by high taxation and artificially low crop prices enforced by the Polish magnate oligopoly. Now populous enough to repel the magnates' exploitation, the Cossacks increasingly displayed their social and economic discontent. The big Polish landowners, mostly absentees and members of the nobility, responded by increasing taxes arbitrarily and instructing their Jewish tax-farmers to collect the revenue. Those unable to pay, for whatever reason, were reduced to a rank lower than serfdom, a state of virtual slavery. The moneys were invested, as it were, in the magnates' gambling habits and pursuit of luxury; none was used to improve the properties.

Thus, unable to pay for seeds and tools with which they might feed their families, the frustrated and angry Cossack and peasant farmers were accosted by Jewish tax collectors who, acting on behalf of an absentee landlord, confiscated a last cow, horse, or even chicken. Even though it was clear that the Jews were only the agents of the nobility, it was chiefly against them that the rising hatred of the Cossacks was directed. That the Jews practiced a different faith and were considered foreigners in the Ukraine merely fueled the emotions.[43]

It was Sigismund Augustus who had first created a Cossack armed force,[44] which became a regiment of the Lithuanian army during the wars of Sigismund III Vasa. The regiment was garrisoned in the southeast of the Ukraine and, when not engaged in battle on behalf of the king, subsisted on booty confiscated from communities of Turks, Tartars, Mongols, Poles, Jews, Russians, and others.

Between 1637 and 1640, their raids developed into ongoing revolts and insurrections. By the latter year they had been joined by the so-called Cossack serfs, who preferred to fight than to cultivate their estate land without reward, and by escaped peasants and miscellaneous adventurers. The Cossack hordes became so dangerous that the magnates and *boyars* had to deploy troops to defend their estates.

An especially fierce Cossack rebellion erupted in 1648 under *hetman* Bogdan Chmielnicki, who had succeeded in inciting the dissatisfied serfs and even the peaceful peasants. He organized the Ukrainians and the Tartars, who were only too willing to join the battle. Their main targets were the Jesuits, the Polish magnates, the nobility, and the Jewish communities. Whole villages and even cities were looted, torched, and leveled. Thus the Polish landowners and the Catholic churches and schools paid a heavy price for their high-handedness and the harsh feudal society that they had created in the steppes of the Ukraine.[45]

The Cossacks sustained their rebellion for almost two decades and carried it into Belorussia, Lithuania, and Poland. As they advanced, they acquired powerful allies. The Orthodox Churches of Alexandria, Constantinople, and Moscow gave Chmielnicki massive support. Tartar bands helped him gain and sustain sovereign power in the Ukraine. As the insurrectionists became more powerful, so did they become more aggressive, fomenting trouble and disorder wherever and whenever they appeared. The resulting orgy of carnage had few parallels in history at the time. The murder of Jews was *de rigeur.* In Nemirov (Podolia) alone, 6,000 Jewish men, women and children were murdered in June 1648. They were only the first victims of widespread slaughter. The monks who recorded the authentic and folk history of the period glorified such deeds and invested them with piety when they were coupled with looting of Jewish property.

For the Ukrainians, Chmielnicki was and remains a revered hero. A massive commemorative statue of the Liberator of the Ukraine stands in the center of Kiev, the country's capital, where the main square bears his name. For the Jews, as surely as mention of Vilna evokes memories of the Vilna Gaon, so does mention of Chmielnicki evoke recollections of pogroms and terror. Lost in the turmoil was Wladislaw Vasa. By the time the uprising marked its first anniversary, Wladislaw was dead and the Commonwealth, whose crown he had assumed on a tide of popularity, had embarked on the path of decline.

Wladislaw's Jewish Charters, ordinances, and miscellaneous rules and regulations provide evidence of his benevolence towards this national minority. In return, he expected the Jewish communities to help his economy by financing his armed forces, the general needs of the country, and his own private expenditures. They complied. Wladislaw fought many wars with various countries, some of his own choosing, most imposed upon him. Most damaging to his rule, and painful to him personally, was the internal strife within his own government. He died a broken man in the town of Merkine in Lithuania.

John Casimir (1648-1668)

Wladislaw's successor was John Casimir, the dead monarch's brother and the last of the Vasas to rule Poland and Lithuania. With respect to the Jewish community, the new monarch took initial actions reminiscent of those of his predecessors: he warned the municipalities not to harm Jewish tradesmen or workers and reconfirmed their Charter of 1633, permitting them to engage without interference in any activity other than that of the guilds.

A former Church Primate, John Casimir reached the Polish and Lithuanian throne from France in a most difficult period for the Commonwealth in general and the Jewish communities in particular.

Governance was weakened by interfactional intrigues and quarrels, rampant corruption, and, above all, poor leadership. The nobility sabotaged the work of the Sejm and the Senate by frivolously vetoing the decisions of over 40 biennial sessions. At a time when new burdens were to be assumed, the king was forced to surrender prerogatives. Taxation was heavier than ever. Were it not for this disarray, Chmielnicki would not have been able to invade Polish territory so successfully.

With the Cossack invasion of Poland, thousands of Jews sought refuge in Lithuania, where the Jewish communities welcomed them as brothers and sisters. Others fled to Central Europe and destinations as distant as Turkey, Egypt, and North Africa. Jewish communities mourned the victims, proclaiming days of fasting in their memory. The Council of the Lithuanian Jewish communities imposed a special tax to support and aid the refugees. For this purpose, council members often took loans, using their own homes as collateral.

In 1653, smelling blood, the Russian Army invaded Lithuania from the south and the Swedes moved in from the North. Vilnius was occupied in 1655 by combined Russian and Cossack forces and burned for 17 days. Throngs of Jews and Poles fled the city; many others were massacred. Plagues and epidemics savaged cities and villages.

The condition of Lithuanian Jewry at this time is described by Moises Rivkes, a member of the community who, together with his family and others, fled to Amsterdam:

> The whole of Lithuania is suffering from bands of Russians and Cossacks, who destroy cities and kill the people. Thus fell Polock, Vitebsk, and Minsk. In Vilnius, *Voivode* Christopher Radziwill II and his army, as well as many citizens, fled. The murderers looted the houses before burning them. Most of the Jews escaped, some by horse and cart. Others, carrying their children and Torah scrolls, walked for miles in search of shelter.

> I left my beautiful house, abandoned my inheritance, my books, my goods, and also my work on the [Talmudic] tractates *Zevahim* and *Menahot*. We went into exile, not knowing where to go, accompanied by the cries of the terrified refugees. We reached the German-Prussian border, where the Swedish army stripped us of the rest of our belongings. We boarded a ship and came to Amsterdam.

> There, the Sephardim and their scholars took pity on us and kindly gave us lodgings, food, and clothing. Some ships with refugees were sent off at their expense to Frankfurt and other communities. Everywhere, the Jewish communities received the refugees with kindness. I was invited to stay by Chief Rabbis Saul Halevi Morteira and Isaac Aboab, and their

philanthropists provided me with a comfortable home where I
might dwell.[46]

Rabbi Rivkes spent another six or seven years in Holland before returning to
Vilnius, where he died in 1671. Indeed, Lithuanian refugees continued to
return for several years, and records attest that a boat carrying Lithuanian
Jews from Holland sank in 1692. This is not to imply that their return was
uneventful or unimpeded. Czar Alexis Michaelowitz, commander-in-chief of
the united Russian and Cossack forces, excluded Jews from the occupied areas
until the Polish army liberated the area in 1661. At this point, both Polish and
Jewish refugees returned to their homes. For the first time ever, Jesuit priests
helped the Jewish communities reestablish themselves by tendering
considerable sums in back rent for the use of Jewish properties vacated during
the years of persecution. The king, too, helped the Jews rebuild their
communities after the war.

The Jews now faced a new rival: the increasingly powerful middle class,
whose power was exploited unreservedly for political pressure in cohorts with
local municipal authorities. The middle-class enmity was two-tiered. As
owners of small factories and shops, members of this class were in constant
competition with the Jews. As Christians, they never accepted the Jews as
equals and now became envious and resentful of successful Jewish
businessmen. They vented their hostility by spreading hatred and organizing
pogroms in order to eliminate their Jewish competitors, fanning religious
emotions as a pretext and a means to accomplish their aims. In 1663,
merchants and guilds predicted that if the Jews were granted special
privileges and renewal of their Charters, Lithuania would again suffer
"punishment from On High."

By 1665, Jews were under physical and political assault. In the latter
sense, the Royal Court was asked to exclude Jews from trade in meat, salt,
herring, hemp, and flax. In most instances, the court decided in favor of the
burghers and the guilds. The number of Jewish trading days was reduced, and
Jews were no longer allowed to deal in meat on Fridays and Ash Wednesday.
They were forced to tender the churches an annual "contribution" for the
privilege of using candles. In 1669, the Royal Court banned Jews from all trade
in fish and barred them from work as silversmiths, goldsmiths, tanners, and
manufacturers of bristles.[47]

After Chmielnicki's death in 1657, Czar Alexis of Russia annexed the Polish and Lithuanian territories that the Cossacks had occupied. Neither he nor the Poles, however, were able to control the Cossack bands, which rebelled at every turn. In 1667, the Governments of Russia and Poland-Lithuania signed a truce meant to bring the situation under control. The accord included a religious clause entrusting Czar Alexis with responsibility for all Orthodox Church adherents within the Commonwealth, now alternately termed a Republic. After the truce went into effect, Lithuania recovered the cities of Vilnius and Grodno, as well as the surrounding areas. The Cossacks, though repelled, remained as bellicose as ever within their own borders.

The war had caused rampant poverty and destruction. Over 400 Jewish localities had been destroyed and thousands of Jews had been killed, raped, or maimed. Forced conversion claimed many in Poland, Lithuania, and the Ukraine. Innumerable families were homeless. Local Jewish communities set up committees to help them, but the burden was too heavy for them. The Council of the Four Lands and the Council of Lithuania assumed responsibility for support of the victims of the destroyed communities. Again Jews went into debt to rescue their brethren – sometimes by borrowing from Christian clergy and churches.[48]

Shabbetai Zevi – The False Messiah

Just as the Jewish communities reached a nadir of despondence and despair, a ray of hope appeared. Letters bearing the glad tidings of imminent salvation began to arrive from Palestine, Salonika, and Izmir. A redeemer had arisen in Israel! His name was Shabbetai Zevi, and news about him and his message roared across the Diaspora, from Yemen to Lithuania. Simple Jews were swept away with excitement, enthusiasm, and hope. Many rabbis and scholars, initially skeptical, later joined the masses in their belief that the Messiah had come and would soon redeem the Children of Israel from all their suffering. Return to the Land of Israel, a better life, and a new and brighter future were imminent.

Many followers of the new Messiah packed their bags for the trip. Businesses and properties were sold; wealthy believers began to make arrangements to rent ships for the poor.

But skeptics remained, especially among the learned. Many expressed their doubts, others their disbelief. Writings began to appear against the new Messiah and his antinomian practices, strongly criticizing him and branding him a false prophet. In 1666, Shabbetai Zevi shattered the hopes and expectations of the Jewish masses by converting to Islam and resurfacing as Aziz Muhamed Effendi. The Sublime Porte rewarded him for his apostasy by giving him the honorary title *kapici-bashi* (Keeper of the Gate).[49]

The Jewish community was shattered. No few of Shabbetai Zevi's many followers went underground. Anti-Shabbetaean rabbis attacked and persecuted them, forcing the rank-and-file to face reality, return to strict adherence of traditional practice, and await the true Messiah. Still, there remained sizable groups of followers in many Jewish communities, including Lithuania. Among them were several well-known rabbis, who attempted to interpret and explain the false Messiah's antics in the light of novel Shabbetaean interpretations of Lurianic Kabbalah.

Some Jews even followed Shabbetai's teachings after his death, practicing Islam in public and a form of Judaism in secret. They were known as the *doenmeh* (strangers, outsiders), and remnants of this sect exist in Turkey to this day. Others preferred the opposite model: public profession of Judaism and secret adherence to Shabbetaeanism. Groups of this kind survived for more than 100 years after Shabbetai's death. To keep their beliefs surreptitious, they concealed the name of Shabbetai Zevi in their writings and amulets. If discovered or denounced as followers or sympathizers of the false Messiah, they were punished by the mainstream clergy and their families banished from their communities.

An exemplar of public Shabbataeanism in Lithuania was Jehoshua Heshel b. Joseph Hatsoref of Vilnius, author of *Sefer Hatsoref.* He joined the movement in 1666 and proclaimed Shabbetai Zevi as the Messiah, son of David. In fact, he was Shabbetai Zevi's spear carrier in Lithuania for 30 years. Hatsoref later moved to Cracow, where he had a number of followers. Another well-known Shabbetaean in Lithuania was Zadok of Grodno. Judah Hasid of Shidlov was suspected but never conclusively uncovered. He organized a "Holy Society of Judah Hasid," whose members journeyed to Palestine to await the Messiah there. On their way, they visited many Jewish communities to which they preached about the imminent coming of the Messiah, without mentioning Shabbetai Zevi by name.

King Michael Wisniowieski Korybut (1669-1673)

The general state of the Commonwealth and its Government was one of instability and indecisiveness. Fratricidal conflicts and dangerous civil wars nearly brought Poland to its knees; the Sejm in Warsaw repeatedly stepped in to enforce truces and make border adjustments. The last blow was struck by Grand Hetman George Lubomirski, who instigated a rebellion against John Casimir in order "to defend the integrity of the land of free elections and save the Constitution from reform." Under the weight of national strife and his own frustration, John Casimir abdicated the throne in 1668 and fled to France. With his departure, the Vasa dynasty and tradition in the Polish-Lithuanian Republic came to an end.

The Sejm filled the gap with a compromise candidate: King Michael Wisniowieski Korybut, a descendant of King Algirdas, son of Gediminas, Duke of Vitebsk. The new monarch was evidently chosen on the merit of his famous father, Jeremy Wisniowieski, a great border magnate who heroically fought against the Cossacks in the days of Bogdan Chmielnicki. The Wisniowieski Korybut family was well disposed toward the Jews, with whom they maintained cordial business relations for many years. Indeed, the newly elected king intervened on behalf of his Jewish subjects in their struggle with the guilds and the anti-Jewish rulings of canon law.

The country, however, reeled in the wake of war and its byproducts, poverty and destruction. Conflicts of interest arose between the central government, the municipalities, and the army. Anti-Jewish hostility grew under the encouragement of fanatical priests, especially Jesuits. In 1670, the central government, the Court in particular, had no choice but to intervene in the common interest. The king himself attracted bitter, active opposition because of his marriage to Eleonora Maria, sister of Emperor Leopold of Austria. This antipathy was exploited by Sobieski, the Polish Grand Hetman and Prazmowski, the Church Primate. Concurrently, the Turks under Sultan Mohomet IV and Ahmad Kuprili invaded Podolia and the western Ukraine. To contain their appetite, the king agreed to pay annual tribute. The Polish response was different: in 1673, they rejected the Turks' offer of a peace treaty at Buczacz. Rallying under Sobieski, they marched against the Turks and triumphed at Chocim. Lithuania contributed nothing to this *tour de force*; seeking greater freedom under the provisions of the Union of Lublin, Michael refused to fight alongside Warsaw. As if to drive the point home, the

Lithuanian monarch suddenly and unexpectedly died one day after the victory.

John III Sobieski (1674-1696)

Michael was succeeded by John III Sobieski, a renowned military commander. Internal chaos continued to predominate; six out of 12 meetings of the Diet were dissolved in the anarchy. The source of the unruliness, which dominated the affairs of state during most of Sobieski's rule, was the magnate class. In its Lithuanian manifestation, the magnates' antipathy focused on the lesser gentry, which returned punch for punch until the armed forces intervened, often resulting in bloodshed. The magnates were represented first by the Pacas family and then by the Sapiegas family; the latter acquired enormous power and tended to solve the problems of the magnate class by Draconian shows of force. Its aim was to demonstrate independence not only from the Polish Sejm but also from the Catholic Church, and its tactics included occupation of Church estates and clashes with the bishops.

Sobieski preferred and favored his Ruthenian estates; throughout his reign he showed little concern for the Grand Duchy of Lithuania. His wife, Mary d'Arquien, promoted and supported nunneries and maintained a special relationship with the Church, showering the Jesuits with public funds and sundry privileges. Sobieski himself was an enlightened monarch who was tolerant of all religions and denominations. In 1683, he suppressed anti-Jewish riots and a violent uprising and pogrom in Brest-Litovsk, punished participants in this mayhem, and ordered the Sejm to contest and actively oppose the blood libel, which was invoked frequently.

Sobieski's main claim to fame in Europe was his victory, as head of a combined Christian Army, over the Turks in 1683, thus delivering Vienna from Muslim/Turkish occupation. He continued his crusades against the Turks.[50] To maintain his power base at home, he fought off internal intrigues and struggled against the increasing number of parties in the Sejm. This put a serious drain on his finances and helped maintain his favorable attitude toward the Jewish population of the country.

Life in the Jewish communities of Lithuania was becoming more complex. The authority of the *Kahal* was beginning to collapse, especially after the Shabbetai Zevi debacle, when many Jews openly rebelled against the religious establishment and its rulings. Converts to Christianity were automatically accepted into the ranks of the gentry and awarded tax relief and other privileges. In spite of those inducements, there were few converts; most defections coincided with pogroms. There were some exceptions. Small groups of followers of a new false messiah, Jacob Frank, accepted Christianity in 1756, together with Frank and his daughter, Eva.[51]

Indeed, it was the controversies surrounding the false messiahs that sent the *Kahal* institution into decline. The *Kahal* had originally been democratic, although suffrage was limited to Jewish homeowners and landowners. Now, with the communities divided internally, the wealthy families fought among themselves for control of the community institution. Nepotism became rampant. Another problem was finance, which began with an array of state and municipal taxes that the Jews remitted through their community agencies. Jews were liable to a head-tax and, unlike non-Catholic Christians, had to pay a "charitable" subsidy to the clergy. Numerous other levies were legislated by the Diet for the benefit of the national treasury. Various communities' *Kahals* brought their grievances about the heavy tax burden to the Radom Fiscal Tribunal, which had been established to supervise all fiscal matters in the Commonwealth.[52] After paying their state-imposed taxes, the Jews remitted ever growing sums of protection money to various malefactors: the Jesuits, other church agencies, the *Schlachta*, government dignitaries.

The *Kahal* institution was caught in a vise: mounting financial needs and diminishing sources of income. This diminished the effectiveness, and therefore the authority, of the *Kahal* leadership vis-a-vis the rank and file. Aggravating the problem was a change in Lithuanian business practices. The gentry now tended to circumvent middlemen, a class strongly populated by Jews, in its import trade.[53]

This period coincided with the ascent of Vilnius as the most important and powerful Jewish center in Lithuania. (One reason may have been the status of this city as the seat of the Lithuanian Supreme Court.) So great was the religious and educational influence of Vilnius that Jews referred to it as "the Jerusalem of Lithuania."[54]

The Jewish communities maintained their far-reaching autonomy throughout this period, and this is often considered evidence of the authorities' tolerance and goodwill. The fact, however, is that the Jews' privileges were bestowed solely because of governmental self-interest. The Jewish institutions not only administered their communities' affairs but collected and remitted taxes imposed upon Jews by the Sejm. Since they had no political ambitions, the Jews were perceived by the government, the Sejm, and the Court as being more trustworthy than non-Jewish residents of the country. Nor was autonomy unique to the Jewish community; other minorities in the Commonwealth lived under similar formulae. Where the Jews differed was in the lack of a national homeland that might defend their rights, their property, and their lives.

Sobieski dealt sympathetically with Jews when they could not pay their taxes. He renewed for another ten years the moratorium first granted them by John Casimir. He was closely acquainted with several Jews. (His personal physician was a Jew named Emanuel Ben-Yona; his customs farmer was one Bezalel.) He was outspoken in his condemnation of the blood libel, with which Jews were often charged during his reign, and of the pogroms and the destruction of Jewish houses and property by those who believed these accusations. This was no trifling matter: ritual-murder accusations and the damage they caused were so extensive as to overwhelm the *Kahals*, which turned to the king again and again.

Several edicts of Sobieski's attest to his concern for Jewish lives and well-being. He prohibited the kidnapping of Jewish children for forced conversion – an occurrence especially prevalent in Lithuania at that time. He regulated conversions to Christianity to safeguard Jews' rights, stipulating that any would-be Jewish convert had to appear before a mixed commission of Jews and Christians and openly declare that his decision had been taken of free will. Once converted, however, there was no return. In this matter, Lithuanian practice followed Church law as practiced in all Medieval Catholic countries.

The Wettin-Saxon Dynasty

Sobieski died in 1696, his reign marked by years of internal crisis. Eighteen foreign candidates vied for the succession. Each had his own supporters in the Sejm, and each dangled bribes and recruited foreign emissaries to lobby among the gentry and the magnates.

The strongest candidates were Louis Conti, Prince of Bourbon, and Frederick Augustus II, Elector of Saxony. Louis Conti, who called himself "God's attorney on earth," was supported by the Churches of France and Poland. His allies in the Sejm paid the Sapiegas family (Lithuania's dominant family) 100,000 thalers for its endorsement of their candidate. Frederick Augustus belonged to a dynasty that was respected throughout Europe. Nicknamed Augustus the Strong, he was an accomplished athlete, a hedonist, an egoist, and a man of immense sexual appetite. Enterprising and wealthy, he squandered most of the Court's funds to satisfy his personal whims and fancies. To prepare for the monarchy election, Frederick Augustus II renounced Lutheranism for Catholicism and entered a monastery near Vienna in order to "cleanse" himself. His wife, Christina Eberhardina Hohenzollern-Bayreuth, was and remained a Lutheran.

This was the first such contest in which the Jews wielded electoral power. They did so for several reasons: the community had become more wealthy; Jews wished to show that they were a force to be reckoned with; and the large number of candidates gave the Jews an opportunity to support the one most sympathetic to community interests. After studying the candidates' attitudes toward the Jews (as well as their general views), the community pledged its collective strength to Frederick Augustus and provided him with financial assistance.[55] (Jewish suffrage, let alone Jewish candidates, was a very distant reform at this time.) At the end of the interregnum, which lasted for almost two years, Frederick Augustus II was coronated in Cracow in 1697. His opponents christened him the "unworthy German Prince" and considered him a usurper.

His first act belied the charge: he returned Silesia, which Germany had annexed and superficially Germanized, to the Poles, to whom ethnically and culturally it belonged. Then he began to dismember the Commonwealth by bargaining away parts of Poland and Lithuania for accommodations with its enemies.

This period marked the beginning of constitutional reform and two important administrative changes. One of the latter curbed the powers of the Grand Hetman and Treasurer. The other, made by the Sejm in 1697, replaced Ruthenian with Polish as the official language of Court decisions in Commonwealth affairs. By this time, the Lithuanian magnates, gentry, and even *boyars* were literate in Polish, and internal official documents used this language.

In 1700, strife between the powerful Sapiegas brothers (Casimir, the Grand Hetman, and Benedict, the Treasurer) and the Catholics under Bishop Brzostowski engulfed the Grand Duchy in civil war. Frederick Augustus, whose election the Lithuanian magnates had opposed, had no sympathy for either side and let the combatants fight it out for two years. When he finally intervened, he brought about a truce by summoning the Diet of Lublin, invoking the Confederation of Sandomierz, and posting a Saxon army in

Palange. The Lithuanian magnates, dissatisfied with the terms, fomented further insurrection. The resulting battle at Lapunai ended in victory for the forces of the gentry, which crushed the Sapiegas armies and cruelly decimated the family. In exchange for recognition of their status, the gentry accepted the authority of Frederick Augustus II as absolute monarch of the Grand Duchy of Lithuania with hereditary rights.

In the meantime, Frederick Augustus II had joined forces with Czar Peter and Frederick IV of Denmark to demolish and partition the Swedish Empire. The result was a debacle. King Charles XII of Sweden first subdued the Danish and Russian forces and then repelled Frederick Augustus' Saxon army at Riga. In 1702, his troops occupied Samogitia, Kaunas, and Vilnius, Warsaw, and Cracow. To secure his victory, the Swedish monarch returned the Sapiegas to power. Two years later, he replaced Frederick Augustus with Stanislaw, son of Rafael Leszcynski and Palatine of Poznan (a Sapiegas family friend with much influence), who was considered a liberal and a humanist.

Charles XII and the Poles were at loggerheads. The Swede regarded the squires' prerogatives as thinly disguised anarchy and believed they knew nothing of the rules of monarchy, aristocracy, and democracy. The Poles accused Charles of subjecting the Commonwealth to a policy of plunder and abuse. The rulers of Russia observed greedily and made plans; it was their feeling that the Poles and Lithuanians were incapable of ruling an independent state, even after 800 years of history. Indeed, the civil war continued. Compounding it were the severe winters of 1708-1709 and the accompanying plagues, which combined to wipe out tens of thousands.

The Sejm served only the conqueror of the moment. The magnates and gentry chose sides in disregard of the national interest. The Lithuanians supported the Swedes or the Russians; the Poles, the Saxons or the French. The Swedes, Saxons, and Russians not only lived off the territories they had occupied but looted them systematically.

However, the Commonwealth's enemies were unable to form a viable alliance. Charles the Swede overreached himself and failed to unite the Polish and Lithuanian gentry in support of the new King Leszcynski. In 1709, two years after marching through the cities and villages of Lithuania along the river Neris, Charles met his defeat in the southern Ukraine at the Battle of Poltava. Wounded, he fled with several hundred soldiers to Turkey. Before the year was out, the armies of Peter the Great overran almost all of Poland and Lithuania with the help of the Saxons. Frederick Augustus II returned to the Commonwealth. In 1710, under pressure of the Russian army, the Sejm officially reinstated him as king; in gratitude, he ceded Estonia, parts of Finland, and Livonia to Russia. At this point in time, the Commonwealth had two kings, two primates, two grand hetmans, two general confederations, and two political systems.

It took only four years for Frederick Augustus' domestic opponents to mount a rebellion against him and his Russian allies, who, of course, fought back with equal vigor. The Czar's delegate, Dolgoruky, stepped in, marking the beginning of Russian involvement and meddling in the internal affairs of the Polish-Lithuanian Commonwealth. The Diet of 1717, surrounded by Russian troops, accepted Dolgoruky's proposals and terms. The gentry agreed to restore the old balance of forces: monarchy (king), authority (Senate-Diet), and freedom (for the nation). Bribes were considered acceptable as "rewards for men of merit," to use the conventional Polish phrase. The gentry forfeited its right to confederate; the Hetman recovered his powers. The armies of the Commonwealth were to be limited to 25,000 men: 18,000 for Poland and 7,000 for Lithuania. The Saxon army of Frederick August II was to be sent home to Germany.

Frederick Augustus II chafed under these terms. Seeking to elude them, he found two allies. One was Emperor Charles VI of Austria, whose authorized Court Jew, Bernard Lehmann, proposed in 1719 that Austria accept Polish territory in exchange for support against the Russians. The second ally was George I of England. Across the divide was Czar Peter of Russia, who signed a treaty with Frederick, Elector of Prussia. Both sides coveted Polish and Lithuanian territory for their own needs, and rationalized their schemes by arguing that the Commonwealth was incapable of governing itself and caring for its own people. Indeed, the Commonwealth economy and society were in shambles. The suffering caused by Swedish terror, Russian deceit, and Saxon intrigue had broken national morale and ushered in a period of apathy, skepticism, and moral decline.

Most of the Diets convened by Frederick Augustus II were dismissed without resolving the problems of state and nation. A combination of the *Liberum veto* and Russian bribery caused the Diets of 1719 and 1720[56] to adjourn in chaos. Both countries of the Commonwealth slipped into anarchy and disaster.

Reformation and Counterreformation: Lithuanian Society in Flux

Before refocusing on the Jewish community, this chronicle steps back to the sixteenth century for a brief review of the Protestant Reformation and the reaction to this upheaval, the Counterreformation, as these occurred in Lithuania.

While Western Europe advanced toward the era we know as "modern," medieval feudalism continued to flourish in Lithuania. Most land, including newly-acquired estates, belonged to the magnates or the Crown. There were various grades within the nobility, who represented about ten percent of the population. The important grades were two: the gentry (*Schlachta*), landowners who controlled peasants who tenanted their lands; and landless nobles, who aligned themselves with various magnates as hangers-on or hired mercenaries.

The magnates, the princes, the counts, and the barons received their titles from the Papacy, the Holy Roman Empire, or the king, sometimes for some good service rendered, but more often for large amounts of money. Once empowered, they acquired vast estates, villages, townlets, and even large parts of some towns. Even though a crude form of democracy had developed in the Commonwealth, as it had not in Russia and Germany, the elites controlled Lithuania and everything within it. The only classes to which they had to give thought were the burghers, whose potential power had to be checked, and the Jews, who could be exploited to bring this about.

The functionaries who dealt with ordinary Lithuanians derived from the nobility: the *voivode* (the powerful governor), the *hetman* (army field marshal), the *castellan* (governor of an estate and the land controlled by it), the *palatine* (estate functionary), and the *starosta* (constable). Members of rich and powerful families accepted appointments for all of these. However, the poorer relatives of these families, who possessed nothing but unbounded hauteur and a proud name, were always willing to marry rich girls even from the lowest strata of society, so that they could pursue lives of indolence and pleasure. The very thought of work or the pursuit of a trade was demeaning to them; in any case, they possessed no skills or handicrafts and had no taste for commerce. Thus they preferred life in the capital, at the royal court, and in the large towns, where their penchant for amusement and adventure might be quenched.

Although feudalism was far from dead, the agrarian reforms gave rise to three new elements in Lithuanian society: merchants, craftsmen, and semi-liberated serfs. The artisans included builders, gardeners and other town-dwelling craftsmen. There were two types of semi-serfs: *ondosadniks*, bonded servants who could afford to buy their freedom and provided the chief source of labor, but were tied to the land of their noble or magnate; and *boyars*, horse-owning serfs, who could join the army or become mercenaries. A *boyar* who prospered might even ascend the social ladder. An occasional farmer might join the small-landholder or petty nobility classes by sequestering pieces of land from the magnates or the kings by various devices.

Beneath all of these were the peasants, whom the ruling classes regarded as sub-humans who lacked the intelligence to learn or change their ways. These persons – *muzhiks* or *klumpii*, so called because of their wooden shoes – accounted for a vast majority of the population. Their status as virtual slaves was prescribed not by law but by circumstance. Their houses belonged to their masters; they were not allowed to move to other villages or areas without permission. They were illiterate and deemed uneducable, dishonest, and untrustworthy. Their owners considered them capable of diligent work only under the strictest discipline, for which they often substituted brutality. These disempowered *untermentschen* were bought and sold together with the land; even their children belonged to the master. Social mobility was not known, let alone practiced. Not until the nineteenth century did they gain certain freedoms, some release from age-old misery, some token of land ownership.

The Catholic and Orthodox churches in the Commonwealth fully identified with this attitude. The churches neither supported nor protected the peasantry, nor did they attempt to improve its conditions. No religious leader felt the need to behave differently: since the peasant was created by God to serve and slave, it was God's will to abuse him and his family.

The newly ascendant groups were in competition with the Jews and thus resented the Jewish middlemen and tax collectors. This, however, did not foment antisemitism as it did in Poland. One reason for the difference was the Lithuanian practice of disregarding Polish law. Another reason was the ambiguous attitude of Lithuanian society toward the Catholic Church and the religious orders. While Lithuanian Catholicism did not lack commitment – most affluent Catholic families, linked to Rome, sought to dedicate at least one son to the clergy – society at large did not identify with the Church and the orders as did Polish society.

Relations of Church and State in Lithuania were synergetic. The two establishments often collaborated and complemented each other's efforts. The Holy See confirmed coronations and endorsed marriages and births in the Royal Court. The civil authorities, in turn, helped enforce Church discipline and bring sinners to justice. The Church and the clergy firmly supported the State and the authority of the nobility and the wealthy landowners. It even supplemented local government in what would now be considered essential human services, such as education, paupers' hospitals, and hospices. In this role, the Church, pursuant to its age-old tradition, was concerned more with the maintenance of control than with its duty to serve. The Crown and nobility were well aware of the influence of the priesthood and treated it as a matter of the highest political importance. Even in the country's remotest backwaters, the government knew it had a reliable ally. The Church always identified itself with political success. Thus it gladly followed wherever power led, and no one, from the cardinal down to the lowliest monk or friar, ever doubted that the path had been paved by God.

Literacy in the early Middle Ages was confined to three groups: the upper classes, the clergy, and the Jews. Almost all Jews in Lithuania spoke and wrote Yiddish; many of the men were literate in Hebrew. Most Jews in the Commonwealth spoke Polish, Lithuanian, or Russian, and some also knew how to write in these languages. Literate Jews were termed *utzony yevrey*, learned Jews, and many of them served as scribes for those unable to write in the required language.

This kind of work was plentiful, since most Poles, Lithuanians, and Russians were unilingual and illiterate. The peasants and the urban poor relied on their priests or the *utzony* (the learned) for their written needs. Only the affluent minority spoke more than one language. Many wealthy Lithuanians knew German or French; others had studied Greek and Latin. They knew nothing of Lithuanian language and culture, and preferred to use Polish as their vernacular. Those who followed this fashion left it to their managers or the Jews to deal with the peasants and their tenants.

The Polish schools were strictly religious. French and Italian humanism, however, permeated the universities and made inroads outside these institutions. At the time of Nicolas Copernicus, who was educated in Cracow, there was an interest in classical studies, including Latin, Greek, Hebrew, and

Roman law. A transition from Medieval to modern learning was made; the Polish Renaissance even fueled a short-lived national and anticlerical trend. Magistrates patronized the fine arts and sponsored an architecture that transformed the appearance of the capital and other cities and brought forth an intellectual elite.

The Reformation, the Protestant revolution, swept through the upper classes and even became fashionable for a time. In Poland it left a nucleus of intellectuals, humanists, and small groups ready to fight for tolerance and freedom of worship. All of this, however, had little effect on the masses. For the masses, religion was an integral part of daily life, and the Reformation did nothing to change it. Ordinary Poles and Lithuanians regarded their priests as holy men who spoke with the voice of Jesus. The priest provided comfort, advice, and help in time of need, and was requited with unbounded gratitude and love. His censure or blame, especially when expressed in church, evoked deep fear and remorse. The Church and its local embodiment, the priest, also wielded great political power, which was invoked as a medium of control.

In the ensuing Counterreformation, the Polish Church acted vigorously to restore doctrinal uniformity among the religious congregations and orders, especially the Jesuits. Classical studies were eclipsed; emphasis was placed on religious drama and the history and lives of saints and local martyrs. By 1656, the Catholic leadership went so far as to have the Black Madonna of Czestochowa crowned Queen of Poland. (The Polish Church renews its vows to the Madonna each year.) Study became ossified. Repetition, recitation, and interminable lectures replaced such scientific inquiry as the Reformation had brought. Religion invaded the language and harbored folk superstitions. The clergy condemned heretical books and persecuted their authors. Music was not spared. Religious decorative art underwent an efflorescence; encouragement from on high brought the Baroque style to the fore, its purpose being to assert the glory of God. As the convents and churches flourished, they accumulated great wealth through endowments, bequests, and business and rent income.

For all this, the clerical establishment was insecure. Thirty percent of the Polish population belonged to ethnic minorities that had their own religious denominations. The ruling Church refused to recognize them and challenged their patriotism. Prejudice against minorities became endemic, almost a way of life – a view nurtured and defined by Roman Catholic writers. While all were despised (Germans, Ukrainians, Belarus, Russians), none were despised more than the Jews.

Predictably, the Reformation and the Counterreformation affected Lithuania and Poland in different ways. The Reformation was publicly preached and advocated in Lithuania as it never was in Poland; chiefly because a Protestant vassal state had been established in neighboring Prussia. It also revealed the degree to which the Lithuanian nobility and magnate classes had become "Polonized," and it showed how influential the Catholic Church had become. The Reformation appealed to the Lithuanian gentry because it offered them an opportunity to increase their privileges. It inspired the gentry to seek its Lithuanian roots and take pride in Lithuanian culture and language. Lithuanian books began to appear; the University of Vilnius began to offer courses in Lithuanian studies. One of the pioneers in this effort was John Tartila, a former Catholic priest who, despite a prohibition by the Royal Court against Lutheran and Anabaptist teachings, published an explanation of Luther's theology.

In the years 1535-1540, under Tartila's influence, a group of prominent magnates, including the Radziwills, began to attend German-language Protestant services and enroll their sons[57] in a pro-Protestant school in Vilnius. When the school was closed down by royal decree, the renegade magnates sent their sons to German schools and universities abroad, for which they were fined. Despite official opposition, German studies infiltrated the Lithuanian upper classes and the aristocracy. Calvinism made important inroads in the Grand Duchy and attracted many ardent and open believers who associated themselves with the anti-Trinitarians, the Bohemia Brethren, and other groups. Even though these groups never enjoyed official sanction, the first Synod of the Reformers convened in Vilnius in 1568 and it was there that the famous "Lithuanian Unit", a Protestant society, was founded in 1570. Calvinist parochial schools were established in Vilnius, Ukmerge, Birzai, Nesvyzius, Brasta (Brest), and other towns. As time passed, the Protestants became a small but powerful minority in the Diet of the Grand Duchy.

The lesser gentry followed the magnates' example and the peasants followed suit, as they always did under the principle "Cuius regio, ejus religio." Enjoying its new numerical clout, the gentry now sought to remove the peasantry from Catholic clutches once and for all by closing churches, expelling priests, and urging clergymen to convert. Two mainstays of the Catholic establishment, however, were immune to such tactics. One was the bishop echelon. The Lithuanian bishops had either been chosen by the Royal Court or had purchased their dioceses from it; their membership in this group automatically gave them membership in the Grand Ducal Council, even though many of them were neither Lithuanians nor ordained priests. The second was the vast network of Catholic properties and institutions, which the Royal Court placed under its protection.

The Protestants were gravely factionalized. Historians mention about 30 denominations in Lithuania and Poland, each teaching and preaching different dogmas and interpretations of the New and Old Testaments. This diversity was anchored in legislation, first promulgated in 1563 and reconfirmed in 1568, that allowed freedom of worship and ecclesiastical affairs. This proliferation of sects made concerted enforcement of the Reformation an impossibility. The establishment by Bishop Protasevichius of the so-called Society of Jesus in Vilnius in 1569-1570 invigorated the local Counterreformation. The Society founded a college in Vilnius that became a Catholic stronghold in the country, and its proponents engaged Protestant scholars in public disputation, as the Church had done everywhere in Europe for centuries previously. The failure of Lithuanian Protestantism was confirmed when the most powerful of the magnates, about 300 in number, abandoned the new creed. Individual members of the gentry continued to adhere to Calvinism and Lutheranism, as did others even within the families of the magnates who had returned to Catholicism. The numbers of Protestants grew in subsequent generations, under German influence.

The Reformation in Lithuania was a phenomenon of privileged social strata. It did not improve the lot of the poor, nor did it concern itself with abuses, intolerance, and injustice. It did, however, open a window to the influences of neighboring countries and their universities and culture generally. In this sense, its impact on the insular but multireligious and multinational Lithuanian society should be considered favorable.

The Jewish Connection

The attitude of the Lithuanian Reformation toward the Jews was ambivalent at best. Reformation forces targeted and abused members of all denominations, and attempted to convert Jews with the intensity that Catholics employed at the time.

In response, the Jewish communities invested greater efforts in the consolidation of their own schools and community institutions. Jewish schools proliferated and expanded in the Reformation and Counterreformation period. New yeshivot were opened and the publication of new and old religious works was encouraged. Taking advantage of official tolerance, their own equality under the law (if not in society), and the Christian infighting and strife, they were able to obtain the breathing space needed to strengthen their internal society and consolidate the Council institutions. Thus they were now able to reach out to other Jewish communities – neighboring ones in Europe and more distant ones in Palestine, Turkey, and other lands. They were also able to attend to current problems and to adapt to their new circumstances.

Synagogue at Prenai, Lithuania, 18th century

Chapter 2

LITHUANIAN JEWRY IN FORMATION

Coalescence of Jewish Community Institutions

The Synod of the Four Lands and Va'ad Lita

The formation of Jewish community institutions in Lithuania dates from 1581, when King Stephen took the most sweeping pro-Jewish action to date: endorsement of a Jewish parliament of sorts, the first of its kind in the Diaspora, for the communities of Little Poland, Greater Poland, Belorussia, and Lithuania. The new institution was named the Synod of the Four Lands (Hebrew: *Va'ad arba' ha-aratsot*). The Synod was not meant to replace the individual community organizations, now known as the *kehilla* (pl. *kehillot*); both institutions were needed for internal and external reasons. The government fully supported the work of the Synod and recognized its power and ordinances, resulting in a form of Jewish autonomy that exercised its prerogatives with government endorsement. The government profited from this arrangement in two ways. First, the collection of taxes and other levies from the Jewish community was now the responsibility of the Jews' own elected leaders. Second, the government was absolved of having to regulate the Jews' internal affairs. As Jewish communities proliferated in the late sixteenth century, the government found it more convenient to deal with a centralized, elected leadership than with each community separately.

The concept of the Synod was a Jewish one, an outgrowth of the rabbinical courts that convened on the market days at the fairs. These ad hoc tribunals gradually evolved into a central rabbinical court, so recognized because of the importance of its members. Four of these rabbinical courts, each located in one of the large old cities, and each augmented by wealthy merchants, lay leaders of individual communities, and other eminent rabbis, formed the basis of the Synod. It is true that a local Lithuanian framework of this type, the Jewish Regional Council, had represented all Lithuanian Jews since 1520. Furthermore, the term "Council of the Four Lands" appears in documents dated as early as 1534. The Synod exercised some authority even before Stephen recognized it and expanded its powers to embrace Jewish affairs in both Poland and Lithuania. In 1568, eight years after tax collection in the Jewish communities was centralized, the Synod chose two delegates to deal with taxation in the name of all Lithuanian Jews.

The monolithic Synod, however, was short-lived. In 1590, acknowledging its constituents' specific needs and power prerogatives, it split in two. The newly named Council of Lithuania (Hebrew: *Va'ad Lita* or *Va'ad ha-medina*, "Council of State") was given official status in Lithuanian law and functioned separately and independently within the Synod.

There were constant problems between the Polish and Lithuanian councils. For one thing, the Lithuania council always depended on its Polish counterpart to plead its case before the central union government. The Council of Poland expected the Lithuanians to share various financial burdens, including the cost of gifts for magnates, members of the Sejm, and the king. The Council of Lithuania considered these demands excessive. The two councils also clashed over the jurisdiction of border communities, commercial rights, and the movement of Jews from one country to the other. In 1623, reacting to the recurrent contretemps with the Council of Poland and specific disputes with the Lithuanian administration, the Council of Lithuania declared its autonomy and seceded from the Synod altogether.

While it lasted, the Synod convened twice a year in Poland at the great fairs of Lublin and Yaroslav, and in Lithuania in the five principal cities: Brisk (Brest-Litovsk), Pinsk, Vilnius, Slutzk, and Gardinas (Grodno). For many years the delegates met in Brisk in honor of R. Meyer Whal, who had become too elderly to travel. Three ledgers (Heb. *pinkasim*, sing. *pinkas*) were kept: in Grodno, Brisk, and Vilnius. Each community sent voting delegates to the Synod. The Synod dealt with important problems affecting the entire country;

each kehilla retained its autonomy in dealing with its particular problems and those of surrounding villages.

The principal *kehillot* were known as *kehillot rashey beyt din* – seats of rabbinical courts. Individual communities acted on disputes within the *kehillot*, including questions of taxation and religious and social bylaws. The Synod was vigilant in view of dangers and threats to the community as a whole, appeasing the appropriate authorities with gifts when it deemed this necessary. The Synod was also a legal instance that took up the cause of Jews in distress and punished perpetrators of internecine injustice. Educational problems were discussed and requests for permission to publish books debated, the overarching principle being common action for the common weal. Apart from the Synod's official agenda, the meetings were used to conduct private business, arrange marriages, and, above all, exchange news and information among the participating communities. The Synod helped unite the communities and, by creating respect for authority, did much to ensure internal law and order.

The breakaway Council of Lithuania met 37 times between 1623 and 1764, in venues determined by the circumstances. Assemblies were held every two or three years, except when emergencies required special meetings. All householders were entitled to participate in *kehilla* elections, but few Lithuanian Jews were householders, as opposed to leaseholders, and few of those eligible actually exercised the franchise. At the end of the Council's existence, fewer than one percent of Lithuanian Jews were electors, although the figures in the five principal communities were considerably higher (7 percent in Vilnius, 10 percent in Grodno, 20 percent in Pinsk). To ensure the availability of most electors, elections were held during the intermediary days of the Passover festival. To regard this structure as democracy in the modern sense, however, would be to overstate the case. The Council leadership was oligarchic, as was that of the individual communities. Community leaders repressed any attempt to organize internal opposition, and knew they could count on the Council's full support in so doing. Independent organizations were strictly prohibited upon pain of *herem*, a potent sanction described below.

Relations between this institution and the Karaite community were testy.[58] For some time, the Council of Lithuania taxed the Karaites as well as the "Rabbanites"; in 1646, this factor, coupled with economic rivalry with the "Rabbanites," inspired the Karaites to demand that King Wladislaw IV expel the Jews from Troki – a demand to which the king acceded. This notwithstanding, Karaites often turned to the Jewish courts in order to benefit from their power and prestige. (The Karaite leadership in Grodno had actually encouraged the community to do this in 1558). In 1665, the Karaite leadership, the Council of Three, forbade the practice. This ordinance was obeyed in Vilnius and Brisk, but ignored in Grodno.

As the years passed, the Council of Lithuania met with difficulties caused by the growing complexity of its environment. The refugees of 1648 still required care; wars exacerbated existing economic problems and caused new ones. In 1700, to treat these matters, the Council of Lithuania admitted additional *kehillot* and established a 15-man standing committee composed of the two leaders and the *av beyt-din* (president of the rabbinical court) of each of the five most important communities. The chief officials of the Council were the head of council (*parnas*) and the presiding officer at the assemblies, who were responsible for both internal and external affairs. The second level of the hierarchy was occupied by the trustee (*ne'eman*), who handled financial matters and acted as both Treasurer and Chief Secretary. His was a salaried position, which could also be held by a rabbi. There was also an interceder (*shtadlan*), whose task it was to represent Jewish interests vis-a-vis the government, the royal court, and the Sejm. This official was well paid. Notably, the President of the Rabbinical Court of Brest-Litovsk (a succession of offspring within one family) chaired the Council of Lithuania for quite some time.

Each council kept a *pinkas* (official book of record) containing its resolutions and budgets. Only a few remnants of the *pinkas* of the Synod of the Four Lands survive, but that of the Council of Lithuania is intact for the years between 1623 and 1764, when the Council ceased to exist. The ledger was edited and published by historian Simon Dubnow in 1925.

The smaller communities often attended Council meetings in order to request tax relief and solicit the Council's advice on their particular problems. The Councils regulated the communities' affairs and guided the social, ethical and legal aspects of Jewish life. In disputes between communities or between individual members of a community, the *dayanim* (rabbinic judges) functioned as arbiters.

The most important aspect of the Council's work was the promulgation of ordinances and regulations which, endowed with the force of law of the land, had the effect of creating a Jewish autonomy. Such "legislation" included special regulations for business dealings, leasing of land, and negotiations with the barons. All lawmaking by the Council required unanimous approval.

To enforce their ordinances and rulings, the Council invoked *herem* (excommunication), which was decreed at the fairs and announced in synagogues.[59] The gravity of *herem* in sixteenth-century Lithuania is barely conceivable today. A Jew under *herem* was to be treated as a non-Jew, to the extent of removing the *mezuza* from his door. *Herem* extended to the wrongdoer's family, denying the offender's children the right to circumcision, expelling them from schools, and barring his wife and relatives from the synagogue. In the event of his death, the excommunicated one was denied the honors due to Jewish dead. In view of the insularity of Jewish communities in that period, treating a Jew as a non-Jew amounted to civil death. It is therefore no wonder that some authorities, most notably R. Joel Sirkes of Brest-Litovsk (1561-1640) (subsequently *av beyt din* of Cracow), sharply condemned the Council's use of *herem* and recommended that it be replaced by a set of sanctions including fines, expulsion, and "extradition" to non-Jewish authorities.

The *kehilla* obtained its budgets, for both external and internal services, by dunning individuals in accordance with their means. Each community or province remitted its taxes annually to the Council. When expenses exceeded income, as they almost always did, the communities were forced to borrow at high rates of interest to meet their obligations. To increase their income, the communities levied additional taxes on bakers and traveling merchants, monopolies such as silk, wine, salt, and candles, and even from betrothals, dowries, and circumcisions.

Business transactions of all kinds were taxed. For example, *kehillot* received four percent of the purchase price of houses and other real estate and as much as 10 to 20 percent on the purchase of kosher meat. With their taxation and arbitration powers, the councils became the Jewish communities' most important political organ for both internal and external affairs. It would be no exaggeration to describe their function as parliamentary.

To avoid competition for land leases, the Council of Lithuania instituted the *hezqat-arenda*, a system of leaseholding rights. *Hezqat-arenda*, often hereditary, applied to houses, market stalls, shops, and other immobiliers. Such regulations not only helped the Council meet its budget but kept Jews from undercutting one another in dealings with the nobility, barons, church, and the government.[60]

The Lithuanian community leadership issued, from as early as 1600, ordinances (*taqanot*, sing. *taqana*) regulating members' religious behavior not only in personal observance but also in dealings with non-Jews. To safeguard personal reputations and the good name of the Jewish community as a whole, individuals were instructed to act with honesty and integrity in all matters, lest their behavior be deemed *hilul ha-shem*, desecration of God's name. In one instance, the Council of Lithuania warned that "any Jew whosoever, who out of the violence of his heart provokes or assaults a non-Jew, shall not be helped by a single penny, even if he should be put to death as a result."

A spate of *taqanot* followed the Chmielnicki massacres of 1648, when refugees flooded the country. The Council of Lithuania introduced two measures to protect the rights of local Jews against the newcomers: *hezqat yishuv* (settlement rights), safeguarding rights of residence and community membership, and *hezqat 'ironut* (municipal residence right) to protect domicile in the towns. They also provided financial assistance to the Chmielnicki refugees and subsequent influxes (e.g., the Russian and Cossack occupation of parts of Lithuania in 1654, and the Swedish invasion of 1677).[61]

Throughout, the councils protected community rights vis-a-vis the government, which occasionally sought to erode Jewish prerogatives in response to various incidents. They vigilantly rebutted blood libels and persistent charges of Jews' having desecrated the Host. They relentlessly pursued murderers and assailants of Jews and spared no effort to have them brought to trial.[62]

The councils concerned themselves with education and culture. They strongly encouraged the publication of new books.[63] In 1652, the Councils of Lithuania and Poland ruled that any community that had its own rabbi should support a yeshiva for both adults and youth. Scholars were exempt from taxation. This caused yeshivot to proliferate in Lithuania and Poland, where they soon became influential within their communities and renowned throughout Europe.

Although there were exceptions, most Jews took pride in the councils' work. The communities' decisions were accepted and their rulings implemented in all respects — religious, economic, social, and educational. The councils, however, did not rule in a void. The predominant factor in Jewish life at the time was spiritual commitment coupled with moral discipline nurtured and enforced by Jewish teachings. It was this intangible force that provided the communities and the councils with the power and influence that enabled them to ensure Jewish continuity and survival.

Collapse of the Commonwealth: Lithuanian Jewry Engulfed

Lithuanian Jewry shared the uncertainty, ambivalence, and turmoil that coincided with the disintegration of the Commonwealth. In 1712, although confirming all the Jewish Charters and privileges, the king signed a new anti-Jewish decree including the following assertion: "The perfidious, faithless Jews have shed the blood of Christian children secretly and outrageously; their actions cry out for Divine vengeance." A spate of ritual-murder charges ensued, perhaps influenced by the king's personal belief in the veracity of the blood libel. In one tragic incident, a baptized Jew, a former rabbi in Slutsk and Brest-Litovsk who had become deranged and taken the name Michael Neophyt, confirmed the blood libel at the Ecclesiastical Court in Sandomierz.

When the king increased the Jewish head-tax to 60,000 Lithuanian *shoks*, the Council of the Four Lands and the Council of Lithuania sent two delegates, Dr. Gordon and Judah b. Isaac, supported by Bishop Sinkiewitz, to plead against the decree. They obtained a moratorium; the king gave the Jews special documents guaranteeing protection and freedom of worship. Twice, in exchange for a large sum of money, Frederick Augustus granted the Councils a ten-year moratorium to help them pay the heavy taxes and special levies imposed on them. Even Wisniowiecki, commander of the Lithuanian army, realized how heavy this burden weighted upon the Jewish communities. Aware that the Jews would find it most difficult to gather the required sums, he gave them a deferment.

To compound their woes, the Jewish communities were beset with memorable fires in these years. In 1731, most of Slobodka and part of Kaunas/Kovno burned to the ground. Three years later, many Jewish lives were lost as the Jewish Quarter of Vilnius/Vilna,[64] including the Great Synagogue and many houses of study, went up in flames in what is known as the Great Fire. Appeals for assistance were sent as far as Amsterdam; in response, the Ashkenazim and Sephardim of Amsterdam donated some 600 guilders in relief.

There was no peace for the Jewish communities. Some even accused the Jews of responsibility for the calamities that struck them. They struggled to safeguard their lives and their right to make a living. Against them were the municipalities, the burghers, the guilds, the gentry, and the Church. They petitioned the king, the Sejm, and the magnates for help; these greeted them with little sympathy or understanding. The rules and regulations were riddled with contradictions. The Christian majority often met their entreaties with mini-pogroms. The Royal Court that sat in judgment on their grievances generally ruled in favor of the municipalities and imposed fines on the Jews. In 1726, the Voivode and some court officials in Vilnius attempted to ensure payment of the fines by closing the synagogue[65] and taking possession of several Jewish houses. Some magnates and, oddly, several priests who owned adjacent properties came to their help. Several bishops offered their assistance, having witnessed their suffering first hand. Prominent among them was Sinkiewitz.

In 1730, the communities and the Council of Lithuania faced a new problem: the onset of a great missionary campaign among Lithuanian Jewry under Father Turchinowitz. His efforts were aided by a special law that prevailed until 1764, by which Jewish converts to Catholicism automatically joined the lower nobility and were granted their privileges. Although Turchinowitz made little progress among the men, he persevered among women and the poor. By the time of his death in 1773, he had converted some 500 young Jewish women.

There were several rare instances in the eighteenth century in which Catholics, particularly members of the magnate class, took special interest in the Jewish religion. A conspicuous example involved one of the Radziwills, Martin Nicolai Radziwill of Kletzk. A scholar of ancient religions, he mastered the Hebrew language, studied Bible and Talmud, and began to practice Jewish rituals including dietary law and the Sabbath. His horrified family forcibly removed his children from his care, sent them to a Piarist convent in Warsaw, and drove Jews off some land that they owned in Kletzk. Martin Nicolai moved to Slutsk, where he continued to practice Judaism until his death in 1756. He was buried in the family plot in Neswiz, never having officially converted to Judaism.

According to an unsubstantiated but widely believed legend, Graf Valentine Potocki, a scion of the well-known Potocki family, converted to Judaism in Amsterdam after spending some time at the papal academy in Rome. A friend of his, one Zaremba, converted with him and settled in Palestine; Potocki returned to Lithuania and lived as a Jew near Vilna, under the name Abraham ben Abraham. (*Ben Avraham*, literally "son of Abraham," i.e., the Patriarch, is the Hebrew surname conventionally adopted by converts.) In 1749, the legend says, Potocki was burned at the stake in Vilna for having converted to Judaism. A local Jew, Eliezer Ziskes, posturing as a Christian, managed through bribery to obtain some of Potocki's ashes and one of his fingers; these were later buried in the Jewish cemetery. Over his grave grew a tall tree that became an object of pilgrimage for Vilna Jews on the Ninth of Av and the High Holidays; the anniversary of his martyrdom was marked with recitation of *kaddish*.

Difficulties and problems aside, the Jewish communities in Lithuania continued to expand and multiply. In 1713, Jews were allowed to move into the townlet of Kalvarija. (Such relocation required a permit.) The community of Slobodka-Wiliampole installed its first rabbi in 1720 – an act that required special permission of the Government – and enlarged its institutions. New communities were established in Shadov and Zhager in 1731. The Jews of Shavli (Siauliai) were permitted to enlarge their community.

The reign of Frederick Augustus II was in its death throes. In a last desperate effort to secure the succession of his son to the Polish-Lithuanian throne, the monarch enlisted the help of Stanislaw Poniatowsky, former ambassador of Charles XII, and tried to obtain the support of the powerful Lithuanian Czartoryski family. He died in 1733, having made no headway.

In the interregnum, some groups favored the late monarch's son, Frederick Augustus III. His advocates included Austria, Prussia, and Russia, which, however, attached political stipulations to their support. A large faction of powerful magnates wished to recall former King Stanislas Lesczynski from France, where he now resided. To be on the safe side, the Jewish communities (like other groups) gave both candidates financial support.

The first candidate brought up for a vote in the Diet of Pragha-Warsaw (1736) was Lesczynski. When he failed to win a majority, the electors proclaimed Frederick Augustus III King of the Commonwealth. The backing of the three aforementioned foreign powers, as well as Czarina Anne, was blatantly evident. It was clear that Poland and Lithuania had lost the freedom to choose their own monarch and that the Commonwealth was increasingly dependent on Russia.

The new king, father of five sons and five daughters, immersed himself in the pleasures of hunting, banqueting, and the opera. Of his 30-year reign, he may have spent two years in Poland and Lithuania. His tenure was marked by national decline, disorder, and inactivity. The Government introduced no new domestic or foreign policies. The Diet, hamstrung by the *Liberum veto*, neither enacted new legislation nor imposed urgently needed taxes. Bloody clashes erupted between the warring parties of the Diet and their supporters among the gentry. With no armed forces to speak of, the Commonwealth was harmless, friendly to the neighboring powers, and ostensibly and officially neutral. The king entrusted the highest offices in the land to his Saxon minister Heinrich-Henry von Bruhl. Bruhl, although a great administrator and diplomat, cared only for the king's personal interests, those of the Saxons, and his own pocketbook. The Poles and Lithuanians regarded Bruhl as a parasite. High-ranking positions went to the highest bidder; great fortunes were accumulated through marriages of convenience and passed on by inheritance. In Lithuania, the newly appointed treasurer, Fleming, worked mainly with and through the powerful families, to the extreme distress of the gentry.

Foreign influence was rife and ramified. As noted, Russia was increasingly influential in political affairs. Lithuanian society, however, turned to France for cultural and intellectual stimulation and to Italy for inspiration in the arts. Officials tried to learn from the English and the Dutch how to solve the country's economic problems and attempted to master Swedish precedents in constitutional matters. In fiscal, administrative, and military affairs, the Austrians and Germans brought the greatest influence to bear. So unruly had the Commonwealth become, however, that none of these foreign powers was able to reap the benefits of their influence.

It was the time of the Ukrainian *Haidamack* (from the Turkish word *haida*, to "move on"), organized bands of serfs and peasants who joined forces with impoverished townsfolk and social outcasts to savage the Commonwealth's eastern periphery. Although they regarded themselves as successors to Chmielnicki, they had no political aims. Indeed, the Russian administration and the Orthodox Church clergy used them in their struggle with the Catholic Church and the Poles. Their reign of terror spanned the years 1734-1768.

The Jews were easy targets of *Haidamack* attacks. Orthodox Church propaganda, vigorously spread by other denominations, intensified *Haidamack* hatred of the Jews. The Polish authorities were unable to defend their own nationals, let alone members of an unfavored minority. As a rule, small prey were chosen: traveling Jewish merchants, Jewish tenant farmers, and outlying *shtetlakh*. Several *Haidamack* assaults, however, turned into large-scale massacres. One example was a murderous assault on Poles and Jews in the town of Umman, led by the *Haidamack* chieftain Gonta,[66] who spared neither women nor children. The *Haidamack* revolt was finally suppressed by a combined Russian-Polish effort; the legacy of these brigands lingers on in Ukrainian nationalist lore and literature.

Ignoring the declared neutrality of the Commonwealth, foreign armies marched through Poland and Lithuania twice at this time: in 1735, when the Russo-Turkish War broke out, and in 1740-1763 during the Austrian wars of succession. Young Poles and Lithuanians were forcibly drafted into the Russian and Prussian armies, which plundered the land to meet their needs. In 1742, Czarina Elizabeth's army occupied part of the Commonwealth and expelled Jews wherever they were found.

A runaway gentry destroyed respect for higher authority in Lithuania. Elected officials answerable to the gentry gained control over the financial affairs of individual towns, thereby infringing on the magnates' private townships and destroying what remained of sound governance there. The gentry then dominated the burghers, peasants, and Jews. Finally they surpassed the king in political influence and became the most powerful force in the Commonwealth. They wrested control of the export trade in corn, potash, hemp, and cattle from the burghers and the Jews; as time passed, they increased their share of the local market as well.

As economic opportunities contracted and money became scarce, Christian antisemitism increased markedly. Anti-Jewish feelings were fomented by an actively antisemitic mayor of Kaunas, who confined the Jewish population to a ghetto, and by fanatical clergy, particularly the Jesuits. (To mitigate the Jesuits' anti-Jewish activity somewhat, the Councils paid them an annual "fee" for distribution among the most rabid student agitators.)

Accusations of blood libel and witchcraft became so frequent that the Councils of Poland and Lithuania dispatched an emissary to the Holy See, who ordered Lorenzo Cardinal Ganganelli, subsequently Pope Clement XIV, to look

into the charges. The Cardinal submitted his report in 1759. Quoting former
Church authorities, especially Popes Gregory IX and Innocent IV, Cardinal
Ganganelli branded the accusations false and recommended that the Church
act to protect the Jews against the blood libel.

The record of Frederick Augustus III on the Jews is mixed. In 1738, he
reconfirmed all the Jewish Charters and privileges and allowed the Jews to
open new shops and sell liquor. In the same year, he imposed a 1,500-zloty
head-tax on city dwellers. No one could afford this, but the Jews were
especially affected because, apart from their many commitments in support
of their own communities, they bore the heaviest burden of taxation in the
land. Frederick Augustus III, like his father, gave the Jews a ten-year
moratorium and absolved the Jewish Councils from interest payments on
their tax liabilities. The king was ambivalent in his support of the Jews in
legal struggles with the burghers and the municipalities, siding chiefly with
the latter in their claims against Jewish citizens.

Meanwhile, the Commonwealth stumbled on. Power resided in the hands
of the aristocracy, a handful of magnates, and several thousand squires. The
great families neglected their civic and local duties in favor of endless
squabbles. The free peasantry and the yeomanry slid into serfhood. Many
self-serving aristocrats steadily stripped once-flourishing towns of wealth
and influence. Corrective efforts were made. Bruhl, backed by the powerful
Czartoryski family, tried to restore sound governance by amending the
constitution to abolish the *liberum veto* and form a standing army. He failed.
In 1744, Antoni Potocki tried to save the cities from ruin by presenting the
Grodno Diet with a manifesto.

In 1761, Frederick Augustus III, Bruhl, the Polish treasurer Wessel, and
the Lithuanian Fleming transferred the mints of Poland and Lithuania to
Leipzig and Dresden, where mintage of the Commonwealth coins was
entrusted to the Jewish firm of Efraim Gumpetz Itzig and Company.
According to the terms set forth by the king and his advisers, the precious
metals used in this coinage were to be debased and the "savings" remitted to
the king. The king profited vastly from this arrangement that year and
ordered the Jewish firm to continue its work. When the fraud was discovered,
European merchants declared the coins valueless and refused to accept them.
The Commonwealth is believed to have lost several million zlotys through the
transaction. The king and his treasurers allowed their Jewish subordinates
to take the blame; the resulting antisemitic turbulence throughout the

country did incalculable harm to the reputation of the entire Jewish community.

These were the Dark Ages in the annals of Poland and Lithuania, and prominent among those who experienced the brutality and corruption were the Jews. Following a Polish practice, Catholic-controlled municipalities in Vilnius, Brisk, Novogrodek, Gardinas, and elsewhere incited hooligans to assault Jewish men, women and children and to loot Jewish homes in pursuit of otherwise uncollectible taxes. In 1728-1730, the Government prohibited the leasing to Jews of the franchise to collect customs duties. The Jewish Council supported this proscription for ethical as well as political reasons. Most Jews involved in these dealings, however, managed to overcome the ban by taking on well-known Christian partners. As late as 1756, there were complaints that Jews held leases in Vilna, Kovno, Grodno, and other cities. It was known, for example, that Jacob Perez, brother-in-law of Rabbi Asher of Vilna, held the lease on liquor in that city, although he and many others were officially represented by a gentile magnate named Mintkiewitz. Mintkiewitz, to be sure, was unable to help Perez when the municipality sent soldiers to beat and torture him.

It became customary for Jews to supply the Voivode and his assistants with luxuries such as Turkish furs and boots and commodities such as salt, sugar, and spices. They were expected to pay the wages of the Voivode's guard and servants plus sufficient remittances to provide most of the services he needed. Even when this practice was banned in 1745, municipal officials continued to expect and, indeed, insist that the Jewish community shower them with even more money, goods and services. The Jews understood that these senior officials expected these gratuities to enable them to maintain their indulgences. In 1756-1759, senior officials simply looted Jewish homes, synagogues, and businesses in Vilna, Minsk, Brisk, and elsewhere whenever they needed money. In his autobiography, philosopher Salomon Maimon describes looting by Voivode Karl Radziwill. Junior officials merited different treatment, since they were the executors of the law. For them, outright bribery was needed.

The Church did not interfere with the patrimonial administration of justice by the barons, which made some of these petty nobles the masters of life and death of their subjects. The majority of the clergy did not lift a finger to protect the serfs and peasants, who could be bought and sold like any other chattel. Many absentee landlords were at the mercy of estate overseers. So, too, were Jews who happened to live near baronial estates; these barons were able to deprive them of their *servi-camerae* status as well as their material goods and well-being.

Municipal leaders wished to terminate the involvement and interference of the Russians, Prussians, and Austrians in the internal affairs of the Commonwealth. They pleaded for peace and sponsored the so-called Sarmantian Movement. They preferred the simple life, as reflected in their very mode of dress. Their policy called for free elections, clean government, the retention of the *liberum veto*, tolerance of all religious denominations, and maintenance of the status quo in economic affairs. When the Russian and Saxon-occupied territories were liberated and returned to the Commonwealth in 1736-1737, the squires regained their power over the peasants. Some in the movement sought to purge the country of Western influence; a few favored deposing the king. Matrimonial alliances by Frederick Augustus III with France and Austria (1748) dashed all hope of this kind. In desperation, the Czartoryskis, who had previously supported Frederick Augustus and Bruhl, now appealed to the Russian royal court through their nephew, Stanislaw Poniatowski, Jr. This was no trifling individual; he was the Saxon minister at St. Petersburg, a favorite of Czarina Elizabeth (1741-1761) and the German Duchess Catherina, princess of Anhalt-Zebst, who, in turn, became the Czarina Catherine II after the death of Elizabeth and the assassination of Peter III. Seeing that all was lost, Frederick Augustus III and Bruhl left for Saxony in 1763. They settled in Dresden and hoped from there to negotiate with the Czarina. The king died later that year. His supposed last words were: "My life was one of unceasing sin. May God have mercy on me."

The Last King of Poland-Lithuania

The Commonwealth was disintegrating. The treaty of St. Petersburg in 1764 allowed Czarina Catherine II and Frederick II of Prussia to decide the future of Poland and Lithuania. Again a foreign power – two powers, to be precise – would elect the king. The chosen one was Stanislaw II Poniatowski, a nephew of the powerful Czartoryskis who had won the heart of Catherine II. Many leading families, hoping to secure the Crown for a scion or friend, had presented their own candidates to no avail.

Poniatowski was the last king of the Polish-Lithuania Commonwealth. The combined population of the two countries was roughly 11.5 million at the time. Dissatisfaction with the new king was rife. It embraced Protestant and

Orthodox adherents, who, although constituting the greater part of the population of Lithuania, had no political rights and restricted religious and economic liberties.

Poniatowski tried to function as an independent ruler with Czartoryski support. His first act was an attempt to introduce constitutional reform; Nicholai Repnin, representative of the Empress of Russia, vetoed it. Then the king sought to curtail the powers of the hetmans and treasurers and the use of the *liberum veto* by establishing commissions – ministries of sorts – of war and finance. Repnin and his Prussian counterpart would not hear of it, insisting that the Commonwealth first grant equal rights to the Protestant and Orthodox minorities. In 1766, the Sejm, to which only practicing Catholics could be elected, refused.

In 1767, the lesser gentry recognized Catherine II as the Protectoress of the Commonwealth. Repnin reciprocated by encouraging this class to form its own confederation in Radom, and helped them by sending important personalities in the opposition, including bishops, ministers, and hetmans, into exile. The Czartoryskis, too, lost their power and were replaced by the Russian representatives of the Czarina. The lower nobility then demanded further restrictions on the rights of foreigners and Jews, most of whom were Commonwealth citizens. Specifically, these undesirables were to be excluded from the offices of tax collector, customs agent, and border inspector. A census of Jews was to be conducted in order to increase poll tax revenues. Finally, Jewish trade and residence rights were to be restricted, lest Christian merchants meet with harmful competition.

Poniatowski endorsed this program, and both the king and the Sejm approved the demands of the lower gentry simultaneously. The Government now discovered that the two Jewish Councils had been collecting larger sums than their tax assessments warranted, using the surplus for community needs and, at times, private purposes. From 1765 onward, all Jews irrespective of age and gender were assessed an annual poll tax of two zlotys. (In the same year, however, the king extended the Lithuanian Jewish Charter and privileges for another 20 years and exempted Jewish farmers from the poll tax.)

The community institutions organized to fight the decree. A supremely important actor in this effort was the *shtadlan*, the community pleader, Arieh Leib Meitess. His gravestone bears the following testimonial: "He brought great salvation to the Jews by his wisdom in the year 5544 (1784)," when, supported by the powerful Vice Chancellor of Lithuania, Joachim Chreptowitz, the Jews of Lithuania resecured their rights of domicile and economic privileges within the law. Antisemitic campaigns by municipalities, artisan class, and the burghers continued, but were resolved by the Royal Court to the Jews' satisfaction. By that time, the Commonwealth as it had existed thus far was no more.

The First Partitioning of Poland and Lithuania

Domestic integrity continued to unravel. In 1768, a small group of gentry joined forces with several magnates to form the Confederation of Bar. The result was an armed uprising in Podolia against the Russian influence and such reforms as were afoot. The king sided with the Russians against the opposition and destroyed the Confederate forces, although pockets of Confederate partisans pursued the lost cause for another four years.

In 1769, serfs and peasants in Vilnius, Trakai, Kaunas, Vilkaviskis, Pinsk, Minsk, Brisk, Gardinas, and Nougardukas rebelled against their oppressive conditions. The insurrection was quashed with great loss of life and property but led to several pieces of reform-minded legislation. The gentry firmly opposed the new laws, which had in the meantime been gazetted in the country's legal code; they regarded the entire code as preparing the way for the liberation of the serfs and the townspeople.

In 1772, the outside forces that truly controlled the country stepped in. Catherine II of Russia, Frederick II of Prussia, and Joseph II, son of Maria Theresa of Austria, signed a treaty that led to the First Partition of Poland and Lithuania. Russia occupied Polock, Vitebsk, and Mtislavl on the eastern border of Lithuania, as well as Livonia. Austria seized Galicia and the southern part of Poland as far as the Vistula. Prussia acquired northern Poland, which it renamed Western Prussia. The annexations were effected without armed opposition. Poniatowski accepted the terms of the partition and, one year later, assembled the general Sejm of the Commonwealth and asked it to ratify them. When the Sejm balked, the Russian and Prussian representatives were obliged once more to apply intimidation and bribery to achieve their aims.

Now Poniatowski reorganized his Government administration, having first obtained the approval of his Russian masters, of course. He created a permanent National Council with 36 members: 18 senators and 18 Sejm deputies, two-thirds from Poland and one-third from Lithuania. He established five departments – foreign affairs, war, finance, justice, and police – and a national education commission that was instructed to form a countrywide school system. The latter project was an outgrowth of an additional upheaval of the era: the dissolution of the Jesuit Order by papal action in 1773. Since the Jesuits had organized and managed most schools in Lithuania and Poland until that time, the government simply confiscated the Order's vast holdings to finance the new state-run system.

Jewish affairs were not at the forefront of Poniatowski's concerns. The Royal Court indeed realized the valuable services that the Jews provided the country in its economic development and foreign trade. Not until 1784, however, were Jews allowed to engage in any business or vocation they wished. At this time, their terms of existence were rendered more or less equal to those of other citizens. The special annual taxes were abolished; Jews were liable only to the residence taxes that other citizens faced. If they had grievances or wished to appeal their tax assessments, they were allowed to petition the Royal Court against municipal councils. As before, Jewish taxes (i.e., those remaining after the elimination of the annual tax) were collected by the *Kahal* and forwarded to the municipalities.

Many Jews (and burghers) lost additional privileges because of general reform efforts made at this time. In 1776, the Sejm deprived the towns and villages of the home-rule rights that the Magdeburg Laws had given them.[67] The people of the smaller towns were reduced to near-serfdom, although they were paid for the work they performed. Jews who had collected state revenues under Grand Ducal concessions now became small shopkeepers or lessees of inns and taverns.

Several economic improvements were made under the new regime. Bridges and highways were built, as was a canal linking the River Niemunas with the Dnieper, thus connecting the Baltic and the Black Sea. Since Jews were well represented among the timber merchants, they pioneered the use of the waterways to transport their goods. Count Anthony Tyzenhaus, the so-called father of Lithuanian industry, founded his business empire in Grodno and brought in experts, many of whom were Jewish, to expand his activities through Lithuania.

This is not to imply that Lithuania had abandoned its previous ways; nor was it fully immune to foreign entanglements.[68] Just the same, new trends had become evident. Under the leadership of Lithuanian Marshal Ignatius Potocki, the Sejm introduced a series of social reforms with the king's support. These novelties were evidently influenced by the ideals of the American Revolution and the French Revolution, which had swept the civilized world and reached deep into the consciousness of the people of Poland and Lithuania. Of special importance in this context was the question of individual rights.

Marshal Potocki's social reforms gave towns people administrative and judicial autonomy, as well as representation in the Sejm, which now made its decisions by a majority vote. The infamous *liberum veto* was no more. The National Council was replaced by a Cabinet of Ministers. Two-thirds of the cabinet might levy taxes, but only a three-quarter majority could declare war or endorse a treaty. In all state institutions shared by both countries, the number of Poles and Lithuanians was to be equal.

In 1790, the Sejm, which sat between 1778 and 1792 as stipulated by its new constitution, elected a special deputation to review the laws governing the status of the Jews. However, the Sejm completely ignored the Jewish question in its sessions of the following year. Three changes affecting the Jews occurred at this time: all religions including Judaism were given freedom of conscience; a municipalities law expanded the jurisdiction of municipal courts and stipulated that only Christians would be recognized as citizens; and a new constitution was enacted in 1791, in which individuals' equality before the law was conspicuously absent.

The Jews were upset with the municipal reform; they considered the municipalities hostile to their interests and preferred to be under Voivode jurisdiction. They sought to achieve this revision with the support of Mattiau Butrimowitz of Pinsk, leader of the Sejm deputation. Their pleas were rejected, and the Jewish communities now found themselves under the municipal thumb.

The municipal animosity transcended mere antisemitism. When Jews and burghers clashed (and, for that matter, when Jewish artisans and Christian guilds tussled), the issue at stake was often economic survival, not economic advancement. The competition was stiff, the market limited, and poverty acute. Christian merchants and burghers frequently exploited the misery and distress of Christian artisans in order to incite them against Jewish traders and craftsmen. Exploiting the Jews as scapegoats, the burghers enhanced their own economic status at the expense of their less educated artisan rivals.

The burgher class strongly favored the constitution of 1791, confident that its built-in inequities would keep the ignorant, illiterate peasants, whom the burghers despised, in their place.

The newly downscaled Commonwealth hardly knew the meaning of foreign affairs. Czarina Catherine II granted her agent in Poland-Lithuania, Nicholai Repnin, the title of prince. Repnin's behavior justified this sobriquet; he treated members of the Polish-Lithuanian Sejm as Russian vassals and let them know that it was his duty, and theirs, to safeguard the interests of the Empress of Russia. By 1792, Catherine herself had concluded treaties ending the hostilities with Sweden and Turkey; she therefore felt free to meddle in the affairs of Poland and Lithuania once again. Specifically, the Czarina was displeased with changes made in the constitution of 1775, even though she had previously approved them, and was determined to nullify them by force of arms.

The invading Russian armies were aided in Lithuania by units organized under Joseph Kasankawskas and the Polish fifth column, the Targowitza. Resistance to the Czarina was spearheaded in Poland by Joseph Poniatowski, the king's nephew, and in Lithuania by Tadeusz Kosciuzko, a veteran of the American Revolutionary War.

The Jews of the Commonwealth sided with the loyalists: as hard as life had become for them under local rule, Russian attitudes toward Jews only augured greater suffering. Thus the community leadership in Vilna urged the noncombatants to support the revolt by donating money and supplying information on Russian troop movements. The community leader (*Rosh ha-Kahal*), Noah b. Feibush Bloch, provided Polish troops with gunpowder, Jewish tailors in Vilna donated several hundred uniforms at no charge, and the Council of Lithuania raised approximately 35,000 gulden[69] to support the uprising. A second consequence of the Jewish stance was the formation in Lithuania of a privately funded Jewish cavalry regiment composed of 500 volunteers, initiated and commanded by Colonel Berek Joselewitz of Kretinga, himself Jewish.

The Second and Third Partitions

The hostilities ended with yet another partitioning and foreign annexation of Commonwealth territory. Russia annexed the eastern provinces of Lithuania, including Minsk and Pinsk, and the eastern sections of Poland, comprising Western Ukraine, Podolia, and Wolhynia. Prussia seized Danzig, Thorn, and part of Greater Poland. Austria was not involved. At the request of Russia and Prussia, the last general Sejm met in Grodno to discuss and ratify the terms, as dictated to the parliamentarians by John James von Sievers, the Czarina's ambassador. The delegates to the Sejm were handpicked and carefully screened this time. Just the same, it took threats and violence, backed by the menacing presence of Russian troops, to persuade the deputies to ratify the Second Partition in 1793.

Poniatowski was allowed to remain on the throne, since the Russians preferred to deal with him rather than with the gentry. The National Council and the Commissions for Finance and War were restored, but the Commonwealth armies were downscaled to 15,000 men. Armed resistance erupted again in 1794. At first it seemed successful: Warsaw and Vilna were liberated, and Joseph Kasankawskas, the Russian-appointed Hetman, was hanged along with other traitors. Kosciuzko proclaimed the liberation of all serfs in Poland and Lithuania and supplied them with arms to join the resistance. The Jewish regiment was reorganized and many Jews returned from exile to join Kosciuzko's army. The resurgence was short-lived. The resistance forces were crushed and Kosciuzko was taken prisoner. Joselewitz fled, and most of the soldiers of his Jewish regiment, which fought near Pragha-Warsaw, fell in combat. What remained of Joselewitz was his glory. Polish history regards him as a hero. Songs were composed and stories written about his valor, patriotism, and death. His widow was granted a state pension and she and her children were permitted to reside in a district of Warsaw where Jews were normally banned.

Russia, Prussia, and Austria moved in for the third and final partition of the Commonwealth, which was consummated in 1795. Stanislas Poniatowski formally abdicated the throne and settled in Grodno. After Catherine died in 1796 and was succeeded by her son, Czar Paul I, Poniatowski moved to St. Petersburg, where he died in 1798.

The shared history of Poland and Lithuania, and of their Jewish communities, had come to an end. The remainder of this chronicle will concern itself with Lithuanian Jewry only. Therefore, a summary is in order.

Taking Stock: Formation of a Jewish Community

The Commonwealth of Poland and Lithuania had existed for roughly 400 years, but Lithuanian Jewry, much smaller than its Polish counterpart, remained distinct and unique throughout. Even in their Hebrew and Yiddish pronunciations, one could differentiate between Lithuanian Jews and their Polish brethren. Historian Joseph Klausner explains this uniqueness as a consequence of the many influences that the community founders had brought. Indeed, they were a heterogeneous group of migrants, hailing from the Crimea, Germany, Palestine, Babylonia, Syria, Spain, Italy, and Turkey. The Karaites also left their imprint. The end product was the *Litvak*, the Lithuanian Jew, member of a community with its own perspective of the surrounding Jewish world.

From their murky origins, three principal communities took shape by the early seventeenth century: Brest/Brisk, Pinsk, and Horodno/Grodno. Brisk was by far the largest community at that time, incorporating some 30 smaller *kehillot* (congregations or subcommunities) in its environs; Pinsk only had eight, Grodno seven. The three collectives co-founded the Council of Lithuanian Jewish Communities (*Va'ad Lita*), an assertion of their independence from the Council of the Four Lands, in 1623. Not until 1652, and then only after lengthy negotiations, was the *Kahal* of Vilna, capital of Lithuania, allowed to join the Council.

Electoral rights in the Council were reserved for three types of community members: householders, the affluent, and learned individuals who had earned the titles *morenu* (teacher) or *haver* (fellow). These were formal designations with criteria that had to be met. *Morenu* was reserved for scholars more than 30 years of age who had been married at least ten years and whose main pursuit was devotional. The title *haver* was awarded jointly by the local community rabbi and two *rashey yeshivot* (heads of talmudic colleges) to deserving men who had been married for more than two years; it was a mark of recognition for honest, just, and exemplary behavior.

Once elected, the Council operated on four levels: dealings with the gentile authorities, relations with other Jewish communities, internal community affairs, and the individual domain.

The Council's role vis-a-vis the gentile authorities was twofold. Its most important duty was to collect and forward revenues from numerous and diverse taxes to the royal treasury. The Sejm had taxed Jews for the support of the army as early as 1581, and added a duty for the foreign occupation forces some time later. In due course, the list included poll tax (*poglowne*), householder tax (*podymne*), gate tax (*powrotne*), a special business tax (*solutiones*), tolerance tax, various food taxes, (*nahrungssteuer*), and a beverage tax (*czopowe*). It was the Council's job to dun each community in accordance with its size and wealth. Several classes of Jews were exempt from taxation: the indigent poor, rabbis, rabbinical-court judges (*dayanim*), and yeshiva students. *Kahal* employees were given substantial reductions.

The second area of Council interaction with gentile agencies was legal defense. The Council supervised and protected Jewish economic rights and defended Jews against the blood libel, accusations of desecration of the host, and other calumnies. In these cases, the Council often had occasion to petition the Royal Court.

Within the greater Jewish milieu, the Council functioned as an arbiter in inter-community disagreements and disputes between individual subcommunities and their members. It also administered charity and assistance for the poor, which were important activities not only in the day-to-day life of the individual Jew but also in the organized activity of the Council and the *Kahal*. From 1649 onwards, the Council, in concert with many European communities, invested much money and effort in the redemption of Jewish prisoners[70] whom the Tartars offered for sale in the slave markets of Constantinople. In Lithuania and Poland, this activity expanded to include Jews who had been imprisoned for defaulting on debts.

After 1650, refugees who reached Lithuania were allowed to establish homes and businesses without the need to pay the *Kahal* for these rights (*hazaqa*) during their first year in the country. Each subcommunity, however small, had to provide full support for one poor refugee and his family, and in 1652 the Council itself chose to support 2,000 such refugees for a period of six months. Local indigents who posed as refugees in order to solicit alms were severely punished.

The Brest and Grodno communities undertook to marry off ten poor brides apiece and to provide homes for the newlyweds. Widows and orphans were, of course, supported by their communities. Each *Kahal* kept a doctor, a pharmacist, and a midwife on the staff to take care of the sick and the needy. The *Kahal* also collected donations for various institutions in the Holy Land and assisted community members who wished to settle there.

Within the community, the Council administered Jewish public works, buildings, and courts. It appointed rabbis, judges, teachers, and community functionaries. It provided charity and assistance to widows, orphans, refugees, and the poor. The Council was responsible for yeshivot and *hadarim* (schools for young boys), printing and purchase of books, and the welfare of underfinanced schools.

At the individual level, the Council monitored the religious, moral, and ethical behavior of Lithuanian Jews in all areas of life: synagogue, business, family affairs, even relations between neighbors. It enacted and enforced *taqanot* (ordinances – roughly 100 by the end of 1623 alone!) that governed everything they did. Card games, dice, and lotteries were prohibited. It was forbidden to allow one's wife or children to work for a lender to whom a loan could not be repaid. The dismissal of a fellow Jew from his position or *arenda* (lease) for default on payments was proscribed, as was the offering of large amounts of money to obtain a post already paid for and held by another Jew.

The authority and power of the Council began to decline after 1648 under the weight of resource shortfall, mounting debt, arbitrary new taxes, and internal squabbling. Opposition to the Council and the *Kahal* structure gathered momentum. It was led by the "commoner" class among the Jews (*'amkha*), which was no longer willing to tolerate the leadership of the *Kahal* elders, most of whom belonged to wealthy families. The commoners, like the scholars, tended to despise those who resided below them on the socioeconomic scale, namely the workers, pedlars, and market vendors, whom they scorned as the "unlearned" (*'am ha-arets*).

The lower classes were, of course, disfranchised and unable to influence the decisions of the Council, the *Kahal*, or related institutions, even in matters directly connected with them. In one instance recorded in *Pinkas Vilna*, the Vilna community ledger, we learn that the *Kahal* sold a building that it owned without consulting the 24 Jewish families that dwelled there or considering their needs. In another example, the Council misappropriated funds earmarked for bribery of government officials in order to extend its own powers. In yet another case, annual tax revenues meant for the repair of a synagogue, a ritual bath, and several small prayer-houses (*kloyzn*) disappeared into thin air.

The *Kahal* agencies sometimes sought to augment their inadequate income by selling off or mortgaging properties that they owned. An additional source of *Kahal* revenue was the sale of business concessions, which were usually valid for a period of five or ten years. On rare occasions, they inherited property bequeathed to them by wealthy Jews. More often, they took loans and fell heavily into debt.

In one particularly ugly incident, a Jewish family bought a house from the Vilna *Kahal* without realizing that the property was heavily mortgaged. Unable to obtain redress from its own rabbinical tribunal, the family sued the *Kahal* in the Fortress Royal Court. The sides reached a compromise.

Instances of mismanagement aside, the Council was the agency through which Lithuanian Jewry fashioned a self-sufficient economy. Jews were involved in all kinds of trades and crafts: they were shopkeepers, butchers and bakers, cobblers and masons, brewers and jewelers, goldsmiths and coppersmiths and tinsmiths. They were also chimney sweeps, guards, and fishermen. Their professions included medicine and banking, music and teaching.[71] Some, of course, were brokers, shippers, and timber merchants. Tradesmen and craftsmen formed self-help societies, and several occupations had their own *kloyzn* (small prayer-rooms). One of the most important and powerful societies, common to all Jewish communities, was the *hevra kadisha*, the burial society, to which the most highly respected members of the community belonged.

All religious, social, cultural and administrative activities were concentrated in the *shulhoyf*, a complex that, together with the adjacent synagogue (*shul*), formed a protective court. Here one could find the rabbinical court, the *miqve* (ritual bath), the kosher abattoir, and the *brunim*, the well that served everyone in the vicinity.

The *shulhoyf* was the community's hub. Here Jewish strangers and visitors gravitated; here Jewish merchants returning from afar would report the latest news. It was the venue where one could hear scholarly discourse, catch up on the latest gossip, and discuss arranged marriages (*shidukhim*).

The last-mentioned practice was widespread. It was not unusual at the time for parents to marry off children at the age of eleven.[72] Child-couples would live with their parents, generally those of the girl-wife, until the boy grew up and could support a family. Many Lithuanian Jewish wives, however, sought employment so that their young husbands might continue their devotional studies.

As numerous as the Jews' community taxes were, the revenues marshalled were chronically inadequate. In response, the Council devised the *korobka*, a sales tax of sorts. Initially imposed on the purchase of kosher meat and poultry, it was soon extended to include many other products. As the tax burden slowly but steadily rose, individual communities showed growing manifestations of independence. The first open rift occurred in 1721, when several localities rebelled against the Council for various reasons, chiefly the rapidly increasing poll tax. The Council reacted in a novel way: collective banishment, i.e., excommunication of the recalcitrant communities. The offended parties then sued the Council before the fiscal tribunal of Lithuania. There was also considerable tension between small subcommunities and the larger entities to which they belonged because of allegedly disproportionate apportioning of the tax burden. Within the *Kahal*, members of wealthy families struggled to secure important positions in community institutions for relatives and friends, even though anti-nepotism regulations were on the books.

Consequently, the *Kahal* institution came under fire from two directions. The community rank-and-file pressed the grievances described above and insisted that the local agency retain some of the tax revenues for local needs. Insofar as the *Kahal* acceded to these demands, it attracted the disapproval of the Council.

The Council and the *Kahal* had little real authority to impose their decisions and punish individuals who violated their regulations. Admittedly, gentile courts were available, but Jewish law strongly discouraged recourse to them, *a fortiori* in strictly internal problems. Practically speaking, the most drastic weapon was excommunication. For offenses that did not warrant this measure, the *Kahal* resorted to the *kune*, a pillory in the vestibule of the synagogue, where passersby were invited to subject the sinner to verbal abuse. Abba of Halusk describes the experience in a letter that he sent from Vilna to Berlin:

> I was led to the *kune*. My neck was clamped in iron rings attached to the wall. A piece of paper was laid on my head, bearing the following message, 'This man has been punished for scoffing at the words of our holy teachers.' Thus I was exposed to the large congregation, who spat in my face and called me 'traitor of Israel.' They kept me in this position for one day and one night. The next day, after the service, I was expelled from the city.

Some delinquents were subjected to flagellation (*malqot*) or to confinement in an *arrest-shtibl*, a room used as a prison cell. Chiefly, however, the *Kahal* used moral suasion to urge community members to obey the law of the land, honor the Jewish civil ordinances, and live in accordance with their age-old traditions.

The Jewish institutions applied sanctions for the sake of moral probity, for example, when women took to peddling in response to shrinking economic opportunities and rising poverty in the community. In 1752, the Council forbade women peddlers to offer their wares in non-Jewish homes unless a Jewish male was present. More than modesty was at stake: the Council meant to discourage women from peddling, since this occupation was considered a man's prerogative. The Jewish poor, who sorely needed the side income that their womenfolk might earn, bitterly resented this ordinance. Other rules regulated the leasing of inns by Jews and the quantity of strong drinks they might sell to serfs and peasants. The purpose was to fend off the frequent accusation that Jews were the cause of drunkenness among the peasants. Opponents of these ordinances included the gentile distillers, most of whom belonged to the magnate class, who profited greatly by intoxicating the peasantry. Large, ostentatious weddings and bar-mitzva celebrations, patterned after banquets held by magnates and the nobility, were considered not only dangerous but also sinful and therefore forbidden. An ordinance of similar intent, reenacted in almost every generation, banned the flaunting of expensive silk clothing and jewelry, which was thought to foment jealousy and antisemitism to the extent of pogroms.

Rich and powerful Jews disregarded these sanctions and indulged in the prohibitions to their hearts' content. One reason for their impunity was the abolition of *herem* and other penalties. Another reason was the general decline of the authority of the Council and the *Kahal*, under the weight of Jewish community factors and externalities connected with the magnate regime in Lithuania.

Indeed, the magnates effectively ran Lithuania and Poland throughout the eighteenth century, making the Royal Fiscal Administration virtually superfluous. For the Jews, this had advantages and disadvantages. The war-starved magnates constantly petitioned the kings for special protective duties, ordinances, and charters that would expand their markets. The kings acceded to this; they also approached the Jews for money. While some Jews were adversely affected, others were hired by the magnates to sell farm produce locally and export it to the West through Danzig and Breslau. Jews, in turn, employed Lithuanian or Russian agents to represent them in areas such as Moscow that were off-limits to them. In general, the magnates protected their Jewish intermediaries and tended to their needs. On the other hand, they kept the Jews at their mercy, punished them at will, and dictated their wishes with no recourse in law. And they always wanted their Jews to generate greater revenues.

Thus, in 1764 the magnates and the government tackled a grave problem: the system of Jewish taxation and the debts owned by the community on account of them. The magnates were especially incensed to discover that on one emergency occasion, the Council had diverted poll tax revenues to internal Jewish community needs. The remedy, they believed, was to dissolve the Jewish intermediaries, the Council and the *Kahal*, and introduce direct, individual remissions of taxes to the government. King Poniatowski was more than willing, and with the encouragement of Czarina Catherine the government withdrew its recognition of the Councils' authority and recommended their abolition. In January 1765, the Sejm ordered the Council of Lithuania to dissolve.

Every Jewish male and female was now liable to a poll tax of two zlotys – a considerable sum for the poor. A census taken that year, showed that 157,300 Jews in Lithuania were liable; Jewish historians believe the true number to be over 200,000.

The *Kahal*, although officially disempowered, still had to act as the government's agent for collection purposes. Furthermore, when the enormity of the Jews' debts to the magnates, burghers, and priests (and their inability to repay them) became known, the government also insisted that the Councils continue to exist until all outstanding moneys were raised. Special combined government-Jewish committees were formed to deal with these problems, and the *Kahals* and the Councils continued to meet and function until 1772. At that time, after the First Partition, the Russian Government reempowered the old institutions.

In 1776, the Lithuania *Kahals* began issuing passports to community members.[73] Concurrently, the Councils were officially dissolved again. The Treasury appointed a liquidation commission to investigate the tax indebtedness of each Council, *kehilla*, and *Kahal*; to revise the tax-collection procedures; and to suggest new ways of upping Jewish revenues. The commission demanded that each affected agency submit detailed accounts of its income. *Kahal* officials – rabbis, elders, *shtadlanim*, *gaba'im*, trustees – had to attest under oath, in their synagogues, that the statements were true. The liquidation commission then arranged terms of amortization and payment at compound interest, calculated into the future. A member of the liquidation commission explained: "Pitying the Jews for their poverty and the disasters that had befallen the communities, they agreed to lower the annual interest rate to three percent." Pity aside, the commission was trying to be realistic about the Jews' repayment abilities. The *kehillot* and the outgoing Council knew, however, that even three percent was too much and that the accumulation of further debt was inevitable.

In 1766, the commission disclosed the extent of debt owed by Lithuanian Jewry: some two million gulden, principally to the monastic orders. The liquidation commission forbade the *kehillot* to take new loans and to farm out the collection of taxes. It even banned the use of excommunication, thus asserting its ability to affect the *Kahal's* internal prerogatives. Just the same, in 1773 the Council of Lithuania was forced (and allowed) to borrow half a million gulden at five percent to repay some of their emergency loans and for other purposes.

The liquidation commission failed to extricate the *kehillot* from their financial woes. One reason was that local officials continued to hit the desperate communities with fresh new taxes. In 1786, the government replaced the liquidation commission with a new commission of inquiry and appointed two new controllers: one to audit local officials and another to oversee the finances of the *kehillot*. For the next five years, the incumbents in the latter position came and went. This, however, was not for lack of power. When they felt a show of force was necessary, the controllers would often incarcerate, for several months at a time, elders who had signed promissory notes on behalf of their communities. The purpose was to coerce the elders to pay up from their own resources or with properties they owned.

The new controllers and commissions, too, failed in their cardinal mission. Consequently, the Treasury farmed out the collection of Jewish taxes to a group of Jews who paid the government 60,000 gulden per annum for this concession. The concessions were abolished in 1788, the tax farmers were handsomely compensated, and the problem remained unsolved.

The Treasury now insisted that taxes be remitted directly by each individual Jew, who would be held personally liable for nonpayment. The *Kahal* continued to collect *korobka*, a meat tax with which communities raised funds for their own needs. This was supposed to be a stopgap measure: the government advised the communities that *korobka* and other extra levies would be forever discontinued as soon as all debts were paid. But the debts were never paid; nor could they.

In 1791, the leaders of the Jewish communities in Lithuania gathered in the market town of Zhalva to discuss ways of counteracting the Jewish reforms enacted by the Sejm on May 3 of that year, which were decidedly unfavorable to their interests. Reforms on the Jewish question were an ongoing process. Other items on the agenda included a three-year extension of an ordinance prohibiting Jewish women to wear expensive clothing and jewelry.

The Jewish representatives, 14 of whom came from Lithuania, subsequently convened in Warsaw. Prominent among them was Dr. Shmaryahu Polonus who, influenced by the ideas and slogans of the French Revolution, had written to the Sejm emphasizing the Jewish contribution to the economy of the Commonwealth and demanding Liberty, Equality, and Fraternity for its Jewish subjects. Their most important meetings in the Polish capital were with Father Piatulli, the king's secretary, who promised the Jews freedom of worship and domicile and equal rights with the burghers, except for the right to be appointed to official government positions. This was no trifling achievement; in return for the king's signed approval of this plan, the Jewish community had decided to reward His Majesty with a gift of two million golden zlotys. The dismissal of Poniatowski in 1792 put the idea to rest.

At this point, the Sejm itself seized control of Jewish financial affairs as well as the community organizations themselves. In 1793, the legislature created a set of Liquidation Courts to deal with the problem – a solution not unaffected by antisemitism and lust for retribution. The special tribunals attempted to downscale the debts by a combination of writeoffs and reduction of interest rates; the purpose was not to achieve full collection but to start anew and reconsolidate Jewish financial administration for the future. Just the same, when the Russians occupied the territory allocated to them and established their own administration in Lithuania, they regarded the Jewish financial problems as an inefficiency inherited from the *ancien regime* that would have to be radically changed.

Not only the Russians were unhappy with the way the Jewish leadership had conducted its affairs. Many Jews, too, felt that the *Kahal* institution had

failed in its duty to safeguard their economic interests and protect them and
their property. They were dissatisfied with day-to-day administration and the
way elections were conducted. As their grievances mounted, the prestige of
the leadership diminished.

The Jewish leaders of Vilna and Grodno moved quickly to establish
relations with the new Russian masters, who were amiably disposed toward
Lithuanian Jewry at first. In 1795, just after the third and final partition of
the Commonwealth, Prince Repnin, now Governor of the Russian-occupied
territories, was presented with a longstanding Jewish request: to release the
communities – Vilna and Grodno in this case – from the jurisdiction and
authority of the municipal courts. As Repnin vacillated, the Lithuanian
Supreme Court ruled in favor of the petitioners and reconfirmed their right
to resolve their internal and religious problems in their rabbinical courts, the
batei-din. All other disputes were to be adjudicated in the Fortress Courts,
which were divisions of the Royal Court. This ruling remained in effect until
1808.

The Russians then reempowered the Kahals and expanded their internal
prerogatives. The resurgence was on paper only. Nepotism and corruption
again proliferated. More importantly, the Kahals failed to discharge one
cardinal duty: security. Gentile mobs beset the communities in search of
extortion money, often within the confines of the shulhoyf. Homes and shops
were looted; robberies and assault were endemic. The Kahals were helpless.
They lacked the money to pay for protection, hire guards, or bribe the police
(for which reason they deliberately delayed their arrival to the scene of
attacks). Ordinary Jews, the 'amkha, blamed the Kahals for this disastrous
state of affairs. No longer content to be dominated by the Kahal and eager to
assert their individuality, the rank-and-file rebelled, chiefly in Vilna and
Keidanai. The council and Kahal apparatus soon tumbled into a terminal
decline.

Unlike their power in purely Jewish affairs, the Councils had never been
able to apply more than mild pressure on the government, and then only for
purposes that they considered crucial for Jewish self-defense and survival.
They played no real part in the power politics of the country, nor did they seek
to do so. Nevertheless, the Councils were a state-within-a-state, endowed
with real autonomy – a condition that proved advantageous both to the Jews
and the country, and a modality on which other minorities in the
Commonwealth patterned their own internal affairs.

The formal structure lingered on until 1844. In that year, the Council and the *Kahals* as then constituted were dissolved for good by order of Czar Nicholas I. Self-rule for the Jews of Lithuania, such as it was, had come to an end. All fiscal and administrative authority was transferred to the municipalities and the government courts; the restructured *Kahals* retained one prerogative only: supervision of their own religious institutions.

Thus, much as the formation of Jewish governing bodies coincided with the coalescence of the Lithuanian state, so did they progress together to vassalship and eclipse. Concurrently, the Lithuanian Diaspora soared to world preeminence for its religious and intellectual accomplishments. This story follows.

Synagogue at Vizunai, Lithuania, second half of the 18th century

Chapter 3

THE RISE TO DIASPORA PREEMINENCE

Mitnaggedim and Hasidim in Lithuania

Although the Council was the elected authority of the Jewish communities of Lithuania at the time of the demise of the Commonwealth, the authority of its religious leadership was no less powerful. Indeed, it was this rabbinical leadership that gave the community its fame. Rabbi (hereinafter abbreviated as R.) Elijah ben Judah Solomon Zalman – the Vilna Gaon or, simply, "the Gaon"[74] – was undoubtedly the most prominent of the many outstanding scholars that Lithuanian Jewry produced in the early modern era and in subsequent generations.

The Gaon, born in 1720 in Silitsa near Grodno, mastered most of the Talmud and its commentaries as a child. He studied with some of the most renowned scholars of his time, among them R. Abraham Katzenelbogen of Brisk and R. Moishe Margoliot of Kedainai. At the age of 18 he married Hannah, daughter of R. Judah of Kedainai. His piety was austere and intellectual, characterized by total subservience to *halakha*, Jewish religious law. At the age of 25, he wandered incognito throughout Poland and Germany in the observance of a custom much in vogue among the very devout of that time: *oprikhtn golus* (self-imposed exile), a method of atonement for one's sins. By this time, even before he settled in Vilna, the Gaon was known as a *hasid* – a saint, but most definitely not a follower of hasidism, as we shall see – for his punctilious performance of the religious commandments. He was renowned for his devotion, modesty, and strict morality. He was said to have mastered all Talmudic and rabbinical literature. Although study was his all-consuming love, he did not confine himself to dry legal tomes; his passion embraced the classics of mysticism and the works of Maimonides. Although the Gaon was a great admirer of the latter, he disapproved of his philosophical writings because, to him, study of *halakha* and its application in everyday life were of paramount importance.

The Gaon never held an official position. His life was one of love, fear, and worship of God. His power, carefully reasoned and couched in legal, practical terms, was purely moral and exercised only in matters of injustice or the perversion of truth. The Gaon's contemporaries in every country submitted to his authority; for Lithuanian Jewry, he was the undisputed leader. Stories about the Gaon, spread by his disciples and the rank-and-file alike, described not a miracle-worker but a man of towering stature, intellectual prowess, and moral perfection. In time, he became a role model and an ideal that Lithuanian Jews might only strive to attain. Generations after his death, his personal characteristics inspired religious movements and trends that spanned the entire Jewish world.

The Jews of his time were beset by controversies right and left, and the Gaon was often asked to proffer an opinion that would inevitably be treated as law. In 1757, for example, he was asked to take a stance on an accusation by Rabbi Jacob Emden to the effect that Rabbi Jonathan Eibeschutz was a sympathizer or follower of Shabbetai Zevi. In this case the Gaon kept his own counsel, arguing that he was too young to intervene.

It was in 1768 that the Gaon settled in Vilna, when a relative and admirer, Eliyahu Pesseles, built for him a *beit midrash*, a devotional study hall, where he taught outstanding yeshiva students. In due course, most of the great scholars in Lithuania considered themselves *mi-talmidey ha-Gaon*, disciples of the Gaon. There was, however, an inner circle, composed of R. Hayyim of Volozhin (Volozhiner), R. Menachem Mendel and R. Simcha Bunim of Shklov, his own sons Arieh Leib and Abraham, and his son-in-law R. Moishe of Pinsk.

These disciples not only recorded the Gaon's teachings but disseminated new, innovative methods of Talmud study that he had introduced. The best known of these had to do with seemingly conflicting passages of the Talmud. The traditional solution in the yeshiva world was *pilpul* – dialectic casuistry meant to reconcile the differences. The Gaon rejected *pilpul* emphatically, choosing whenever possible to accept the *pshat*, the surface level of the text.

In his quest for true understanding of the Talmud, he was able to prove that many of the ostensible contradictions were caused by textual inaccuracies. His corrections appear in the margins of every edition of the Talmud today.

Another innovation of the Gaon was his critical method of studying the Talmud and its vast corpus of related literature. He preached the unity of all Jewish devotional study.[75] Almost alone among scholars of his time, he devoted much attention to the study of the Bible. He stressed the importance of mastering Hebrew grammar as well as any secular science that would promote better understanding of the devotional text. In 1778, to drive this point home, he commissioned his disciple and friend R. Baruch of Shklov to translate Euclid's *Geometry* into Hebrew, the only language he knew, apart from Yiddish. In the introduction to his translation, R. Baruch summarized the Gaon's doctrine as follows:

> If a man is deficient in the sciences, he will be deficient a hundredfold in knowledge of Torah, for Torah and science go together.

In addition to his all-consuming love of religious study, the Gaon placed great emphasis on the perfection of character, asserting that only among the pure of heart can Torah be effective. Since purity of heart and moral perfection were inconsistent with a hedonistic, pleasure-seeking life, the Gaon prescribed rigorous frugality and restraint of passion. For himself, the joy of study and worship was sufficient reward.

The Gaon became a model of emulation in these contexts and others. One exception, at least during his lifetime, was his aborted voyage to Palestine in 1783, undertaken alone with an intention to arrange for his family to join him later. He never explained the reason for his return, and the enigma has not been resolved.

His income came from two sources. One was a meager weekly allowance given to him by the community; he used part of it for his own family – often leaving his children hungry – and distributed the remainder to the poor. The other was a small supplement from a rich relative, Moishe Rivkes, who had established a fund to support the many scholars in his family. The Gaon rejected all other forms of financial aid.

He was an inflexible and uncompromising man, his strictness with himself carrying over into relations with others. In 1770, for example, he endorsed a rabbinical court decision to flog the Maggid (itinerant preacher) of Halusk for daring to question the method of Biblical exegesis used by the great commentator, Rashi. In general, however, he approved of the *maggidim*. One of his few close friends was R. Jacob ben Ze'ev Kranz, the Maggid of Dubnow, whose visits he welcomed and in whose company he relaxed somewhat.[76]

The Gaon also became embroiled in a tumultuous controversy that persists to the present day: the *hasidic-mitnaggedic* schism. Indeed, today's protagonists on the *mitnaggedic* side trace their doctrines to the Gaon and are known, irrespective of country of origin, as *lita'im* – Lithuanians.

Hasidism (lit. "pietism") was in great measure a reaction against the hegemony of the religious establishment and the prevailing social structure of the period. It aspired to achieve spiritual reformation by emphasizing the emotional and mystical content of Judaism, and preached the need to serve God joyously, in song and dance. It addressed the problems of the common people, the *'amkha*, and raised their morale and self-esteem by placing them on a par, in the eyes of God, with the scholars and the rich, who, generally speaking, held the common folk in contempt.

Hasidism began to spread in Lithuania shortly after the death of the movement's founder, R. Israel ben Eliezer, the Baal Shem Tov or "the Besht" (1700-1760). It was not met kindly. The epithet *mitnaggedim*, "opponents" (sing. *mitnagged*) was coined by *hasidim* to denote those who rejected the new trend on ideological grounds or simply failed to join. It was a name proudly accepted and acknowledged by an overwhelming majority of Lithuanian Jews, who rallied behind the Gaon and the lay leadership in their efforts to stanch the *hasidic* tide.

Although the *mitnaggedim* were repelled by the uninhibited religious emotionalism of *hasidism*, they might not have responded as vehemently as they did had it not been for a related development within hasidic communities: formation of courts around charismatic personalities, the *tsadikim* (sing. *tsadik*, lit. "saints," alternately *rebbe*). These leaders tended to exact blind obedience from their followers, who venerated them and sought their advice and help in all matters spiritual and material. In its extreme manifestation, the institution of the *tsadik* became a virtual intermediary between Man and Creator. *Hasidism* was also attacked for alleged incorporation of secret teachings of Shabbetai Zevi and, in particular, the nearly contemporaneous Jacob Frank. With this, the Gaon's implacable enmity was aroused. He termed *hasidism* a dangerous innovation, its doctrines a deviation from historic Judaism, its texts blasphemous.

The anti-*hasidic* struggle was more than a war of words and ideas. It raged in bitter internecine strife for some thirty years and continued to smolder for generations thereafter. The opening round took place in Vilna in 1772, when the community leadership ordered the closure of a small *hasidic shtibl* and excommunicated all adherents of the movement, which the Gaon had branded as heretical.

The *hasidim* initially sought a rapprochement. In 1779, R. Shneor Zalman of Liadi (the first Lubavitcher Rebbe) and R. Menachem Mendel of Vitebsk sought to meet with the Gaon, explain the principles of their movement, and ask him to call off his attacks. The Gaon refused to meet them, as he continued to do until his death in 1797.

The controversy flared anew in 1780, when R. Jacob Joseph of Polnnoye, a disciple of the Besht, published his book *Toldot Ya'aqov Yosef.* Not only was this the first work to articulate the basic teachings of *hasidism*; it also fiercely criticized the traditional Jewish leadership and its scale of values. The *mitnaggedim* regarded it as a statement of contempt of scholarship, rejection of intellectual leadership, and unconcealed disrespect for the role of the rabbi.

In 1781, the Gaon reaffirmed the ban on *hasidism* and the excommunication (*herem*) of its followers. Henceforth they were to be excluded from community membership and harassed in every way possible until they repented. The *herem* was ratified at the fair of Zelva by the community leaders of Brisk, Grodno, Pinsk, and Slutsk. Notice of the decision was forwarded to all communities in Lithuania and Belorussia.

Tumult broke out wherever *hasidim* and *mitnaggedim* lived in proximity. Members of the two factions neither prayed together nor accepted each other's prayer service ritual. Their children did not intermarry. They refused to eat in each other's homes; they challenged the halakhic reliability of each other's ritual slaughterers. They burned each other's books. Three *hasidic shtiblakh* in Vilna – Karliner, Liosna, and Stolin-Liachowitz – were forcibly closed.

Just the same, *hasidism* survived in Lithuania and Belorussia. However, it acquired a different form, less deviationist and more respectful of Torah scholarship and scholars.

Chief among the Lithuanian *hasidic* branches was Lubavitch, known also as Habad, the acronym for *hokhma* (wisdom), *bina* (understanding), and *da'at* (knowledge). Additional *hasidic* courts – Karlin, Stolin, and other Belorussian groups – gradually established a presence in some Lithuanian towns. They were among the first *hasidim* to establish yeshivot and to introduce scholarship in *hasidic* studies. Together with other hasidic groups in Poland and the Ukraine, they developed their own literature and folklore, based on tales of *tsadikim* and their miracles and parables, as well as a singular, specific form of Biblical exegesis known as *hasidishe toyres*.

By this time, the Vilna Gaon had become for Lithuanian Jewry what the *tsadik* or rebbe was for his *hasidim*. The Gaon is even credited with having performed a miracle, although he would have been the last to consider it as such. When the troops of Czarina Catherine II besieged Vilna in 1792, the Jews of the city begged the Gaon to help them. He led them in public recitation of the 20th Psalm...whereupon the Czarina's army lifted the siege and moved on. For many years afterwards the Jews of Vilna celebrated the anniversary of the Gaon's miracle of deliverance.

Strife between *hasidim* and *mitnaggedim* broke out again in 1796, when the *hasidim* alleged that the Gaon had regretted his ban against their movement. The Gaon responded by sending special emissaries to the communities of Lithuania and Belorussia bearing a letter refuting the rumor; the *hasidic* counter-rumor challenged the authenticity of his signature on the letter. The Gaon then condemned *hasidism* in stronger terms than before, terming the movement "a sore on the body of Israel" and its followers "sinners."

Elijah ben Solomon, the Vilna Gaon, died in 1797, as did his wife Hannah. As word of his death spread through the city that, under his leadership, had become the center of *mitnaggedism*, the mainstream community plunged into grief and the *hasidim* – with the exception of Habad – erupted in glee. *Mitnaggedim* at his funeral vowed to fight *hasidism* to the finish. This did not happen, for two reasons: the consolidation of *mitnaggedism* in Lithuania and the advent of the Haskalah (Jewish Enlightenment) movement, the common enemy of all observant Jews. Over time, the bitterness and fury of the *hasidim-mitnaggedim* controversy subsided.

The main campaigns in the war on Haskalah occurred after the Gaon's death. Haskalah leaders in Lithuania were wont to refer to the Gaon as a forerunner of their movement, citing his scientific approach to Talmudic studies and his erudition in secular science. But while the Gaon's influence broadened the horizons of all Lithuanian Jews, he was surely no *maskil*. He considered the Haskalah an assimilationist movement that would estrange

Jews from their values and traditions; he even approved the burning of their books.

The Gaon wrote more than 70 works, of which some 50 have appeared in print. None were published during his lifetime; several have been lost. His writings include commentaries on most of the Biblical canon and several orders of the Mishna. They also include glosses, commentaries, and novellae on the whole of the Babylonian Talmud, various parts of the Jerusalem Talmud, the Zohar, and other sources of kabbalah. He also managed to write a Hebrew grammar and several books on mathematics.

Writing only in Hebrew, he was immune to the influence of Greek, Arab, or Latin scholars, unlike other important Jewish philosophers and thinkers, especially in the Middle Ages. In this sense, he was a more authentic representative of classical rabbinic Judaism than they were. Beside his many books, the Gaon left numerous disciples and followers who put his ideas into practice, including settlement in the Holy Land.

Elijah of Vilna was undoubtedly one of the greatest spiritual and intellectual Jewish leaders in modern times, a man whose personality towered over Lithuanian Jewry and influenced its cultural life centuries after his death.

Lithuanian Yeshivot: The Golden Era

This chronicle now examines the metamorphosis of Lithuanian Jewry after the Gaon's death. Central to this development was the unique Jewish institution and way of life known as yeshiva (pl. yeshivot) – literally "sitting," customarily translated as "rabbinical academy."

In their wanderings and exiles, Jews carried and transmitted a singular manner of living based upon rabbinic interpretations of the Bible, the Talmud, and their commentaries. Rabbinic sources define the study of legal codes and texts (all aggregated under the heading "Torah study") as a religious command emanating from Mount Sinai. Consequently, Jews throughout the Diaspora committed themselves to a lifetime of scholastic endeavor in which notions such as "completion" or "graduation" were unknown.

Until the advent of Haskalah, Torah study was universal in Poland and Lithuania. It is no coincidence that the Talmud was first typeset in Lublin (1563 and 1623). Formal religious studies began in early childhood in *heder* and continued at yeshiva, synagogue, and home. Council ordinances often provided guidelines for yeshivot and Torah study. War, pogroms, and poverty might vitiate this commitment but could not override it. The last Slutzk Council, convening under dire pressure in 1679, managed to recommend the study of at least one chapter of Mishna each day after morning prayers. The Council also lamented the eclipse of Torah study in Lithuania, blaming this on the scarcity of books.

As time passed, the yeshivot came under fire from the 'amkha, the common people. Some yeshivot admitted young men who had motives other than study for its own sake. Some students expected to be supported for the rest of their lives. R. Hayyim of Volozhin (Volozhiner), disciple of the Vilna Gaon, responded to the critics by agreeing with them. Yeshiva applicants should be examined for their purity of motive and should disabuse themselves of expectations of lifetime support. Public dissatisfaction with the prevailing yeshiva ethics, he asserted, had caused financial support for needy religious institutions to decline. Affluent Jews in particular were increasingly unsympathetic to yeshiva students and their financial needs. The abolition of the Council of Lithuania at this time had made things even worse.

The Talmud itself was no longer widely studied in Lithuania; the popularity of books on Jewish ethics had brought this new discipline into vogue. The *tsadik* (construed in Lithuania as a man of good deeds and high moral values, as opposed to the hasidic rebbe) became a role model who was more highly regarded and respected than the Talmudic or law-learned rabbi. Needless to say, the rabbis of Lithuania viewed this new trend with alarm, regarding it as an attempt to deny the yeshiva student and the scholar their rightful place in society. In 1803, they asked R. Hayyim of Volozhin to set matters right by forming new yeshivot and revitalizing existing ones.

R. Hayyim scoured the country for support and met with a warm response. He recruited many new students, persuaded scholars of renown to teach them, and solicited funds from individuals (not only of the wealthy or middle class), synagogues, and communities. Thus, rapidly and, generally speaking, under the leadership of one man, the Lithuanian yeshiva world was revitalized.

This accomplished, R. Hayyim of Volozhin overhauled the method of supporting these yeshivot and their young students (*bahurim*), which became the basis for a pattern used by almost all yeshivot elsewhere. The previous method was to arrange the "adoption" of students by individual families, which provided clothing and daily meals (hence the name of this practice, *esn*

teg, lit. "eating days"). R. Hayyim asked his benefactors to remit all assistance
to the yeshiva itself, which would meet its students' needs in order to spare
them any feelings of humiliation or dependency. He also insisted that the
students dress neatly and look no different from other young men.

Then came R. Hayyim's most radical innovation: a new system of teaching
and study, based on the methods of his mentor, the Gaon. *Pilpul* was discarded.
The purpose of study was to attain true understanding of Talmudic texts
through logical reasoning, without the need to resort to questionable
subtleties.

This was a departure from tradition, which regarded *pilpul* as a mental
exercise that supposedly sharpened the students' intellect. Thus it was
opposed by many leading scholars and rabbis of the time, including R. Moshe
Sofer (the "Hatam Sofer" of Pressburg) and his teacher, R. Pinchas Horowitz
of Frankfurt. For the Lithuanian yeshivot, however, this methodology soon
became universal. Today, yeshivot that practice it, wherever located, are
known as "Lithuanian."

Throughout the long history of Lithuanian Jews, yeshivot remained the
indispensable venue of classical Jewish education for young and old. Almost
every synagogue maintained its own *beit midrash*, supported by the local
rabbi. The aim of every Jewish family was to send its sons to a yeshiva, even
though State schools were available and the influence of the Enlightenment
was considerable.

The underlying concept was study for study's sake, *Torah li-shma*. It
began in *heder*, a rudimentary but rigorous elementary school where no
secular subjects were taught. The next stage was *yeshiva qetana*, literally
"little yeshiva," a prep school of sorts for *yeshiva gedola*, "large yeshiva" or
yeshiva proper. Very few students who ventured this far did so with the aim
of studying for the rabbinate or preparing for a profession.

In the nineteenth century, this very fixity of purpose presented yeshiva
life with one of its major challenges: the incursion of secular study among the
devout. Two forces triggered this breach of unity: the Haskalah and
government coercion, nowhere more pronounced than in Russian-controlled
Lithuania. Each yeshiva, each community, coped in its own way. Collective
action came later. In 1911, a conference of Russian rabbis in St. Petersburg
resolved that before accepting their first rabbinical post, those intent on
entering the rabbinate should take enough secular courses to pass
matriculation examinations. This, it was thought, would prepare them to

confront the *kazioni rabbiner*, government-appointed rabbis. A minority view at the conference, represented by R. Israel Meir ha-Kohen (the "Hafets Hayyim," 1838-1933), dismissed secular studies as "a waste of time." This polarization and various compromises made to resolve it are evident in yeshiva education today.

The history of the Lithuanian yeshivot is told below in abbreviated form, focusing on six of the most important academies: Volozhin, Telz, Slobodka, Ponevez, Radin and Lida.

Yeshiva of Volozhin

The yeshiva that R. Hayyim personally founded, that of Volozhin, grew quickly in size and reputation. Gifted *bahurim* throughout Lithuania and in neighboring countries chose it over all others. Volozhin also attracted scholarly laymen, who went out of their way to stop there in their travels to attend a few lectures in Talmud. These people then joined study groups that met regularly if not daily; these multiplied throughout the country and were joined by young men and older boys whose thirst for learning was insatiable. Thus the Lithuanian Jewish tradition of constant Talmud study by laymen was revived.

Since Volozhin and the other yeshivot were unable to meet the demand, only the most gifted and those who appeared to be the most dedicated were admitted. Inevitably, the selection standards were very strict. Those who were rejected but still longed to study traveled to small cities and townlets, where they enrolled in local *batey midrash* (smaller yeshivot housed in synagogues). If their parents were unable to support them, they were "adopted" by members of the local community using the *esn teg* method. Students who had no lodging would remain in the *beit midrash* and sleep on one of its hard wooden benches. Some seemed to prefer this arrangement because it maximized their potential study hours. Such scholars were known as .*perushim*, a term signifying modesty, piety, and introversion. Highly respected throughout Lithuania, they filled *batey midrash* and small synagogues in localities of all sizes.

When R. Hayyim Volozhiner died in 1821 at the age of 73, his son Isaac was invited to succeed him in his two capacities: head of the yeshiva, which was now named Ets Hayyim (literally "tree of life," figuratively "monument to Hayyim," in memory of its founder), and rabbi of the town of Volozhin. In addition to his Talmudic erudition, R. Isaac was well versed in worldly matters

— an astute political observer and a fine orator, who knew mathematics and spoke several languages.

His official reign was truncated in 1824, when the Russian Government ordered the yeshiva to shut down. This was much to the joy of the maskilim, who considered Ets Hayyim a fountainhead of benightedness and reactionism. Unofficially, the yeshiva continued to exist under R. Isaac, sometimes under the most difficult of circumstances. It took 20 years and all of R. Isaac's talents to obtain permission from the Government in St. Petersburg to reopen the yeshiva.

As strenuously as the leading maskilim hated the Yeshiva of Volozhin, they respected R. Isaac personally. One of the most prominent Haskalah writers, Dr. Max Lilienthal, travelled to Volozhin to consult him on several matters. R. Isaac even endorsed an edition of Moses Mendelssohn's commentary, the 'Biur'," and several Jewish textbooks meant for use in government schools for Jewish children.

By the end of his life, R. Isaac's extensive community activities left him no time for day-to-day management of yeshiva affairs. These he entrusted to his two sons-in-law, R. Eliezer Isaac and R. Naftali Zevi Judah Berlin, the latter known as the 'Netsiv' for his Hebrew acronym.

Upon his death in 1849, R. Isaac was succeeded by R. Eliezer Isaac. When the latter died five years later, however, an internal dispute broke out. Some scholars opposed the natural successor, the Netsiv, in favor of a new star on the Talmudic horizon, R. Joseph Ber Soloveitchik, R. Hayyim Volozhiner's grandson. After the intervention of some of the most eminent rabbis of the period, the Netsiv was appointed rosh yeshiva (yeshiva dean or head) and R. Soloveitchik was named his deputy. The controversy continued. By 1856, the student body itself had split into rival Netsiv and Soloveitchik factions. R. Soloveitchik resolved the matter by leaving the yeshiva and accepting an appointment as rabbi of Slutzk. The Netsiv was now the sole head of the Volozhin Yeshiva. Several years later, he named none other than R. Hayyim Soloveitchik, son of his former rival, as his deputy. R. Hayyim Soloveitchik had in the meantime married the Netsiv's granddaughter.

It was hardly a case of nepotism; even before his appointment, R. Hayyim Soloveitchik had become a towering personality in his own right, famed throughout the Orthodox world as a scholar and teacher. Thereafter, the most gifted and committed students streamed to Volozhin from all of Lithuania, the Pale of Settlement, and even Germany. No academy could match the

intensity and love of religious study that emanated from this little town and
its great yeshiva.

But there was more to Volozhin than Talmud. According to contemporary
writers, the yeshiva of the Netsiv and R. Hayyim Soloveitchik was a nonpareil
breeding ground for the concept of settling in Palestine, the Holy Land, *Erets
Yisrael*. Secret societies took shape within the yeshiva; their members, often
among the most brilliant and dedicated of the students, vowed to devote their
lives to the cause of Eretz Israel. One such society, called Nes Tsiyona (Banner
of Zion), required new members to take the following oath:

> By the name of the Lord God of Israel, by the name of our Holy
> Land, and by the name of all that is dear and sacred to me, I
> swear faithfully, in God's Name, to serve the aims of our Society
> loyally and to attempt, so long as I live, to fulfill the ideal of
> settling Erets Israel. I further swear to reveal the secret of our
> society to no man before he, too, enters its covenant by taking
> this oath.

When the Russian police discovered the society and ordered it to dissolve, a
new society with the same ideals quickly formed. This group called itself
Netsah Yisrael (after an expression in I Sam. 15:29, lit. "eternity of Israel,"
possibly a euphemism for God) and, like its precursor, required members to
settle in Erets Israel.

The Yeshiva of Volozhin had a second undercurrent: study of Haskalah
literature. The academy had gained the reputation, principally beyond the
borders of Lithuania, as a place where one might study Torah by day and
Enlightenment by night. Some students enrolled for this very purpose. The
Haskalah was their true passion; the yeshiva was merely a transit stop on the
way to Berlin, the center of the Enlightenment.

The maskilim were neither amused nor grateful; in 1858, by their
prompting, the government again closed the yeshiva down. As previously, the
academy maintained its program of lectures and private studies
surreptitiously and without interruption. A year later, again as a result of
maskilic denunciations, the government demanded that the yeshiva
curriculum find room for Russian language and other secular subjects. The
Netsiv disregarded the order, confident that it would be rescinded.

He was mistaken, although the denouement was long in coming. In 1887,
Alexander Zederbaum, editor of the Haskalah organ *Hamelitz*, enlisted a

small group of yeshiva students and openly denounced the academy for failing to implement the government's decrees and demanded that the changes be introduced forthwith. The Jewish lay leadership in St. Petersburg, increasingly concerned, convened a rabbinical conference in that city with the participation of the Netsiv and R. Joseph Ber Soloveitchik, now the rabbi of Brisk. The conference yielded to the secularist pressure and resolved to include Russian and arithmetic as compulsory subjects in the Volozhin Yeshiva syllabus.

It was not enough. In 1891, the government issued another decree limiting studies at the yeshiva to ten hours per day, six of which (9:00 a.m. - 3:00 p.m.) would be reserved for secular studies. Nighttime study was prohibited. The Netsiv rejected the *diktat* contemptuously. Thus in January 1892, after 90 years as a center of religious studies, having turned out thousands of rabbis, teachers and scholars, the Yeshiva of Volozhin was closed by order of the Russian government. Two years later, after making several futile attempts to annul the decree, the Netsiv, R. Naftali Zevi Judah Berlin, died in Warsaw.

The yeshiva building stood empty for three years, until R. Meir Noah Levin, rabbi of Volozhin, asked the government to let the facility reopen as a synagogue. His explanation – that the Jews of the town did not have enough prayerhouses – was accepted. As soon as the yeshiva doors reopened, R. Levin began giving Talmud lectures that dozens of students attended. When the lectures evolved into lessons, the nucleus of a new yeshiva took shape. R. Levin did not stay long in Volozhin, but his successor was R. Rafael Shapiro, son-in-law of the Netsiv, whose fame as a Talmudist made Volozhin attractive to scholars once again. The Yeshiva of Volozhin was back on its feet, albeit unofficially. Although it never regained its former glory, it recovered its status as one of the great yeshivot of Lithuania, to which students streamed from all parts of Russia.

The yeshiva was inactive during World War I. R. Rafael Shapiro moved to Minsk, where he died in 1926. The next year, his son, R. Yaacov Shapiro, was invited to return to Volozhin and attempt to revive the yeshiva. He succeeded, although the yeshiva never regained its former reputation. R. Yaacov Shapiro died in 1936 and was succeeded by his son-in-law, R. Hayyim Wolkin, who proved to be Volozhin's last *rosh yeshiva*. When World War II erupted, Rabbi Wolkin fled with his family and some 50 students to Vilna, where he began to reorganize the yeshiva. Shortly thereafter, they were all murdered at Ponar (in Lithuanian: Paneris) together with thousands of other victims of the Nazi terror.

Yeshiva of Telz (Telshiai)

The Yeshiva of Telz was established in its modern form in 1875 and existed until 1940, when the Soviet Union invaded Lithuania. Founded by R. Eliezer Gordon, who was assisted by his son-in-law, R. Joseph Leib Bloch, and by R. Shimon Skop, who was later appointed Rabbi of Grodno, the yeshiva (known simply as "Telz") became renowned throughout the Orthodox world for the quality of its scholarship.

Telz reached scholastic prominence after the easygoing practices of R. Gordon were replaced with strong discipline administered by R. Bloch. His was the rigorous regime for which yeshiva life is famous, and he was precisely the authoritarian, all-dominating individual who could impose it. The students rebelled at first. Although the majority eventually accepted his authority and learned to respect him, others either left for other academies or continued to foment tension. R. Bloch therefore decided to leave Telz, first for Varno and then Shadov, where he established his own yeshiva, in which some of his former Telz students enrolled. He was succeeded at Telz by R. Hirsh Rabinowitz, former head of the Slobodka Yeshiva.

R. Gordon died in 1910 in London, where he had gone to solicit funds for his financially strapped academy. R. Bloch was invited to return to Telz to function as both town rabbi and yeshiva head. This time the students greeted him warmly and enthusiastically; none disputed his authority by now. His tenure in both positions was a signal success; he earned the respect (but not the affection) of laymen and students alike.

Unlike other yeshivot, Telz encouraged its teachers and students to participate in the social, political, and public life of the Jewish community. Students were active in the non-political Tse'irey Israel movement; others joined Agudath Israel, whose Yiddish-language bulletin, *Der idisher lebn*, was published in Telz.

Telz introduced several instructional novelties: "tracking" in five classes ranked by level of knowledge, compulsory attendance, regular tests. The study of Musar (Jewish ethics) was introduced and emphasized. Telz also became known for its focus on the development of logical analytical skills.

The Telz Yeshiva continued to function during the general evacuation of Jews from Lithuania in 1915, since most of the Telz community was not affected by the expulsion order. In 1926, pursuant to a government ruling, the yeshiva introduced a four-year program of secular studies. Instead of robbing the academy of its piety, this act elevated the yeshiva to a position of decisive influence on the life of the entire Jewish community. A cradle-to-grave system of religious education was established under its control: a kindergarten with sex-segregated classes; a secondary school for girls; a teachers seminary with separate men's and women's programs; and a *kollel* (advanced yeshiva for married students who trained for the rabbinate).

In 1940, when the Soviet Union invaded Lithuania, the yeshiva was closed and its buildings were confiscated. Most of the students left Telz and continued their studies under their rabbis in other towns; some teachers and students made their way to the United States. There, in 1941, they re-established the Telz Yeshiva in Cleveland, Ohio, under R. Elijah Meyer Bloch, who had taught at the original Telz Yeshiva since 1917. A yeshiva township near Jerusalem, Telz Stone, is part of the old Telz Yeshiva of Lithuania.

Yeshiva of Slobodka

Slobodka Yeshiva was founded in 1861 and, like its counterparts, functioned until the Soviet occupation of Lithuania in 1940. It was a small, insignificant institution until 1882, when R. Nathan Zevi Finkel made it world-famous as a center of scholarship dedicated to the ideals of the Musar movement.

The guiding mentor of Slobodka was R. Moshe Mordechai Epstein, who was appointed to co-direct the academy in 1893, took over as sole yeshiva head in 1896, and remained in this capacity until his death in 1933. It was he who gave the curriculum its specific Musar ambiance by adding a daily half hour devoted solely to perusal of Musar literature, and by giving Saturday night Musar lectures before the entire student body. To signify the change, those loyal to the ideals of R. Finkel and R. Epstein renamed the yeshiva Knesset Yisrael in honor of the founder of the Musar movement, R. Israel Lipkin of Salant (Salanter).

R. Epstein's emphasis on teaching Musar was so controversial as to cause the yeshiva to split in 1897. The opponents created a new yeshiva that they named Knesset Beit Yitzhak in memory of R. Isaac Elchanan Spektor, (Chief Rabbi of Kovno). After World War I, this yeshiva moved to Kamenetz, Poland. Slobodka itself continued to grow, its enrollment exceeding 300 by 1899.

Slobodka suffered an unusual pounding in the twentieth century, even by the standards of the yeshiva world. The yeshiva was forced to relocate during World War I, first to Minsk in Belorussia and then to Kremenchug in Russia, returning to Slobodka only at the end of the war.

In 1921, one of the yeshiva instructors, R. Zalman Permut of Kobrin, founded a Slobodka *kollel* and persuaded the Lithuanian Ministry of Education to recognize it as a theological seminary. Three years later, the authorities revoked this status on the grounds that the students did not take a secular curriculum as required by law. Apart from interfering with the curriculum, the government thereby exposed the students to the draft. The yeshiva's response, taken in 1925, was to open a branch in Hebron, Palestine. Under the stewardship of R. Moshe Finkel, son of the founder, the new academy soon had an enrollment of more than 150. After 25 of the students were murdered in the infamous Arab massacre in Hebron four years later, the facility relocated to Jerusalem, where it has been known since as Hebron Yeshiva.

In the meantime, the original Slobodka yeshiva continued to function under R. Isaac Sher, son-in-law of R. Nathan Zevi Finkel. Enrollment, which had contracted to 230 in 1926 after the Hebron move, peaked at nearly 500 in 1938. The yeshiva was dissolved during the Soviet occupation of Lithuania in 1940; most of the teachers and students perished in the Holocaust.

Slobodka Yeshiva reopened in 1947 in Bene Beraq, Israel, under R. Isaac Sher. Following his death in 1950, his son-in-law, R. Mordechai Shulman, headed the yeshiva until his own death in 1982. He was succeeded by his son, R. Nathan Shulman.

Ponevez Yeshiva

Ponevez Yeshiva was founded in 1909, when Luba Gavronsky, daughter of the wealthy Moscow tea merchant, Kalman Ze'ev Wissotzky, established an endowment fund for this purpose in memory of her husband, Baruch Bened. The interest from this fund was to provide for the support of 20 outstandingly gifted students, of whom eight were to be married. By recommendation of R. Hayyim Soloveitchik, R. Isaac Rabinowitch, an acknowledged scholar popularly known as Reb Itsel Ponevezer, was appointed to head the new academy. Reb Itsel's reputation as a scholar and teacher was such that to be known as one of his students at Ponevez was, in itself, an indication of excellence. Indeed, the Ponevez students were hand-picked and generously supported.

Fate and European realities conspired to give Ponevez Yeshiva only five years to gestate. When most of the Jews of Ponevez were expelled after World War I erupted in 1914, the yeshiva moved to Mariopol in the Ukraine. It continued to receive support from the Wissotzky family until 1917, when the Russian Revolution forced the Wissotzkys to flee and their fund to collapse. Seeing no future for a yeshiva in the new Communist state, Reb Itsel returned to Ponevez in 1918 to reassume his position as town rabbi. Only one student returned with him: R. Ze'ev Kirzner, who would subsequently hold rabbinical positions in England, South Africa, and the United States.

Reb Itsel had not realized that Ponevez was as firmly under Bolshevik control as Moscow until the new rulers ordered him to close down the town's *Talmud Torah* (boys' religious school). Shortly afterwards, in 1919, he passed away. Eight days after his death, R. Joseph Kahaneman was appointed Rabbi of Ponevez and immediately began to reconstitute the yeshiva on the basis of a *yeshiva qetana* that he had established in the town while passing through in 1916. Gathering its 27 graduates, he reopened Ponevez Yeshiva in the summer of 1919.

R. Kahaneman's enterprise met with great difficulties. At first the town was still under Soviet occupation. However, as Lithuania recovered its independence and Jewish conditions improved, the yeshiva began to flourish. It even benefited from the Communist evacuation of Ponevez; when the retreating forces moved into Belorussia and captured Grodno, 40 students from the yeshiva there fled to Ponevez and joined the new academy. A second influx came about when R. Yerucham Leibovitch, one of the best-known luminaries of the Musar movement, was appointed as the yeshiva's *mashgiah* (literally "overseer," actually a powerful clerical dean in charge of students' spiritual development). R. Yerucham, subsequently famous throughout the world of Jewish scholasticism as the *mashgiah* of Mir Yeshiva, brought many of his own advanced students to Ponevez. The reputation of the academy spread, and students streamed to Ponevez in such numbers that the yeshiva building could no longer accommodate them.

The personal qualities of R. Kahaneman deserve special mention. Aside from his prowess as a scholar, teacher, and orator, he was a masterful organizer and administrator. He possessed great charm, warmth, and charisma. In addition to his many duties as *rosh yeshiva*, he was heavily involved in community and political matters in the newly established Republic of Lithuania, especially after being elected to the Seimas and the National Jewish Council. He was considered one of the leading Jewish activists in the country.

None of R. Kahaneman's community affairs distracted him from his responsibilities to his yeshiva. He was a superb fundraiser and often went abroad for fundraising purposes; his favored destinations were the United States and South Africa, where many Lithuanian Jewish emigrants had settled. Under his baton, the yeshiva continued to expand and grow into the 1930s until, with an enrollment of 200, it joined Slobodka and Telz as the leading yeshivot of Lithuania. Looking ahead, R. Kahaneman used several large overseas donations to purchase a new yeshiva building and several houses meant for dormitory use.

The outbreak of World War II shattered all of his many plans. The invading Soviet forces (1940) requisitioned the yeshiva buildings; the academy now moved from one cramped set of quarters to another. When Nazi Germany occupied Ponevez in Operation Barbarossa (June 1941), all Jews in the town, including all but two or three yeshiva students, were brutally murdered within a three-day period. All that remains of the Jewish community of Ponevez are three mass graves.

R. Kahaneman emigrated to Palestine during Passover of 1940 after making every (futile) effort to save his family and his students. Unbroken in spirit, he established a new Ponevez Yeshiva in Eretz Israel in 1941. Today, Ponevez Yeshiva, with its thousand students and its magnificent hilltop quarters in Bene Beraq, is one of Israel's largest and most influential institutions of religious scholarship. It stands as a memorial to its former counterpart in Lithuania.

Radin and Lida

Other Lithuanian yeshivot of importance included that founded in 1869 by R. Israel Meir Ha-Kohen of Radin, author of *Hafets Hayyim*, an exposition and halakhic code devoted to the great importance of the laws against slander, gossip, and talebearing. Such was the impact of this work that R. Israel Meir Ha-Kohen, despite having authored additional halakhic treatises of great importance, has since been known as "the Hafets Hayyim".

The Hafets Hayyim had not intended to establish a yeshiva. His saintly personality, his integrity, his piety, together with his books, created such an attraction that students flocked to his home until the yeshiva took shape by itself right there. Only 45 years after its founding, in 1914, did the Radin or Hafets Hayyim Yeshiva move into a spacious building of its own and appoint a full-fledged *rosh yeshiva*, R. Naftali Trop.

At its inception, Radin Yeshiva was similar in form and outlook to many other small-town Lithuanian centers of learning. After several years of diligent study, its 30-40 students usually moved on to Volozhin or other major yeshivot. But where most such centers stagnated or closed down after a while, Radin developed into one of the great yeshivot of Lithuania and Poland. The reason was its special emphasis on correct religious behavior in interpersonal as well as devotional affairs, to be mastered through study of the *rosh yeshiva*'s works on Jewish ethics, as exemplified by his personal conduct.

The Hafets Hayyim refused to accept payment for his work; after his marriage, his wife supported him from the earnings of a small grocery store. He published 21 books, of which the best known and most widely studied is *Mishna Berura*, a six-volume commentary on *Shulhan Arukh*. For Ashkenazi Jews, this work is the authoritative guide to everyday religious practice.

When World War I broke out, the Hafets Hayyim left his home together with his family and students, and peregrinated from Belorussia to the Northern Ukraine until 1920, when the USSR and Poland concluded a peace treaty. When word of his return spread, students again flocked to Radin and the yeshiva soon regained its former glory. By the late 1920s, it had some 300 students, including some from the faraway United States.

The Hafets Hayyim died in 1933 at the age of 95, but the yeshiva maintained its lofty standards and reputation until the Wehrmacht rolled into Poland in September 1939. Vestiges continued to exist until early 1940, when the USSR occupied Radin as part of its partition of Poland under the Ribbentrop-Molotov pact. Some of the students and teachers relocated to Vilna, capital of still-independent Lithuania, in order to escape the Communists and continue their studies. A few stayed on in Radin. Many of them were exiled to Siberia; a handful managed to escape to the United States or to Palestine. When the Germans overran Lithuania a year later, those who had fled to Vilna now fell into the hands of the Nazis.

This marked the sad end of the existence of a yeshiva that, for 70 years, had spread the inseparable messages of scholarship and high moral values among thousands of students, many of whom became famous scholars and rabbis serving countless Jewish communities worldwide. In tribute, many yeshivot and religious institutions in Israel, the United States, and elsewhere perpetuated the memory of the Hafets Hayyim and the Radin Yeshiva by taking on these names.

The second yeshiva discussed here is that of Lida, established in 1905 by R. Jacob Reines (1839-1915), a founder and leader of Mizrachi (the Religious Zionist movement). This was a modern yeshiva, in which secular studies were taught side by side with traditional Talmudic and rabbinic studies, all in an environment of strict Orthodox observance. It is hard to imagine how revolutionary this concept was at the time. R. Reines had previously attempted to fulfill it while serving as rabbi of Swentzian, but failed a few months later under the fanatical opposition of many of his colleagues. The new initiative was reinforced by a resolution taken at the Second Mizrachi Conference, held in Lida in 1903.

The Yeshiva of Lida was a novelty in that its curriculum sought to train qualified rabbis fully versed in both Talmudic and general secular studies. These clerics, once ordained, would defend their communities against hostile clergymen, cabinet ministers, and miscellaneous officials, and eventually replace the government-appointed *kazioni rabbiner*. Thus, R. Reines's yeshiva drew up a formidable syllabus: the standard Talmudic content plus studies in Bible (an aspect that most yeshivot ignored); Hebrew language, literature, grammar; and Jewish history. Secular studies included spoken and written Russian, Russian and general history, world geography, mathematics, and some of the natural sciences.

The yeshiva offered a six-year program divided into six grades, with annual promotion by examination. Students were to receive regular stipends, which would increase each year. Four supervisory committees were established consisting of rabbis for the curriculum of Jewish studies, scholars and writers for secular studies, laymen for financial affairs, and students for all matters affecting their own welfare. Special attention was paid to every student's scholastic progress, religious and general behavior, and good manners.

The announcement of the yeshiva's forthcoming inauguration was greeted with great enthusiasm. Hundreds of students flocked to Lida from all over Russia; many more were turned away for lack of space. The appointment of R. Solomon Poliachik, a well-known scholar, to the yeshiva staff enhanced its reputation and attracted additional hundreds of student candidates.

R. Reines's task in running the yeshiva was not an easy one. The Russian and Russian-Jewish political situation was touchy. (It was the time of the Russo-Japanese War and the Kishinev pogrom.) Hostile rabbinical colleagues spread false but damaging rumors about his yeshiva and inveighed against its Religious Zionist philosophy. Consequently, the Jewish community at large gave him neither the moral nor the financial backing that he had had good reason to expect. R. Reines did marshall some assistance from Baron Ginzburg, R. Jacob Mazeh (Chief Rabbi of Moscow), and the Wissotzky family. Despite the difficulties and disappointments, the yeshiva maintained its high standards and progressed steadily.

As with all other institutions of its type, the Yeshiva of Lida was shattered by the outbreak of World War I. Many long-time students were drafted, others left Lida to avoid conscription, and new students did not enroll in their stead. When the German army approached the city, the remaining students and their teachers fled. But the yeshiva suffered its most serious blow just before the German invasion: the death of R. Reines in September 1915.

The yeshiva relocated in Elizabethgrad after much wandering but failed to withstand the hardships of World War I and its aftermath, i.e., the Russian Revolution and the ensuing civil war. Many students and teachers perished; a few were able to escape abroad.

The Yeshiva of Lida was gone, never to return. In its integration of devotional and secular study, however, it served as a model for Yeshiva University in New York, Bar-Ilan University in Israel, and similar institutions elsewhere. All are living testimonials to the vision of R. Isaac Jacob Reines.

Volozhin, Telz, Slobodka, Ponevez, Radin, Lida. Small towns in a small country. Their names will survive forever by virtue of the centers of Jewish learning that they had hosted. The yeshivot described here are but a sample. Academies of similar nature proliferated throughout Lithuania and Lithuanian-Poland. Each, however, was a world unto itself; each made its specific contribution to what is still called the "yeshiva world." All drew their inspiration from the legacy that the Vilna Gaon had bequeathed to the Jews of Lithuania.

The Musar Movement

Nineteenth-century Lithuanian Jewish scholasticism produced yet another innovation that set this Diaspora apart from all others: the Musar movement.

As a religious educational discipline, Musar (lit. moral instruction or ethics) strove to train the individual in strict ethical behavior as prescribed by *halakha*. It was conceived in response to hasidic accusations that Lithuanian Orthodoxy had become severe, soulless, cold, and dispassionate, a doctrine of dry devotional study and prayer. The Musar movement was a specifically Lithuanian Jewish phenomenon; it passed the Jewish communities of Poland without leaving a trace.

One factor explaining this peculiarity was the development of general Polish and Lithuanian society through the mid-nineteenth century. Although the two countries had been united for hundreds of years, their peoples had retained distinctive characteristics. Lithuanians in general lacked the romanticism, idealism, and manners of the Poles; they were more down to earth, more practical, simple and hardworking, a peasant people.[77] Despite frequent invasions, the people of Lithuania retained their language and culture and took little interest in alien ways.

These characteristics affected the Jews of Lithuania in many ways. Barely affected by external cultural influences, largely uninterested in local or national politics, they lived in a world of their own, their society insular and segregated. By and large, they were content to live modestly on modest incomes, as long as they were left in peace and allowed to maintain their Jewish life. Lithuanian Jews knew little joy and sought few luxuries; the glory of the Torah was their predominant concern. Even in this respect, their houses of study and prayer were as drab and poor as were their homes and diet.

The mortar that cemented the integrity of Lithuanian Jewry was the community's sense of cultural superiority. Thus it invested all efforts in devotional study, making Lithuania an ideal center for this activity. Consequently, Torah study in Lithuania developed its own unique form of spiritual vitality.

The most respected and honored individuals in the community were the *talmidey hakhamim*, those who had reached the pinnacle of the scholastic meritocracy. Every Jewish family in Lithuania, however poor, sought to dedicate at least one son to a lifetime of religious study or to find a scholar as a son-in-law. Children's education was a cause of utmost importance; parents were vigilant about the moral fiber of the teachers they employed. In one of its ordinances, the Council of Lithuania warned: "Do not accept a teacher for your children unless he brings a letter of recommendation from his local rabbi and written consent of his wife to leave his home."

It was in this milieu that the modern Musar movement took shape. Founded by R. Israel Lipkin of Salant (hence "Salanter," 1810-1883), it drew its inspiration from the ethical writings of earlier rabbinical scholars such as R. Solomon Luria of Brisk, "the Maharshal" (1510-1574); R. Shabbetai ben Meir ha-Kohen of Vilna, "the Shakh" (author of *Siftey Kohen*, 1621-1662); R. Jehiel Heilprin of Minsk (1660-1746), R. Ziskin of Grodno; and, towering over them all, the Vilna Gaon.

All of these luminaries had stressed the importance of ethics study and its application in daily behavior. R. Israel Salanter's movement, however, was novel in its attempt to confront the specific challenges of his time. Chief among these challenges was a threat that Lithuanian Jewry had not known until the nineteenth century: a rising tide of secularist assimilation, which, fueled by the Enlightenment, reached crisis magnitudes by the mid-1800s. The *shtetlakh* of the Russian Pale of Settlement were engulfed in poverty that overwhelmed the Jews' willingness to do without. Antisemitism, malnutrition, illness, and the collapse of Jewish authority as represented by the councils, sowed tension and bitterness within Jewish society. Internal dissent grew as the years passed. Upheavals in Russia, Haskalah-driven secularization, the influence of the German-gestated Reform Movement in its battle against Orthodoxy, the allure of hasidism – the effects of all of these dragged the leadership of Lithuanian Mitnaggedism to the brink of disintegration. Even some yeshiva graduates had abandoned the strict practice of Orthodox Judaism.

R. Isaac Blaser, a colleague and disciple, summed up the Mitnaggedic view of the situation in his introduction to R. Israel Salanter's book *Ohr Yisrael* (Light of Israel): "Fear of God has deteriorated terribly; sins proliferate...unity is shattered. Without fear of God, knowledge of Torah, too, will ultimately disappear." In modern terms, the expression "without fear of God" denotes a state of moral degradation.

The community had experienced similar, if less acute, problems in the past, and had formed partial solutions. To reinforce the concept of *torah lishma*, study for its own sake, R. Hayyim of Volozhin had pioneered the coupling of Torah ideals and charity. R. Joseph Feiner, better known as R. Yossele Slutzker, had popularized written works on Jewish ethics and ethical philosophy among his students. Some of the truly learned had formed study circles known as *hevrot shas* ("Talmud societies"), and some of the less scholarly congregated in groups known collectively as *Menorat ha-Maor* (lit. "Candlestick of light," an allusion to the candelabrum in the Temple and the title of a fourteenth-century ethical work by the Spanish sage, R. Isaac Aboab).

Under the impact of the nineteenth-century challenges, however, Lithuanian Mitnaggedim questioned the very possibility of preserving a traditional yet dynamic way of Jewish life based mainly on study and intellectuality.

R. Israel Salanter was uniquely positioned to offer an alternative. Israel ben Ze'ev Lipkin was born in 1810 in Zhagory, where his father was the town rabbi. At the age of 12, when he was married, he enrolled in the yeshiva of R. Zevi Hirsh Broide in Salant, where he was considered an *'ilui* (prodigy) and referred to by his teacher as "the little Alfasi." R. Broide taught him the basic principles of Musar and laid the foundation for his understanding of the importance of the role of ethics and morals in Jewish life. However, it was R. Joseph Zundel of Salant, a great scholar but a singularly modest and humble man who supported himself in business, who had the greatest influence on him. Attracted and impressed by R. Zundel's personality, R. Israel regarded him as his teacher and mentor. The maxim that he preached all his life — "Study ethics, and you will be a truthful, honest and virtuous person all your life" — was R. Zundel's.

R. Israel Salanter's explicit purpose was to formulate a popular philosophy that both scholar and *'amkha* would find meaningful. This philosophy, he hoped, would unite these groups in their faith in and service of God; it would also improve their character, behavior, and manners. His central theme was a tripartite unity: man and God; man and fellow man; and man and himself.

R. Israel first attempted to tackle the problems of the time by direct appeal to the communities. In 1849, he wrote to the Vilna community leadership proposing the establishment of a *musar shtibl*, a special room where busy merchants might gather for the sole purpose of moral reflection and self-improvement. In particular, he condemned the sin of financial fraud.

Subsequently, he suggested to the leadership that women, too, should concern themselves with the study of morals and ethics.

R. Israel's first *musar shtibl* was founded in 1849 in the home of Reb Zalman b. Uriah in the Vilna suburb of Zaratziah. His study program for self-improvement and self-examination was based on the perusal of two important ethical works: *Mesilat Yesharim* (Path of the just) by R. Moshe Hayyim Luzzatto and *Hovot ha-Levavot* (Duties of the heart) by R. Bahya ibn Paquda.

People flocked to R. Salanter's lectures and sermons. He spoke both to *'amkha* and to scholars, each group in its own idiom, and was admired by all. The *'amkha* were particularly flattered that this famous yet modest and pleasant scholar addressed them in a way they could easily comprehend. They were also relieved to discover that R. Israel did not use his rabbinic pulpit to solicit donations for worthy causes, in the fashion of the time. He actually rejected this practice on principle as an abuse of the dais. The correct purpose of the rabbinical sermon, he believed, was to educate and inspire. His own themes were the ethical and moral values of Judaism, including consideration for people, cultivation of good manners, and empathy with the sufferings of others. He reduced lofty concepts to easily remembered adages: "Goodness and honesty bring one closer to God;" "Fear and love of God is a wisdom to be acquired; it does not come automatically with the study of Torah." He preached against being "a saint at others' expense," and cautioned that only "words from the heart can penetrate the heart of another." The merit of his message and his lack of ulterior motives convinced his audiences to accept him as an authority on the problems of the Jewish community.

R. Israel Salanter's fame spread. He traveled throughout Lithuania and the Pale of Settlement, where he delivered innumerable halakhic discourses, invariably advising his audience beforehand of the subject and sources of his forthcoming lectures. Scholars who attended these sessions came prepared with their most difficult questions and came away enchanted by his clear and intelligible answers. By 1860, when he settled in Vilna, Musar had become a movement.

During his seven years in Vilna, R. Israel popularized and strengthened the movement and made the Lithuanian capital one of its strongholds. His tenure ended in 1867 after the maskilim of the town (who respected him greatly) had urged him, indeed pestered him, to accept the deanship of the government-sponsored rabbinical seminary. R. Israel failed to convince them that the seminary was nothing more than an instrument by which the Russian government hoped to weaken, dilute, and dominate Russian Jewry. The graduates of the seminary would, in his view, be expected to carry out government directives not only in Jewish community policy but in matters of religious ritual and practice. When it became clear that R. Israel would not give the seminary the seal of approval that the government had sought, the maskilim entreated the government to force his hand. Instead, R. Israel moved to Kovno, where he consolidated the Musar movement and gave it a centralized organization. Only after his death in 1888 did the Lithuanian maskilim attack the movement he had founded.

From his new base, R. Israel Salanter put his education and Musar program to the test in the *kloys* (prayer and study house) of Reb[78] Ze'ev Neviazner in Zhamut (Zamut). There he gathered a number of exceptionally gifted young men, including some who were married, even though normally the two groups studied separately. Among his most important disciples were scholars and rabbis who later became famous in their own right. These included rabbis Eliezer Gordon of Telz, Yerocham Leib Perlman of Minsk, Jacob Joseph of Vilna (later of New York), Isaac Blaser of St. Petersburg, Yerucham Leibovitch of Mir, Simcha Zisl Ziv of Kelm, and Naftali Amsterdam, all of whom helped spread the teachings and philosophy of Musar throughout the world.

Shortly after this, R. Israel stepped down as head of the Movement, naming R. Eliezer Gordon his successor. He wished to devote his time and energy to struggle against the Enlightenment, in order to ensure the continuity of traditional Judaism in Lithuania. His was a singular form of struggle: R. Israel believed that the best way to counter secularization and estrangement caused by enemies from within was to create cadres of disciples, all spiritually mature and themselves professing an enlightenment based purely on religious and ethical studies. The most important task of the Musar teacher, he believed, was to set his followers an example by means of his own behavior, backed by sincerity, honesty, and credibility.

R. Israel Salanter did not inveigh against secular education as such. He believed that Jews, especially religious Jews, should acquire and excel in useful professions such as medicine and the law. He admired R. Azriel Hildesheimer, dean of the Orthodox rabbinical seminary in Berlin, and R. Samson Raphael Hirsch of Frankfurt, proponent of the Torah *'im derekh erets* (combined religious and practical training) philosophy. However, he considered the latter doctrine ill-suited to the yeshivot of Lithuania; these, he believed, should confine their curricula to Torah, Talmud, and ethics.

It soon became evident that the Musar movement would not attain one of its founder's goals. Unlike hasidism, it did not sink roots among the 'amkha. Although democratic in its conception, rank-and-file Jews found its teachings too difficult to understand and follow. R. Israel Salanter himself believed in limiting the rabbinical calling to morally, spiritually, and ethically mature scholars. Hence, in the long run, it was only among the elite of the yeshivot that the Musar movement achieved its principal success. Even here, however, the Musar movement was not well received in all quarters. With its emphasis on self-improvement through the intensive study of ethical texts and the need to constantly examine one's behavior and strive for the highest degree of moral and ethical purity, it was time-consuming – to the detriment of Talmudic studies and in competition with them. Thus the Musar movement acquired vigorous opponents amid the very circles for which it was intended.

The Musar movement eventually split into many different groups and schools, usually named after the yeshivot in which each was located. The methods and aims of these groups were often at cross purposes. Some wrapped themselves in an aura of mysticism; others created insular "secret societies." A few urged their adherents to attract ridicule in order to suppress their egos. Still others became snobbish and antisocial, much in contrast to the original concept of Musar.

Thus metamorphosed, the Musar movement caused a serious rift in the religious leadership of Lithuanian Jewry. R. Isaac Elchanan Spektor, Chief Rabbi of Kovno, and many other important rabbis objected to the study of Musar in yeshivot. In the famous Volozhin Yeshiva, where Musar was an "elective," most of the students opted out.

The Knesset Israel Yeshiva of Slobodka provides a good example of what happened. Its dean, R. Nathan Zevi ben Moses Finkel (known as the *Alter* or "the Grand Old Man" of Slobodka), was a disciple of R. Israel Salanter who treated his students as if they were his own children and sought to control not only their thoughts but their deeds. Some of the free spirits among them, disenchanted, left for other yeshivot. Others who could not conform to R. Finkel's standards were politely asked not to return to the yeshiva after the end-of-term vacation. Most, however, learned to accept R. Finkel's authority and strict supervision, and chose to remain. Now that the winnowing was complete, Musar became more influential than ever at Slobodka. Its adherents strove to dominate yeshiva life from head to toe; students whose submission was less than total were frowned upon, if not ostracized.

Many Lithuanian rabbis, especially those who were concerned that Musar was diverting too much time from the principal task of teaching and studying Torah and Talmud, condemned these tactics. This did not stanch the formation of new Musar groups throughout Lithuania, especially in the *kollelim*. Although many of these groups were attended by fewer than ten students, each was considered a gain for the movement. The *kollel* deans often acquiesced, against their better judgment, to the inclusion of Musar in their curricula.

The controversy at Slobodka reached a Solomonic denouement. Several influential rabbis, headed by R. Zevi Hirsh Rabinowitz of Kovno and R. Moishe Danishevsky of Slobodka, decided to put things in order by establishing a second yeshiva in the town. The now-venerable Knesset Yisrael yeshiva would continue in the Musar tradition, and the new institution, called Beit Yitzhak and headed by R. Zevi Hirsh Rabinowitz, would pursue the tradition of the Yeshiva of Volozhin. It worked. Peace reigned in Slobodka. Each yeshiva studied in its own fashion; students and teachers of the two institutions were on friendly terms. Interestingly, it was the Musar Yeshiva, Knesset Israel, that now attracted the larger number of students; it grew dynamically and flourished under the leadership of R. Isaac Sher, son-in-law of the Alter.

But it was only an armistice. The controversy erupted anew when R. Joseph Zusmanovitz, known as "the Yerushalmi" (literally "the Jerusalemite") because he had studied in Jerusalem for a time, was appointed Rabbi of Slobodka. The Yerushalmi was a gifted, charismatic scholar, whose teaching attracted many students and whose preaching drew large audiences. He was also an opponent of the Musar movement. His appointment so embittered the leadership and supporters of Knesset Israel that they named a second cleric, R. Zalman Ossovsky, to the same position.

Since Slobodka was too small a community to have two chief rabbis, the town divided into enemy camps. Synagogues, schools, and even families were torn apart in ugly, bitter strife. R. Zusmanovitz finally bowed to the powerful pressure of the Musarists and left Slobodka to assume the position of rabbi of Wilkomir. It was there that he, together with his family and most of his community, perished at the hands of the Lithuanians and Germans in July 1941.

By the early twentieth century, Musar study had, in one form or another, become part of the curriculum of most Lithuanian yeshivot. The movement gradually developed its own education system and promoted a social unity that clung to its exponents even after their yeshiva days were over.

R. Israel Salanter left only one major written work, *Ohr Yisrael*, edited and published in 1900 by his disciple, R. Isaac Blaser; several of his articles had been collected and published earlier in a special work called *Imrey Bina* (Sayings of understanding). Although his movement eventually struck roots in Israel, the United States, and Great Britain, it was indigenous to Lithuania and flourished nowhere else in Eastern Europe.

Musar had been meant in part as an antidote to hasidism, a popular movement with a small elite at its head, a movement that absorbed its adherents in a warm family-like community, a movement that absolved them, through the personality of the Rebbe, of the need to make difficult, personal decisions. The Musar movement, by contrast, focused on the individual Jew and ordered him or her to seek self-improvement and self-fulfillment. It summoned the individual to a daily, never-ending struggle to attain new heights of religious performance and behavior; it ordered the individual to make himself or herself into a better Jew and a better person. The world of Musar was harsh, joyless, difficult, always analytical – much like that of the Lithuanian Orthodox intelligentsia that had nurtured it.

The Lithuanian Maggidim

Maggid (preacher, pl. *Maggidim*) is the name used to describe popular preachers, often itinerant, who acted as teachers and messengers, spreading knowledge and news in the communities they visited. The *Maggidim* occupied a special place in Lithuanian Jewry.

Although itinerant preachers date back to Biblical and Talmudic times, the tradition and institution of the *Maggid* developed in the late Middle Ages and was popularized in Europe by R. Ephraim Salomon Lunschitz in the second half of the sixteenth century. The function took two forms: appointed *Maggidim* who received salaries from their local communities, and itinerant preachers who were paid for their sermons by the synagogues or communities they visited. The itinerants lived a life of poverty, constantly wandering alone from community to community, families left behind, sustained principally by their own dedication and the love and adulation of their audiences.

As religious, political, and social upheavals proliferated in the seventeenth and eighteenth centuries, so did the *Maggidim*, both itinerant and locally appointed. Their stature, too, increased; halakhic scholars, heads of rabbinical courts, authors of halakhic and homiletic works, and even chief rabbis of cities were attracted to this vocation, as were, at times, learned businessmen.

In the nineteenth and twentieth centuries, Lithuanian *Maggidim* played an important role in the Musar movement and the struggle against hasidism. The typical Lithuanian *Maggid* combined profoundly sincere faith in the Almighty with a passionate sense of mission to preach His word to the masses. Some of the *Maggidim* were scholars who used Enlightenment tools to enrich their preaching styles and teaching methods; others were well-meaning souls who made up in passion what they may have lacked in erudition. Either way, their sermons were replete with social criticism and homilies meant to improve listeners' social behavior.

The Lithuanian towns and *shtetlakh* were fertile ground for the homilies of both official and itinerant *Maggidim*. The audiences were well versed in traditional Jewish sources, rich in spirituality, and sincerely respectful of knowledge in general and Jewish learning in particular. The advent of the *Maggid* was a bright moment in an existence perpetually beset by hateful Christian neighbors and occasional pogroms – an existence often blighted by great personal and, sometimes, national suffering. The *Maggid's* parables, questions-and-answers, and comments on the problems of Jewish existence in the Diaspora were music to his listeners' ears. He comforted them, took the sting out of their lives, and helped alleviate their suffering. He inspired them to take pride in their Jewishness, to rejoice in their ability to transmit their Jewish heritage to their children, and, while doing so, to continue waiting patiently for the Messiah.

Each sermon lasted for hours. To keep the audience alert, the *Maggid* varied his delivery between soothing words and fire and brimstone. Some *Maggidim* commented on problems of the time; others dealt exclusively with themes of social justice, honesty, morality, and ethical conduct. In times of great suffering – during pogroms or looting of Jewish homes – some *Maggidim* had the effrontery to question God. Pointing a finger heavenward, they would cry: "How can You do this to us? Are You not a God of justice and mercy?"

Delivered in the mournful singsong that characterized the *Maggid*'s delivery, these words moved audiences to tears, whereupon *Maggid* and audience together would weep in yearning for an end to the Exile and their spell in the Diaspora.

The most famous Lithuanian *Maggid* was R. Jacob ben Ze'ev Kranz, better known as the Maggid of Dubnow or the Dubner Maggid. Born in 1741 in Zietl, near Vilna, Kranz was appointed preacher and rabbinical judge in Dubnow, hence his sobriquet. Just the same, he spent much of his 19-year tenure circulating among many other cities and communities, which had invited him to preach. The Dubner Maggid was an erudite scholar who fashioned halakhic, kabbalistic, and ethical works into popular parables, fables, and tales that captivated and enchanted scholars and simple people alike. Even exponents of the Enlightenment, including Moses Mendelssohn and his circle (whom the Maggid met in Berlin), were charmed and impressed by him. As noted, he was a close personal friend of the Vilna Gaon, who greatly admired his talents and was able to relax at times by listening to his storytelling. The Maggid, in turn, considered himself a disciple of the Gaon and used his skills to combat hasidism and hasidim. His works, all of which were published by his son, included *Ohel Ya'aqov* (Tent of Jacob), an anthology of homilies on the Pentateuch; *Kochav mi-Ya'aqov* (Star out of Jacob) on the *haftarot* (selections of Prophetic writings appended to the weekly Sabbath Torah reading); and *Kol Ya'aqov* (Voice of Jacob) on the Five Scrolls. He also wrote *Sefer ha-Midot* (Book of virtues), based on *Hovot ha-Levavot* by R. Bahya ibn Pakuda, in which he discusses the Jews' spiritual relationship with God and the observances and practices that this relationship warrants. The Dubner Maggid died in 1804.

As in the case of the Dubner, the position of *Maggid* was often combined with that of *dayan* (rabbinical judge), leading to an elaborate job description: *Maggid meysharim u-more tsedeq*, literally "preacher of uprightness and teacher of justice." (The latter was a synonym for the office of *dayan*, rabbinical judge). Whenever a community leadership appointed a *Maggid*, it gave him the official title *Maggid de-mata* (local Maggid) or *shtotmaggid* (town *Maggid*). The office of *shtotmaggid* of Vilna was highly prestigious and much in demand; only the most respected and outstanding scholars were welcome to apply.

The Lithuanian rabbis favored the institution of the *Maggid* as an important tool in the dissemination of the knowledge of Torah, Musar, and piety and often incorporated their own sermons into their published works as suitable material for *Maggidim*. An example is *Beit ha-Levi* by R. Joseph Ber Soloveichik; its homilies became popular with the preachers. Among the best-known *Maggidim* were Ze'ev Hirsh Dainov, the Slutzker Maggid, who was suspected of Haskalah leanings, and the great itinerant Moshe Yitzhak Darshan of Kelm.

The most exalted *Maggid* in the country was the *shtotmaggid* in Vilna. The status and stature of this office is shown by the fact that Rabbi Zevi Hirsch Rabinowitz, who occupied the position for eight years, was invited to follow his father, R. Isaac Elchanan Spektor, as Chief Rabbi of Kovno after the latter's death.

The reputations of quite a few *Maggidim* crossed borders and oceans. R. Hanoch Zundel Luria, the *Maggid* of Novaradok, was popular with rabbis and maskilim alike for his learned homilies, in which he quoted secular scientists and great Hebrew and Greek philosophers profusely. For this, he was often attacked by religious extremists who could not fathom his thinking.

R. Velvele, initially *Maggid* of Dorotzin and subsequently appointed *shtotmaggid* of Vilna, was famous for his moving funeral oratory. One such speech created a graveside scandal: his critical remarks at the burial service of Maskil and author Mordechai Aaron Ginzburg. The angry and immediate maskilic response was committed to writing by Hebrew poet Adam Hacohen Lebensohn.

Another *Maggid* in Vilna, Jacob David Vilawsky, travelled to the United States in 1900 in order to seek help in the publication of his many halakhic, exegetical, and homiletical works. Three years later, he was appointed Chief Rabbi of Chicago but left for Palestine in 1905, where he settled in Safed and founded the Yeshiva Torat Erets Yisrael.

R. Jacob Joseph (1848-1902), another Vilna *shtotmaggid*, was renowned in his time as the best preacher in Lithuania and the Pale of Settlement. A great Talmudic scholar and Musar movement activist, he was popular among scholars and the masses. His admirers would follow him from city to city to listen to his preaching. In 1888, R. Jacob Joseph was installed as Chief Rabbi of New York in an attempt by several Orthodox congregations there to create a central religious authority. The undertaking failed; he died in poverty in 1902. Rabbeinu Jacob Joseph Yeshiva in New York bears his name.

The "Zionist *Maggidim*" most of whom were born in Lithuania, were in a class of their own. However, they were direct successors of the traditional and

Musar *Maggidim*. It was they, through the skill and art of their oratory, who helped spread the ideals of *hibat tsiyon* (Love of Zion) and were among the first members of the Hovevey Tsiyon movement. Their fame as Talmudic scholars gave them great credibility among the masses, who flocked to hear them during their constant travels.

Hayim Zundel Maccoby was born in Kobrin in 1858 and was appointed as preacher in Kamenetz at the age of 18. He left that city in 1879 and, already famous as the Kamenetzer Maggid, preached in many cities. In 1883, he became the first official preacher of the Hibat Tsiyon movement and, as such, traveled continuously throughout Lithuania, Russia, and Poland. Over many rabbis' opposition, some 300 societies for settlement in Eretz Yisrael were founded due to his influence. In 1890, he moved to England where, as in Eastern Europe, he attracted large audiences and pioneered the Hibat Tsiyon movement in that country. His Zionism, however, was by no means secular: for religious reasons, he became one of Herzl's strongest and most articulate opponents until his death in 1916.

Zevi Hirsch Masliansky, another important Zionist *Maggid*, was born in Slutzk in 1856 and taught at the Yeshiva of Pinsk, where one of his students (for a short while) was Chaim Weizmann. Outraged by the pogroms of 1881, he joined Hibat Tsiyon and became one of its most enthusiastic proponents. Ahad Ha-am, Menachem Ussishkin, and Leo Pinsker, among other Hibat Tsiyon leaders, encouraged him in his activity as a roving preacher for Zionism. His fame as an orator spread and huge audiences gathered to listen to him. Forced to leave Russia in 1894, he emigrated to New York after a preaching tour of Central and Western Europe. As a popular Yiddish orator and the most eloquent *Maggid* of his time in America, he helped popularize Zionism among Yiddish-speaking Jewish immigrants there. He died in 1943.

It should be reemphasized that the *Maggid* was much more than a preacher of sermons. Locally based or itinerant, he was a communicator who could impregnate large audiences with ideas by dint of his rhetorical skills. He spoke wherever a podium was available: synagogue, marketplace, conferences, fairs.

Much of the *Maggid*'s impact flowed from his emotive attitude. *Maggidim* were sensitive to the spiritual needs and suffering of their people. They comforted and rebuked, threatened sinners with hellfire, taught and entertained, always attuned to the problems of their day. Commensurate with their country's Jewish community, Lithuanian *Maggidim* were on balance more scholarly than their colleagues elsewhere. Thus their influence reached both the community leadership and the simple people, spreading love of Torah and Eretz Israel for generations to come, wherever they appeared.

The Lithuanian Haskalah

The Haskalah, the Jewish Enlightenment movement, originated in the general European Enlightenment that dawned in the late 1700s. Haskalah adherents, who termed themselves *maskilim* (sing. *maskil*) considered themselves rationalists in the secular humanist sense, and taught that reason was the yardstick by which all should be measured. Such a prescription could only lead to conflict with traditionalist forces.

Haskalah first germinated in Austria and Germany; it took some years to spread to Eastern Europe. There, and in Lithuania in particular, the conflict first centered on religious opposition to secular education. Rabbinical objections were twofold: the very introduction of general studies would divert Jewish students from the Torah and Talmud; and the contents of such study would alienate them from traditional beliefs and practices. Contemplating the changing patterns of Jewish life in Germany and Austria, the rabbis blamed Haskalah philosophy, with its insistence on changes in behavior, language, and dress, for the general increase in assimilation that had occurred.

The early maskilim in Russia stressed Jewish emancipation as distinct from assimilation, and regarded the spread of Enlightenment as a precondition to the full attainment of this goal. Thus they, like their colleagues in Central Europe, emphasized the importance of modifying Jewish social patterns by urging the masses to engage in productive labor such as agriculture and crafts. Thus the Russian Haskalah set itself a two-phase strategy: first to effect social and cultural changes within the Jewish community itself; and then to campaign for the improvement of Jewish legal rights and social status in Russian law and society.

All of this was anathema to the rabbis. Insofar as education had become the arena of conflict, their counterprescription was a solely devotional, Torah-only curriculum.

Lithuanian Jews had never formed a movement that championed secular education. Gifted individuals, sometimes supported by patrons but mostly from wealthy families, had occasionally engaged in study of this or that profession. Jews from Lithuania had long been known to travel to Italy for medical studies at the University of Padua. In 1692, for example, the wealthy Gordon family of Vilna had sent one of its sons away for this purpose; other relatives followed. Jews from Brisk, Grodno, and other Lithuanian cities attended medical schools in France and Germany; Frankfurt-am-Oder was a favored venue. Graduates who returned home were offered attractive physicianships or consultancy positions on princely estates or in the royal court. However, the modest outflux dissipated at the end of the eighteenth century, when the newly formed medical school at the University of Vilna allowed several Jews to enroll.

Consequently, Haskalah found fertile soil in Lithuania. The forces of resistance, too, had been weakened in the Pale of Settlement. No longer could rabbis or lay councils apply sanctions such as excommunication. Thus there was nothing to prevent or hinder the coalescence of a local Haskalah movement by individuals who were already maskilim by conviction. The indigenous maskilim received occasional encouragement from the Russian authorities, who offered it for reasons of their own.

By the early 1890s, cheaply produced Yiddish translations of foreign, especially Russian, literature were peddled throughout the Pale and snapped up by an eager clientele. Since women were generally excluded from religious studies but had become literate in Yiddish, they were among the most enthusiastic customers. In this fashion the lowly peddler, albeit unwittingly, helped distribute foreign literature and ideas in every corner of the Pale where he sold his wares. Ironically, the Vilna Gaon contributed his share to the spread of Haskalah in Lithuania. His favorable attitude toward general knowledge – rooted in his quest for better understanding of the religious sources and commands – now fomented a measure of tolerance and openness to secular study for secular aims.

Several Lithuanian scholars figured prominently in Moses Mendelssohn's circle in Berlin. One was Salomon Maimon (1753-1800). Once a child prodigy in the *beyt midrash*, Maimon became an expert on Kant and published many philosophical works in German. His Hebrew writings included commentaries on Maimonides' *Guide to the Perplexed* and on Ibn Ezra's commentary on the Pentateuch and Psalms. His autobiography is an important source for the study of Jewish life in Eastern Europe at that time. Considered a heretic at the time of his death in Germany, Maimon was interred outside a Jewish cemetery.

Solomon Dubno (1738-1813) was another important Lithuania-born member of Mendelssohn's group. A Bible scholar and Hebrew poet, he lived and studied first in Amsterdam and then in Berlin, where Mendelssohn engaged him as a private tutor for his son Joseph. It was by Dubno's suggestion that Mendelssohn translated the Bible into German and penned the Hebrew commentary known as the *Biur,* to which Dubno contributed in part. In the middle of this project, Dubno was prompted by his friends in Russia, who disapproved of his association with Mendelssohn, to leave for Vilna. He later returned to Germany but finally settled in Amsterdam, where he wrote his own commentaries, much Hebrew poetry, and a geography of Palestine. Dubno's commentaries were the first Jewish sources that dealt with the structure and style of the Bible; they also provided many explanatory remarks on history and geography.

Mendelssohn and his circle set firm limits on the degree of assimilation that they would permit. As firmly as they sought to reeducate the Jewish masses and introduce them to the German language and culture, they opposed co-education of Jewish and non-Jewish children. Mendelssohn also objected to the *Toleranzpatent,* the Edict of Tolerance, issued by Emperor Joseph II of Austria in 1782. Haskalah leaders originally welcomed the educational and other reforms proposed by the Edict as harbingers of a Jewish emancipation; Mendelssohn, however, soon perceived it as an instrument of a policy meant to lead Jews to conversion. In his book *Jerusalem,* Mendelssohn denied any intention to deviate from the Law of Moses in order to gain civil rights.

Just the same, Mendelssohn and his followers inveighed against many pillars of traditional Jewish life. One was the Yiddish language, which they were loathe to use even for translation purposes. They respected the authority of the Oral Law but belittled the study of Talmud for the masses – the very focus of all Jewish education up to that time. Their doctrines reverberated loudly in Lithuania by means of Mendelssohn's *Biur* and his German translation of the Bible. Interaction with scholars, merchants, physicians, and various periodicals and books by German maskilim reinforced the message until an indigenous maskilic cadre took shape in the backwater vassal province of Muscovy.

Although several early Lithuanian maskilim maintained close and direct relations with their colleagues in Berlin, they regarded themselves as disciples of the Vilna Gaon and based themselves on his writings. Several prominent members of this group are described below by way of example.

One of the most important was Baruch Schick, also known as Baruch of Shklov (1740-1812). Schick, ordained as a rabbi at the age of 24, served as a *dayan* in Minsk. Attracted to the Enlightenment before reaching adulthood, he traveled to London to study medicine. After graduating, he moved to Berlin where he met Mendelssohn and others of his circle and adopted their philosophy as his own. In 1777, he published two books that demarcated his fields of interest: a scholarly commentary called '*Amudey ha-Shamayim* (Pillars of heaven) on a work of Maimonides, and an anatomy for the masses. On his way back to Minsk a year later, he visited Vilna and joined a group that associated itself closely with the Vilna Gaon, in whose name he issued a statement on the need to study secular science for a better understanding of Torah. Acting on the Gaon's advice, he translated several scientific works into Hebrew, including the first section of Euclid's *Geometry* from the Latin. By 1784 he published another two books: *Derekh Yesharim* (Way of the righteous), a treatise on medicine and hygiene printed in The Hague and a geometry and trigonometry text translated from English, printed in Prague. At this point he returned to Minsk and then to Shklov, his birthplace, where he was active among the maskilim. He later moved to Slutzk, where he served both as *dayan* and as court physician to Count Radziwill. He dedicated his remaining years to the dual missions of convincing Jews in the Pale of the need to study science and the arts and urging a revival of the Hebrew language. He died in Slutzk in 1812, leaving behind several manuscripts including a translation of the second section of Euclid's *Geometry*.

By 1820, many Haskalah associations or societies existed in the Pale of Settlement. They were especially active throughout Lithuania and used Vilna as their headquarters. Their members dressed in the German fashion and were referred to as *Deychn* or *Berliner*. Unlike their German counterparts, who wrote and published their works in German, the maskilim in Lithuania and Russia used Hebrew and Yiddish, although some advocated a transition from Yiddish to the German language or Russian, which were deemed "pure." The lives of several important members of these groups are described below by way of example.

Abraham Mapu (1808-1867), a major Haskalah exponent and the creator of the modern Hebrew novel, was born in Slobodka. Given a traditional religious education, he was considered a brilliant student of Talmud at an early age. As an adult, he began his career by teaching Bible and Talmud in Kovno, within the traditional system. In view of his religious background and knowledge, as well as the Biblical style and setting of his early novels, the religious public initially received Mapu's works with favor; rabbis later greatly frowned on them.

Mapu's first novel, *Ahavat Tsiyon* (Love of Zion), represented a landmark in the development of modern Hebrew literature with its Biblical setting and florid language, reminiscent of the French Romantic school. It expresses the yearnings of a people, fettered in economic, political and social shackles, for a better, fuller life. As such, *Ahavat Tsiyon* was not only the first Hebrew-language novel but an important and influential work as well. It was printed in some 16 editions and was translated into many European languages as well as Yiddish, Ladino, Judeo-Arabic, and even Judeo-Persian.

The second Mapu novel (1858), *'Ayit Tsevu'a* (literally, The painted vulture; figuratively, the hypocrite) portrays contemporary life in Lithuania, satirizing the outward piety of those whose religion is only skin-deep and emphasizing the need for social and educational reform. The influence of this book, too, reverberated in various directions. Subsequent Hebrew writers such as Mendele Mocher Seforim and Judah Leib Gordon were especially affected by it; rabbis and the Orthodox circles were incensed.

Mapu published several nonfiction books meant to improve the primitive educational methods of his time, but it is for his Biblical novels that he is best remembered as a pioneer of the Haskalah. By stimulating pride in Jewish national history and calling attention to the centrality of Eretz Israel in Jewish life, *Ahavat Tsiyon* and his other fictional works contributed importantly to the rise of the Jewish national movement, which subsequently found its political expression in Zionism.

The Haskalah-religion dichotomy should not be overstated. Vilna, termed the "Jerusalem of Lithuania" by Napoleon as he contemplated its ecclesiastical splendor, had sufficiently broad horizons to accommodate the epicenter of Lithuanian Haskalah as well. Most, if not all, of the early maskilim drew their inspiration from traditional Jewish sources, which continued to inspire their writings and their ideals throughout their lives even after they had discarded ritual observance, as many of them eventually did. One maskilic group even established its own synagogue in Vilna, Taharat ha-Qodesh, in 1846. For a better understanding of this ostensible paradox, one need only refer to Bialik's poem *"Im yesh et nafshekha lada'at"* (If you wish to know):

> If you wish to know the source from which your brethren drew their strength...then turn to the beyt midrash, the house of study -...

> And then your heart will tell you that your foot treads on the threshold of our House of Life, and you will peer into the treasure trove of our soul.

This is the background from which Yehuda Leib Gordon, one of the most ardent exponents of Haskalah, came forth to create modern Hebrew poetry.

Gordon was born in Vilna in 1831. His father, a learned and cultured man in the maskilic sense, hired a student of one of the Vilna Gaon's disciples to teach the boy. Educated in the light of the Gaon's method, which advocated study of Bible and Hebrew grammar before study of Talmud, Yehuda Leib was considered a prodigy by the age of 14 and soon became remarkably proficient in many areas of talmudic and rabbinic literature. Under the influence of his brother-in-law, the Yiddish poet Mikhel Gordon, Yehuda Leib then began to study European languages and culture, and at the age of 22 graduated from the government teachers' seminary in Vilna. For 19 years, 1853-1872, he taught French and other secular subjects in government schools in Kovno, Ponevez, Shavli and Telz, where he became the principal of the Hebrew public school and later established a girls school. In 1872 he moved to St. Petersburg, where he served as secretary of the Jewish community and director of the Society for the Promotion of Culture among Jews.

Accused of anti-Czarist activities, he was imprisoned and banished in 1879; exonerated a year later, he returned. The community did not reinstate him to his former position, and for lack of other income he accepted an offer to become the editor of *Hamelitz*. This journal expanded from semiweekly to daily during his tenure. For a time, Gordon was also the general and science editor of a Russian-language Jewish monthly and a contributing editor in matters of Jewish history and Hebrew literature for an 82-volume Russian encyclopaedic dictionary, on whose staff he worked. Gordon died in St. Petersburg in 1892.

Yehuda Leib Gordon, a master of the Hebrew language, utilized his vast knowledge of Aggada, Mishna, and Mediaeval Hebrew literature to produce a unique style much different from his predecessors' pure Biblical rhetoric. A versatile writer, Gordon produced poems, novels, and essays, but his fame rests principally on his poetry. Within this genre, too, he displayed his versatility, turning out epics, narrative verse, polemic poems, and fables. Love poems and nature poems are conspicuously absent. Although he deals with injustice and suffering generally, his major concern is with Jewish life, both past and present.

Gordon's best known works are his epic poem *Ahavat David u-Mikhal* (The love of David and Michal), based on the Biblical theme, and *Mishley Yehuda* (Judah's fables), a Hebrew translation of writings by Aesop, La Fontaine, Krylov, and others, including several fables and parables of his own based on Biblical and midrashic themes. The title page of the latter work, which became very popular, described the contents as a collection of musar (ethical) parables and fables and whetted the readers' appetite with a famous Midrashic quotation: "Do not disparage the parable (or fable), since it is the means by which one may best understand the message of Torah."

His polemical poems and articles championed diverse causes of the common people, the poor, and the oppressed. His most famous work in this category is the poem *"Kotso shel yod"* (The point on the top of [the Hebrew letter] yod[79]), in which he advocates the rights of the Jewish woman, especially the *'aguna*, the deserted wife.

Gordon was the author of a motto that became the watchword of maskilim everywhere. In a poem entitled *Haqitsa 'ami* (Arise, my people), he urged members of his people to "be a Jew in your home and a man in the street." He believed, in his early adult years, that Jews should cast aside their self-segregation, their Yiddish language, and the rigidity of their old customs in favor of integration into their general surroundings. This, he maintained, would improve relations between Jews and the people around them. As time passed, however, Gordon, became disillusioned with Russian liberalism because of its inability to cope with growing antisemitism. He also rejected the ultra-assimilationist trends of the younger generation of maskilim, who repudiated Jewish values and abandoned the Hebrew language. His poem *"Le-mi ani 'amel"* (For whom do I toil) decries those "enlightened brothers who have learned science and mock the old mother," and who urge Jews to "forsake [Hebrew] and take up the vernacular, each of his own country." He wondered aloud, "Perhaps I am the last of Zion's poets and you, the last readers." All of this led Gordon to reassess his attitudes toward Diaspora Jewish life.

Gordon never went so far as to join Hibat Tsiyon, which advocated emigration to Eretz Israel as a solution to the problems of Russian Jewry. He believed, as he wrote in *Hamelitz* in 1882, that "our redemption can come about only after our spiritual deliverance." He did, however, become an active supporter of the Zionist cause. It was an 1866 article of his in *Ha-Carmel*, a Hebrew weekly published in Vilna, that inspired an association of pro-Palestine pioneers to adopt the name Bilu. Ahad Ha'am, the forefather of spiritual Zionism, acknowledged his indebtedness to Gordon in the introduction to his *'Al parashat derakhim* (At the crossroads).

A remarkable phenomenon of the Haskalah was the considerable number of Jewish apostates, converts to Christianity, who continued with their Hebrew writings and Jewish activities. Some remained in touch with the Jewish community; others burned their bridges. All were savants who wrote in Hebrew and made important contributions to Jewish scholarship in one form or another. On the whole, the maskilim despised these turncoats, who harmed the movement by alienating Jews from Haskalah philosophy and reinforcing rabbis' warnings of the dire fate that awaited all those who flirted with Haskalah.

The biographies of Daniel Chwolson (1819-1911) and Abraham Uri Kovner (1842-1909), both born in Vilna, shed light on the nature of this group. They had accepted Christianity in order to gain admission to Russian society and the improved economic conditions that supposedly awaited it. Wits of the period commented that Chwolson and others embraced Christianity out of conviction – conviction that conversion would help a Jewish boy make good in Russian society.

Chwolson, the son of devout Orthodox parents, received a traditional yeshiva education but left for Germany in 1841 to study Oriental languages in Breslau. In 1855, after moving to St. Petersburg, he converted to Russian Orthodoxy and accepted an appointment as Professor of Hebrew and Semitic languages at the University of St. Petersburg. His writings dealt with every phase of Oriental life and religion, and he made major contributions to Hebrew paleography. He joined Hever Mefitsey ha-Haskalah, the Society for the Promotion of Culture among the Jews, but was forced to relinquish his membership under a torrent of hostile Jewish public opinion. Nevertheless, Chwolson remained on good terms with many Jewish scholars and leaders.

He actually helped the Orthodox establishment on many occasions by intervening on their behalf when the Russian Government threatened yeshivot with closure or sought to ban new printings of the Talmud. As a member of a government commission set up to investigate charges that Jews were indeed guilty of the blood libel, he rendered the Jewish community an important service by proving the baselessness of this charge in Talmudic and related Jewish literature. For a large fee, Chwolson argued the Jewish community's case in defense of ritual slaughter, which the Russian authorities sought to ban. He published studies on early Hebrew printing and was an active collector of Hebrew incunabula and rare books. Chwolson assembled a rich library that he presented to the Russian Academy of Sciences. He lived to the age of 92.

Abraham Uri Kovner attended various Lithuanian yeshivot and helped pioneer modern Hebrew literary criticism. Married at an early age, he left his wife in order to study Russian language and secular sciences. At the age of 20, he published two essays on Hebrew literature in *Hamelitz*,[80] a Hebrew-language Haskalah weekly founded in 1860, whose declared aim was "to mediate between Jews and the Government and between the faith and Haskalah." In these essays, as in later works such as *Heqer davar* (Research), Kovner was sharply critical of the Hebrew authors of his day, accusing them of disregarding contemporary realities and engaging in frivolous dalliances with Hebrew poetry and irrelevant stories of the past. The modern Hebrew and Yiddish literature of his time, he maintained, were transitional genres; all future Jewish literature would be written and would flourish in the vernacular of the country in which Jews lived.

Kovner's writings provoked such bitter controversy that *Hamelitz* accused him of being a nihilist. Kovner denounced *Hamelitz* to the Russian authorities, claiming that it had supported a plot to purchase Palestine and establish a monarchy under the House of Rothschild there. His last Hebrew work appeared in 1868, after which he began writing in Russian. By this time he urged the authorities to close down yeshivot and replace them with modern rabbinical seminaries. Antisemitism and the Jewish question, he argued, were rooted in economic factors and would no longer exist once general social conditions improved.

In 1875, Kovner was arrested in St. Petersburg, where he worked as a bank clerk, on charges of forgery. He was convicted and sentenced to four years of hard labor in Siberia. After his release, he converted to Christianity and married a non-Jewish woman. He subsequently settled in Lomza, where he continued to take an interest in Jewish affairs and topics through various kinds of writings, including correspondence with the likes of Tolstoy and Dostoyevsky on the Jewish problem.

Although Kovner's main prognosis for the demise of Hebrew literature did not come to pass, he had much to do with the development of this literature. He also pioneered, through his attacks on the writers of his day, the art of literary criticism in the Hebrew language.

The maskilim did more than turn out social and philosophical prose, poetry, and essays. They developed a purely secular literary form of expression in both Hebrew and Yiddish, dealing with day-to-day problems and local, Pale, and world news, as the Jewish world had not known theretofore. In view of their upbringing and religious education, the early maskilim generally retained a healthy respect for the moral and spiritual strengths inherent in Jewish values. This, however, did not inhibit them from severely criticizing what they considered rigid conservatism on the part of rabbis and community leaders and, therefore, to urge radical change in the name of progress. Thus, under Haskalah influence, the Yiddish language, for centuries used solely for religious writings and folklore, was now invoked for criticism and ridicule of the old ways, coupled with demands for reform. As time passed, the caustic tone of these writings was tempered somewhat by a sympathetic awareness of the harshness and helplessness of Jewish existence in the Pale. This gave rise to a series of educational works that attempted to teach Jews the ways of the new world and inspire them to expect and hope that they might break free of their isolation by discarding their particularism. Such an emancipation, in turn, would lead to a better understanding and appreciation of the Jews as a people and to their ultimate integration into general society.

The founders of this new genre, which used the Yiddish vernacular to reach and teach the masses, were Shalom Jacob Abramovitch (1835-1917), better known as Mendele Mocher Seforim; Shalom Aleichem (1859-1916), whose real name was Sholem Rabinowitz; and Isaac Leib Peretz (1852-1915).

In their struggle to bring Enlightenment to the Jews; the maskilim turned to the Russian government for support – an odd thing to ask of an Empire that withheld enlightenment from citizens of other denominations. Naively they petitioned government offices, requesting of them to impose reforms on the masses, to force them to change their manner of dress, and to limit the total number of Hebrew publications at the expense of books on religious themes. The government accepted and enforced these schemes, using the Haskalah movement to further its own aims of assimilating and converting the Jews.

Between 1840 and 1850, the Russian authorities established a network of Jewish schools throughout the Pale, with German and Russian as the languages of instruction. The first administrator they named to head this system was the well-known educationalist Max Lilienthal. Lilienthal, backed by the maskilim, promoted the Haskalah agenda but suspected that the government had something else in mind. This suspicion was confirmed when the government demanded the excision of Talmud study from the curriculum. Unwilling to preside over an instrument that, he believed, had the long-term aim of converting Jews to Christianity, conscious of the government's intention to use him, and aware that he would never succeed in persuading the Jewish masses to accept secular education, he left for the United States in 1844. There he accepted positions as a Reform rabbi, first in New York and then in Cincinnati.

To further its assimilationist policies, the government established rabbinical seminaries in Vilna and Zhitomir to turn out secularly educated clerics and teachers. The function of the graduates, the *kazioni rabbiner* – government-sponsored rabbis – was to register births, marriages, and deaths, and deliver sermons in praise of the government. These "official" rabbis, elected by the Lithuanian and Russian communities between 1857 and 1917 by government order, were generally treated with contempt and hostility. Many had scanty knowledge of Judaism; some were morally suspect. The maskilim supported the institution of the *kazioni rabbiner* in accordance with their philosophy, but the true religious influence in the communities remained with the traditional rabbis. In time, the official rabbinate provided many maskilim with a source of livelihood. Several members of this group rendered great service to their people and were exceptions to the *kazioni rabbiner* archetype. They included Zionist leaders and writers such as Jacob Mazeh (1859-1924), the official rabbi of Moscow, and Shmaryahu Levin (1867-1935), who held a similar post in Grodno.

As the Lithuanian Haskalah moved into its second generation, the nature of its exponents changed. Most of the early maskilim were autodidacts in secular affairs and well-schooled in Judaism and Biblical and Talmudic literature. The second generation, although well educated and proficient in

Russian and secular studies, were largely ignorant of and, indeed, estranged from Jewish tradition and learning. A polyglot group that was well versed in mathematics and various disciplines, they formed a large and growing class of Jews who, on this basis, were qualified to occupy government positions and obtain government contracts. To meet the requirements of a changing society, they discarded their traditional garb, dressed in European fashion, shaved their beards and cut their earlocks, abandoned religious observance, and pursued Russian culture avidly. This vogue spread like wildfire throughout the Pale, including Lithuania, during the reign of Czar Alexander II (1855-1881). Jewish and Russian newspapers and journals published by the maskilim were a decisive force in this development. Among the most important of these publications were *Hamelitz, Tsiyon* (Zion), *Kol Mevaser* (The Manifesto), and *Hashahar* (The Dawn), all of which appeared in Hebrew, and the Russian-language *Razvet* and *Voskhod*.

Both the early maskilim and the successor generation favored the government's Russification policy. Irrespective of its motives, it offered the Jewish masses secular education, and here, they believed, lay the solution for their problems in the Pale. They fully believed that Russia would soon join the rest of Europe in emancipating the Jews and would grant all Jews in Russia the rights previously awarded to selected groups only: the rich and the intelligentsia in 1859, craftsmen in 1865, and Russian-educated Jews in 1874. Eventually, they were sure, the Russian Jew would be treated as a real citizen with equal rights and obligations under the law.

As for assimilation, the Russian Haskalah movement was of two minds. One attitude favored the assimilation of Jews into the Russian nation; in extreme cases, this led to conversion, as in the two cases described above. Holders of this view dealt in Jewish scholarship and learning for its own sake, following the Wissenschaft des Judentums (Jewish Science) model. The second attitude, much more widely held – especially among those who were active from 1870 onward – promoted a Jewish national awakening, driven by Hebrew language and literature as vehicles for the teaching of Jewish values and inculcation of the awakening itself. They argued their case in a plethora of newspapers and publications in Hebrew, Yiddish, Russian, and German.

New circumstances further fissured the Haskalah movement. The first was the emergence of a powerful movement that overtly preached antisemitism. Writers, intellectuals, government officials, and important clergymen enlisted in this cause, skillfully using their writings and, especially, the Russian press to incite the masses against the Jews. The clergy was particularly adroit at arousing the illiterate Russian *muzhiks*, who needed little encouragement, to hatred of the Jew.

Every new social and economic problem that bedeviled the Empire – and there were many – exacerbated the friction. The assassination of Czar Alexander II in 1881 triggered four years of pogroms and led to severe restrictions on Jews' privileges, which were limited to begin with. Especially onerous to the maskilim was the government's endorsement of a quota system in the high schools and universities that was later termed *numerus clausus*. (Such an issue did not arise in the civil service, from which Jews were barred.)

As a movement, Haskalah failed to respond to these developments with one voice. Some, in spite of all the difficulties, refused to surrender their dreams and still believed in the goodwill of Russian society. They resolved to continue their struggle for change, progress, and eventual emancipation. Many Jews who held this view joined various revolutionary movements in Russia, convinced that a new, just regime would solve the Jewish problem once and for all by granting all Jews equality, thereby absorbing them into the Russian nation.

However, a much larger group of maskilim and intellectuals, supported this time by many of the common people and the traditionalists, turned to Jewish nationalism. They were the founders of Hibat Tsiyon and Hovevey Tsiyon, proto-Zionist movements that regarded emigration to and productive agriculture in Eretz Israel as the sole solution to the Jewish problem.

Yearnings for Zion and the Zionist Movement

Yearning for Zion among Jews began with the destruction of the Second Temple by Rome in 70 C.E. and the subsequent expulsion of the Jews from their devastated homeland. The sanctity of Eretz Israel, coupled with longing for return to it, soon became a central plank in the Jew's daily existence. It was a major theme in the daily devotion, the Grace after Meals, and, especially, the festival rites. Thus the Jewish religion played a unique role in keeping the collective territorial memory alive. The persecution and oppression that Jews almost always faced during their lengthy exile merely reinforced their aspirations and invigorated their hopes. Consequently, religious faith and national aspirations fused to form an all-pervasive element in Jewish life.

Jews clung desperately and unequivocally to the belief that the Messiah would eventually come and carry them back to their ancient homeland. This explains why the urgings of every false Messiah attracted such enthusiastic responses. Even when these expectations gave way to disillusionment, sorrow, and gloom, Jews never forfeited their hopes.

The threadlike connection with the Holy Land was maintained across the centuries by travellers of various kinds. None was more important than the *meshulah*, the fundraising emissary from Eretz Israel, armed with letters of recommendation. Lithuanian Jewry gave every arriving *meshulah* a warm welcome, great respect, and assistance in the fulfillment of his mission. Every synagogue in Lithuania had collection boxes into which the devout might slip coins to help some institution in the Holy Land. A Council of Lithuania ordinance, dated 1623, appealed "for help for our brethren in the Holy Land" and urged every synagogue to raise funds for this purpose on all Jewish festivals, including Yom Kippur and Rosh Hodesh (the first day of each lunar month in the Jewish calendar). The ordinance was reissued in 1652 and in 1655 – precisely the time at which the community was swamped with refugees and devastated by the Ukrainian uprising.

Some *meshulahim* evidently "postponed" their return to Eretz Israel for an inordinately long period of time, perhaps preferring to remain in the Diaspora. In 1664, this brought forth another ordinance: emissaries might remain in Lithuania to solicit funds for two years and not a day longer. Those who overstayed their welcome, the Council ruled, should be deprived of further support, and their letters of recommendation should be considered null and void.

An ancillary function of the *meshulah* was to preach the importance of the commandment of living in Eretz Israel. From the sixteenth century on, as Europe stabilized and the Ottoman Empire, the sovereign in Palestine, entered its golden era, the number of Lithuanian and other Jews who fulfilled the precept of *'aliya* – settlement in Eretz Israel – indeed began to increase. Thus contacts and communications between Lithuania and the Holy Land also gained strength and intensity. In 1548, R. Kalman Kalonymus ben Jacob of Brisk, son-in-law of R. Solomon Luria (1510-1574) ("the Maharshal," a famous scholar and Talmudic commentator), was named the first Ashkenazi Chief Rabbi of Jerusalem. In 1588, he was succeeded by R. Ephraim Katz-Fish, also of Brisk. Rabbi Katz-Fish's grandson R. Ephraim of Shadl, too, held this position, as did R. Jacob Zak of Vilna, father of R. Zvi Hirsh Ashkenazi (1660-1718) ("the Hakham Zvi") and grandfather of R. Jacob Emden.

Many of the older, wealthier Jews who moved to the Holy Land left their savings or other moneys with the Councils or private individuals for investment, arranging for annuities on which they might live in Palestine. For example, the Koppel family of Lutzk, which emigrated in 1678, left behind 940 gulden that yielded a guaranteed yearly income of 150 gulden; R. Johanan Prager of Vilna received 200 gulden annually for the 1,200 gulden that he had invested with the Council before his departure.

Lithuanian Jews were well represented among seventeenth-century 'olim (Jews settling in Eretz Israel). The fundraising meshulahim knew which names to drop in any community they visited. However, the fundraisers were neither exclusively Lithuanian nor even Ashkenazi. Sephardi representatives came to Lithuania too; in 1694, for example, Simon ben Jacob of Jerusalem visited Vilna, Brisk, and Shklov to make sure his Sephardi institutions received their fair share of the charitable funds emanating from Lithuania.

The first "mass immigration" of Lithuanian Jews, a group of some 125 led by R. Judah Hasid of Shedlitz (near Grodno), left for the Holy Land in 1700. They were joined by many others en route until the group finally numbered about 1,500, a third of whom died on the way. Those who reached the Holy Land almost doubled the Jewish population of Jerusalem, which peaked at 1,200.

They received a chilly welcome, for the Jerusalem community suspected them of being followers of the false Messiah, Shabbetai Zevi. Indeed, there were several known Shabbetaeans within the group; prominent among them was Hayyim Malakh, who had become closely associated in Vilna with the Shabbetean prophet, Hershel Tsoref, after an early career as a highly respected rabbinic scholar, kabbalist, and preacher. Malakh and his followers had joined Judah Hasid's group to await the advent of the Messiah, whom they understood to be Shabbetai Zevi, in 1706. Two years after the deadline, with no Messiah in sight, Malakh returned to Lithuania as an emissary to raise funds for his group, whose Shabbetaean connections he denied. Denounced in 1710 in a circular by the rabbis of Constantinople, he returned to Poland, where, in Podolia, he founded a radical sect that gave birth to the movement of Jacob Frank.

In 1705, after the death of R. Judah Hasid, a synagogue in his memory was built within the compound of the Ashkenazi community of Jerusalem. Arabs leveled this synagogue and the entire compound in 1720; the area was left as a ruin (Heb. *hurva*) for some 140 years, at which point a new synagogue, known as the Hurva, was erected on the site.

The Hurva courtyard served as the center of the Ashkenazi community of Jerusalem until 1914. Apart from the synagogue itself, it housed the offices of the Etz Hayyim Talmud Torah (boys' religious school), the *kollelim* of the Vilna *Perushim* (disciples of the Vilna Gaon who had settled there in the early 1800s – see below), a hospice, and rabbinical court and offices of the Chief Rabbinate of Jerusalem.[81]

The story of pre-Zionist *'aliya* combines several well-known failures, specifically those of R. Israel Baal Shem Tov (the Besht), the founder of hasidism, and the Vilna Gaon, with steady success. In 1747 a vanguard group of hasidim, followers of the Besht, left Europe en route to the Holy Land. A second and much larger contingent followed in 1764, including Lithuanian hasidim from centers such as Shklov, Vitebsk, and Vilna. A third group, approximately 300 in number, left Lithuania under the leadership of R. Azriel of Shklov eight years later.

The hasidim settled and established their centers in three of the four holy cities of Eretz Israel – Jerusalem, Hebron, and Tiberias – where they soon enjoyed cordial relations with the Oriental Jews who had previously settled there. Rapport with the Sephardim of North Africa was especially convivial. The two groups respected each other's customs and traditions; even their prayerbooks shared the same ritual, the *nusah ha-Ari*, alternately known as nusah Sepharad, formulated by kabbalist rabbi Isaac Luria. They intermarried and, from 1780 onward, sent emissaries into the Diaspora together to raise funds for their institutions and alms for their poor.

Generosity had its limits. The *Kahal* organizations in Lithuania encouraged only the wealthy, who would be no burden to them, to make *'aliya*. Several communities earmarked their help for specific centers in the Holy Land, presumably because former members had settled there. Thus an entry in the *pinqas* (community ledger) of Tiktin, dated 1785, speaks of "adopting" the Hebron community as the beneficiary of this town's Jewish charity.

A Vilna contingent of a different kind set out for Eretz Israel in 1808. They were the *Perushim*, disciples of the Vilna Gaon, led by Rabbi Mendel of Shklov. A second group, under R. Riveles-Rivlin, followed a year later, and a third group, led by R. Israel of Shklov and R. Hayyim Katz, arrived in 1810. The last of these groups included several wealthy families, such as the Zeitlins, who soon established and supported their own *shtiblakh* (prayer and study rooms). It was a well-organized emigration of entire families with many young children. R. Hayyim Katz summed up the results in a letter penned soon after his arrival in Eretz Israel: "Here, if you have money, you can live happily and enjoy both worlds."

Most of the *Perushim* settled in Jerusalem and, originally, Safed, where they joined earlier groups of *landsmenner* who shared their philosophy and way of life. After an earthquake in 1837 devastated Safed, nearly all the *Perushim* in that town relocated to Jerusalem, giving that city a Jewish plurality that it never relinquished. The influx also caused housing density in the walled city that was countered in the 1850s by construction of the first extramural neighborhoods of "new Jerusalem." The Me'a She'arim quarter in Jerusalem, for example, was considered a *Perushim* stronghold by the time it was completed in 1881. Interestingly, the acrimony between Lithuanian hasidim and mitnaggedim (the *Perushim* were nonpareil affiliates of the latter group) did not pursue the two groups to the Holy Land; when several Habad hasidim moved into Me'a She'arim, no opposition arose. The two factions, which originated in the same regions of Lithuania and Belorussia, understood and respected each other. The same could not be said of relations between Lithuanian *Perushim* and hasidim from Poland, Galicia, Hungary, Romania, and even the Ukraine.

Many of the newcomers had arrived penniless, although they had been asked to make financial arrangements before departure. The Vilna *kollel* in Jerusalem now became the conduit for *haluqa* – alms for indigent *Perushim* scholars and others – and the *gemah*, a free-loan fund for craftsmen and the destitute.

The Vilna *kollel* in Jerusalem soon sent its first *meshulah* to Lithuania, and the emissary appealed to R. Hayyim of Volozhin and the Vilna community. R. Hayyim not only pledged the requisite assistance but arranged for regular forwarding of funds and encouraged his disciples to join the *Perushim* already in the Holy Land. The largest share of the philanthropy went to *Perushim* families and institutions in Jerusalem and Safed. The Vilna *kollel* was joined by similar bodies affiliated with other Lithuanian cities, including one from Raseinai, headed by R. Judah Leib Menuhin, whose grandson Yehudi became a world-famous violinist and conductor. The affiliated-*kollel* model was also used by *'olim* from other countries and regions of Eastern and Central Europe – *Kollel* Warsaw, *Kollel* Ungarin (Hungary), *Kollel* Hod (an abbreviation for

Holland-ve-Deutschland), and so on. They bickered and quarrelled to no end, chiefly because of insufficient funds; the same factor explains their bitter controversies with the Sephardim.

In 1866, R. Joseph Rivlin established the *Va'ad ha-Kelali* (General Committee of the Ashkenazi *Kollelim*) to address the problems of community fragmentation and place the entire *haluqa* system under a regime of order and discipline. In fact, the *Va'ad ha-Kelali*, on which each *kollel* had a representative, cared for all general needs of the community at large, including rabbinate, religious education, welfare, health, and the support of scholars. Provisions were made for community members who did not belong to any *kollel*. Management of *haluqa* in Palestine, however, remained in the hands of Lithuanian Jews until the end of World War I, first through the *Perushim kollelim* and then through the *Va'ad ha-Kelali*. Emigrants from Vilna, Minsk, Pinsk, Keidanov, Suwalk, Rasein, and Grodno were among the beneficiaries, according to *Shemesh tsedaqa*, (lit. Sun of charity), the list of *haluqa* charities.

Lithuanian *Perushim* and hasidim continued to flow into the Holy Land, disregarding the dangers and hardships of the long journey, driven by the belief that they were paving the way for redemption of the Jewish homeland for the Jewish people as an augury of Jewish salvation. Many rabbis, particularly the heads of the Yeshiva of Volozhin, supported the eminently practical policy of establishing settlements in Eretz Israel, since the critical situation of European Jewry, especially that of the Russian Empire, warranted their urgent emigration and resettlement in a land of their own.

The first steps toward converting a 2,000-year-old dream into a political reality of return to the ancient Jewish homeland were taken in the late nineteenth century, with the creation of the Zionist movement. This movement, however, was preceded by almost 80 years of advocacy by distinguished individuals, Jews and Gentiles, including many Lithuanian rabbis, who had long preached and published their advocacy of settlement in the Holy Land without waiting for the Messiah, as previous doctrine insisted. Prominent among these clerics were R. Samuel Mohilever (1824-1898), who helped stimulate Baron Edmond de Rothschild's interest in Jewish colonization in Palestine and became an enthusiastic supporter of Herzl, and R. Jacob Reines (1839-1915), head of the Yeshiva of Lida and later, in 1901, the effective founder of Mizrachi, the Religious Zionist movement.

Importantly, however, these rabbis were decisively outnumbered in Lithuania by exponents of the Messiah-first doctrine. To them, Zionism was an act of blatant rebellion against the Almighty's design for His people, and religious Zionism coupled rebellion with betrayal. With the spiritual leadership divided on such a fundamental issue, religious Jews in Lithuania, as indeed throughout the Diaspora, found themselves in a great dilemma that reached its tragic denouement in the Holocaust.

The maskilim were not nearly as divided. The writers and intellectuals of the Enlightenment championed the idea of Palestine as the Jewish homeland and, in 1882, their newspaper *Hamaggid* (The Preacher) became the principal organ of the Hovevey Tsiyon movement, whose associations were mushrooming throughout Lithuania. The associations went by different names in different cities: *Sha'alu Shelom Yerushalayim* (Seek the peace of Jerusalem; cf. Ps. 122:6), in Vilna, *Dorshey Tsiyon* (Seekers of Zion) in Grodno, *Boney Tsiyon* and *Ohavey Tsiyon* (Builders of Zion and Lovers of Zion) in Bialystok.

The Zionist societies were open to anyone who accepted their platform of return to and settlement of Eretz Israel. Their members included hasidim and mitnaggedim, Orthodox and secular Jews, men and women. Their aim was to provide financial and other assistance to agricultural workers and artisans who were prepared to emigrate to Palestine, and to those who had already made the momentous move. The Hovevey Tsiyon societies operated illegally in Lithuania and the rest of the Pale, where political gatherings of any kind were forbidden and thus punishable. All funds collected by the Societies were channelled through the general *tsedaqa gedola* (Great Charity Fund) in Vilna. However, when it was discovered that the Fund leadership had used such revenues to help victims of a pogrom in Balta without the knowledge or consent of Hovevey Tsiyon, the Zionist movement moved its headquarters from Vilna to Odessa, where government supervision and control were laxer at the time.

The year 1881 proved to be a watershed in the history of the Jews of Lithuania and the Pale in general, and of the Russian Haskalah movement in particular. The runaway antisemitism and violent pogroms that followed the assassination of Czar Alexander II in March of that year; the restrictive May Laws of 1882, which barred Jews from the cities and confined their residence to towns and townlets; and the introduction of a *numerus clausus* limiting Jewish high-school enrollment to 10 percent of total enrollment, led to disillusionment, despondence, and the abandonment of all hopes of achieving civil equality as the West had made available. Some Jews, especially the youth, took a radical turn and joined revolutionary movements. Many more, however, emigrated. It is estimated that 2,600,000 Jews left Russia, Lithuania, and neighboring countries between 1881 and 1914, chiefly for the United States but also for England, South Africa, Argentina (the followers of Baron Maurice de Hirsch), and Palestine.

Meanwhile, the Jewish national renascence and the establishment of settlements in Palestine had fired the inspiration of enlightened intellectuals, who, in turn, fueled the masses with aspirations for national liberation in the Jewish homeland. "The Jew," Leo Pinsker declared in his *Auto-Emancipation*, "is everywhere in evidence, nowhere at home, and everywhere considered an alien." Now minions of writers and academicians pledged their talents to the dissemination of Hovevey Tsiyon ideology and supported the movement's practical work in Palestine.

Young people from all walks of life, especially university students, flocked to the proto-Zionist movement, craving to discover and study their heritage to define their Jewish identity. A group of 25 student-organizers from Kharkov toured Russia and recruited some 500 enthusiastic young men and women who declared themselves willing to leave for Palestine immediately to work the land as pioneers. They adopted as their name and motto the acronym *Bilu*, formed from the initials of the first words of Isaiah 2:3, *Beit Ya'aqov lekhu ve-nelkha* – "House of Jacob come, and let us go forth." Members of the movement, who termed themselves *Bilu'im*, established their first settlement in 1882 and called it Rishon Lezion, First in Zion (cf. Isaiah 41:27). In 1887, a large group of Jews from Ponevez emigrated to Palestine with the help and advice of the Hovevey Tsiyon society in Vilna. The following year, the movement formed a women's group in Kovno and Slobodka, which called itself *Benot Tsiyon*, Daughters of Zion. This group supported a Hebrew high school for girls, named Yehudiya, literally "Jewess", which had recently opened in Vilna.

In 1888, a secret society within Hovevey Tsiyon coalesced in Vilna. It called itself Beney Moshe, Sons of Moses, and its spiritual leader was Asher Ginsburg, a Hebrew writer, thinker, and philosopher, better known by his *nom de plume*, Ahad Ha'am. In a history-making article entitled *"Lo zeh ha-derekh"* (This is not the way), he set forth the society's ideology. Ahad Ha'am strongly criticized the Hovevey Tsiyon policy of immediate settlement in Eretz Israel and suggested instead that the movement prepare its members, by means of education and propaganda, for a more dedicated, meaningful, and efficient settlement enterprise than that in progress. If Eretz Israel was to become the spiritual center of the Jewish people, appropriate spiritual preparation for a return to the homeland was of vital importance.

Beney Moshe was a miniscule group with fewer than 200 members. Nevertheless, it attracted most of the Hovevey Tsiyon leaders and as such wielded great influence within the movement. Knowledge of Hebrew was a prerequisite for membership, and Hebrew was the language it used for its meetings and transactions.

Beney Moshe had opponents of many kinds: not only those who treated settlement in Palestine as the supreme value but also Orthodox groups that campaigned against what they considered a new secular ideology.

Beney Moshe moved its headquarters to Palestine, where it was active in education until 1897 when, following the first Zionist Congress in Basel, it ceased to exist.

In 1890, the Russian secret police uncovered several Hovevey Tsiyon cells in the Pale of Settlement, including one in the Yeshiva of Volozhin, as well as those in Moscow and St. Petersburg. The ensuing wave of arrests threw the movement into a spasm of fear and panic. After strenuous efforts by Abraham Lederbaum, editor of *Hamelitz*, and Zeev Berman, subsequently a supporter of Baron Hirsch, Hovevey Tsiyon was granted an official permit to pursue its goals in Russia, including agricultural training and promotion of emigration to Palestine. By this time, government policy favored anything that might cause Jews to leave Russia.

Hovevey Tsiyon remained anathema among many Lithuanian rabbis who, for ideological reasons, opposed the very idea of Orthodox Jews, let alone rabbis, working hand-in-hand with the secularists. To counter the despised movement, they created their own organization, which they named *Mahaziqey ha-Dat* – Keepers of the Faith – and which their detractors termed the "Black Office." It was directed by R. Lifshitz, secretary to R. Isaac Elchanan Spektor, Chief Rabbi of Kovno, whose name he invoked without the latter's consent or approval. *Mahaziqey ha-Dat* fought Hovevey Tsiyon in the Pale and tussled with the movement's supporters in Jerusalem so vigorously that it was believed to have denounced Eliezer Ben-Yehuda and caused his arrest by the Turks in 1894. Hovevey Tsiyon fought back on all fronts. It was no easy struggle, since *Mahaziqey ha-Dat* had warned its sponsored *kollelim* in Eretz Israel that their regular support from Lithuania would be curtailed if they cooperated with the infidels.

Meanwhile, Hovevey Tsiyon gained strength on both sides of the Atlantic. Membership increased; activities were intensified in the Diaspora and in Palestine. It was the Russian Jewish leadership that held the real clout in the movement, and when Leo Pinsker died in 1891, Menachem Ussishkin was elected to replace him as chairman.

The importance of Hovevey Tsiyon lies in its indispensable role in propagating the ideology of return to Eretz Israel as a practical reality. Its success paved the way for the structured political Zionism that followed. When Herzl appeared upon the scene, he found the nucleus of a supportive mass movement ready to respond to his leadership and vision.

In 1894, with the seminal Zionist Congress on the horizon, delegates from Vilna, Grodno, Riga, and many other cities of the Pale convened in Bialystok. It was this conference that introduced the *sheqel*, a membership fee and fundraising device given the name of the Biblical census coin and the mechanism by which the Temple in Jerusalem had been sustained. Most members of the Hovevey Tsiyon societies joined the Zionist movement in this fashion and continued to support settlements in Palestine. Since the movement was still illegal in Russia, its printed material and the *sheqalim* were produced in Vienna.

When Zionism as a political force burst forth in 1897 at the first Zionist Congress in Basel, it was only natural that the most favorable response to Herzl's urgings came from the Jews of Lithuania and the Pale. Targets of intense hatred, subsisting under conditions of political bondage, economic distress, and social hostility, they regarded Herzl's *Judenstadt* as the elixir that would banish their impotence. His reception by royalty and heads of state filled them with pride; his motto – "If you will it, it is no fairy tale" – was embraced verbatim.

From its very beginning, the Zionist movement in Russia and Lithuania was divided on questions of education and culture. Many prominent rabbis had risen to its leadership echelons and played an important role in every aspect of Zionist activity. It was their view that the Zionist Organization program should distance itself from educational and cultural affairs altogether; these issues, they argued, were so controversial that the religious and secular factions of the movement could never agree on them. One of the subsequent Zionist Congresses reached a compromise: two committees were established, one for traditional religious education and another for general progressive education. A key player in fashioning this compromise, which survives today in the form of two separate education and culture departments within the World Zionist Organization, was R. Reines of Lida.

In the meantime, the Zionist movement continued to attract Jewish masses in Lithuania. In 1893, there were 41 societies in four key provinces: 13 in Kovno, 4 in Vilna, 19 in Grodno, and 5 in Suwalk. The number grew to 135 within one year, and by 1901 the same four centers had no fewer than 201 Zionist societies. In preparation for the Fifth Zionist Congress, which took place later that year, members of these societies purchased approximately 6,400 *sheqalim*.

When the Jewish National Fund came into being in 1901, the Lithuanian Zionist societies energetically supported its activities. However, their policy of "a blue and white JNF box in every Jewish home" brought a new opponent out of the underbrush: the R. Meir Baal Haness Fund, which relied on similar collection boxes and feared for its own revenues. The R. Meir Baal Haness leaders were urged on by the "Black Office," which rejoiced in this new pretext to attack, discredit, and besmirch the Zionist movement. Undeterred, the Zionists pressed ahead until JNF boxes were indeed standard equipment in most Lithuanian Jewish homes.

The societies placed much stock in education and culture, pursuing these goals with a single-mindedness that their opponents matched. To begin Zionist indoctrination at early childhood, they set up schools known as *hadarim metuqanim* ("improved heder") in which Hebrew was the language of instruction. This was met with persistent hostility on the part of local teachers (*melamdim*) in various communities. The problem of staffing these schools with qualified teachers was met in part with the establishment of the Grodno Pedagogic Institute in 1908. For adults, Zionist societies created libraries, reading rooms, choirs, and evening classes. They organized their own prayer quorums and study groups for Bible, Talmud, Jewish history, and other subjects. The Kovno and Vilna groups were particularly active in the production and distribution of Zionist books and brochures in Hebrew, Yiddish, and Russian. Yiddish and Hebrew circulars, often displayed in synagogues, provided society members with important propaganda and information material. Itinerant *Maggidim* and gifted public speakers helped spread the message of Zionism by inspiring their audiences, maintaining enthusiasm, and helping found new societies.

Opposition in Lithuania to the Zionist movement and its ideology came from two elements which were, themselves, diametrically opposed to each other. On the left was the Bund (the General Jewish Workers' Union in Lithuania, Poland and Russia), the completely secular, antireligious, Jewish proletarian movement, which regarded Zionism as a reactionary force and indeed expelled members who joined Zionist societies. By 1900-1901, these expellees formed their own groups, which they called Po'aley Tsiyon (Workers of Zion). The history of the Bund merits separate description, which follows shortly.

On the right of the anti-Zionist pincer were the *Mahaziqey ha-Dat* ("Black Office") elements that had fought Hovevey Tsiyon, now joined by others who, although previously sympathetic to the Zionist cause, had turned their backs on the movement following the education and culture controversy. The most important rabbis associated with *Mahaziqey ha-Dat* were Hayyim Soloveitchik of Brisk, David Freedman of Karlin, Eliezer Gordon of Telz, and Hayyim Ozer Grodzinski of Vilna, all of whom wielded great influence in the Orthodox community as respected scholars and heads of great yeshivot.

In 1899, R. Shalom Ber, the Lubavitcher Rebbe at the time, sponsored the idea of an open attack on the entire Zionist movement under the auspices of the Black Office, which congregated in Kovno at the time. The major weapon would be a manifesto, issued under the names of the most prominent rabbis in Russia and influential leaders in St. Petersburg and elsewhere, denouncing Zionism as unpatriotic and antireligious. R. Samuel Jacob Rabinowitz of Alexot (a suburb of Kovno) and the local Zionist group in Kovno uncovered the plan and vigorously denounced it in a series of articles in *Hamelitz*.

A war of writings ensued. The Black Office circulated thousands of copies of letters signed by well-known rabbis, branding Zionism a Shabbetaean cult that aimed "to uproot the tenets of our faith." Counterattacking, R. Samuel Jacob Rabinowitz obtained and published letters and articles signed by over 100 well-known rabbinical personalities in support of the Zionist movement. The Black Office rebounded with a book entitled *Or la-Yesharim* (Light unto the righteous), which contained anti-Zionist letters and opinions from another 100 rabbis.

There was no respite. The renowned R. Shloimele Hacohen of Vilna made the following statement in *Hamelitz*:

The producers of this book (*Or La-Yesharim*) have done a great injustice by characterizing 200,000 Jews who believe in Zionism as heretics, disbelievers, and Shabbetaeans, for they include hundreds of rabbis, eminent scholars, and righteous men. Such a book should not be kept in a Jewish home, for it will merely foment controversy, discord, and grievous disunity among Jews.

Hacohen urged all rabbis to condemn the book and defend the Zionists from their attackers' slander. Few did, but the influence of the Black Office ebbed and the Zionist leadership in Lithuania ignored its calumny.

An important reason for this was the emergence of an Orthodox brand of Zionism. In 1893, by the initiative of R. Samuel Mohilever of Bialystok, a "spiritual center" – *merkaz ruhani/ruchani* in Hebrew, hence the abbreviation "Mizrachi" (the Religious Zionist Movement) – was established to direct the public-relations activities of Hovevey Tsiyon and explain and disseminate its policy of settlement in Palestine. Nine years later, at a well-attended conference of rabbis and laymen in Vilna, R. Isaac Jacob Reines elevated Mizrachi to the status of a Religious-Zionist political party. One of its first actions was the unveiling of a monthly journal in Vilna, *Hamizrahi*, edited by historian Zeev Yavetz.

A one-day visit to Vilna by Dr. Theodor Herzl in August 1903, triggered a tumult within the Zionist movement. He was returning from St. Petersburg, where he had met with Russian Interior Minister Vyacheslav Plehve and other officials to seek government support of the formation of a Jewish State that would take the persecuted Jews off Russia's hands. This in itself was a tour de force for Zionism, which was illegal in Russia and Lithuania and conducted surreptitiously. Herzl spent a memorable day in Vilna, meeting with Zionist delegations from all over Lithuania and with a number of local rabbis, including Shloimele Hacohen, who gave him the priestly blessing. More than 4,000 people packed the courtyard of the Great Synagogue of Vilna and the streets of the nearby Jewish quarter, hoping to catch a glimpse of the famous would-be potentate. The police, observing the unprecedented scene, dispersed the crowd on the pretext of its being an illegal demonstration. Thus Herzl had to meet with a series of smaller groups, some in secret locations outside the city. His travels that day brought him into the homes of many simple Jewish workers – the sort he had never seen before. Huge crowds flocked to the railway station to bid him farewell; the authorities sent Cossack soldiers to scatter them by force. In his diary, Herzl wrote: "Yesterday, Vilna day, was something I shall never forget."

The poverty of the Lithuanian Jewish rank-and-file had moved him to tears. Thus, at the Sixth Zionist Congress in 1903, Herzl presented a British proposal to establish an autonomous Jewish colony in Uganda. Herzl's motives were practical; he does not seem to have intended to abandon the original Basel program. The Uganda scheme, he believed, would create political relations with the British Government that would facilitate future settlement in Eretz Israel. It would also alleviate Jewish suffering in Russia and its satellites.

The plan split the Congress and the Zionist movement in two, its opponents terming themselves Tsiyoney Tsiyon (Zion-Zionists) and its exponents Maginey ha-Histadrut (Defenders of the [World Zionist] Organization). The Russian delegates and a large majority of Lithuanian deputies, representing the very Jewish communities that were to be saved in Uganda, fought the Uganda scheme bitterly. The only destination that concerned them was Eretz Israel. Only by promising to continue his efforts to obtain settlement rights in Palestine was Herzl able to hold the Zionist Organization together – for the moment.[82]

Herzl died of heart failure in 1904. The next Zionist Congress, held in 1906, instructed the Zionist Organization to concern itself exclusively with Eretz Israel, as the Lithuanian and Russian Zionists had insisted. The Congress also decided to establish in Vilna a central office for the entire Zionist movement in Russia. The office was to be responsible for organization, press, propaganda, finances, information, and all the movement's day-to-day problems. It soon became the most important center of Zionist activity in Russia and, because of its location, stimulated the growth and expansion of Lithuanian Zionism in particular. By this time, in fact, Vilna had become the center of all Jewish public activity in Russia, since nearly all organizations established their headquarters and printed their publications there.

An exogenous event further agitated the turbulence within Russian and Lithuanian Jewry: the revolution of 1905. Many Jews flocked to the revolutionary movements, some of them Gentile and several others, especially the Bund, Jewish. Half of the many Hebrew publications were closed down; in Vilna, only *Ha-Zeman* (The Time) survived. Serious antisemitic riots erupted throughout the Pale of Settlement. In protest, a general strike and day of mourning was held in late 1905; participation of Jews in Russia and Lithuania was total. In 1906, struggling for equal civil rights, Jews took an active part in the elections to the Duma, the Russian parliament. Indeed, the electors sent twelve Jewish deputies to the legislature, including six from Lithuania. The Zionist office in Vilna began to sponsor training courses for small vigilante groups. These cells, which postured as physical-education societies known as Gymnastics Clubs, formed the nucleus from which a nationwide self-defense organization would grow.

These operations caused the authorities to reassess their attitude toward ostensibly illegal Zionist activity. Thus far they had treated their own policy with benign disregard, permitting the collection of moneys for the Jewish National Fund and the sale of the *sheqel*. In 1900, they had even allowed the Jewish Colonial Trust to market its shares overtly. In Kovno and Minsk, local permits had been granted for public gatherings. Now, however, the Zionists were taking an interest not only in matters connected with emigration and settlement in Palestine (which the Government thoroughly and enthusiastically endorsed) but also in the civil and political rights of Jews in Russia. This, Russian officials believed, might lead to the coalescence of a unified national Jewish political force. These apprehensions mounted after the Po'aley Tsiyon Conference in 1903 in Vilna, during which the various nascent Jewish socialist groups merged to form a Socialist Zionist party. The revolutionary slogans of the new constellation convinced the Czar's officials that the Zionists were among those seeking to overthrow the government.

Thus a crackdown on the Zionist movement began. Sales of Jewish Colonial Trust shares were banned in Russia; all Zionist meetings and gatherings were carefully monitored. The situation in Vilna was somewhat more relaxed because the provincial governor, Prince Svyatopolsk-Mirsky, was sympathetic to the Zionist cause (though not so sympathetic as to refrain from use of force against the Jewish masses during Herzl's visit). In the Lithuanian capital, the sale of *sheqalim* continued without hindrance and meetings in private homes were tolerated. Public gatherings were forbidden to all.

Svyatopolsk-Mirsky, like the other officials, knew what was going on. A report on the Zionist movement in Vilna, presented to him in 1904, showed that the Zionist idea had spread far and wide among the Jewish masses. Virtually all literate Jews, except for the Socialists and the Black Office extremists, belonged to Zionist societies. Zionist influence among the 100,000 Jews in Vilna and district could not be doubted after Herzl's memorable visit to the city; the Zionist leader, an Austrian citizen with no official standing whatsoever, had been received like a king.

The report divided the Jews of Vilna into two camps: Zionists and Socialists. The former accepted the existing order; most of the latter vacillated between the Zionist movement and the general Socialist groups. Consequently, the Zionists in Vilna should not be considered a menace to the Russian government...yet. The report concluded by noting that a war on Zionism meant a war against the entire Zionist population of Lithuania and Russia.

In 1906, the government banned any political organization that had "foreign connections." Although this legislation was directed mainly against non-Jewish Russian revolutionary societies, the terminology was such that it embraced the Zionist movement, which had its principal leadership in Germany. Nevertheless, individual Zionist societies in Vilna, Kovno, and Grodno were authorized. Although they called themselves "Palestine" and pledged themselves to the study of the Jewish national problems in Eretz Israel, the Russian Senate soon declared this a subterfuge and ordered them to disband. The Government again forbade all Zionist gatherings in 1907. To show that they meant it this time, the authorities arrested several Zionist leaders after searching their homes and confiscating their documents. The men were held for several weeks and then released with a warning.

In 1907, the authorities began to suppress all organized Jewish activities and revoked the permit under which the Jewish Territorial Organization operated in Russia. In effect, all Jewish parties and organizations ceased to exist and indeed disappeared from public life, with the exception of some Zionist elements that managed to survive in the underground. Persecuted and demoralized, these groups turned for help to David Wolffsohn, Herzl's successor as president of the World Zionist Organization.

Wolffsohn (1856-1914) was born in Darbenai, Lithuania. In Memel, where he studied, he was greatly influenced by his teacher, R. Isaac Ruelf, subsequently a leading forerunner of Hovevey Tsiyon. By 1896, when he first met Herzl, he had become a prosperous timber merchant. Captivated by Herzl, Wolffsohn accompanied the Zionist leader on his journey to Eretz Israel to confer with Emperor William II, and on his visits to Turkey. It was Wolffsohn who had suggested the blue and white as the movement's colors and revived the name *sheqel* as the Zionist membership fee. He had established the World Zionist Organization headquarters in Cologne, where he now lived.

In 1909, Wolffsohn presented Pavel A. Stolypin, Prime Minister of Russia, a memorandum explaining that the Zionist movement had no aim other than to solve the Jewish problem by means of emigration to Palestine. He traveled to St. Petersburg to meet personally with Stolypin and other ministers. His hosts, although quite cordial, refused to legalize the World Zionist Organization in Russia. They did, however, grant some concessions for work on behalf of the JNF and the Jewish Colonial Trust.

Returning from St. Petersburg, Wolffsohn, like Herzl before him, stopped for a day in Vilna, where he received a tumultuous welcome. Delegations from Kovno, Grodno, Lida, and many other cities and townlets in Lithuania came to greet him and to pay their respects. He visited the Great Synagogue courtyard and addressed the masses that had assembled there. This time the Vilna police were ordered from St. Petersburg to take no action. Indeed, the Government's attitude toward Zionist activity seemed more tolerant and benign for a brief period after Wolffsohn's visit. The Yiddish-language weekly *Dos idishe folk* (The Jewish People) reappeared in Vilna; JNF activity was again conducted openly.

The reconciliation was short-lived. Early in 1910 the Russian authorities resumed their attacks on the Jewish national movement. Zionist leaders were arrested, tried, and jailed. Homes and offices were searched; documents pertaining to the movement and Palestine were confiscated. A full-scale effort to liquidate the Zionist movement seemed to be at hand.

Organized Zionism continued to function clandestinely in Lithuania, although under constant Russian police surveillance. Meetings were held under the guise of "weddings." Disregarding the peril, many Lithuanian delegates representing the Zionist Central Committee in Vilna and other associations traveled to Basel in 1911 to participate in the Tenth Zionist Congress.

A year later, five members of the Zionist Central Committee in Vilna were convicted and imprisoned for illegal Zionist political activity. The political trial shattered what remained of overt Zionist activity in Lithuania. Even the annual memorial service for Herzl at the Great Synagogue in Vilna was prohibited, as troops and police took up position in the crowded synagogue itself to nip in the bud any attempt to speak in honor of the late Zionist leader.

Factors not directly connected with government behavior wreaked further havoc. A grave economic recession elicited massive emigration, especially among the young. Many towns and townlets had lost more than half of their

Jewish inhabitants. This alone wiped out no few Zionist associations. There
had also been internal strife. The general Zionist Organization found itself
under attack by the Bund on the left, the Black Office on the right, and the
Socialist Zionists and the Territorialists in the "center," insofar as one existed.
The government crackdown on Zionism did eliminate most of these internal
quarrels.

Lithuanian Zionism continued to operate without hindrance in the
underground. The Central Committee in Vilna held regional sporadic
conferences in Grodno, Kovno, and Suwalk, attended by delegates from
neighboring townlets. When the Committee collapsed, organizational
activities were transferred to Kovno and Grodno. "Weddings" were staged in
many cities, and JNF work continued, now directed from the town of Smargon
in Vilna province.

Zionism actually progressed at this time, relatively speaking. In 1911,
Zionists in Bialystok founded an association for land purchase in Palestine
and quickly built their registered membership to nearly 700. The doctrine of
shelilat ha-galut, repudiation of the Diaspora, gained strength among
Lithuanian Zionists. This meant that their efforts focused on one goal only,
settlement of Eretz Israel. For some time they even refused to campaign in
elections to the Russian Duma.

Education of the young remained a priority for the Zionists of Lithuania.
The school system was intact: hadarim metuqanim, teacher training courses
in Bialystok and Grodno, the yeshiva in Lida, the Yehudiya girls school, and
many similar institutions. The government treated the matter with benign
neglect, believing that education of any kind would lead to assimilation. Thus
the message was passed on.

The upheavals of World War I were as traumatic for this sector of
Lithuanian Jewish society as they were for the yeshivot. The climate of
revolution, pogroms, and border changes created general suffering and chaos.
At the beginning of the war, many Lithuanian leaders and functionaries –
Zionist and other – were exiled to Central Russia, where their independent
cultural activities, and indeed their very presence, influenced communities
that had not known them theretofore.

Outside of Russia-Lithuania, Zionism during the war years was chiefly
political as opposed to practical. Governments were petitioned; propaganda
was disseminated. The acknowledged leader of the Zionist movement was
Chaim Weizmann, subsequently the first president of the State of Israel. Born

in the village of Motele near Pinsk in 1874, he had displayed scientific talent at an early age and had left home at the age of 18 for advanced biochemistry studies in Berlin. There he came under the spell of Ahad Ha'am, to whose ideology of cultural and spiritual Zionism he developed an intellectual attraction. After earning his doctorate in Switzerland in 1899 and selling his first chemical patent two years later, he divided his activities between his vocation, science, and his passion, Zionism. It was a combination of these that led to his acquaintance with and influence on Arthur James Balfour who, as Foreign Secretary of the British Government, issued on November 2, 1917, the famous Declaration that bears his name. This brief statement, in which Balfour expressed his government's favorable view of "the establishment in Palestine of a national home for the Jewish people," was to prove a turning point in modern Jewish history.

Back in Russia and its Lithuanian vassal, the war triggered an upheaval that had a much greater immediate impact. The Bolshevik Revolution of 1917 made the struggle for a Jewish national home an important issue among pro-Bolshevik Zionist groups. The resulting debate developed into fierce infighting within the Jewish left-wing intelligentsia, by the end of which the most extreme groups had quit the Zionist movement altogether. These disputes had little or no effect on the Zionist masses in Lithuania and the Pale. Although loyal to Russia and aware of the problems facing the country of their birth, they longed for a normal life for themselves and their children – the sort of life that Russia had never allowed them. Their goal was emigration, their desired destination: their own national home.

In all too many cases, they achieved their goal but were forced to choose other destinations. Wherever they settled, Lithuanian immigrants played a major role in their communities' Zionist and spiritual leadership. In several instances, as in South Africa, they set the tone. In Israel, the origin and development of the formative constellation of political parties, movements, and ideas is directly traceable to the Jews of the Pale.

"The Bund" – Toward a Secular Labor Diaspora

"The Bund" (*Algemeyner Idisher Arbeter Bund in Lite, Polen, un Rusland* – the General Jewish Workers' Union in Lithuania, Poland and Russia), the non-Zionist Jewish socialist party founded in 1897, was a product and manifestation of the burgeoning Jewish labor movement in "Jewish Lithuania" – the six northwestern provinces of Lithuania and Belorussia, centered in Vilna. The Bund drew its leaders and members from the masses of Jewish industrial workers in the Pale (whose numbers reached some 300,000 by 1890). Theirs was a socioeconomically downtrodden class even within the Jewish community, but the Bund gave them a sense of pride, dignity, and the assurance of belonging to a cohesive support group. Once it gathered steam, the Bund spread to Poland and the Ukraine and later opened chapters around the world.

To appreciate the importance of the Bund, one must recall the all-embracing nature of the Eastern European political parties, quite unlike, for example, their American counterparts.[83] The Bund fashioned a vibrant cultural life for its members, including its own secular, Yiddish-speaking school system, seminars and evening classes for adults, and drama societies. This provided the non-Orthodox proletariat with an alternative social and cultural environment to that offered by the community mainstream. Such an alternative was sorely needed, for the traditional leadership and society held the working class in undisguised contempt. By joining the overwhelmingly secularist labor movement, the workers thus severed their ties with the religious community, creating great tension for themselves and their families.

It had taken several decades to emerge. The pre-Bund Jewish labor movement drew its support from two sources: wage laborers and apprentices who, as early as 1870, had organized strikes in the textile and tobacco industries, and such members of the radical Jewish Marxist intelligentsia who still harbored a Jewish identity. Generally speaking, Lithuanian Jewry had attained a higher cultural standard than that of the neighboring Jewish communities, thanks to their renowned love of study and, especially, their famous yeshivot and other religious educational institutions, of which the government-sponsored Rabbinical Seminary of Vilna is only one example. In this respect, the Russian government shot itself in the foot by supporting and promoting, for its own reasons, a fertile breeding ground for the early Jewish socialists and revolutionaries.

In its early stages, the Jewish labor movement (which eventually split in three directions) was deeply involved in Russian politics. Many of its adherents shared the Menshevik view of the revolution, arguing that Russia would first need to develop a bourgeois system that would later give way to a socialist order. In 1887, this group founded a Social Democratic – Marxist labor organization, which merged into the Bund in 1901.[84]

Many of the early Jewish labor leaders were so assimilated that they had to learn or relearn Yiddish in order to reach the masses. They combined Marxist ideology with a commitment to their Jewish identity and a sense of responsibility toward the Jewish poor in general and the Jewish proletariat in particular. The first attempts to expand from labor unionism to the dissemination of socialist ideas among Jews in their own language, and thence to the establishment of a Jewish revolutionary movement, were made in the 1870s by the Lithuanian-born Hebrew writer and early revolutionary Aaron Samuel Lieberman and his circle. His major task, and that of his many successors, was to arouse the Jewish proletariat from its passive acceptance of the existing miserable conditions to an active struggle for better pay and terms of labor.

When the Russian authorities discovered his group in 1875, Lieberman fled to London, where in May 1876, he founded the Hebrew Socialist Union, the first specifically Jewish socialist workers organization. Its purpose was to encourage the formation of similar entities throughout the Diaspora. Lieberman's venture collapsed in December of that year; some of its members later became active in the Jewish workers movement in England.

The first Jewish public library in Lithuania was formed by Jacob Finkelstein in 1872 and managed under Bund auspices. Finkelstein also established study groups in which Jewish workers were taught the importance and significance of employment, the labor union, and use of the strike weapon to improve their lot. Initially, some of these study groups were conducted in Russian; a Yiddish interpreter stood by for the benefit of the audience. The speakers, drawn from the ranks of the Populist and Narodnaya-Volya movements, introduced their Jewish worker audiences to the ideas of Russification and Marxism.

In 1886, the Jewish labor leadership in Vilna took another step forward by founding *artels*, small cooperative labor societies in specific trades, and mutual self-help funds, basically for the needs of strikers and their families. Strike-fund donations were compulsory for union members: five kopeks per week at first, later 25 percent of all salaries. The early struggle was for a ten-hour working day and the amelioration of abusive working conditions, especially but not solely in textiles and tobacco. In their daily struggle against the industrialists they also promoted the interests of their non-Jewish proletarian colleagues. Wherever a rabbi was known to support Jewish bosses, unionists heckled him during his sermons.

The emerging labor movement competed with other sources of influence – general revolutionary tension in the Empire, government-supported antisemitism, the ambivalence of the special Jewish laws – for the sympathies of the Jewish intelligentsia. The most important factor for Jewish intellectuals, however, was the pervasive poverty of the densely populated *shtetl* in the Pale. Many leaders in the intellectual circles gradually turned to the belief that the Jewish proletariat must form its own socialist labor movement, in view of its peculiar circumstances and needs. Those on the radical Left, by contrast, continued to ignore particularistic Jewish needs; disregarding the realities of the pogroms, they concentrated on a general struggle in the expectation that the benefits of victory would belong to the Jewish worker too.

The years 1890-1897 coincided with the ideological gestation, consolidation, and coalescence of the Bund. During this time, Yiddish replaced the Russian language that the pioneers had used as their vehicle of propaganda. Using the vernacular of the masses, they were phenomenally successful in reaching and organizing a majority of the Jewish proletariat and attracting uncommitted members of the intelligentsia. Originally a collection of small, isolated cells, the Bund metamorphosed rapidly into a mass movement under a central committee. The general aim was equal rights for Jewish workers, including domicile and movement. Specifically, Bundists fought for Jewish emancipation within the law and identified with the general struggle for improved labor conditions and land reform for the peasants. To reach the Jewish masses in the Pale in the language they best understood, "jargon committees" were organized in Vilna in 1895. Articles and political brochures and treatises were translated from Russian and German into Yiddish, the purpose being to create a more literate rank-and-file, better equipped to articulate its aspirations. In this fashion the Jewish labor movement became an integral part of a revival of Yiddish language and literature.

For strategic reasons, Jewish workers who identified with the general proletariat joined the Russian labor movement as an equal partner while retaining its independent Jewish organizational framework. This dualism created ideological tensions and political vacillation throughout the existence of the Bund.

In 1896, the embryonic Bund went international when representatives of the Russian Jewish labor circles participated in the Socialist International in London, collectively terming themselves the Jewish Social Democrats, a sobriquet that had been in use since 1891. Upon its return to Lithuania and Belorussia, the group began to publish two periodicals: *Idisher Arbayter* (The Jewish Worker) and *Arbayter Shtime* (Worker's Voice), both of which subsequently became Bund organs. The masthead of these publications described the editorial board as sitting in Vilna, but the editors actually migrated from place to place – Bialystok, Kovno, Grodno, Minsk, and elsewhere – because the Okhrana (as the Russian secret police were known at the time) were always hot on their heels.

The Bund was officially founded at a secret conference held in Vilna on October 7-9, 1897. It was attended by 13 delegates representing some 34,000 members. The leading figure among the founders was Arkadi-Aaron Kremer, son of a maskil and Hebrew teacher in Shventzyany (Vilna province), the moving spirit of the Jewish Social Democrats in Vilna. One year later, when the Bund joined the newly founded Russian Social Democratic Labor Party as an autonomous group, Kremer was elected to the central committee of the latter movement.

The Second Bund Convention was held in April 1898, in Kovno; this location was chosen for the large number of poor Jewish workers who lived in its densely populated suburbs. Solidarity aside, this convention was as illegal as its predecessor and the delegates understood that they might need a broad selection of hiding places. Inspection and harassment by the secret police was also thought to be weaker in Kovno than in Vilna. In fact, 70 Bund activists were arrested at the conference; many of them were exiled. The Okhrana was well informed. Before the year was out, the head of the secret police attempted to split the Jewish workers movement by urging Jewish proletarians in Minsk to form a non-political trade union. A newspaper called *Der Fraynt* (The Friend) made its debut under police authorization. The purpose of this organ was to explain the need for the formation of a licit Jewish labor movement in the Pale, comprised of politically unaffiliated workers' groups and committed to improving Jewish economic and cultural conditions without opposing the general policies of the Czar and his government.

The Bund regarded this officially recognized nonpolitical workers' party as a government stooge meant to subvert the organized left-wing Jewish movement. Be this as it may, the rival entity was abolished by government decree in 1903.

The Bund held its third Convention in 1899, again in Kovno. This time, the discussions focused on the demand for equal civil rights for Jews in Russia. A central question in this debate concerned the nature of the Jewish-Russian affiliation: were the Jews a separate nation or part of the Russian people? If they were nationally distinct, they would need specific national rights in addition to those of all Russian citizens. If they were part of the Russian people, their struggle should aim to achieve rights equal to those of other Russian citizens. The issue engulfed the movement in crisis, split its leadership, and was left unresolved.

The Bund chose Bialystok as the site of its fourth convention in 1901. Here the assembly passed two resolutions that would become integral elements of the Bund political platform. The first, approved by most of the leadership, stipulated that Bund members would foreswear violence or sabotage in their dealings with factory owners and strikebreakers. The mission of the Bund, the resolution explained, was to organize Jewish workers and educate them in the importance of the class struggle, not to engage in economic terrorism. The second resolution resolved the previous year's festering ideological dispute. Henceforth the Bund would envisage the Russia of the future as a federation of nations in which all citizens would enjoy equal rights. Jews would wait for a suitable opportunity to introduce their own specific national demands and should avoid the pitfalls of chauvinism at all costs. The convention also resolved to denounce and attack "Jewish reactionaries who refuse to understand the class struggle." These included Po'aley Tsiyon (the Zionist Socialist Workers Party), other miscellaneous Zionist groups, the Territorialists, and, above all, Orthodox institutions and their leaders. Even adherents of historian Simon Dubnow's Autonomist ideology, which the Bund later incorporated into its program, appeared on the "enemies list" in 1901.

In reality, most of the Jewish workers parties were no less socialist and dedicated to the class struggle than the Bund. But instead of merging or at least cooperating, thus presenting the common enemy – the Russian government and its oppressive Jewish laws – with a united front, the Bund and all the other Jewish workers' parties and splinter groups competed against each other for membership and power in the Jewish community.

In 1902, the Bund acquired one of the supreme needs of all ideological organizations: a martyr. Hirsh Leckert, a shoemaker who happened to be a member of the Bund, wounded Von Vahl, Governor of Vilna, for having ordered the flogging of 22 Jewish and six Polish demonstrators and strikers. After Leckert was executed, the Bund lionized him in songs and plays.

In the years 1903-1905, the Bund had a membership of almost 35,000 in the Russian Empire, including Lithuania, of whom some 4,600 were political prisoners (1904). It offered the range of services that political movements of the time and place were expected to provide, and had become a power that Jewish communities ignored at their peril. After the Kishinev pogrom of 1903, the Bund joined other Russian Jewish organizations in setting up active self-defense systems in the Ukraine and other pogrom-prone areas. Self-defense soon became an important part of the Bund program. The Kishinev atrocity shocked Jews throughout the area; many who had previously hesitated to join movements of any kind, let alone revolutionary ones, now rushed to enlist in various Jewish organizations, including the Bund.

The Bund was a lone wolf in its field. In 1903, it was expelled from the RSDP (Russian Socialist Democratic Party) for having moved to the Russian party's left and asserting excessive independence as a specifically Jewish movement. It was readmitted after making several reconciliatory gestures. The very next year, the Bund delegates stalked out of the Second RSDP Convention for the reasons given above and because the RSDP refused to condemn the pogroms explicitly. By 1905, as the strongest Jewish movement in the Pale, the Bund rejected any form of collaboration with other Jewish organizations including self-defense committees. The Bund also drew its own iconoclastic conclusions from the trauma of the Kishinev pogrom and its aftermath: the inclusion in its platform, by request of its more Jewishly rooted members, of a demand for Jewish national and cultural autonomy in Russia.

In 1905 the Bund founded a youth movement, the Bundishe Yugent, which rapidly developed into one of the largest organizations in Russian Jewry, chosen among many alternatives by the sons and daughters of many middle-class families.

The Bund's ideological struggles – with other Jewish movements (especially Zionist ones) and within its own ranks over ideological issues – intensified. Bund policy lurched hither and yon as leaders attempted to reconcile nationalism with internationalism and define the role of the Jewish proletariat within the all-Russian movement as against its place as part of the Jewish people. Even the general acceptance of the use of Yiddish did not signal ideological agreement within the Bund; Yiddish was chosen on pragmatic grounds as the universal language of the Jewish masses in Russia.

Bund policy never wavered in two respects. One was the importance of class struggle and its implications for the well-being of the Jewish masses in the Pale. Bundists derided the Hibat Tsiyon movements as utopian and the attempt to revive the Hebrew language as useless and pointless, as the resurrection of classical Latin or Greek would be. The other was Zionism, which they now branded a reactionary, bourgeois movement. The Bund opposed Zionism staunchly at all times; the rationale for the moment was the leadership's wish to curry favor with the Russian Social Democratic Party, to which the Bund still belonged. The pogroms did modify the Bund attitude toward the Russian Socialist movements, which, by and large, were indifferent to Jewish suffering. With regard to Zionism, however, the Bund adopted a respectful posture at this time, for the rise of political Zionism and its growing appeal to and influence on the Jewish masses in Lithuania, Poland, and the Pale, had presented the Bund leaders with a serious threat to their cause. They responded by barring card-carrying members of Zionist groups from their unions. (Non-Jews were welcome as always.)

It was Vladimir Medem who steered Bund ideology on the nationalism-internationalism question toward a solution called "Neutralism." Medem's father, a Latvian Jewish medical officer in the army, was so assimilated as to have baptized the boy into the Russian Orthodox Church. Before Vladimir served the Bund, the movement served him by steering him back to his Jewish identity; he later became one of its most prominent leaders. His Neutralist ideology postulated that the destiny of Jewry – survival or assimilation – was impossible to predict. The Bund should make allowances for the development of both trends; it should not feel obliged to promote national continuity.

Neutralism was short-lived; it joined the many casualties of the abortive revolution of 1905. An analysis of the mood in the Pale after the revolution convinced the leadership that the Jews there were becoming disillusioned with Marxism and more concerned with their survival as individuals and as a people. Vladimir Medem, the father of Neutralism, was one of the first leaders to retreat from it, proclaiming the need to work actively to ensure Jewish survival as a national entity. But the failure of the revolution and the ensuing reign of terror tumbled the Bund into serious decline. Only the organizational nucleus survived; the ranks were decimated in the despair and frustration that engulfed the Jewish masses. Now limited in its trade-union and political activities, the Bund concentrated on cultural affairs such as adult education, drama groups, and literary and musical efforts, all conducted in Yiddish.

Thus, at its eighth conference (1910), the Bund resolved to fight for two causes: the establishment of State Yiddish schools and, most surprisingly, the right of Jewish workers to rest on the Sabbath day. Neutralism was widely discredited by this time. The Bund began to participate in conferences of a general Jewish nature and meetings of Jewish community agencies, campaigning for secularization and democratization including greater autonomy for itself. The years 1909-10 were dedicated to a renewal of efforts to reorganize and strengthen the party. Although the Bund had not participated in the Duma elections in 1905, in which six of the twelve Jewish delegates chosen had been Zionists, it did take part in the 1912 elections and won the votes of many non-socialist Jews.

In 1912, when the Bolsheviks and the Mensheviks parted ways for good, the Bund decided to remain within the Menshevik Social Democratic Party, whose policy now favored Jewish national-cultural autonomy, a concept the Bolsheviks strongly opposed.

The Bund had by now come a long way from its former minimal involvement in Jewish affairs. In 1913, it called a strike in protest against the blood-libel indictment in Kiev of Mendel Beilis, a fiction meant to besmirch the entire Jewish people. Tens of thousands of Jewish workers walked off the job. Beilis was ultimately exonerated and set free after spending more than two years in prison awaiting trial.

At its last pre-Revolution conference, held in Kharkov in 1916, the Bund finally acknowledged the existence of a specific international Jewish problem. In a departure from former policy, it now participated in the work of community organizations such as OSE, ORT, and the Jewish-Russian relief organization, Yekopo. In their newspapers *Tsayt* (Time) and *Lebns-Fragn* (Questions of Life and Death) they openly discussed antisemitism and the persecution of Jews in Russia. Their discussions on participation in a World Jewish Congress, however, ended without resolution.

At the dawn of the Revolution, the Bund had a membership of roughly 42,000 in approximately 400 branches, the overwhelming majority of which were within the Pale. Bund activists held leading positions in both the left and the right flanks of the Menshevik movement, demanding in both instances full national and cultural autonomy for the Jews. Bundists participated in Jewish community elections and sent representatives to committees that were organizing a general Jewish conference that had been scheduled for December 1917. Its only iconoclastic stipulation was that such a conference avoid taking resolutions on the rights of Jews outside Russia.

After the Russian Revolution of 1917, the Bund leaders lent their sympathies to the Communists, especially in the Ukraine, where terrible post-Revolution pogroms were raging. In 1919, the Bund in the Ukraine joined the United Jewish Communist Party to form a new party called the Komfarband, which amalgamated with the Ukrainian Communist Party later the same year.

At the twelfth conference of the Bund, labelled "all-Russian" and held in Moscow in 1920, an irreconcilable rift developed when a majority of the delegates favored a resolution urging the Bund to affiliate with the Communists as an autonomous body. (The minority had seceded at the Twelfth Conference in 1919 and formed its own, very short-lived, Social Democratic Bund.) Even though the Communist International rejected this stipulation of autonomous status, the Bund, after its next conference, held in 1921 in Minsk, decided to join the Soviet Communist Party.

Truth to tell, the Communist Party never fully accepted or trusted the Bund, which, in their view, personified Jewish separatism, nationalism, and the lower middle class. In time, many Russian Bund leaders – those who joined the Communist Party and the breakaways – were either exiled or shot by agents of the Soviet regime. Others joined the Yevsektsia, the Jewish section of the Communist Party propaganda ministry (a very powerful agency at this time). The declared policy of this office, as expressed in a resolution taken at its first conference in Moscow in October 1918, was the "systematic destruction of Zionist and bourgeois institutions," with the kehillot, and religious and Hebrew schools, and Zionist parties heading the list.

Dead in Russia, the Bund went on to brighter days elsewhere. Its socialist philosophy, devotion to Yiddish, secular Jewish nationalism, theories of doykeyt ("hereness") and Dubnow's Autonomism, which envisaged the permanency of Jewish existence in dispersion (hence the opposition to Zionism) continued to attract Jews in different parts of the world. The Bund was especially strong in Poland, where it took root in Warsaw in 1914 and did well in subsequent municipal elections. By 1939, just before World War II broke out, the Polish Bund had 498 branches and almost 100,000 members.

Its appeal was due less to its socialist platform than to its active role in fighting governmental and public antisemitism.

During the Nazi occupation of Poland, the Bund was active in the Jewish resistance movement. Former Polish Bundists who survived the Holocaust joined existing Bundist organizations in various countries including the United States; some assumed leadership positions. A number of former Bundists found refuge in Israel, where they established the Bund Organization of Israel. This entity, while faithful to the original principles of the Polish Bund, views the Jewish State somewhat more favorably under the circumstances.

Afterword: The Karaites – From Assertiveness to Denouement

Contention between the Karaites and the Jews of Lithuania, as noted in Chapter 1, transcended religious differences. Even though a separate Karaite Charter based on the Magdeburg rights had existed since 1441, authorities at all times treated Karaites as Jews when this furthered their goals. For example, they dunned the Karaites for all Jewish taxes. Since the collection mechanism in the formative and Commonwealth periods was the Jewish Council (*Vaad ha-medina*), intercommunal controversy on this issue was constant and irresolvable. Specifically, Karaite representatives in the Council deliberations bitterly contested the sums allocated to them by the Council as their share of taxes due.

The Karaites' separatism did not prevent their expulsion from Lithuania in 1495 together with "rabbanite" Jews, nor did it bar their return eight years later. By 1576, they had progressed much as the Jews had. They established a beautiful synagogue in Troki, together with a *Talmud Torah* (boys' religious school) and other community institutions, including police who enforced community bylaws and regulated members' behavior.

If the divide between Karaites and Jews was largely theological, that between the Karaites of Troki and their Christian neighbors was physical. The section of the city in which they resided was given separate municipal status; anyone entering it had to pay a special tax.

The community regulated its affairs by means of a General Assembly, initially held annually and later at irregular intervals. The Assembly convened chiefly to elect religious and secular leaders, to deal with internal problems, and to elect functionaries. One of the latter was the *voit* (secular judge), the community head, whose duty it was to safeguard their guaranteed rights and adjudicate civil cases. The assemblies also elected three *dayanim* (religious judges); these were spiritual leaders who had the power to punish and excommunicate members who acted against the interests of the community. In the Karaites' external relations, the *voit* was much the more important official. He was their official representative to the Grand Duchy, and his appointment required approval of the Voivode (governor), who expected a monetary gift for granting it. As salary, the *voit* was allocated a house, a plot of land, and 10 percent of the sums at stake in the lawsuits argued before him.

By the end of the seventeenth century and for the next 150 years, the position of *voit* passed from father to son, irrespective of the latter's competence.

During the fifteenth and sixteenth centuries, the Karaites sent their sons to be educated in Constantinople and other Karaite centers, but later they took advantage of local Jewish schools. Especially gifted youth attended rabbanite yeshivot. Out of respect for their Jewish neighbors, the Karaites closed their businesses on the second days of the three pilgrimage festivals – Passover, Shavuot, and Sukkot – even though these were of Rabbinic origin. To alleviate tension with the Rabbanites, Karaites refrained from openly challenging the validity of the Talmud and expressing their aversion to its teachings. As time passed, they even took on several Jewish laws and customs that they had previously ignored or eschewed. They heated their ovens for the Sabbath, lit Sabbath candles at home, and sang traditional *zemirot* – table hymns – during Sabbath meals. They refrained from consecrating marriages during the *sefira* period between Passover and Shavuot, and abstained from meat during the first nine days of the month of Av, preceding the Tisha Be'Av fast commemorating the destruction of the First and Second Temples in Jerusalem. They affixed *mezuzot* to the doorposts of their dwellings and inserted several Rabbanite prayers in their ritual.

The Karaite synagogue, known as *knis* (sharing the same grammatical root as the Hebrew *beyt kneset* and the Aramaic *beyt knishta*) was arrayed in Sephardi style, its floor adorned with many precious carpets. Worshippers removed their shoes before entering.

The Lithuanian Karaites communicated regularly with coreligionists in Turkey, Syria, and Palestine, using mail, couriers, and travelers. In 1642, a

Palestinian Karaite named David ben Joshua visited Lithuania to seek not only financial assistance for his community but to recruit at least six Karaite families who might be willing to move to Jerusalem to join the three Karaite families living there at the time. There is no evidence that he succeeded on either count. Indeed, Karaites in Damascus wrote to their Lithuanian brethren in the early eighteenth century to complain that the latter were neglecting the sect's charities in Palestine.

The Karaite community called its rabbis either by this title or *hakham* or *hazan*. Many of these men were great Hebrew scholars and poets. A prominent example was the first important Karaite author in Lithuania, Isaac ben Abraham Troki (1533-1594), who wrote an anti-Christian work entitled *Hizuq Emuna* (Strengthening of the faith). Subsequently translated into German, Latin, and Spanish, *Hizuq Emuna* was studied and widely quoted in Christian theological circles throughout Europe. Also from Troki was Solomon ben Aaron, who in 1700 composed a book against Rabbanite Judaism and Christianity as well as a treatise on Karaism and its major differences from Rabbanism. An accomplished poet as well as a renowned linguist, he published a book on Hebrew grammar and was invited in 1696 to lecture at the Swedish Academy in Riga, Latvia.

Karaites were well represented outside of Troki. More than a quarter of the sect, for example, lived in Neustadt. The Neustadt community was evidently well off, providing more than 45 percent of all tax revenue generated by Lithuanian Karaites in 1705. In the second half of the eighteenth century, Lutzk became an important center of Karaite literary and scholarly activity, turning out spiritual leaders and teachers for four major communities in the Crimea that found these in short supply.

In general, whenever Lithuania went to war or fell into crisis and chaos, as often happened, Karaites and Jews were equally desirable targets for assault and plunder. In 1772, magnate Ignacy Skeender instigated an especially serious pogrom aimed specifically at the Karaites of Troki, leaving a gruesome trail of fatalities and gutted homes and business. The Karaites petitioned the Sejm in Warsaw for redress, and succeeded in having their Charter renewed the following year.

As if taking an example from Poland and Lithuania, which effected their first partition in 1772, the Karaites sought an official divorce from the Jewish community that year. The Jewish Council of Lithuania, to which they had belonged, was disbanded before the year was out. Now the Karaites withdrew from the *Kahals* and petitioned the government for separate legal status and autonomy, emphasizing their Mongol-Tartar origins.

Thus far the Karaites of Lithuania had considered themselves Jews in the sense of regarding their polemics and sometimes violent disagreements as internecine. By 1783, however, the Karaites of Lithuania had embarked on a historical path of their own. It took until 1795 to anchor the new attitude in law. With the Russian control of Lithuania, Catherine II signed legislation establishing a legal differentiation of status between Jews and Karaites, each enjoying different degrees of civil rights.

The distance between the two groups grew as the years passed. In 1829, for example, Karaites were exempted from military service and Jews were not. To accentuate how different they were from Rabbanite Jews, they stressed their opposition to the Talmud, the source text of Jewish Law. They also claimed to possess traits that differentiated them from Jews, such as honesty, industriousness, and loyalty to the throne. Statements to this effect were meant to impress the authorities, and they succeeded. The Russian Government granted the Karaites autonomy and, in 1835, expelled the Jews from Troki pursuant to Karaite urgings.

The next successful move was an official change of name. Instead of "Karaite Jews," they were now called "Russian Karaites of the Old Testament Faith" and later simply "Karaites." In 1840 they were placed on a par with the Muslims and granted the legal status of an independent church. Two Karaite dioceses were established, in Troki and in the Crimea. Finally, in 1863, the Karaites were given rights equal to those of the indigenous Russian population.

The community continued to turn out scholars. The most famous of them in the nineteenth century was Abraham ben Samuel Firkovich (1786-1874), who also spearheaded the struggle for equal rights. In the course of his travels in the Crimea, Palestine, Syria, and Egypt, he discovered many rabbinic and Karaite manuscripts and works that had been presumed lost. Although his writings contained many forgeries and errors, Firkovich made an important contribution to Karaite and, indeed, to Jewish scholarship. His valuable collection of manuscripts and other ancient writings was acquired by the State Library of St. Petersburg.

The twentieth century heralded the denouement of Karaism in Lithuania. At the end of World War I, much community activity relocated to Vilna, which now belonged to Poland. In 1932, the Government of Poland endorsed the election of a former high-ranking Russian official as the *Hakham* of Troki. By this time all but 200 Lithuanian Karaites, most of whom resided in Panevezh, had emigrated.

Karaite separatism spared the community from the Holocaust. In fact, the Nazi murder squads were explicitly ordered to leave the community unharmed. This order was based on a 1939 ruling of the German Ministry of the Interior, stipulating that the Karaites did not belong to the Jewish community by virtue of their non-Jewish "racial psychology." The German authorities appointed several Karaites to important positions in the Crimea and, generally speaking, treated them well.

Nevertheless the Karaite problem continued to trouble the Nazis, who questioned three Jewish scholars on the community's origins: Zelig Kalmanowitz, the Yiddish writer and philologist who edited the *YIVO Bleter*, the newspaper of the Jewish Scientific Institute in Vilna; Meir Balaban, a historian of Polish Jewry and founder and director of the Institute for Jewish Studies in Warsaw; and Itzhak Schipper, a historian and a member of the Polish Sejm. To save the Karaites, all three ruled that the community was definitely not of Jewish origin. The three Jewish experts perished during the Holocaust, but the German racial and anthropological researchers accepted their opinion and spared the Karaites of Lithuania and other Nazi-occupied countries.

The Karaites did not return the favor. They refused to help Jews who sought their assistance in attempting to escape from the Nazis. In some instances they even denounced Jews who posed as Karaites to escape the Nazi clutches. Specifically, some Karaites provided the German and Lithuanian authorities with community membership lists, against which the false identity cards carried by these Jews were easily discovered.

Chapter 4

THE AGE OF TYRANNY AND FEAR

Lithuanian Jewry under Russian Rule

From 1795 until 1914, historic Lithuania – the counties of Kaunas, Grodno, Minsk, Moghilev, and Vitebsk – was part of the "Northwest Territory" of the Russian Empire. Where Lithuania had once been an aggressive occupier and empire-builder, it was now Russia's turn to occupy an expanse of some 350,000 square kilometers, from the shores of the River Dvina in the northwest to the Dnieper in the south east. After the various partitions of Poland and Lithuania, Russia annexed the Ukraine, Belorussia, and other territories that had once been Lithuania's. Thus a vast Jewish population found itself in the embrace of the Russian bear.

These Jews eventually became part of the largest ghetto in history: the *Cherta*, established by the Russian government in 1835 and sustained until 1917. The *Cherta*, better known as the Pale of Settlement, comprised 15 provinces or *gubernias*, nine in Russia and six in Lithuania and Belorussia: Vilna, Kaunas, Grodno, Minsk, Moghilev, and Vitebsk.

Thus, as Russia absorbed historical Lithuania, so did Lithuanian Jewry lose its territorial identity in the eyes of the ruling power. It had become part of a larger captive community. In the intracommunal sense, this meant little: Lithuanian Jewry maintained both its Lithuanian and its Jewish identity under Czarist rule, and the vibrancy of its outpouring is documented above. What follows, then, is a review of the Czarist side of the relationship.

160

The Russian Czars and government were at odds with much of the population under their rule, both domestic and captive. However, they were united in their xenophobia. All strangers were disliked, but none were as hated and despised as the Jews. Moreover, Jews were foreigners by definition, even though they had populated the newly conquered territories for up to 800 years.

Russia itself had never had an indigenous Jewish population. All Jews were officially expelled from Russian soil with the first conquest of 1727 and were driven out of parts of the Ukraine and Belorussia in 1739. When they effected their occupation of Lithuania, the Russians initially had no specific policy or laws concerning Jews. At first they retained the Polish and Lithuanian regulations, although they considered these part of a defective and inefficient system. Gradually they amended the existing laws and introduced new ones, modifying or improvising new Jewish policies as the occasion required. Consequently, the Jews never knew exactly what the law was and what intentions the government harbored toward them.

There was a fundamental difference between the Czars' attitude toward their Jewish subjects and that of the Polish-Lithuanian kings. The Polish and Lithuanian kings, by and large, maintained a sympathetic, tolerant, and benevolent posture toward the Jews. Fully aware of the needs that Jews might be able to meet, they did their utmost to shield and protect them from their Christian neighbors' hostility and violence. The Czars, by contrast, were absolute monarchs – despotic, reactionary, intolerant, and autocratic. The Imperial policy of the Romanovs was one of discrimination, not only against the Jews but also, in somewhat milder form, against Muslims and, in fact, against anyone not affiliated with the Russian Orthodox Church, including Catholics and Protestants. In this respect, the Russian monarchs followed a ruling by the Russian Orthodox Church, even though Catherine II and subsequent Czars had promised to grant the "minorities" all the rights and privileges that they had been promised.

Since the Jews had no one to protect or defend them, their treatment at the hands of the Russian administration, both central and local, was especially brutal. The government not only imposed its own barbarous edicts upon the Jews, but permitted, and indeed often encouraged, local officials to incite the Gentile population to pogroms. The method used was to single out Jewish communities as scapegoats for their own mistakes and failures.

The government's policy toward all the newly conquered people was one of intensive Russification. People were expected to abandon their native languages, change their names, close their indigenous churches, and adopt a new way of life. This met with much resistance, but not on the part of the nobles, the gentry, or the burghers. It was the serfs and peasants, in the main, who retained their native languages. They paid an economic and spiritual price for this, as they had under all regimes.[85]

Czarist rule brought about a radical deterioration in the lot of the Lithuanian people. After living continuously since 1230 in their own free Grand Duchy, they now faced forced assimilation, increased poverty, and the abrogation of rights that had never been generous.

An account of the unhappy Jewish experience under the new regime follows. For chronological convenience, it is presented in the "begats" format used to describe the community's formation in gestational Lithuania.

Catherine II (1762-1796) – A Flicker of Liberalism

In Russian history, the reign of Catherine II, who was influenced by Montesquieu, Voltaire, and Diderot among others, was a watershed period. At first Catherine considered herself an enlightened monarch whose task it was to liberalize her society, including that of the newly acquired territories. She called for the formation of an elected assembly of deputies representing all classes except the serfs and clerics. Nor did her reforms disregard the Jews. Her state tax law eliminated discrimination on the basis of religion. Catherine was even prepared to allow Jews to settle in Russia proper, a privilege denied them by her predecessors unless they converted to Christianity, and granted them unrestricted trading rights provided that they pay a double poll tax. Catherine's new subjects were to enjoy personal rights and freedom of religion, any religion.

All of this was short-lived; Catherine's liberal intentions soon yielded to the will of the gentry and the nobility, whose prerogatives she had expanded. Catherine now invested her energy in foreign politics. Her principal aims were to acquire Polish provinces that had large Russian Orthodox populations and to drive the Turks out of Europe. She failed to achieve the latter aim, but during the first Turkish war between 1768 and 1774, she established Russia's right to patronage over the Christians of Turkey.

Her early liberal inclinations did have some effect. The 1775 Statute for the Provinces, an innovative document, effected improvements in local administration, the judiciary, and self-government that lasted until the reforms of Alexander II. In 1785, she issued a Charter that served the nobility's interests until the serfs were liberated in 1861 and gave the burghers a basis for control of municipalities and self-government. In the same year, Catherine reaffirmed the religious, judicial, and fiscal status of the *Kahal*, the Jewish community organization.

In 1794, with the acquisition of Lithuania, Catherine II appointed Nicholai Vasilevitz Repnin as the ruler of the newly occupied country. Vilna became the official capital of the Lithuanian *gubernias* (counties); the seat of the provincial government and the supreme court, printing press, and censorship office, which concerned itself with Hebrew books among others, was located in Grodno.

Paul I (1796-1801) – Years of Turmoil

Catherine's successor, Paul I, was an unmitigated tyrant whose brief tenure featured perversely inconsistent policies and a special harshness that he visited upon his people, including his own advisors. His rule, reminiscent in manner to that of an Oriental potentate, left no impression on the history of his country. It was during his reign, however, that the Russian Senate began to consider how best to deal with the country's growing Jewish population and to collect material for comprehensive legislation that would govern their status. The burghers, observing the monarch's character traits, petitioned him to expel the Jews from the towns and cities. Paul I rejected this idea, settling for discriminatory measures such as doubling the business-license fee for Jewish merchants. He even granted citizenship and a previously-denied concession to the Jews of the Latvian province of Courland. But he was no philosemite. He endorsed, and placed on record, a statement made by one Derzawin, a senator and poet:

> We have to transform the Jews into a useful element and curb their avaricious pursuits. They should be registered in several categories, urban or rural, burghers, merchants, or agricultural settlers. They should be given family names. Their religious life and synagogue and their rabbis and teachers

should be placed under the authority of a supreme ecclesiastical
tribunal in St. Petersburg. They should be evenly distributed
in specially chosen provinces and should be allowed neither to
hold governmental or municipal positions nor to employ
Christian domestic servants. They should change their dress
and speech. There should be a government printing press for
Jewish philosophical books. Jewish children should be allowed
to study in their own schools until the age of twelve, but should
then continue in public schools.

That illiteracy was rife among non-Jews in the Russian empire was of no
concern to Derzawin.

Another official who pondered the newly discovered Jewish problem was
one Friedel, the German-educated governor of Vilna. According to Friedel,
the root of the problem was threefold: Jewish religion, Jewish attire, and the
Yiddish language. Jews should not be allowed to marry before the age of
twenty, he counseled.

Truth to tell, the Russian Empire had encountered difficulties with the
inhabitants of the newly conquered territories, including parts of Lithuania,
ever since the First Partition of Poland and Lithuania in 1772. Themselves
ambivalent about the nature of the policies they wished to enact in these
territories, they were unable to fashion realistic solutions that the minority
groups would accept. Consequently, four norms prevailed during the Czarist
occupation: tyranny, misrule, a fixation on Russifying the non-Jewish
minorities, and an all-consuming obsession with the problem of all Jews
under their jurisdiction. A fifth trait, if somewhat less prevalent, was
assassination as the vehicle of succession, as in the disposition of Paul I by
court conspirators in 1801.

An afterword to this period of Russian rule pertains to Prussia, Russia's
partner in the partition, new owner of the Suwalki area of Lithuania and its
eastern sector, including Memel-Klaipeda, Tilsit, and other border towns. In
the process of colonizing these areas, the Prussians introduced a
Germanization policy that included the imposition of German language and
culture. Formerly Lithuanian Jewish communities now incorporated into
Prussia were adjoined to the older German Jewish aggregates of Koenigsberg
and Berlin. Prussian law improved their religious, social, and economic

circumstances to a level far superior to that of their brethren under the Russian yoke.

Since strong links continued to exist between the newly Prussianized areas and the Lithuanian Jewish localities in the Pale of Settlement, the Prussian-occupied zone became a corridor through which Enlightenment ideas and the language, literature, culture, and customs of the new communities penetrated the townships of the Pale. From their observation point across the border, the Lithuanian Jews in their cities and villages sought to learn new ways, improve the old, and maintain a specific Jewish character. Both groups still shared the traits of intellectualism and spiritual activism, and their interaction produced a new form of Jewish leadership for emerging new movements in Jewish life.

Alexander I (1801-1825) – Repression Takes Hold

Paul I was succeeded by his son, Alexander I, upon whom the Russian people pinned great hopes for a better future. At first, feeding on their enthusiasm, he, too, was captivated by the liberal tendencies and philosophy of the time, as characterized by the American Declaration of Independence and the French Revolution.

Alexander I made several attempts to enact just and progressive legislation. Anxious to obtain the goodwill and cooperation of his newly conquered subjects, especially those in Poland and Lithuania, the Czar appointed Adam Czartorisky, a friend of his youth and a descendant of the Polonized Lithuanian magnates, as his Foreign Minister. In 1802, Alexander I established a commission to ameliorate the condition of the Jews in the Russian Empire and issued a senatorial *ukase* making Jews eligible to serve in municipal offices. This measure of emancipation lasted only one year in several Lithuanian provinces but went ahead elsewhere.

In 1804, representatives of all the *Kahal* agencies were invited to St. Petersburg to participate in the discussions of another special commission set up to improve the conditions of all the king's subjects. One member of the commission, the Imperial Secretary, Michael Michaelovitch Speransky, recommended a new Jewish policy for the Empire, one of maximum liberties and a minimum of restrictions. He believed that such a policy would induce the Jews to solve "their" problem themselves, to everyone's benefit. The other members of the commission disagreed furiously. Only heavy-handed treatment, they said, would force the Jews to join the mainstream of Russian society quickly. Speransky was outvoted and dismissed from office; in 1812 he was exiled.

The Empire was working at cross purposes. A carrot-and-stick statute passed the same year sought to expel from Old Russia even the small number of affluent Jewish merchants who had been granted permission to live there. Concurrently, the Government strove to motivate Jews in the Pale to acquire a Russian education and, above all, to engage in agriculture. To bring this about, Alexander presented the Jewish community with a ripe "carrot": 80,000 hectares of land in Kherson and exemption of farmers in this area from military service. By 1810, this device attracted 2,000 Jewish families to Kherson. Then came the "stick": one of the economic articles of the Statute of 1804 prohibited Jewish residence in villages that they had inhabited for generations, chiefly in the south of Russia. It also banned certain activities by Jews in these villages, such as the sale of alcohol to the peasants. Since these prohibitions affected the livelihood of many thousands of Jews, the government then declared its intention to let Jews settle as peasants on their own lands or on government lands that would be allocated to them elsewhere.

The expulsion of the Jews from villages and localities in southern Russia began soon after the Statute of 1804 was gazetted. When it became clear that the 101,000 families involved could not resettle themselves in agriculture settlements at the drop of a hat, the expulsion order was suspended; the systematic evacuation of the villages did not resume until 1822. Indeed, a small number of Jews continued to reside in the cities of Old Russia, outside the Pale, and traveled freely in pursuit of their trades. They accomplished this by purchasing special licenses in the form of gold medallions of various kinds. For the Jewish masses, however, the boundaries of the Pale of Settlement were virtually impermeable between this time and 1917.

The density of the Jewish population in the Pale led to fierce economic competition. There were three times as many unskilled laborers, skilled workers, and cottage industrialists as were needed to meet the population's needs. Since Jews were forbidden to move out of the Pale[86] and could not obtain loans for purchase of equipment and materials with which they might expand their businesses, unemployment in the Pale was rampant. From 1808 onward, when Jewish and governmental records in these matters became available, some 45 percent of the Jewish labor force was idle and more than

35 percent of Jewish families in the Pale appealed to Jewish welfare institutions for assistance at least once.

Behind the facade created by a handful of very wealthy Russian Jewish families were masses of impoverished Jews in the Pale, who struggled endlessly for the barest of livelihood. Embittered by their circumstances, they nurtured hopes and aspirations for a better world. Within a generation or so, they or their offspring were well represented in the Russian revolutionary movements and the great emigrationary outflux.[87]

In the meantime, the Czar's Court and the intelligentsia were still obsessed with the Jewish problem, for the real policy goals – assimilation and eventual acceptance of Christianity – were far from fulfillment. Together they explored the possibilities. The Talmud, for example, was known to be a principal obstacle in any attempt to win the Jews over. Its teachings would need to be both curtailed and refuted. Thus the war against the yeshivot, abetted (usually unwittingly) by secularist Jewish voices, began to gestate.

The ascent of Napoleon Bonaparte to supreme command of the French armed forces in 1797, shortly before Alexander I assumed the Russian throne, distracted the heads of state in Russia from their preoccupation with the Jews. Napoleon formulated plans to end the Russian, Austrian, and German occupation of Eastern Europe including Poland and Lithuania. Specifically, he formed a Polish and Lithuanian Legion under Polish commander Jan Henryk Dombrowski and entertained great hopes that the legion would liberate the Commonwealth from its foreign occupiers. Jews supported the resistance by providing money or goods; they were not allowed in the army at the time.

Napoleon's legion failed, but the supreme commander himself assumed the title of Emperor and justified his self-promotion by trouncing the English, Austrian, and Russian forces at Austerlitz in 1805. Napoleon's armies marched into Prussia two years later and then overran the parts of Lithuania that the Russians had formerly occupied.

The French found Lithuania in a state of decline: its economy in ruins, its feudal arrangements crumbling but alive. Most property in the cities was controlled by monasteries, churches, and the petty nobility. In the periphery, many estates and farms were owned by absentee landlords and managed by Jewish leaseholders. Although much of Lithuania's commerce and industry was in Jewish hands, neither Christian nor Jewish merchants amassed much wealth (with a few exceptions). Jews were under the jurisdiction of the

Principality Court, also known as "the Fortress," but later, when the Czars' power diminished, they were handed back to the municipal courts, which invariably ruled against them. Community religious affairs and internal disputes were adjudicated by the *batey din*, the rabbinical courts.

Serfdom was abolished wherever the French took control, although the freed serfs were not given land of their own. The Napoleonic Code was introduced on the personal level, but Lithuania as a country retained its 1588 status under the principle of *plebe nobilus non prefendi* – non-preference of commoners over nobles. The French granted the Jews equality before the law: ghetto gates were torn down and Jews were given a window through which they might view the European world.

The window closed quickly, both for Gentile Lithuanians and for the Jewish communities. The French occupation lasted until 1808, when the Treaty of Tilsit assigned the Polish province of Suwalkai and various parts of Lithuania to Russia. Napoleon and the Czar parted on friendly terms (although the Czar refused to give the French monarch his sister Ann in marriage). Lithuania braced itself for a new round of Czarist abuse.[88]

It came quickly. Impoverished as the country was, Alexander I immediately increased its tax burden. Many nobles, unable to meet the demands, forfeited their estates to the government, which, in turn, handed title to these properties to preferred persons, either as rewards for good service or as incentives to settle in Lithuania. The Czar did have his supporters in the newly occupied lands: a small group of Lithuanian and Polish friends, including Lithuanian magnate Michael Clophas Oginski, who tried to intervene on Lithuania's behalf without notable success.

Napoleon took on the Czar again in 1812. This time Lithuania and its Jewish communities were exposed to both the invading and the retreating armies. Napoleon's forces, 220,000 strong, crossed the River Nemunas at Alexot near Kovno and entered Vilna, where the Emperor himself stayed for more than two weeks.

The occupiers conscripted a Lithuanian battalion, merged it into Napoleon's armed forces, and ordered the civilian population to provide the invading troops with food, lodging, and hospitals for the wounded. Generally speaking, the Jewish community resisted these designs. Yiddish circulars were distributed throughout Russia urging the Jews to pray for the Czar's victory, although one Jew, Smeral Vilky, was exiled to Siberia for spying on behalf of the French. The Russian Governor of Vilna wrote to the Czar commending the Jews of Lithuania "for their patriotism during the French occupation and for their support of the Russian forces." The Czar promised to reward them for their loyalty.

One towering Jewish leader, the first Lubavitcher Rebbe, R. Shneor Zalman of Liadi, openly supported the Czar against Napoleon in the wars of 1808 and 1812, despite Russia's persecution of Jews and Napoleon's promise of liberty and equality. The Rebbe distrusted Napoleon's Jewish policies, especially his plans for a reconvened Grand Sanhedrin. The French Emperor's intentions, he maintained, would inevitably cause widespread assimilation; the Jews would be better off suffering in dignity under the Czar and waiting for better times rather than exposing themselves to Napoleon's potentially dangerous policies. By contrast, the hasidic rebbes and masses in Poland, together with their Gentile counterparts, the Polish nobility and the population at large, strongly supported Napoleon, who, they hoped, would liberate them from the Russian oppressors.

Napoleon's armies advanced, captured Smolensk, and marched on Moscow. The capital surrendered; its inhabitants nearly burned it to the ground to prevent its falling intact into French hands. Napoleon waited two months for a peace treaty. The Russians, however, had time and climate on their side. Napoleon paid dearly for misjudging the Russian mentality. A Russian regrouping, abetted by a bitterly cold winter, drove the invading armies out of Russia and, eventually, from Lithuania. The cities they left behind were paved with casualties and replete with epidemics and misery. After brief local insurrections in 1813 and 1814, Russia reinstated its rule in Lithuania as elsewhere.

Still, the Napoleonic campaign had left a strong and enduring impression on the peoples of Lithuania, Poland, and Russia. The Russian officers were shocked by the contrast between their conditions and those of the French, the arbitrary rule, the abuses, and the corruption of their own bureaucracy and courts, the suffering of the serfs, and the rampant illiteracy in their country. A new generation emerged, university-educated, idealistic, and influenced by the philosophies and romanticism of Kant, Hegel, Fichte, Schelling, and others. They began to probe the Russian national soul, study Russian history, and contemplate its uniqueness and originality. They were fascinated by the *mir*, the old Russian peasant commune, which became the model and pattern for the modern socialist movements that they later created. Theirs became a philosophy totally distinct from Western individualism. Many were uninterested in politics, liberalism, or systems of government. They wanted Russia to refulfill the principles of the Eastern Church – the Orthodox autocracy – that they considered the highest form of civilization. But they were a minority among the Russian intelligentsia. The majority group, which opposed them strongly, was composed of so-called Westernizers, led by Herzen, Belinsky, and Bakunin, to name only three.

Napoleon's impact on the Jewish communities in the cities his armies had occupied was no less dramatic. By inviting Jews to enter the modern world, he had challenged them to become part of general society while remaining completely faithful to their tradition – if they so desired. The resulting debate within Jewry has lasted to this very day.

Czar Alexander I sought his role in the post-Napoleonic world. At the Congress of Vienna in 1815, he postured as the Savior of Europe. In 1818, at Aix-la-Chapelle, the "Holy Alliance" of Russia, Austria, and Prussia reconfirmed the partition of Lithuania and Poland and redivided the sections of Europe that Napoleon's armies had occupied. The Czar was a leading actor in this Alliance, which Metternich, the "honest broker," used to repress all liberal movements in Europe. Russian influence and prestige in Europe soared. Pondering his newly acquired assertive power, the Czar remarked, "The war illuminated my soul. I discovered God and the truth of the Bible and have become a changed man."

However, much else had changed with him. The Napoleonic tidal wave had shattered the age-old feudal patterns, opening up new economic and political options for Jew and Gentile alike and leading to a civil emancipation process that swept the established order aside.

Returning home after the Congress of Vienna, Alexander I attempted to be an enlightened monarch and introduce liberal ideas, following to some extent in the footsteps of the French. First he asked the nobles and the gentry to liberate their serfs voluntarily and grant each family a plot of land. Only some 5,000 serfs were liberated in this fashion. His next step, the Ukase of 1817, sought to improve the condition of his new subjects in the Russian-occupied territories. The major effect of this measure, meant for implementation by the Czar's brother, Grand Duke Constantine (commander-in-chief of the occupied territories), was to enforce and intensify Russification. The Lithuanian intelligentsia resisted this process, as they always had. The Ukase of 1817 was never implemented. In the face of force majeure, however, they temporarily sacrificed their national and cultural aspirations, as well as their language, by opting for Polonization rather than Russification. Polish replaced French and Latin at the University of Vilna; Lithuanian schools taught Polish language and culture.

In the meantime, the Czar reassumed his former posture as a Christian mystic and religious reactionary. In 1818 he asked his ambassador to Warsaw, N. N. Novosiltsov, and a trusted adviser in matters of reform, Prince N. P. Kochubey, to prepare a constitution for the Russian Empire that later became known as the May 3rd Constitution. The new document revoked rights that the Jews had acquired under the Napoleonic Code.[89]

Alexander I, although preoccupied with the Jewish problem, now entrusted the handling of this crucial matter to Prince Alexander Golitzyn, his Minister for Religious Affairs. Golitzyn, president of the Russian Orthodox Bible society, was a religious fanatic who concerned himself with the spiritual succor of the Jews by "saving their souls." In 1817, Golitzyn set up an Israelitish-Christian Society which, under royal patronage, offered financial and legal concessions, free land, and other privileges to baptized Jews. An advisory board including six Jewish deputies was established to work with Golitzyn to solve the Jewish question in Russia. A conference held in Vilna in 1818 to discuss the problem was attended, not voluntarily, by 22 delegates from the *Kahals* of 11 provinces. All these efforts ended in an utter fiasco; the Israelitish-Christian Society was dissolved by Czar Nicholas I in 1833.

In general, Alexander I followed Catherine's policies toward the Jews and enforced the laws she had enacted against them. One of these provided for State-sponsored elementary schools for Jewish children; this was expected to promote assimilation and eventual conversion to Christianity. However, Jews were excluded from Russian high schools and universities. A group of professors attempted in 1811 to populate these and similar schools by appealing to the *Kahals*. Czartorisky, now concerned with the education of Jews in addition to his other priorities, urged the Czar, in an 1817 memorandum, to teach the Jews Russian culture first; only then, when thus prepared, should they be baptized. This, Czartorisky ruled, would serve the causes of humanity, politics and, above all, religion. Alexander I even attempted to effect a mass conversion of Jews to Christianity; he failed.

At precisely this time, Alexander faced a new phenomenon: the emergence of a religious movement of peasants in Central Russia who called themselves *subotniki* (Sabbath observers), and were perceived to have converted to Judaism. An indignant Alexander subjected the *subotniki* to terrible abuse, including deportation to Siberia. Although no Jewish connection or influence was involved – no Jewish communities existed in provinces where the *subotniki* flourished – officials held the Jews collectively responsible for *subotnik* religious ideas. Consequently, all promises to improve the conditions of the Jews were forgotten. Indeed, additional anti-Jewish legislation was enacted. Candidacy for positions of community elders and rabbis was restricted to those who wrote and spoke Russian, German, or Polish, and wore modern clothes. No longer were official or public documents gazetted in Yiddish or Hebrew, as had previously been the case. *Kahal* prerogatives were further curtailed: *Kahal* work would henceforth be supervised by the gubernia (district) governor. The *Kahal* would be held responsible for timely payment of State taxes by all Jews. Public schools were opened to Jewish children (to encourage assimilation), although communities were allowed to keep their own schools if instruction took place in the vernacular.

Jews in various localities faced mass expulsion. In 1820, after the Jews in Kovno were given permission to expand their presence, protests of such intensity erupted that a decree expelling the entire Jewish community from this city was issued. After a hard fight, R. Hershel Neviazner succeeded in nullifying it. A famine in Belorussia in 1823-24 resulted in the expulsion of 20,000 Jews. Subsequently, large numbers of Jews were driven out of Lithuanian villages into the towns, where they were subjected to intensive propaganda meant to encourage them to take up agriculture at some future time. Many thousands of Jews, suffering from hunger, cold and disease, thronged the larger cities, where the *Kahals*, miscellaneous Jewish organizations, and individual Jews came to their aid generously. In 1827, the Jews in the Lithuanian city of Telz came under the blood libel and were accused of desecrating the Host. Such charges soon became a favorite pretext for attacks and pogroms.[90]

Alexander I fretted about Napoleon's Grand Sanhedrin plan. Although the French autarch had departed the scene, the Czar feared his scheme as a propaganda ploy meant to mobilize the Jews of Europe, including Austria, Prussia, Turkey, and most ominously, Russia. Counterattacking, the Czar ordered his governors to convene provincial assemblies where Jewish representatives would discuss ways of improving the status of Jews in Russia. As a gesture of goodwill, he suspended the village expulsion edict...and ordered local authorities to implement it a short time later. The results – suffering among the expellees and congestion in the towns and cities to which they were herded – led to the appointment of yet another commission, this one to study the effects of the decree. The commission reported that the expulsions had brought no benefit to the Russian and other peasants who remained in the villages from which the Jews had been evicted; it advised the Czar to rescind the prohibition of Jewish residence in the villages and to allow them to manage the inns once again. The government quickly accepted the commission's findings.

In so doing, Alexander and his officials signalled their apprehension of a new problem: a rebellion by Gentile Lithuanians and Poles, which the oppressed Jews might join. The Russification program and the extensive nationalization of estates in the occupied areas aroused the opposition of Lithuanian writers, historians, and philosophers such as Adam Mickewitzus, Sylvester Valinas, and Klementas. By 1821, a Patriotic Society had coalesced to orchestrate the resistance. Within a year, many of its leaders were arrested and expelled to Siberia or imprisoned locally. The Czar, increasingly autocratic and egocentric, surrounded himself with the likes of Novosiltsov, Golitzyn, and Prince Constantin, sycophantic friends and advisors who denied the need to abolish serfdom or constrain the absolute power of the Czar, the Father of Holy Russia, in any way. Czartorisky resigned in frustration.

In Lithuania and Poland, as throughout the Russian Empire, the Russian language assumed an almost mystical supremacy and replaced all other languages as the language of instruction in the schools and universities. Teaching of Russian culture was intensified at all levels. In his final years, Alexander I became obsessed with fear of an impending uprising against him by his own people and the population of his newly conquered territories. He died in Taganrog in 1825.

Nicholas I (1825-1855) – The Iron Czar, Policeman of Europe

Alexander I was succeeded by his younger brother, Nicholas I, a crude, ignorant man noted for his cold, introverted personality and his limited capacity to understand anything. His reign was characterized by oppression and cruelty. He was constantly preoccupied with the "problem" of the new citizens of his empire, and continued, indeed intensified, his brother's policies of assimilation and Russification of the minorities. Thus he incorporated the Grand Duchy of Lithuania, with its mostly Catholic population, into Russia proper and gave it provincial status. As a Russian Orthodox fanatic, although no mystic, Nicholas believed in the divine mission of converting his citizens to his own brand of Christianity. To achieve this, he first shut down most Catholic monasteries and converted them into Orthodox churches. This he regarded not only as a religious duty but as an integral part of his Russification program. The Ruthenian and Ukrainian Uniate Churches and their parochs (priests) fared no better. Not only were their buildings reconsecrated in the Russian Orthodox denomination, but their ritual was aligned with that of Russian Orthodoxy.

In due course, Nicholas' repression of disliked Christian denominations evolved into a campaign against all free thought. His subjects responded with fear and hatred. Revolutionary leaders Rilayeff and Trubetskoi launched an insurrection in St. Petersburg in December 1827. It failed; most of the insurgents, who became known as the Decembrists, were either hanged or exiled to Siberia. Nicholas then hinted at the possible introduction of liberal reforms contained in the political platform of his Decembrist enemies. At no time, however, did he follow through.

Firmly convinced of his divine selection as the agent to control and suppress all liberal thinking, Nicholas I laid the foundations for a new secret police force. With the enormous power that it accumulated over the people, it was emulated by all subsequent Russian governments until the most recent times.

As for the Jews, Nicholas I's personal attitude and official strategy were motivated by hatred, distrust, and religious extremism. The general thrust of Nicholas I's Jewish legislation was to reduce their numbers in the Russian Empire, forcibly reeducate them so as to deprive them of their individuality and, thereby, rob them of their religious and national particularity, and render them "harmless" to the Christians, "both economically and morally." The first action of this kind, taken in 1827, was a ukase prescribing the conscription of all Jewish boys at the age of twelve for a period of 25 years, the better, he believed, to win new souls for the Russian Orthodox Church. In view of the treatment that these children-conscripts were given, the objective was clearly forced conversion.

Each Jewish community, through its *Kahal*, was given a quota of "Nicholas soldiers" or "cantonists"[91] that it was to provide. Boys of eight or nine were sometimes kidnapped by professional "snatchers," *khapers* in Yiddish, whom the *Kahal* employed for the purpose of filling its quota. In all, more than 50,000 boys were torn from their families in this fashion. For decades, Russian Jews retained the memory of that terrible era by recounting the abuse and suffering visited upon these children, as well as the many tales of individual courage and heroism in resisting conversion. These stories, articulated by numerous Russian Jewish authors, documented Nicholas' implacable hatred of and inhuman decrees against the Jewish people. They described the beatings, corporal punishment, and, in some cases, the death penalty to which "cantonists" were subjected. The servitude of these children was described as "worse than the punishments meted out by the Spanish Inquisition," which, it was pointed out, had been directed against adults. Most "cantonists" served the prescribed 25-year term, if they lived so long; others, snatched away at a younger age, served 35 years.

No parents were secure with their sons. Zvi Gittelman describes the moral extremis that the situation brought to the surface:

> Little wonder that all sorts of subterfuges were used in attempts to avoid military service. One can even understand the willingness of the wealthy and of the communal officials whom they supported, to shield their own children from service by substituting others as was allowed by law. The hapless substitutes were almost always the children of the poor and the socially marginal....
>
> A Yiddish folk song of the time expressed the sentiment poignantly:
>
> "Rich Zushe Rickover has seven sons,
>
> But not one puts on the uniform.
>
> But Leah, the widow's only child,
>
> Becomes the scapegoat of a communal sin."[92]

The children were usually abducted in the dead of night and hauled away to destinations far from their homes. Some of the younger boys failed to last the journey. The survivors were entrusted to the custodianship of a *diadka* ("uncle"), a mentor and educator who would usher them into the new faith. Roughly half of the young conscripts yielded to the might of the Russian Orthodox Church. Many others perished. Some others, however, refused to yield. They withstood years of physical and mental torture until their forced army service came to an end. The few among them who remembered where their homes were returned to their native cities and villages, proudly displaying their tiny four-fringed garments and prayerbooks, the only articles they had taken with them when snatched away. Others, who had forgotten whence they had come, settled in existing Jewish communities, particularly in Siberia, Estonia, and Finland.

Nicholas I was particularly sensitive to the perceived danger of political influence on education in schools and universities. Political activity was banned in all such institutions, even though the privilege of higher education was restricted to the upper classes, families of the gentry, the upper echelons of the bureaucracy, and a very small number of exceptionally gifted youngsters. Jews were rarely seen in this milieu; most of those who penetrated it were converts.

In Lithuania, the peasants and serfs were the first to rebel against the Russian Orthodox Church, whose tradition was imposed on them, and their forced induction into the Russian army. An uprising that began in Telshiai in 1830 spread throughout the old Grand Duchy. A similar revolt erupted in Poland in 1831, joined by several petty nobles in Vilnius, Kaunas, and other cities. The insurgents were defeated at Ostrolenka.

The Lithuanian revolutionaries paid a heavy price for their participation in the insurrection. Leaders and principal activists were exiled to Siberia or sentenced to death. The rebels' landholdings were parcelled out to court favorites and other Russians in a far-reaching colonization process that led to a large Russian influx. Russian was declared the official language of the country, its use in schools made mandatory and strictly enforced. Imperial offices intensified their activity and strengthened their control of the country.

By 1835, the government believed it time to regulate the legal situation once and for all. A Statute for the Minorities legislated that year was comprised of 17 articles that codified all restrictions and strictures enacted since 1804. The Lithuanian Statute of 1588 was abolished five years later. Infractions of the law were punished swiftly and severely, even though most Lithuanians, illiterate, could not understand what was expected of them.

A new constitution subjected Lithuanians, Poles, and other minorities to all sorts of repressive measures. In Lithuania, every manifestation of nationalism was banned, including national costumes and songs. Jews termed this document the "Oppressive Constitution."

Nicholas' minister of education, Sergei Semyonowitch Uvarov, believed that the path to Jewish reform was one of rapprochement with the general population through education. Thus he proposed the establishment of a network of government schools in the Pale of Settlement, to be financed by special taxes imposed on the Jews themselves. It was Uvarov who, in 1841, appointed Max Lilienthal to direct this project. One year later, several prominent Jewish religious and lay leaders, including R. Menachem Mendel Schneersohn, the Lubavitcher Rebbe, were invited to join a Jewish Education Committee that would devise a curriculum. Legislation for the creation of these government schools was passed in 1844 and remained in effect until the end of the Czarist regime.

The schools, first situated in heavily Jewish-populated cities in the Pale such as Vilna, Riga, Odessa, and Kishinev, failed abysmally for lack of enrollment. Lilienthal resigned in 1844 and slipped out of Russia, evidently convinced, as noted, that the government meant the schools to serve as instruments for conversion, not education.

That same year, by order of the Czar, the *kehillot* were disbanded and the Jews placed directly under the jurisdiction of the police and the municipal authorities. However, a substitute Jewish authority of carefully selected individuals was created to deal with problems of the "cantonists," the modern schools, and the Jewish taxes, especially the *korobka*. Religious and community needs formerly met by the *kehilla* were now entrusted to volunteer Jewish societies.

It was at this time that Jews, Lithuanians, and Poles, equally threatened with oppression and cultural extirpation, found common cause. Members of all three groups collaborated to smuggle Lithuanian and Hebrew books, printed in Germany, across the Lithuanian-German border. Adam Mickiewitz, the famous Polish-Lithuanian author, paid tribute in his writings to the Jews who had smuggled volumes of his books into Lithuania. In a Polish Legion journal that appeared clandestinely during the Revolution of 1848, Mickiewitz referred to the Jews as "our elder brother Israel," who merited "respectful and fraternal" treatment and assistance in the achievement of "equal rights in every matter."

Back in the Pale, the stream of legislative harassment continued to flow. An 1850 census showed a Jewish population of 2.4 million in Russia, including, of course, Lithuania. The poll itemized citizens as "productive" – wealthy merchants, artisans, and farmers – and "unproductive." Most Russian Jews

found themselves in the latter category. In 1851, Jewish males were forbidden
to wear traditional garb and sidelocks (*peot*); married Jewish women were
ordered to stop shaving their heads.

By now, the Czar's oppressive policies toward the Jews aroused indignant
protests from Jewish communities and statesmen in the West. As early as
1839, while visiting London, the Czar had been presented with a petition by
prominent British political leaders, urging him to annul an *ukase* ordering
the expulsion of Jews from towns and villages within 35 miles of the German
and Austrian borders. The decree was in fact allowed to lapse, but only
because it proved harmful to state interests. In 1846, Sir Moses Montefiore
received a tumultuous welcome in Vilna and Kovno, which he visited while
traveling to St. Petersburg on a mission of intervention on behalf of his Jewish
brethren. Even the titled, wealthy, and influential Montefiore failed to
persuade the Iron Czar to modify his Jewish policies.

If an extent of rebellion and intervention might have helped the Jews
under Nicholas, one may attempt to estimate it by considering the case of the
Lithuanian serfs, a much larger group that pressed for its rights – of which
it had absolutely none – without the pernicious baggage of Russian
antisemitism. There were more than 550 peasant uprisings during the reign
of Nicholas I. Obtuse as he seemed, the Czar was distressed by the endless
insurrections that characterized his tenure, especially those of the Lithuanian
serfs, whose situation had deteriorated as a result his administration's
crackdown. Most of the peasants farmed lands owned by the Crown; they were
worked to the bone and heavily taxed. Others labored on private estates, and
their plight was even more pitiable. When estates changed ownership, the
serfs were handed from one master to another. They were often flogged,
imprisoned, tortured, and abused, and the tradition of *jus primae noctis* was
widely invoked. The 25-year forced conscription into the Russian Army
applied to them, too, and was a special source of resentment for people who
needed every spare hand to support their families. Straining to curb the serf
uprisings, Nicholas I attempted to regulate and restrict the landowners'
authority somewhat. His efforts were neither taken seriously nor
implemented.

The Czar established many secret commissions in search of a solution to
problems connected with the peasants, the minorities, and other new citizens.
In 1842, by recommendation of one of these commissions, the Czar issued an

ukase abolishing personal serfdom throughout the Empire and establishing a scale of payments for labor.

After the Polish revolution of 1848, fought inter alia to improve the peasants' lot, Nicholas I became even more fanatical in his religious outlook. The Czar proclaimed his conviction that God was with him, guiding and protecting him in the conduct of the Russian Empire's internal and external affairs. Another group ran afoul of the tempestuous Czar at this time: the intelligentsia, which he blamed collectively for the revolution. Individual intellectuals directly accused were persecuted and severely punished. Uvarov, whom the Czar considered "too liberal," resigned. His successor as minister of education was Prince P. A. Shikmatov, who sought to "base all teachings on religious truth and morals." In his view, education of this nature would bring salvation to the whole country and solve most of its problems, all of which originated in sin. Many writers, philosophers, and academicians did not share Shikmatov's views. Some of them were imprisoned; others were exiled.

In 1853, Nicholas picked a fight with the Turks that eventually resulted in the Crimean War. One of his motives was his ambition to seize control of the Holy Places in Jerusalem and be seen as the patron and protector of the Orthodox Church in the Ottoman Empire. When the battle progressed auspiciously, Nicholas assumed the role of protector of all Christian subjects in the Ottoman Empire. England, France, and Austria vigorously opposed this move, as well as Nicholas' ambition to control the Dardanelles, and declared war on Russia in 1854. This spelled further agony for the Jews, since Nicholas I needed additional cannon fodder. In 1856, after a bitter struggle with heavy casualties on both sides, the Russians were defeated.

Nicholas I did not live to see this outcome. He died in St. Petersburg in 1855, a broken, disillusioned man, depressed by the realization that he had failed his people and his country. For the Jews, his reign, particularly because of the "cantonist" decree, is remembered as one of the darkest periods of life under the Czars.

Alexander II (1855-1881) – Fear Sets In

Nicholas was succeeded by his son, Alexander II. In the early years of his rule, he was influenced by Western liberal ideas and viewed himself as an enlightened monarch. He greatly admired the works of Zhukovski and believed that this liberal poet's ideas and philosophy should be the basis for a new liberal system of education for the whole of Russia. He contemplated an important role for Russia in Europe and was sensitive to Europe's attitudes toward his status and authority. He was thus greatly disappointed when, in 1856, after Russia's defeat in the Crimea, he and his Government were displaced by the Austro-Hungarian Empire as protectors of the Christian churches in the Ottoman Empire. Still, Alexander II accepted realistically his country's defeat and its effect on the Empire.

At his coronation in 1856, he declared that Jews would be conscripted into the Russian Army on equal terms with non-Jews, with the exception of "Jews who lack a permanent domicile or are not engaged in productive work." Mention of such a matter at a royal coronation is itself an indication of the importance given to Jewish issues in nineteenth-century Russia. Thus Alexander II finally put an end to his father's "cantonist" outrage. Then he reduced the term of military service from 25 years to 16 for all citizens, irrespective of class or minority affiliation.

Alexander II's reforms marked a turning point in Russian history. For the Jews, still shaking off the harsh effects of Nicholas's reign, he was viewed as a savior and benefactor.

In 1858, the government of Alexander II permitted Jews to move from one locality to another within the Pale and allowed the Jews of Kovno and Slobodka to build a new cemetery. A *ukase* issued the following year permitted some Jews to leave the Pale and settle anywhere in the Empire, provided they met certain criteria and restrictions. The Jews thus liberated were the university-educated, the artisans, merchants, distillers, and possessors of various kinds of special medals. Jews otherwise confined to the Pale were allowed to leave temporarily for education or occupational purposes. By 1860, new groups of Jewish farmers began to appear both within and outside the Pale, at first to a limited extent, but soon in steadily growing numbers.

Alexander II's greatest achievement was the liberation of the serfs in 1861. He was convinced that the living circumstances of the Russian peasant were intolerable and would inevitably lead to widespread revolt and revolution – unless the government itself took the initiative by abolishing serfdom by law. Indeed, unrest was rampant throughout the Empire; the chorus of demands for liberty and freedom was rising in tenor. In the same year, the Patriotic

Movement in Poland promised in its Manifesto to grant emancipation to all in a free Poland, "including Jews."

The Russian regime's intentions were put to the test that year, when the Jewish community of Shavli was visited with the blood libel and several Jewish leaders were arrested by local authorities. The government appointed a commission of inquiry, headed by General Nezimov and including Tolstoy and Levanda. After five years of investigation and discussion, the libel was pronounced a fraud and the arrested Jews were released. In terms of the times, it was a small step forward. Such advances were few and far between. Further incremental progress occurred in 1862 when, after a disastrous flood in Kaunas, the Government provided relief for all victims equally, including Jews.

A larger breakthrough occurred the following year, precipitated by a major failure of Alexander's regime. The Czar's liberal ideas and good intentions overlooked Lithuania and Poland. Alexander II had not abolished oppressive laws against Catholics and other non-Russian Orthodox Christians; nor had the government changed its attitude toward these minorities. The vassal nations were unable to make the necessary adjustment.

Thus another revolt broke out in 1863, led by rebels who had survived the Polish-Lithuanian uprising against Nicholas I in 1831. These revolutionaries, fighting against the colonization of their villages and for the preservation of their language and culture, urged the Jews in their midst to participate in their struggle. Although most Jews supported the government forces, Jews were killed on both sides during the fighting. A new pattern had been set: Jewish participation in Gentile affairs was solicited.

During the uprising, Alexander appointed a new governor-general for the area comprising Lithuania and Belorussia: Michael Muraviev. Headquartered in Vilnius and known as the hangman of Lithuania, Muraviev executed many of the insurgents on the gallows in Vilnius's marketplace. The rebellion continued for almost two years; then it slowly died out. Despite its failure, it had given the Jews a one-year period, in 1863, during which they were allowed to purchase land. One year later, both Jews and Poles were forbidden to acquire or settle on Lithuanian soil.

Alexander II continued to introduce reforms. In 1864, the Russian administration was reorganized, with provincial *zemstva*, land councils, established in the *gubernias*. These councils were vested with authority over hospitals, medical services, education, public welfare, roads, and food provision. In essence, they provided the rural communities with local self-rule. In a further reform, carried out the same year, the judicial system was modernized with the introduction of trial by jury, replacing the secret procedures practiced theretofore.

Acknowledging the new climate, Jews finally began to take advantage of the Russian schools that had been opened for them; by 1864, 7,500 Jewish students had enrolled. By 1865, some 100,000 Jews had moved out of the Pale under Alexander's liberalization.

Alexander II did not betray the hopes that he had aroused in the first half of his reign. However, even after the serfs had been freed, most landowners and members of the gentry continued to oppose the changes, fearing for their economy and way of life. For a brief time, Count V. N. Panin, a well-known reactionary and defender of the landowner class, took over the leadership of a commission that phrased various laws connected with the reform. But despite Panin's attempts to circumvent the spirit of the new laws, the serfs were finally free.

Alexander II did not abandon his predecessors' desire to integrate and assimilate the Jews of the Empire into the population at large, but he was prepared to accomplish this on the Jews' own terms and at their pace. For this purpose he organized a new Jewish Commission, composed of businessmen and intellectuals, to suggest ways to effect the integration "insofar as the moral condition of the Jew permits this." The Commission recommended that Jews be admitted to the bar, allowed to hold certain judicial offices, and participate in rural self-rule. The Czar balked. Another request that he resisted had been presented to him by Jewish soldiers who wished, after their 25 years or more of military service, to settle outside the Pale upon discharge. This privilege, Alexander believed, was for educated and advantaged Jews only. Not until 1867, after realizing that part of the Russian press and several high-ranking military officials saw matters the Jews' way, did he relent.

Great changes were taking place throughout the Empire. At the end of the reign of Nicholas I, only seven newspapers and some 20 monthlies, all heavily censored, had been published. In the first years of Alexander II's rule, there were more than 70 newspapers and 158 monthly journals. Hope for true reform was in the air, not only in freedom of expression and human rights but in the amelioration of economic, political and social injustices. A laissez faire philosophy was current, spelling the destruction of the monopolistic bureaucratic patterns of the *ancien regime* and highlighting the need for a new social order. New business opportunities increased the velocity of commerce; the development of new industries caused the middle classes to expand.

The Jews were strongly affected by these changes. Attracted by the new business opportunities and prompted by their own entrepreneurial instincts, many Jews who were not officially permitted to move out of the Pale did so anyway. Theirs was a perilous life, requiring constant bribery of police or other officials (*nachalniki*). Several Jewish capitalists became active in developing and expanding various industries; Jews were prominent in sugar refining, textiles, tobacco, timber, grain exports, and even railroads and shipping. For the first time, there was an outflux of Jews from more developed to less developed regions, where their presence and enterprise were welcome indeed. There was also substantial Jewish migration within the Pale, from backward villages and underdeveloped districts to areas of greater economic potential.

These changes affected neither the persistent anti-Jewish propaganda of the government nor the antisemitic teachings and preachings of the Church, which continued unabashedly to foment antisemitic public opinion.

Even Alexander II himself underwent no profound change. Despite his liberal talk and seemingly enlightened policies, the Czar refused to surrender his unlimited prerogatives as an absolute monarch and uncompromisingly opposed any constitutional limitations on his powers. It was said that Alexander's liberalism ended when the Russian people took his reforms seriously and tried to implement them, however slowly. Whenever it came time to implement the government's declared policies, the bureaucracy responded with intolerable delays, vacillations, and procrastination. Consequently, public opinion became increasingly restive and the revolutionary movements burgeoned.

In 1866, one D. Karakazov, a leader of the *Narodniki*, the Populist Party, attempted to assassinate the Czar. The plot failed, but Alexander became a different man. Frightened and angry, he discarded the liberal image he had tried to create and surrounded himself with conservative, reactionary nationalist advisers whom he believed he could trust. Within a short time, these new counselors prevailed upon the Czar to repudiate his reformist policy and rescind even the few liberalizations that had already been implemented.[93] Policy toward the minorities remained ambivalent. Use of languages other than Russian in official documents, including business correspondence, was proscribed.

The Jewish problem was aggravated by the advent of a Lithuanian-Jewish apostate named Jacob Brafmann, born in 1825 in Kletzk. After embracing Russian Orthodoxy, Brafmann was appointed to teach Hebrew in Minsk at the request of the Holy Synod. Like many previous converts, he had become a venomous antisemite and missed no opportunity to attack and denounce the Jews, their religion, and their institutions. Brafmann, who thus ingratiated himself with the Church, was promoted to the office of censor of Hebrew and Yiddish books in Vilna and St. Petersburg. By this time (c. 1865), he also propagated Christianity among the Jews and continued his attacks on the *Kahals*. World Jewry, he insisted, was a "state within a state" that fomented hostility against Christians and the Russian government and was orchestrating an international conspiracy to gain control of the world. This "secret Jewish government" must be destroyed. In his numerous public assaults on the Jews in various Russian periodicals, Brafmann distorted passages from Talmudic and Responsa literature. Where these did not suffice, he published real or falsified excerpts from *Kahal* records that he had stolen. In 1869, Brafmann unveiled his *Kniga kagala* (*Kahal* book), which purported to be a Russian translation of the Minsk *Kahal* ledger, but was in fact a distorted and perverse misrepresentation of this document. The Government published this book and circulated it among its offices and officials, the better to educate the bureaucrats about, and against, "the enemy within."

Kniga kagala was exploited as an important instrument in fomenting antisemitism in Russia. Jewish community representatives petitioned the Government; distinguished Jewish scholars turned out learned essays. All attempted to refute Brafmann's distortions and falsifications and to discredit him by exposing his ignorance of Jewish sources. All failed. *Kniga kagala*, a thematic forerunner of the 1928 forgery subtitled *The Protocols of the Elders of Zion*, was officially championed and used in much the same fashion that the Nazis utilized the subsequent libel.

By 1873, the government apparently gave up its hopes of inducing Russian Jews to assimilate en masse through education, for that year the government-sponsored rabbinical seminaries in Vilna and Zhitomir were closed, as were the special government high schools established under Nicholas I. However, the regime still thought it necessary to lure youngsters from the *heder* system of education, and opened more than 100 elementary schools and several teachers seminaries.

A more important policy change was made in 1874. One of several statutes enacted that year abolished the principle of community responsibility for individuals' misdeeds. This new policy gave Jews equal status – in this respect – with other subjects of the Empire but, in so doing, abolished many of the responsibilities and social ties that had held Jews together. In some towns, in keeping with this new policy, Jews were allowed to run for municipal office.

This period also saw the beginning of radical change in Jewish economic and social life. Now that the serfs had been liberated, the Jew moved from his traditional middleman role toward participation in the industrialization of the country. Many Jews gravitated to manufacturing, some as plant owners but many more as workers. This, coupled with the very low wages paid in the Pale, elicited the emergence of a large Jewish proletariat. Other Jews found their way to commerce and the liberal professions, where an acculturation process ensued – even though converts to Russian Orthodoxy enjoyed a distinct advantage in advancement and promotion.

Even though the out-migration of Jews from the Pale of Settlement had been large enough to allow new communities to form throughout the Empire, the vast majority of the Russian and Lithuanian Jews still lived in the Pale under appalling conditions. Unemployment was endemic; such work as was available hardly sufficed to provide a subsistence standard of living. Hunger and sickness were prevalent, aggravated by general despair. As many as 12 families shared dwellings of three or four rooms. The average worker took home 15 kopeks per day, a few cents in modern terms. Almost 40 percent of Jewish families in the Pale received welfare assistance of some kind, chiefly from overseas Jewish communities. Four-fifths of the Jewish population of Vilna lived from one day to the next, and Vilna was typical. Jews in the *shtetlakh*, the townlets, fared even worse; their diet was comprised of a few potatoes and seasonal vegetables.

Nevertheless, this period coincided with great cultural advancement and enlightenment for Jews in the Pale. Apart from the elementary schools and religious seminaries mentioned above, girls' schools opened at this time. Furthermore, the *heder* paradigm flourished alongside with the modern system. The Haskalah and Hibat Tsiyon movements thrived; scholars and writers published important books in Hebrew and Yiddish. New newspapers and scholarly journals appeared in both languages as well as Russian.

Concurrent with this was an uninterrupted outpouring of religious and rabbinic literature by outstanding rabbis and scholars, who continued to establish new yeshivot and other centers of learning in Lithuania and throughout the Pale. Jews were also involved in a general Lithuanian cultural reawakening, influenced by Lithuanian publications and newspapers smuggled into the country from eastern Prussia.

One unforeseen effect of this policy was the exposure of the Russian-educated Jewish and Lithuanian intelligentsia to the idea and ideals of Russian radicals such as Herzen and Pissarev. They found the Populist and early Marxist philosophy especially attractive. Although Populism placed its hopes on peasant support, the initial participation of the Jewish intelligentsia in general revolutionary activity was "representative" of the peasant classes. Gradually, however, perhaps because of the pervasive and deeply rooted antisemitism of the Populist movement, Jewish intellectuals turned their attention to the suffering Jewish proletariat. Together they faced the pogroms, countered the blood libels, and contested other false accusations.

In 1875, a small Jewish group in Vilna, collaborating surreptitiously with Russian circles in Moscow and St. Petersburg, attempted to form a Lithuanian-Jewish revolutionary organization. The cell was composed of former yeshiva students, some of them full-fledged Talmudic scholars, and graduates of university and teachers seminaries. In their view, "the revolution" itself would solve the Jewish problem in Russia, as it would the woes of mankind in general. These Jewish revolutionaries served as liaisons between the organized Russian underground revolutionaries and their friends and supporters in the West. They helped smuggle forbidden literature into the Empire and assisted comrades who were hunted by the police.

Alexander II was assassinated by revolutionaries on March 13, 1881. Following this, devastating pogroms broke out in almost 200 communities in the Pale. The Jewish world was shocked. Especially stunned were the Jewish assimilationist circles, whose philosophy had been shown to be an illusion. Few suspected that the government itself had instigated and helped foment the pogroms. The Czar's regime was more frequently accused of having remained passive, doing nothing to crush or prevent the devastation. However, the pattern of the pogroms following the assassination of Alexander II was so similar as to reflect the implementation of a specific model on the basis of detailed instructions. The behavior of the police indicated as much.

They were passive as a rule; insofar as they intervened at all, it was against the Jews, who, if forewarned, sometimes attempted to organize their defense.

Lithuania and Belorussia were spared from serious pogroms for some time, since the Governor-General of Vilna province, Count France Edward Ivanovich Totleben (Todleben), had made it clear that he would not tolerate them. It is now apparent that Totleben's concern for "his" Jews was due less to his humanitarian sentiments than to his fear of epidemics and fires, which might devastate the Vilna and gubernia economy. But to no avail. The pogromists eventually avenged themselves on the Jews and the local government through large-scale arson. By this time, it was clear to all that the pogrom campaign had indeed been organized and directed by the government, which sought in this fashion to distract public opinion from its reactionary policies and the suffering they had caused.

Pogroms continued to erupt from time to time for almost 25 years. Jews were used as scapegoats to mask the government's failures, corruption, and inefficiency. Subsequent evidence leaves no doubt about the organizers' identity: senior army officers and important court officials, most affiliated with the "Sacred League," a far-Right terrorist group, who moved from city to city to direct the atrocities. One of the most notorious leaders of this band was Von Derenteln, Governor of Kiev, mastermind of many pogroms in the Ukraine and an especially efficient agent of government antisemitism.

Alexander III (1881-1894) – The Reactionary Czar

Alexander III, who succeeded his father in 1881, continued to steer the Russian Empire back toward feudalism but with greater efficiency. His reign was characterized by the use of violence as a political instrument. His attitude towards all Russian religious minorities, including Jews, was strongly influenced by the Holy Synod and especially by its Procurator – his former tutor, mentor, and trusted advisor, Konstantin Petrowitz Pobiedonovstzev, whom historian Theodor Mommsen compared to the infamous Torquemada of the Spanish Inquisition.

It was Pobiedonovstzev who cynically prophesied the disposition of Russian Jewry: one-third forced to emigrate, one-third baptized, and the remainder starved to death. The fulfillment of the first part of his prophecy had already begun, for the terrible pogroms of 1881 precipitated a mass emigration of Jews from Russia. The rest of his prediction seemed farther away, but the continuing pogroms suggested that it, too, might be imminent.

Alexander III conceived of himself as divinely chosen to defend the absolute power of the monarchy. However, he promised to adhere to his father's early reforms and was opposed to pogroms. He chose as his Minister of the Interior, Count N. Pavlovitz Ignatiev (1832-1908), a determined, ambitious politician and a strong supporter of the Slavophiles. Ignatiev promised not to tamper with existing municipal policy and pledged to alleviate the peasants' lot. He reduced land prices, abolished the poll tax, and regulated land rents. These minor reforms did little for the peasants and nothing at all for the lower classes, to which most Jews belonged.

Ignatiev used every means to distract the public mind from the general situation. Although the Slavophile government treated all their minorities as second-class citizens, the Jews remained the most convenient scapegoats for the general misery. After all, they had no mother country that could act on their behalf or field their complaints. When some censorship restrictions were waived in 1882, the press lost all inhibitions in vocalizing its attitude toward the Jews, attacking them venomously for their "enslavement of the Russian masses."[94] In addition to copious local antisemitic writings, similar works and pamphlets were imported from other countries, mainly Germany, then translated and distributed throughout the Empire. Newspaper articles and pamphlets on this theme were often recited aloud by agitators to inflame the illiterate masses. Sometimes the agitators, as if not trusting their props, gave the throngs their own written or oral instructions, citing, for example, alleged Imperial ukases that gave the local population only three days in which to savage the Jews.

The many pogroms were a turning point in Russian Jewish history. They brought death, maiming, and suffering on a very large scale and uprooted masses of Jews who suddenly found themselves homeless and with no country of their own to which to turn. After the first spate, the communities proclaimed a fast and special prayer gatherings. For years thereafter, Russian Jews observed the fast on its anniversary in commemoration of the victims and martyrs. Powerful new national and political ideologies were beginning to develop among Russian Jews. Many young, well educated members of the community, notably those from affluent families, joined radical revolutionary movements. Others prepared to flee the country. Interestingly, Spain extended an open invitation to the new Russian Jewish exiles, an offer that few emigrants utilized.

World opinion was disgusted by Russia's behavior. Impressive crowds — comprised mostly of Jews and augmented by non-Jewish liberal elements — turned out in London, Paris, New York, and Washington to protest against the pogroms and persecutions. Reports on the pogroms, smuggled out of Russia, appeared in leading newspapers throughout the world. Diplomats forwarded eyewitness accounts to their governments. The Russian authorities were bombarded with protests against the atrocities. An American immigration commission toured several of the pogrom sites and reported home from Moscow.

The Pale began to disgorge its desperate Jewish inhabitants. Two of the favored destinations were the United States and South Africa, but many settled in England, Germany, the Netherlands, and other European centers. Hundreds of Lithuanian, Polish, and Russian *landsmanshaften*, emigres' societies, sprang up all over the world to help refugees from their former cities or *shtetlakh*.

Interior Minister Ignatiev, speaking for the government, claimed that the pogroms were manifestations of popular indignation against the Jews for their exploitation of the peasants and their financial manipulations. Ignatiev even set up "Committees for Review of the Jewish Question" and commissioned reports and recommendations. To create a facade of evenhandedness, two Jewish members were co-opted onto each committee of this kind, but their oral statements were ignored and their written memoranda neither presented nor discussed. After investigating the Jews' economic activities and discussing the findings at length, the committees advocated even more repressive measures than had been enacted thus far. These, they said, would teach Jews the virtues and values of "loyalty, civility, and citizenship." The Russian press, led by *Novoya Vremya* (New Times), editorially supported these recommendations, reasoning that it was preferable and effective for the government itself to put the Jews in their proper place than to leave this task to the rabble and the pogromists.

For the record, several cabinet ministers expressed their horror that such acts of violence were taking place in Holy Russia. This may be written off to embarrassment; after all, word of the pogroms was circulating abroad and Russia's image in world opinion was plummeting. Ignatiev gave the matter more thorough treatment. Although responsible for internal security, he had turned a blind eye to what was going on during the pogroms. Now he brought criminal charges against more than 5,000 ruffians who had participated in the pogroms. Fewer than 200 were found guilty, and the penalties they received were too mild to serve as a deterrent. Then Ignatiev argued that the true culprits were the terrorist revolutionaries and the Jews themselves: the former for struggling against the government; the latter for their own behavior. When Jewish delegations entreated Alexander III in St. Petersburg to intervene in view of the rampant pogroms, blood libels, and other accusations spreading throughout the Empire, the Czar simply repeated this formulation.

The Jews, Ignatiev elaborated, were at fault because they were greedy innkeepers and merciless moneylenders. However, a joint investigating committee composed of Russians, some of them clergy, and Jews had established that most of the early pogroms had occurred in villages and townlets where there were neither Jewish innkeepers nor moneylenders – only poor, hardworking Jewish families. The committee also proffered conclusive evidence that both the pogrom instigators and the arms they had used had been brought in from outside the affected areas. In the face of all this evidence, Ignatiev maintained that if the Jews were unhappy with their lot, they should leave Russia. The western borders were always open for them, he noted, and many of their coreligionists had chosen this option in the past.

In May 1882, after coordinating the reports of his various committees for revision of Jewish questions, Ignatiev introduced a package of orders that became known as the May Laws, briefly referred to previously. By terming them "provisional," Ignatiev was able to circumvent the State Council, where opposition might arise. To present his legislation to the cabinet, Ignatiev needed only the signature of the Czar, which he obtained without any difficulty. The provisional May Laws remained on the books until the Bolshevik Revolution of 1917.

The May Laws have been described as a perpetual administrative pogrom. First, Jews were no longer allowed to do business on Sundays and Christian holidays, traditionally their most profitable times for trade with the peasants. This restriction had the further benefit of penalizing Orthodox Jews, who closed their businesses on their own Sabbath and religious festivals. To appreciate the impact of this blow, one must bear in mind the extent of poverty in the Pale. Gentiles were hardly better off than Jews in this respect. The burghers had lost their protective Magdeburg Laws in 1878. Life was a struggle for mere existence; semistarvation had become a norm for the majority, both Jew and Gentile. An absurd tithing system was in effect: a reserve of meager resources for bribery of government officials.

Second, Jews were no longer allowed to purchase property, obtain mortgages for farmland, make leasing arrangements on landed estates, or obtain power of attorney to manage or sell such properties or even to extend existing leases. The intent of this provision was to forbid Jewish ownership of land and residence in or dealings with agricultural areas. This and other provisions of the May Laws boosted the incomes of government officials, who, for a fee, would interpret or apply them more leniently than otherwise. One official simply disregarded the new legislation altogether: Ignatiev himself. This Slavophile count, who seemed to have every reason to prefer the services of Russian Orthodox Slavs over those of Jews, always used Jews to arrange the extension of leases on his own family estates – before the enactment of the May Laws and long afterward.

Third, the May Laws limited the Jews' right of domicile within the Pale itself, establishing a veritable Pale within the Pale. Without warning, entire regions, towns, and townlets were renamed and borders redrawn. Marketplaces and hamlets were marked as villages. In all these Jews were now forbidden to reside, although their families had lived there for generations. Thus, unless they were willing and able to tender huge bribes, as very few were, they were evicted from their homes.

In 1882, in response to bitter infighting among his ministers and the continuing protests from abroad against government policies, the Czar replaced Ignatiev with Count Dimitry Tolstoy, another reactionary who retained the May Laws and introduced additional anti-Jewish legislation. Despite official censorship, isolated reports made their way into the foreign press, leading to further outcries against the Czar and his government.

In 1883, a new Commission on the Jewish Question was established. Chaired by Count Phalen, a former minister of justice, it invested five years in its deliberations, meaning that no liberalization could be forthcoming for that time. As for further strictures, an old law passed in 1858 but never implemented, prohibiting residence of Jews within 35 miles of the German and Austrian borders, was suddenly enforced in 1884. The purpose was to stanch the spread of German Jewish influence in Russian-controlled territories. Accordingly, several Lithuanian Jewish communities within that radius were evicted. From this time on, permits allowing Jews to reside or work outside the Pale were very difficult to obtain. The residence privileges previously given to Jewish ex-soldiers (apart from "cantonists"), professionals, and trained artisans were wiped out overnight. Some 220,000 individuals were affected.

The policy of encouraging Jews to acquire an education and enter the liberal professions was reversed that year. The famous Rabbiner Seminar in Zhitomir was closed on the pretext that it was training its students in trades or professions with which they would exploit the Russian population. Jewish enrollment elsewhere, as previously noted, was subjected to quotas. Relatively wealthy Jews sent their offspring to Germany, Switzerland, France, or Italy for their higher education. In 1887, Russia withdrew its recognition of diplomas earned abroad.

When the Phalen Commission concluded its deliberations in 1888, it found that there were some 650 laws specifically affecting the rights and restricting the freedom of Russian Jews. A majority of Commission members considered these laws unjust and recommended a new policy that would gradually grant Jews economic freedom. The government favored the views of the reactionary minority. Briefly stated, the Phalen Commission did nothing to alleviate the plight of the Jews in the Empire. Expulsions continued and were brutally enforced, at short notice and without compassion. By 1891, when another two-year spate of serious pogroms erupted, approximately one million Russian and vassal Jews had emigrated.

A missing element in the turmoil came into play at this time: the hitherto apathetic masses in the Empire were aroused by the great famine of 1891. The new Marxist movement turned to the masses of industrial workers and the peasants for support. The farm crisis worsened in view of heavy taxation, falling grain prices, and a decline in the value of the ruble. When the Treasury came under pressure, the new Minister of Finance, Count Sergey Yulyevich Witte increased customs and excise duties and awarded the government a monopoly on the sale of liquor, a popular commodity in Russia then as now. This automatically excluded Jews from a trade in which they had traditionally been prominent.

Although this new measure deprived many Jews of their livelihood, the community leadership was quietly pleased: the reform deprived the antisemites of one of their favorite pretexts for agitation and, in due course, showed it to be a blatant falsehood. Antisemitic propaganda in Russia had long portrayed the Jew as a greedy innkeeper, constantly encouraging impoverished peasants to drink and, in this fashion, exacerbating the general social malaise. Russians drank as heavily under the new, Jew-free government monopoly as they had before.

Still, Alexander III and his ministers continued to blame "the Jews" and "the revolutionaries" for peasant laziness and middle-class greed. They were blind to their own responsibility for the general corruption and mismanagement of the Empire's affairs; nor could they appreciate the aroused feelings of the people.

The 1890s marked a general renascence of assertive nationalism in Europe. Minorities everywhere were caught up in the fever; none more so than the Lithuanian minority in Russia. All elements of Lithuanian society were involved, including the peasantry. In the Lithuanian case, unlike that of Russia and Poland, there was no temptation to exploit traditional antisemitism for political advantage. On the contrary, the Lithuanian leadership invited the Jewish population of the country to participate in the struggle for an independent Lithuania, with the promise of full citizenship once freedom was achieved.

Alexander III died in 1894 in Livadia at the age of 50, a frightened man who saw revolutionaries under every bed and enveloped himself in police protection. He was succeeded by his eldest son, Nicholas II, a reprobate under whom the Romanoff dynasty would come to a bloody end.

Nicholas II (1894-1917) – The Last Czar

Nicholas II, son of Alexander III, inherited a politically divided people and found himself in the midst of a tragic and complicated situation. As the Czar, he commanded a measure of personal respect and served as the axis around which the machinery of government aimlessly revolved. His was a vast but exceedingly backward empire that controlled its population by means of a large, oppressive police apparatus. After decades of internal and external pressure for reform, nothing had budged.

Many historians have noted the strong Jewish representation among the leaders and members of Russian revolutionary movements. Antisemites, displaying their pathological hatred of the Jews, have claimed that Jewish radicals relentlessly, almost demonically, sought to resolve all the world's problems in permanent fashion by means of constant revolution, disregarding the general desire among Russians to revamp their own social and political order. Jews in the Empire struggled desperately to integrate into Russian society, but their efforts failed to diminish the forces of antisemitism or alleviate its pernicious effects.

The Jewish revolutionaries who had only recently emerged from the Pale and who were attracted to socialism and its messianic belief in a better world were in a quandary. The existing circumstances could no longer be endured. The traditional Jewish world was beginning to collapse; the historic Jewish leadership, comprised of the wealthy and the religious scholars, could not cope with the new exigencies and knew of no way to maintain or shield the fabric of Jewish life. With these terms of reference, the Jewish revolutionaries and socialists regarded themselves as the vanguard of the Jewish people, which would lead the masses and teach them a new way of life. Most of these young idealists refused at first to comprehend that the struggle for the Jewish right to an independent national existence was incompatible with the concept of a comprehensive revolution meant to solve all problems, including the Jewish problem, as the international revolutionary socialist movements prescribed.

The contradictions quickly rose to the surface. In fact, very few of the millions of Jews in Russia were attracted to the international radical movements; even fewer became involved. This tiny minority denied the very existence of a specific Jewish problem and actually rejected the possibility that a distinct Jewish entity and way of life were worthy of being sustained. Most of the Jewish revolutionary leadership, by contrast, synthesized its own theories and solutions to the Jewish problem by combining socialism and national existence in various degrees of importance. They created or joined diverse political parties and attempted to translate their theories into a political program, each group professing to represent the Jewish people.

After the 1917 revolution, the radical ideologues purged their political programs of their Jewish component and sought to integrate into the international Communist movement and general society. One such ideologue, Isaac Deutscher, termed these people "non-Jewish Jews." The new Communist order, however, would have none of it. Once a Jew, always a Jew, a stranger, and a usurper.

Still, many young assimilated, Russified Jews – mostly students, no few of whom came from well-to-do families – were accepted by the *narodniki*, the various factions of Populists. Their goal was to "descend" to the people, and the people in this case were not their own Jewish poor but the *muzhiks*, the

Russian peasants. Although born Jewish, they took no interest in Jewish life or in mitigating the agonies of Jews in Russia. The peasantry was another matter. Eagerly they sought to encounter the peasant commune, the *obschinamir*, which they idealized as a simple, uncorrupted collective on which future democratic Russian society would be patterned. They were inspired by their vision of the "beauty of the life of the Russian peasantry," which they previously met only in Russian literature.

The Jewish *narodniki* who joined the idealistic, utopian revolutionary movements dreamed of a Paradise on earth, where there would no longer exist national differences or ethnic prejudices, where all Russian citizens, in unity, would enjoy liberty and freedom. Their sympathy was totally with the oppressed poor and the *muzhiks*, for whom they, together with the other *narodniki*, were prepared to risk their personal liberty and perhaps their lives. Divorced from political reality and ignorant of human nature, their like clung to the populist ideal until the 1890s.

When they finally met the peasants in their villages, most of them were cruelly disappointed. They beheld the peasants as most of them really were: a brutish, crude, boorish, superstitious lot, influenced by an obscurantist, reactionary clergy. Theirs was a social class in which individuals brimmed with hatred and bitterness toward each other, their feudal lords, and all strangers, especially if they were not Russian Orthodox. Their priests had taught them to hate Catholics because of the authoritarian hierarchy in Rome, Protestants for their individualism, and above all Jews, who had "killed Christ." They believed in the blood curse, the New Testament explanation of Jewish suffering, which they invoked to excuse and justify pogroms and shedding of Jewish blood.

If the Lord was their Father, so was the Czar. They accepted their sufferings in this world as being just punishment for their sins. So the Church taught; so it must be. They participated happily in pogroms and persecution of all aliens: Jews, Poles, Finns, non-Christians, non-Orthodox. Anyone of non-Russian descent, including those not born in their own vicinity in Central Russia, was suspect. Their officials regularly apprised them of the laudability of their actions in the eyes of the press and government propaganda. Such intermediation was needed because most of the peasants were illiterate.

Imagine, then, the reception these xenophobic peasants gave the purveyors of a new godless gospel of salvation.

The Jewish revolutionaries were not only shocked by the ferocity of the pogroms that followed the assassination of the Czar and two government ministers in 1881,[95] but by the reactions and, perhaps equally, the interpretations given to the atrocities by their non-Jewish party colleagues. The *Narodnaya-Volya* bulletin of 1882 described the pogroms as a rehearsal for a future general peasant rebellion: "Today the Jew, tomorrow the Czar and the *kulaks* (landowners)." The lesson was learned: the ostensibly phlegmatic Russian masses could, with proper leadership, be spurred to rebellion. The revolutionaries would henceforth attempt to direct the peasants' anger and resentment to the true oppressors: the government, which sanctioned the exploitation of the workers, the peasants (who formed a majority of the population), and, above all, the Czar.

This troubled the Jewish revolutionaries (and some of their non-Jewish colleagues) gravely. The lessons of the French Revolution and other upheavals had taught them that bloodshed during a rebellion was often unavoidable. Nevertheless, they were dismayed by the extent of the pogroms, the rape and brutal slaughter of innocents, and the focus on one particular group, their own.

While some of them continued to believe in the power of the general revolution to solve the Jewish problems, including equality of the Jew before the law, others were so disturbed that they felt the need to join existing Jewish Socialist groups or establish their own. This was especially true of revolutionaries who had once attended Jewish schools, yeshivot, or the rabbinical seminaries in Vilna and Zhitomir.

It was during such stirrings in Russian Jewish life that Nicholas II took the throne. He was neither fit nor suited for this function, and he knew it. Initially reluctant to accept the responsibility, he resolved, upon accepting it, to discharge it to the fullest. *Samoderzhetsvo*, the principle of absolute, God-given autocratic power, including the right of succession, was at stake.

In 1894, Nicholas II married Alix of Hesse, thereafter known as Alexandra Feodorovna. They had four daughters and one son, Alexander. When the latter proved to be a hemophiliac, the Czar's family, and especially the Czarina, consulted innumerable doctors and specialists, many of questionable repute, and surrounded themselves with "holy men" of various kinds. The most famous of them was Grigory Rasputin, whose influence on the entire royal family can only be described as a spell. Under his tutelage, the Czarina became a religious fanatic and mystic, wholly divorced from reality.

Hers were not the only delusions in the Empire. For a short time after the succession of Nicholas II, hope flickered among some liberals, radicals, and even Jews, that his would prove to be a more enlightened reign than that of his father. Their hopes were dashed when, at his coronation, Nicholas II proclaimed that people's participation in government was a "senseless dream." On the contrary, he vowed to do everything he could to defend his Divine autocratic rights, as his father had.

This caused two differentiated groups to form a secret alliance in order to oppose Nicholas II and contest his policies. One was the liberal-kadets, a party of Constitutional Democrats that included some Jewish members; and the radicals, a faction of social revolutionaries that had broken away from the Social Democrats, with a membership including Jews and non-Jewish proletarians and peasants, such as the Trudoviki and Zemtsvo. Their tactics included agrarian strikes and protests, terror, and the assassination of despotic officials. Their campaign made its debut in St. Petersburg in 1896, when more than 30,000 workers struck for economic changes. Agrarian riots and terrorism continued; cabinet ministers Bogolepov and Sipiyaghin were assassinated. To suppress the violence and crush the revolutionaries, the Czar chose Vyacheslav von Plehve, a leading reactionary and an enthusiastic disciple of the antisemite Pobiedonovstzev, as his Minister of the Interior.

Plehve adopted a systematic anti-Jewish policy, promising to stanch the uprising "in the blood of the *zhidi*" (the Russian pejorative for Jews). Pogroms erupted throughout the Empire and ritual-murder trials were held in two Lithuanian cities, Vilna and Luknik.

Loyal officials fell victim to the anti-Jewish madness. During the eviction of Jews from the villages, Count Totleben, Governor-General of the Vilnius gubernia, had allowed some Jewish refugees to settle not only in several of the least crowded suburbs of Vilna but also, in clear contradiction to the Czar's ukase, in several villages just outside the city. Vilna had been engulfed in an epidemic, Totleben explained to the cabinet. When apprised of Totleben's action, Nicholas II reprimanded the Governor in writing. *Zhidi*, he ruled, must not be allowed to settle in villages outside Vilna, epidemic or not. A *ukase* had to be obeyed at all cost. In this missive, as in all of his speeches and writings, Nicholas II referred to the Jews only by the pejorative *zhidi*, never as *yevrey*.

The Czar and his government attempted to justify the Jewish persecutions and anti-Jewish laws. Jewish revolutionaries were at fault for the pogroms, they maintained, since they had provoked the anger of the Russian people. The press went one step farther, implicating the entire Jewish community for having instigated and influenced the uprising.

What was happening, of course, was the beginning of civil war in Russia. The Czar and his government were able to sweep most of this under the rug, disregarding the calamitous situation of the population. Nevertheless, the revolutionary movement expanded rapidly, not only in numbers but in the intensity of public involvement. For the first time, there were stirrings even within the Orthodox Church, i.e., several processions in which icons were displayed and prayers offered in an attempt to call attention to the country's problems.

Minority and national groups across the Empire had begun to assert themselves, organize, and demand their rights. Lithuania was no exception. In 1900, attempting to reach new adherents and alleviate economic distress, a Lithuanian revolutionary group formed the first consumer cooperative in the country. It proved to be a great success. The 1905 revolution magnified the need for co-ops of this kind, and their numbers in Lithuania alone grew to 120 by 1910, and 162 by 1915.

Anti-government groups in Lithuania, Poland, and the Ukraine were largely unimpressed and unaffected by the attempts of the government-controlled press to turn the Jews into scapegoats for all the Empire's evils. Most ordinary people, however, including some of the intelligentsia, firmly believed what they read in the government's numerous publications, and these writings speedily assumed the dimensions of an antisemitic crusade. The widespread unrest exacerbated existing racial antagonisms. Of course, there were Jews who participated in the general struggle for liberty and human rights; others sided with the revolutionaries in the class struggle as proponents of the dictatorship of the proletariat. Many such Jews were imprisoned, exiled, or hanged for their activity; others emigrated. But the government, for its own purposes, greatly overstated the Jews' role in these movements, thereby fueling the flames of the Jewish problem.

On April 6-7, 1903, a particularly savage pogrom rocked Kishinev, capital of Bessarabia. Forty-nine Jews were brutally massacred and another 495 were wounded, eight of whom died in the hospital. Seven hundred homes and 600 businesses and shops were looted and destroyed. Over 2,000 families were left homeless. The action was precipitated by agitation on many levels. A blood libel had been circulated during the two days of Easter that year. The pogrom was inspired and fomented by a vicious antisemitic campaign conducted by a fanatic journalist, Pavolaki Krushevan. Krushevan's series of articles on "The Jews' Program for World Conquest," which he published a short time later in the St. Petersburg newspaper *Znamya*, formed the nucleus of the *Protocols of the Elders of Zion*. Ranking Bessarabian officials, including the deputy governor and the local police chief – apparently backed by Plehve – had helped prepare the riots, which took place in full view of the police and the city's military garrison, neither of which intervened.

The civilized world was shocked. News of the pogrom elicited widespread public outcries; protest rallies were held in Paris, London, and New York. Jewish communities worldwide presented Von Plehve with a united appeal to end the persecutions. Petitions poured in – from the Vilna headquarters of the Zionist Central Committee, from individual influential Jews. Efforts were made to enlist the support of Russian Christians and foreign dignitaries. Plehve responded with increased repression and a further crackdown on Zionist political activity. Theodor Herzl rushed to St. Petersburg to plead with the Interior Minister on behalf of the Jews and the Zionist movement. Plehve informed him that the Russian Government supported the work of the Zionist movement insofar as it advocated the mass emigration of Jews from the Empire. However, it would neither permit nor tolerate Zionist nationalist propaganda, for this might incite other minorities within the Empire.

Plehve's policies were not unanimously endorsed by the Cabinet. Count Witte, the Minister of Finance, opposed them because they encumbered Russian efforts to obtain loans on the international capital market. Thus he objected to the persecution of the Jews, arguing that the anti-Jewish laws were responsible for active Jewish participation in Russian revolutionary movements, rather than the other way around. In view of this heresy, Nicholas II dismissed Witte later that year.

On July 15, 1904, several months after the Russian Fleet was defeated at Port Arthur in the early stages of the Russo-Japanese War – for which 30,000 Jews had been recruited – Plehve was assassinated when a revolutionary hurled a bomb at his carriage.[96] Nicholas named Prince Svyatopolsk-Mirsky to succeed him. Svyatopolsk-Mirsky, known for his liberal views, was chosen in an attempt to placate the people and win over part of the intelligentsia. Mirsky granted the Lithuanians the right to publish in their own language and use the Latin alphabet, two matters that had been denied them theretofore.

In May 1905, with Mirsky's permission, 40 leaders of Jewish communities met in Vilna to form the Union for the Attainment of Complete Emancipation of the Jews of Russia. At this meeting, a 22-member executive committee was elected and a headquarters in St. Petersburg was chosen. One of the committee members, representing Vilna, was Dr. Shmaryahu Levin, subsequently famous as a Zionist leader, orator, and writer. The Union undertook to fight the League of True Russians in the cities and the infamous Black Hundreds in the provinces. This was a formidable task: the two organizations were fanatical groups that deserved much of the blame for the terrible pogroms of October 1905, in which 730 Jewish communities were plundered and many Jews killed, wounded, or raped. One of the chief instigators of the pogroms was the infamous monk Fiodor Iliodor, a fanatic antisemite and spokesman for the Black Hundreds, who openly advocated the extermination of the Jews. In 1912, Iliodor publicly repented and repudiated his own teachings, expressing regret for the murder and suffering he had helped inflict.

Professor Julius Brutzkus, future Minister for Jewish Affairs in the independent Republic of Lithuania (appointed in 1921), compiled a report on Jewish life in the Pale in 1903-1904 for the Jewish Colonization Association (ICA), founded in 1890 by Baron Maurice de Hirsh to provide potential emigrants with places of settlement in North and South America. Brutzkus' report included the following observations:

> The Jews of the Gubernias of Vilna, Grodno, and Kovno influence all Jewish life in Lithuania and Belorussia. They are in the forefront of the struggle for equal rights and the extension of permitted areas of settlement, presently limited by the Government. They are the spearhead in the battle for Jewish equality as citizens as well as for recognition of the Jewish contribution to the Russian army. They are particularly active in contravening the pressures on Jews by the Russian Orthodox Church to convert. During the past ten years, only one conversion has been cited in Kovno.

After a lengthy period of silence, prominent Russian litterateurs such as Maxim Gorky and Leo Tolstoy came out in defense of the Jews. The Jews were not at fault for the economic crisis in Russia, they asserted; the entire Russian population was a victim of the corrupt bureaucratic regime. They denounced the influence of antisemitic literature and its "state within a state" argument, a treacherous libel that it never tired of repeating. The Emancipation Union placed advertisements in the Russian press to thank the authors for their statements, expressing hope that many more would display similar courage and that all honest Christians would join them in defending Jews against the many false accusations that they faced.

With the appointment of Prince Mirsky, the public again hoped that the Czar might be about to try a more liberal policy. Nicholas II shattered these hopes by refusing to make concessions on a demand for a representative assembly.[97] The Revolution of 1905 was at hand.

It began on January 9, 1905, with a march of thousands of proletarians led by Father Georgy Gapon, holding icons high and singing religious hymns on their way to "their Czar," with whom they demanded an audience. The military opened fire on the defenseless crowd, leaving more than 1,000 dead. In retaliation, revolutionaries set off a charge in the Kremlin that killed Grand Duke Sergius, a relative and favorite of the Czar. Mirsky resigned and was replaced by a ministry bureaucrat. Strikes, agrarian uprisings, and interminable political struggles, meetings, and conferences followed, culminating with an Empire-wide general strike in October of that year.

Nicholas II contemplated abdication but was saved by Count Witte, who had in the meantime concluded a peace treaty with the Japanese. Witte was recalled and appointed Prime Minister. The Czar signed a manifesto, prepared by Witte, which promised human rights and freedom of thought, speech, and association but retained the Czar's title of autocrat. A series of violent demonstrations organized by reactionary elements ensued, followed by a further wave of pogroms. This time the police and army openly supported the rioters and protected them against the Jewish self-defense groups. There was an armed uprising in Moscow but the rebels were dispersed. By the end of the year, the revolutionary movement and its leadership had been ruthlessly and cruelly crushed.

In Lithuania, too, there had been renewed stirrings of hope for liberation from the Czar's autocratic rule. Lithuanian deputies representing all political views and social groups had united to demand autonomy for their homeland. As part of their campaign, they urged their compatriots to stage a tax strike and opposed the induction of Lithuanians into the Russian Army. Freze, the acting Governor, moved to placate the vassals by promising democratization on the village level. In December 1905, before the revolution in Russia had been put down and before its reactionary aftermath ensued, the Grand Diet of Vilna asked the Czar and his government to grant Lithuania autonomy within the Russian Empire. The dictator responded with two limited concessions: a compromise on the language issue and the appointment of several Lithuanian officials.

For Russian and Lithuanian Jewry, the revolution of 1905 catalyzed the growth of political self-consciousness and national self-awareness. In spite of their social and political differences, and even more so their divergent attitudes toward a solution for the Jewish problems, all Jewish groups collaborated to present a united list for the elections of the First Duma (Assembly), which met in April 1906. Twelve Jews were elected. For the first time, a majority of Jews voted not for a Social-Democrat radical nor for a Zionist nor for a Bundist, but for a candidate who ran for election as a Jew: Naftali Fridman of Kovno, who represented Jewish rights as citizens. Russian and Lithuanian Jews were finally emerging from the ghetto and learning to defend themselves, voice their collective opinion, and give their representatives a mandate to demand rights rather than to beg for privileges.

Despite their efforts, the Jewish delegates were unable to attract the Czar's attention and prevail upon the Duma to denounce the pogroms. Anti-Jewish violence continued throughout Russia, engulfing more than 300 cities. The elections to the First Duma had been comparatively unrestricted and had given Constitutional Democratic Party (Kadets) and the Peasants (Trudoviki) a majority; these forces demanded radical agrarian reform, not succor for the Jews. However, the powers of the Duma had been curtailed, even before it first convened, by the passing of important new legislation (by Ivan Goremykin, the Minister of Finance) that maintained the prerogatives of the Czar. The political struggle within the Duma between the Government and the delegates continued relentlessly, until in July, barely three months after the inaugural session, the government dissolved the Duma on the pretext that one of the latter's declarations during the debate on agrarian reform had been an illegal appeal to the country. In response, some 200 delegates moved to Finland to protest and organize passive resistance in case the government refused to convene a new Duma.

The fate of the First Duma had been sealed even before it met, for Count Witte resigned after the Duma elections had given his political opponents a majority. By obtaining a loan from France shortly before his resignation, he had left the Czar free to do as he pleased. In the meantime, Pobiedonovstzev had resigned and was succeeded by another absolutist and Slavophile, Prince Sergei Uvarov.

Before his death in 1915, Witte published three volumes of memoirs that have much of interest to say on the history of the Jews in Russia. In these memoirs, Witte characterized the Black Hundreds as murderous gangs responsible for the killing and raping of innumerable Jews. These thugs, he asserted, were the true, secret love of the Czar and the Czarina, who considered them exemplary Russian patriots. The Czar, he wrote, glorified them as the "pride of the nation." The Okhrana (the Czar's own secret police), by contrast, knew the Black Hundreds to be ordinary thieves, hooligans, and murderers, all with police records, the kind of people with whom "decent Russians do not shake hands." Their prime objective was to harass and persecute aliens: Jews, Poles, Finns, and others. They were proud and happy only when they were able to show proof of having "killed or mutilated a few peaceful *zhidi*." Witte described the period as one of continuous, widespread persecution of Jews; the agitators themselves, he said, did not know what they expected to achieve by their conduct. Never before, according to Witte, had the Jewish question in Russia been dealt with in such a cruel way; and never before had Jews been subjected to such abuse. As for political attitudes toward these practices and events, Witte added that "One who is not a Jew-hater cannot achieve a reputation as a true conservative."

The Second Duma did in fact convene in February, 1907. Despite government pressure and coercion, it proved to be more radical than the First; the ultrasocialist groups nearly formed a majority. The Lithuanian Jewish delegates cooperated closely with the Lithuanian national faction, led by Antanas Smetona and Antanas Tumenas, and again petitioned for the abolition of the Pale – to no avail. The government, again alarmed, sought a pretext to dissolve the new assembly and found one when the chamber vacillated about denouncing revolutionary terrorism. The Second Duma lasted four months.

To ensure a more quiescent Third Duma, the government gazetted a law diminishing the minorities' representation and increasing that of the gentry. It also applied brutal pressure during the elections. Thus the Third Duma convened in November 1907, and served until June 1912. The Fourth Duma was in session between November 1912, and March 1917. In neither assembly could the Czar's government silence or suppress the opposition parties. However, with the assent of the Duma, Prime Minister Pavel A. Stolypin succeeded in taking further measures against the Jews and the Ukrainian national movement. In 1911, having lost his credit with the Duma and his usefulness to the Czar, Stolypin was assassinated. As for the identity of his killer, evidence pointing to a revolutionary was produced. Rumors at the time ascribed the killing to a police plot.

Throughout this period, the entire Russian system rested on widespread, unbridled corruption and bribery. Officials of all kinds, high and low – police, judges, bureaucrats – were on the take, and Jews were vulnerable prey. Antisemitism pervaded every aspect of life and all walks of society. The Czar, although consumed by his obsessive hatred of Jews and, indeed, all the Empire's minorities, nevertheless found time to demonstrate his contempt for the simple, poverty-stricken Russian masses as well.

A glimpse into the day-to-day life of Lithuanian Jews, who formed an integral part of the Pale, is provided by Julius Brutzkus' contemporary reports. In 1911, he wrote, two-thirds of the Jewish population of Lithuania earned their living by serving as "hewers of wood and carriers of water" (a Biblical phrase denoting unskilled workers and menial service providers), coachmen, brickmakers, and other servile capacities. Poverty was endemic, sanitary conditions extremely primitive. More than one third of the Jews depended on charity; money forwarded by relatives provided some with their sole income.[98]

When World War I broke out in 1914, most parties in the Fourth Duma formed a patriotic union. All other issues, including the struggle against the Government and the system, were forgotten for a while. Although unhappy about and profoundly enraged by the lack of change, the population was disciplined and obedient. The government might have taken the opportunity to moderate its repression and brutality, but did not.

Under the leadership of Prince Georg E. Luvov, head of the Union of Zemstva Party, the last Duma was progressive, rather than radical, in its approach. As such, the assembly proposed to the Czar that he form a national unity government to deal with the reforms that were so desperately needed at a time of war and emergency. The Czar, oblivious to the seriousness of the situation, took the advice of Ivan Goremykin, the Minister of the Interior: no national unity government, no reforms. The denouement began. The army, convinced that only a change of regime would make victory possible, sided with the Duma. Goremykin was forced to resign. His successor, B. Strumer, was an ignorant, comic figure who served only to highlight the weakness of the whole system. With the Czar as commander-in-chief stationed at army headquarters and thus absent from the capital, it was the Czarina, surrounded by a clique of sycophantic advisers and her trusted confessor Rasputin, who virtually ruled the Empire. Ministers were shuffled and reshuffled; the government always at loggerheads with the Duma. Everyone who could command the Czar's attention – friends, royal cousins abroad, even foreign diplomats – warned him that he would have to make concessions and introduce reforms in order to prevent a revolution. Nicholas II did not budge. Even the assassination of Rasputin did not affect the Czarina's obduracy.

Disorder broke out in Petrograd, as St. Petersburg was newly named, during a session of the Duma. The meetings adjourned for good on February 26, 1917. The Russian Revolution, which was to change the face of the world and affect the lives of millions of Jews within the Empire, broke out the following day.

There were indeed two revolutions, marking two very different phases in the history of Russia and of mankind: that of February 1917, which resulted in the overthrow of the Czar and the House of Romanov and that of October of that year, which was fought in the name of Marxism and international revolution. The former, in which the Bolsheviks took no part, eventually led to the formation of a provisional government under Alexander Kerensky, which survived until the outbreak of the Bolshevik Revolution. It was the very liberalism of the provisional regime that enabled Vladimir Lenin and Leon Trotsky to prepare for the second revolution.

Jewish community life roared into action after the February upheaval. *Kehillot* in the Pale and throughout Russia held elections. A Jewish congress convened in Petrograd; a Zionist candidate list earned a plurality. Many young Jews expressed a desire to emigrate to Palestine – to make *'aliya* to Eretz Israel. The Bolshevik Revolution in October nipped the renascence in the bud. As unrest, riots, and civil war swept the country, Jews suffered enormously. Pogrom followed pogrom and murderous gangs roamed the countryside, especially in the Ukraine, killing Jews en masse. As the Red and White armies clashed across Russia, the Jews were caught up in the middle; the Whites were especially abusive.

Lenin's closest circle included a small number of Jewish revolutionaries, of whom Leon Trotsky is the best known. Although born Jewish, Trotsky took no interest in Jewish affairs and had nothing in common with other Jews. The philosophy of this group addressed itself to the universal good as against that of the individual, and to international problems and solutions as opposed to national concerns. These men were untroubled by, indeed oblivious to, the pogroms and the existence of antisemitism within their own camp. Nevertheless, they were generally identified as Jews, especially by the opponents of Marxism. Russian Jewry and other communities paid dearly, at this time and later on, for the prominence of their non-Jewish Jews.

As for Czar Nicholas II, his reign and his three-century dynasty came to an end in March 1917. Upon his overthrow, he requested permission to depart for Great Britain. Instead, he and his family were arrested. On the pretext that he and his family were about to escape from their place of confinement at Yekaterinburg to Omsk, where a White Army admiral had established a counterrevolutionary government, "citizen and citizeness Romanov" and their family were executed without trial on the night of July 16, 1918.

Chapter 5

THE GREAT WAR AND AFTER: JEWISH NATIONAL AUTONOMY IN REBORN LITHUANIA

Ethnic Interrelations in a Heterogeneous Society

Germany's declaration of war on Russia (August 1, 1914) led to total mobilization throughout the Empire. Lithuanian and Russian Jewry rallied to the flag; more than half a million Jews served in the Czar's armed forces.

The main frontier between the Russian and German armies crossed Lithuania close to the German border. Russian military authorities, suspecting that Lithuanian sympathies lay with their German enemies, took a harsh, hostile attitude toward the local population in general and Lithuanian Jews in particular. Russia's eastern front stretched through the Pale of Settlement, the small area (barely four percent of the Empire's territory) in which more than 90 percent of the subject Jewish population was concentrated. The Jews of Lithuania, many of whom had sons in the Russian Army, tried to be as neutral as possible. Despite their feelings toward Russia, they offered the German forces no assistance.

The Lithuanian economy was predominantly agrarian; almost 80 percent of the inhabitants eked out their existence by living off the land. Although Russia had abolished serfdom in 1861, the socioeconomic paradigm in Lithuania remained largely feudalistic. A serf class was still identifiable; a landed gentry mainly composed of Poles continued to dominate the serfs and the peasants on its vast estates.

Within this deeply stratified society, the Jewish population comprised the middle class, as it had for centuries. The agrarian ratio was reversed in their case: nearly all Lithuanian Jews resided in towns and villages (*shtetlakh*). Jews comprised half of the total urban population of historic Lithuania and the entire populace of some villages. More than 80 percent were small merchants, artisans, and laborers; about six percent owned a small number of large businesses or found employment in the liberal professions.

In all, historic Lithuania had roughly 15 million inhabitants of diverse ethnic origin, composed as follows:

Origin	Population	Percent of Total
Lithuanians	4,500,000	30
White Russians	4,500,000	30
Jews	2,500,000	15
Poles	1,500,000	10
Miscellaneous*	2,250,000	15

* Russians, Germans, Ukrainians, Letts, Tartars, and others.

After World War I, a new Lithuania was fashioned, comprised of the counties of Kaunas, Vilnius and Suwalki. This entity may be termed "Ethnic Lithuania." In its area of 21,419 square miles, a heterogeneous population of 2,167,000 lived side by side in separate but relatively harmonious ethnic communities, as follows.

Ethnic Group	Pct. of Total Population
Lithuanians	67.2
White Russians	12.9
Jews	8.9[99]
Poles	6.5
Miscellaneous	4.5

The diverse ethnic groups worked vigorously to maintain their distinctive cultural identities, religions, and customs. So strong was their ethnic identity that all previous attempts at Polonization and Russification had failed; from the Late Middle Ages until the early twentieth century, the heritage and traditions of each culture succeeded in flourishing from generation to generation.

Friction among these groups was a function of time and circumstances. For example, although the exclusively Catholic Lithuanian population was prone to intolerance of the Orthodox Belorussians, the prewar tension did not affect relations between these groups, since their material interests did not conflict and both had suffered equal political oppression under the Czarist regime. With the Poles, by contrast, acute and overt antagonism was clearly in evidence, due largely to Poland's historic efforts to impose its own culture on the population at large. Lithuanian and Belorussian peasants who toiled on Polish estates resented their "masters" deeply; tribunals[100] were inundated by complaints lodged by peasants against alleged injustices by Polish overlords. This distrust, hatred, and suspicion was definitely exacerbated by the advent of war.

Surprisingly, Poles and Jews interrelated more cordially in Lithuania than in Galicia or Poland itself, because both were minority groups who needed each other's support. Even so, the Jews did not trust the Poles entirely and were not quick to fraternize with them. They were always aware of the massive influence of the Polish Church and press on local Poles. Jews knew that the Poles' political affinity gravitated so strongly to the mother country as to have created a "Little Poland" in Lithuania.

Thus, generally speaking, Jews, Lithuanians, and Belorussian peasants were on reasonably amicable terms in the Grand Duchy. Their intellectual classes made cooperative efforts and had compatible viewpoints, and their political solidarity was reconfirmed in all elections for the Russian Duma.

Stirrings of Lithuanian National Identity – The Jewish Connection

The modern Lithuanian national identity emerged in an evolutionary process, its power base resting with the middle classes and educational fraternities that had been developing since the late nineteenth century in response to Russian attempts to restructure society by abolishing serfdom.

A new element entered the political scene with the formation of Marxist groups. These Lithuanians – young, intellectual, and politically conscious – sought to assert their social and cultural independence from their Polish and

Russian overlords. Thus, in 1917, a "Patriotic Center" was formed in the university town of Vilna. The Center was politically sympathetic to Russia, and it expected Russia to show its gratitude by granting Lithuania national and cultural autonomy. Russian Premier Ivan Goremykin did not respond on behalf of his government; these Lithuanian dreams were dashed against a wall of official Russian indifference.

In the buildup to the Great War, the Lithuanian nationalists, anticipating an Allied victory, looked to the West – especially the United States – for assistance and support. Their Lithuanian-American brethren provided them with great financial and moral encouragement. The worldwide political tension, however, denied them the fertile ground they needed to nurture their nationalistic ambitions, and further development was temporarily thwarted by the realities of impending war.

The eruption of World War I found Lithuania on the front line. From the very outset, the country was dealt two serious economic blows: industrial plants were relocated to the Russian interior, depriving Lithuanian laborers of their means of livelihood; and financial assistance from Lithuanian emigres dwindled, bringing disaster to thousands of families that depended largely on this income.

The Russian military authorities, aping their civilian counterparts in St. Petersburg, treated the Lithuanian population with hostility and the Jews with particular venom. This is clearly illustrated in proclamations and press releases in semi-official publications such as *Novoya-Vremja*, *Groza*, and *Ruskoe Slowo*, to name only three. An article in *Groza* on August 12, 1914, contains the following policy recommendation:

> The Jews should be sent to places that may fall into enemy
> hands. When our army retakes these places, the Jews may then
> be expelled as foreigners.

A military bulletin issued by Corps Commander Fedotov contained a libelous retelling of events that maligned the Jewish population as an aggregate of traitors that was assisting the German forces. This calumny was subsequently reprinted in the official government newspaper *Pravitelstveny Viestnik* and then forwarded to the Petrograd Telegraphic Agency for wider dissemination.

Several members of the high military command belonged to the antisemitic League of True Russians; others sympathized with the Black Hundreds, the perpetrators of vicious antisemitic propaganda and pogroms.

Collectively speaking, the Jews responded to these recurrent antisemitic outbursts by proclaiming their patriotic allegiance to Russia. Community leaders in Vilna, for example, described theirs as the oldest community in Russia and the largest near the front; they urged fellow Jews to discharge their civic duties and provide the "beloved Russian Government" with all possible assistance. The Russian Jewish press fully supported the government's aims despite its anti-Jewish policies. Indeed, many Jews made the supreme sacrifice, although their numbers cannot be cited with precision. Acts of valor by Jews were rarely reported; when reported, the military authorities did not disclose the heroes' Jewish identity.

The Russian officials who sat in judgment of these manifestations of Jewish solidarity were Prince Nicolai Nicolayewitz, uncle of the Czar, and General Yanuskewitz of the High Military Command. Proclamations aside, they regarded the Jews as traitors by definition. Accordingly, as the fighting began in August 1914, officials unveiled a campaign to propagate anti-Jewish suspicion, hatred, and hostility among the Russian populace. Overt antisemitism became an official government policy guideline; legal restrictions on Jews were toughened. The ever-present threat of pogroms and persecutions, backed by the press and given popular support, posed a very tangible threat to Jewish existence in Lithuania.[101]

The defeat of General Paul Renenkamf's troops in May 1915, precipitated a string of reversals on the eastern front. The armed forces' honor and morale were at stake; a scapegoat had to be found. The Russian government and the army openly accused Jews of betraying the army by aiding the Germans. Their Yiddish dialect was said to be the treacherous medium of communication between the invading forces and the Jewish fifth column. Espionage trials were held; although evidence of culpability was not forthcoming, convictions were obtained. Those found guilty were dispatched to prisons in the Russian interior.

The Kuzhi Incident: The Expulsion of Lithuanian Jewry

The next step was the expulsion of the Jewish population of Lithuania. It was not long in coming, but a pretext had to be found. A minor incident on April 28, 1915, in the village of Kuzhi, near Siauliai – where no more than six Jewish families lived – gave the Russian army the excuse it needed.

When the German army captured the village, eight soldiers visited several Jewish homes in search of food and other provisions; having acquired what they sought, they left immediately. When Piatigorski's 131st Battalion recaptured the village two days later, the Jews warned the Russian troops of the proximity of the German forces. That very night, the Germans shelled and torched the village. The Russian military authorities then accused the Jewish villagers of having given the German forces information that they had used to destroy Kuzhi.

The incident attracted such infamous publicity that it was debated by the Fourth Duma in May 1915, and a commission under Alexander Kerensky was appointed to conduct an on-the-scene inquiry. The Kerensky commission found the story, as related by the military authorities, to be a total fabrication. For the Jews of Lithuania, however, the damage in local public opinion was irreparable. The articles on the subject had achieved their desired effect: incitement of the people and propagation of blind hatred against Jews.[102]

Several relatively liberal and progressive Russian newspapers (*Retch, Russkaya Vedomost, Bourse Gazette, Novosti*, etc.) treated these accusations very cautiously, insisting on further investigation and research before publication of such damning conclusions. Several journalists protested the government-sponsored libel. The most vehement comments of these types appeared in the writings of Boris Smoliar:

> According to the strictly confidential document N-6 dated January 4, 1915, the High Command ordered Jewish soldiers on the front lines to be positioned in the most forward positions and, at times of retreat in the rear, always in the first line of fire.[103]

On May 8, 1915, Deputy N. M. Fridman of Kaunas, read a declaration in the Duma which contained the following passage:

> As Jews, we have been and still are suffering extreme hardships due to our inferior legal status. Nevertheless, we have always thought of ourselves as Russian citizens, and have indeed remained loyal to our country at all times.

Despite this rhetoric, the process of expelling Lithuania's 200,000 Jews was sent into motion.

The first document prescribing the mass expulsion of Jews from 40 locations in Plotzky County was signed by General Pioter J. Ruzky on January 25, 1915. Orders to expel Jews from Courland County came through on April 24 and 28.[104] Similar instructions for Kaunas, Gardinas, and Suwalki counties followed in May.

The negativism and mistrust on the part of the Russian military toward Jews and other ethnic groups, while widespread, was not absolute. Examples of consideration for minorities are evident. Commanders displayed a more humane attitude in several large towns, such as Siauliai, where Jews formed a quarter of the population, and Panevezys, where more than one-third of the inhabitants were Jewish. Several commanders threatened the local population with punishment under military law for inciting hatred against Jews or harming them in any way.

The expulsions continued anyway. Even foreign protests failed to halt them. Jewish families were moved at random; almost half a million Jews were refugees by the end of 1915. Some of them (and some Lithuanian nationalists as well) sought haven in the deep interior of Russia – the counties of Bochmat, Mayopol, Yekaterinoslav, Poltava, and elsewhere. Those who decided to remain were mistreated by German occupation forces near the Polish border. Roving Polish bands assaulted Jews in Vilnius and Suwalk.

The horrors of war took their full toll on the Lithuanian people – Christians and Jews alike. Uprooted by advancing troops, refugees were continually on the move. Unemployment, destitution, hunger, and disease were the stark new realities. Military requisitions and looting of villages and towns became the norm. Control of several districts of Lithuania, especially in the vicinity of Vilna, changed hands nine times. The battle-scarred landscape was witness to minor pogroms and the use of forced labor.

Relief efforts were made. A Lithuanian Welfare Committee was set up under Martynas Ycas, a Lithuanian delegate to the Duma, to distribute financial aid. A corresponding Jewish organization came into being under the Russian acronym Yekopo (*Yevreisky Komitet Pomoschtzi*). Together the two groups attempted to ease the burdens of war for thousands of Lithuanian families.

Quite a few towns and townlets were simply overlooked by the Russians' mad dragnet. Jews in these localities kept their institutions intact, although they often approached the American Jewish Joint Distribution Committee for help. For example, Marijampole asked for financial assistance in order to establish a clinic, an old-age home, and refugee accommodations, and, most importantly, to pay the salary of a Hebrew teacher. The American relief funds were forwarded to their destinations in Lithuania through Zionist relief offices in The Hague.

The Jews of Lithuania and Russia had no reason to support the corrupt government of the Czar and became increasingly doubtful of their future in the Empire. As time passed, growing numbers of Jews evaded conscription orders and deserted their units. This fueled the antisemitic flames and made the community's position even more precarious. But the greatest tragedy of Lithuanian-Russian Jewry, indeed of Jews throughout Europe, was to find themselves pitted against other Jews on the battlefield. They found it exceedingly distressing to risk and inflict death, especially when their coreligionists were involved, in the service of a distant, hated authority that denied them equal rights, failed to protect them in the never-ending cycles of pogroms, and preferred to see them emigrate.

In the German Orbit: Hope Flickers

After 120 years of repressive Russian rule, Jews and other minorities in Lithuania responded to the German occupation of their country with a measure of optimism.

Indeed, Lithuania had a pro-German streak. Many Lithuanians who had been educated in Germany or Switzerland, and some anti-Russian nationalists such as Bishop Matthew Valancius, had long felt close affinity to the German nation. Their response to Russian press restrictions had been to smuggle manuscripts over the border for printing in Eastern Prussia. They had maintained regular contact and liaison with influential German delegates to the Reichstag such as Mathias Erzberger, who encouraged them in their national aspirations and promised them help and support.

Haskalah-minded Lithuanian Jews, educated in Enlightenment Germany, looked to Prussia for cultural inspiration and were aided by contraband publications that found their way across the border. The German intellectual outlook permeated the philosophical tenets of the Zionist and Jewish-Socialist movements that gathered considerable momentum before the war and during the German occupation.

As the war raged, Lithuanian Gentiles and Jews alike harbored the hope and expectation that the Germans' arrival would alleviate suffering and reestablish an appreciation of human rights and equality for all minorities. These beliefs were reinforced by the supreme commander of the Kaiser's forces, Paul von Hindenburg; his Chief of Staff, General Erich Ludendorff, and other commanders of the German Eastern Army of Occupation. The Jews were greatly encouraged by an expression that Ludendorff had used in one of his manifestos: "*Meine Liebe Juden!* (My dear Jews!): We have come to change your lives!"

It was in September 1915, that Germany completed its occupation of the whole of Ethnic Lithuania (Kaunas, Vilnius, and Suwalk counties). The occupation forces established a complex military administration with the Ober-Ost Verwaltung as its center of power. This special office, headed by Maj. Von Gossler and Lt. Col. Duke Franz-Joseph Isenburg-Birstein, with Maj. Gen. Herman Hofmann functioning as Chief-of-Staff to the Commander-in-Chief of the Eastern Front, was responsible for incorporating each newly conquered piece of Lithuanian territory into a single administrative unit entitled the Land Ober Ost. As the Germans tightened their grip on Lithuania, the purpose of this elaborate mechanism became apparent: annexation.

Many Jewish officers and men served in the occupation force. All of them, including the Orthodox, were great patriots who firmly believed in the superiority of their German culture and tradition. With very few exceptions, this was their first encounter with their eastern coreligionists (*Ostjuden*). They felt little if any kinship for these people; they regarded their Lithuanian brethren as objects to be reeducated and taught to imitate the manners of civilized Germans.

The occupation force put Jews to work as intermediaries and advisers. Thus Herman Struck, the famous artist, served as a liaison officer to the local Jewish population and later headed the Jewish Department of the German army. Educationist and writer Leo Deutschlander was placed in charge of Jewish education in Lithuania as an appointee of the German occupation regime. In December 1915, by request of the German military authorities and with their support, Deutschlander, together with Dr. Joseph Carlebach, subsequently Chief Rabbi of Hamburg, founded the Yavneh Gymnasium in Kovno, a religious high school in the Orthodox Frankfurt style. Yavneh opened with no more than 50 students; by 1918 it had developed into a complex comprising two separate-but-equal schools for boys and girls, with a combined enrollment exceeding 250. Although many classroom hours were reserved for Jewish studies, the language of instruction was German. After Lithuania attained independence, several of these German-Jewish educators stayed on and had much influence on the development of the Jewish education system in Lithuania.

The result was a hybrid system. The modern Hebrew and Yiddish schools were linear successors of the *heder* and yeshiva, although these, too, survived in their original form. Along with the German-Jewish influence, Jewish refugees from Russia (Lithuanian Jews returning home and Russian Jews fleeing the Revolution) brought their influence to bear on the development of modern education, especially in the fields of instruction and writing. As time passed, all the Jewish political parties and the Jewish press did their share in the building of this model system. Although these Jewish schools were not formally affiliated with the Jewish autonomous system that emerged in postwar Lithuania (discussed at great length below), leading personalities such as Drs. Menachem (Max) Soloveitzik and Simon Rosenbaum supported them and furthered their refinement and development.

Disillusionment: The Plight and Resurgence of Lithuanian Jewry

Disarray under a Harsh Occupation

Lithuanian Jewry began to prepare for the kind of autonomy it had known under the Va'ad Lita in the sixteenth century. A Jewish committee was formed in Vilna under Dr. Jacob Wygodski, with the participation of Dr. Zemach Shabad, Mendl Lithauer and Joseph Izbicki, for the purpose of organizing and representing Jews who dwelled in German-controlled territory. However, the committee was overwhelmed by the problems the community faced – food, health, housing – and the Germans soon dissolved it in favor of a military and civil administration of their own. Official notices, once published only in German, Polish, and Lithuanian, now began appearing in Yiddish as well.

The occupation forces quickly demonstrated that their sole preoccupation was the advancement of German interests at the expense of the local population. Practices such as requisitioning to meet the occupation forces' needs, conscription of labor, and, whenever possible, forced export of goods to Germany, became standard operating procedure.

Economic conditions worsened. In 1916, the Germans allowed some Lithuanians to emigrate and ordered others to leave the cities and resettle in townlets and villages, where food was more plentiful. Industry and trade were virtually paralyzed. Growing numbers of Jews and Christians alike depended on charity; the *Jewish Chronicle* of February 23, 1917, reported that some 57,000 people had registered with charitable societies in Vilna alone.

Hundreds of Lithuanians and Jews were deported as laborers to the coal mines of the Ruhr region and Upper Silesia; others were forcibly employed on the docks at Tilsit and Memel. Standard remuneration for a day's work was 30 pfenning (a few American cents);[105] conditions were atrocious. A Reichstag committee for the East upbraided the Chancellor for permitting what amounted to slave labor.[106]

In Lithuania itself, the Germans conducted three censuses within a period of several months in 1916-1917, in order to ensure a regular supply of labor. Local work conditions were abominable. Hundreds of people toiling in frost and snow, many without proper clothing or even boots, fell ill and died. An eyewitness expressed incomprehension at the extent of poverty and suffering experienced by the people of Vilna and estimated that 50-60 people starved to death each day. Typhoid epidemics swept the city in 1916 and 1917; several cases of cholera were discovered. Medical care was almost nonexistent and living accommodations were primitive.

Protests surfaced as the plight of the Lithuanians verged on the unendurable. In many instances, Jews joined other ethnic groups to voice their opposition to the Germans' forced-labor decrees. After the Jewish Central Committee witnessed the brutal treatment of 5,000 forced recruits in mid-1916, Dr. Wygodski and R. Isaac Rubinstein, together with Poles, Lithuanians, and Belorussians, lodged a strong protest with the authorities and advised the population to ignore these and subsequent work orders. The dissidents also threatened to expose the gross unfairness of the work decrees before the neutral countries. The Germans were not dissuaded. When one of their subsequent labor summonses was ignored, they marshalled the brigades with a show of force. Dr. Wygodski spent more than a year in a German prison camp for his good efforts.

There was one avenue of escape from the dismal fate of forced labor: ransom, for those who could afford it. A payment of 600 marks sufficed to place a Lithuanian Jew (or Gentile) in one of the categories exempt from forced labor: clergy, Talmudic students, physicians, pharmacists, and teachers.[107] Overseas relief arrived in 1916, some from Lithuanian-Americans and some from the Joint and Jewish organizations in Western Europe. According to the *Jewish Chronicle*, American groups provided Yekopo with the equivalent of 100,000 marks in those difficult times. For the beleaguered populace, it was all a drop in an ocean of misery.

Cultural and Organizational Recovery

Even under the arduous German occupation, Lithuanian Jewry in wartime continued to pursue its traditional goals of erudition, culture, and charity.

New Hebrew- and Yiddish-speaking schools were opened; the religious elementary schools, *Talmud Torah* and *heder*, continued to function in Vilna and other large towns. Evening classes for adults were offered in various locations. Libraries had not been shut down; they played a central role in promoting appreciation of the arts. Students and workers alike were encouraged to form discussion societies. Concerts were held, as were Yiddish and European plays.

Charitable associations went about their efforts, not only furthering their own causes but helping maintain community cohesion. One of several especially active organizations at the time was the nonpolitical Help Through Work Society, which specialized in care of and assistance for children.

Political consciousness, always an important aspect of Jewish collective existence, reached new heights during this period of adversity. The impact of diverse political organizations – Zionist, Socialist, the Bund, and the ultraorthodox Agudath Israel – during the three-and-a-half years of German administration was an augury of things to come in the subsequent period of Lithuanian independence.

Two significant historic events that occurred at precisely this time greatly exacerbated the legendary rivalry among Jewish political groups: the Bolshevik Revolution of October 1917; and the Balfour Declaration in November of that year. Each became a focal point for ongoing polemics and internecine bickering, and conflicting views were expressed in the only Yiddish newspaper that the Germans permitted for publication, *Di Letste Nayes* (The Latest News). Despite the strict censorship, each group managed to present the Jewish public with its platform. This accomplished, they relied on parlor meetings, study groups, and group discussions to continue politicizing the Jewish community.

Denouement and Implications of the German Occupation

Notwithstanding its flagrant abuses, the German occupation of Lithuania brought certain indirect benefits. In their three-and-a-half years of rule, the Germans improved the prewar judicial and educational systems and attempted to improve communications and the public health system. They had found the economy in a shambles, since the Russians had dismantled and hauled away entire factories. In order to meet their own needs, the German authorities helped revitalize the economy as long as the war continued, an act from which the entire country profited.

By the end of the war (November 1918), Lithuania had been wholly integrated into the German economic orbit, its economic ties to Mother Russia severed after 120 years. From 1916 to 1918, the German Office for the Jews in the East, headed by Herman Struck and R. Dr. Wilhelm Lewy, campaigned for Jewish rights and equality under German law. In September 1917, the Central Committee of German Zionists urged the German authorities to support Jewish claims for national and cultural autonomy in Lithuania, including Jewish participation in the government of the new state.

After lengthy, intricate negotiations, a Lithuanian National Conference was held in Vilna on September 12-18, 1917, attended by 214 regional delegates from all parts of the country. A 20-member provisional council, the Taryba, was established as the temporary governing body; it elected Antanas Smetona, the head of the nationalist Tautininkai Party, as president.

Germany did not support Lithuanian national aims without setting its price; the military government preconditioned its recognition of the Taryba on the formation of an "external union" with Germany. Other proposals by the occupation regime were somewhat more benign; one was that representatives of three minority groups – Jews, Poles, and Belorussians – be invited to join the Taryba.

Lithuania's political status and the legitimacy of the Taryba became urgent questions that provoked worldwide debate. Two gambits connected with Lithuanian independence were attempted in Russia. On May 27, 1917, a provisional Lithuanian Parliament (alternately termed the Diet and the Seimas) convened in Petrograd, attended by some 336 delegates who digressed from their more immediate concerns, e.g., the spreading Russian Revolution, to call for an independent Lithuanian state. The assembly was sponsored by the Kerensky government in an attempt to bring affiliates within the Russian orbit; the delegates were pro-Russian. Some time after the war, a Conference of Lithuanian Jews was held in Petrograd, on the initiative of a deputy to the Duma named Fridman. The participants in this gathering resolved to elect four Jews (headed by Fridman) to the Lithuanian Council in Petrograd, each representing various Jewish political parties including Zionists and Socialists.[108]

In Germany, Mattias Erzberger, a Reichstag delegate and later Foreign Minister of the Zentrum Party, undertook to promote the Lithuanian struggle for self-determination in late 1917 by wresting a declaration of independence from the German government. On October 12-17, 1917, German Zionist leader Dr. Arthur Hantke visited Vilna to discuss Jewish demands for representation in the forthcoming elections to the Taryba. On his return to Germany, he presented the government with a Zionist petition asking the Germany military authorities to allow Lithuanian Jewry to convene a community-wide conference in which one-sixth of the seats in the Taryba would be apportioned among Lithuanian Jewish community leaders.

On February 16, 1918, as political debate over external recognition and legitimation of the Taryba continued, the Lithuanian people took the decision into their own hands by declaring independence. At the end of March, Kaiser Wilhelm II recognized independent Lithuania, with the proviso that the new entity must sign an "everlasting alliance" with Germany and help finance the cost of the war. A constitutional monarchy was envisaged at first. The crown of Lithuania was offered to Wilhelm von Urach, the Catholic Duke of Wurrtemberg, and the name King Mindaugas II was chosen. The offer was later withdrawn; the decision regarding the future form of government was referred to the constituent assembly, which favored a parliamentary republican structure.

On November 11, 1918, the Taryba instructed Professor Augustinas Voldemaras, one of its members, to form the first provisional Lithuanian government. In December 1918, a Zionist conference in Vilna nominated three delegates to the new cabinet. These were Dr. Jacob Wygodski, a Zionist who became Minister for Jewish Affairs; Dr. Simon Rosenbaum, a Zionist who was appointed Deputy Minister for Foreign Affairs; and Dr. Nachman Rachmilewitz of Agudath Israel, who was named Deputy Minister for Trade and Industry.

At this stage, Voldemaras noted the military vulnerability of the new republic and took immediate action to form a Lithuanian army. In view of the war-induced turmoil in the region and the neighbors' unsatisfied territorial demands, Voldemaras' precautions, taken none too soon, were too late. On April 20, 1919, Polish forces marched into Vilna, creating upheaval and panic among Jews and Lithuanians alike. Soon the entire country was engulfed in tumult.

As internal and external forces battled for Lithuania, the Jews' attitude was strictly harmonized with the views of their Christian neighbors. Two powers now claimed sovereignty over the country: Soviet Russia and Poland. Refusing to accept the rule of either, the Jews of Lithuania formed a united front with Gentile countrymen who favored an independent Lithuanian nation. They were active participants in the birth of the new state.

The provisional government welcomed Jewish support, believing that Jewish participation in the struggle for independence would bolster goodwill and assistance from abroad. Indeed, in response to a request by Lithuanian Jews, German Jewish leaders were instrumental in helping the fledgling state obtain a much needed loan of one hundred million marks from a Berlin bank.

In December 1918, members of the Taryba decided to establish a stronger, more representative provisional government. The person they instructed to form it was Attorney Mycolas Slezevicius, the leader of one of the largest political parties, the Laudininkai (Populists). The result was a wall-to-wall coalition including the Christian Democrats, the Populists, the Social Democrats, the Nationalists, and the minority parties.[109]

In its first Bulletin, the Slezevicius government announced that the Taryba had declared its readiness to recognize the Jews as the most important minority in Lithuania and to grant them equality, full political rights, and cultural autonomy.[110] With this, the Jews, already represented in the machinery of state, prepared to participate more actively in its workings.[111]

Vilna, however, was lost. As Polish legionnaires continued to pour into the ancient capital, which was still occupied by German forces, the government decided to evacuate Vilna on January 1, 1919. When two ministers, Dr. Wygodski and Antanas Janulaitis, refused to abandon the city, the government fell apart. The Germans pulled out on January 4, 1919, and the path to Polish domination was clear. The government designated Kaunas the provisional capital of the Lithuanian state.

Twelve days later, an eight-day Conference of State began in Kaunas, during which eight new members and 160 deputies were elected to the Taryba. A decision was taken that elections for the next Constituent Assembly would be based on equal, direct, secret, and proportional elections. Dr. Max Soloveitzik, head of the Jewish faction in the Kaunas Municipality, was chosen by a provisional Jewish Council to represent the Jews as Minister without Portfolio for Jewish Affairs. This precipitated a breach in the prevailing harmony. The pronounced trend toward minority representation came under fire from the Christian-Democrats and the Nationalists, who attacked Premier M. Slezevicius for his liberal civil-rights policy and his promises to the minorities.

In the meantime, the Independent Republic of Lithuania acted to cement its viability. By July 1919, it had strengthened its armed forces to the extent that no one of consequence continued to challenge its legitimacy.[112] Seeking to terminate the country's reliance on Germany, the Cabinet sought economic assistance from the Allies. M. Slezevicius, in one of his first speeches to the Taryba, made this clear: "For the future of our country, we must depend especially on England and America, and not on Germany." This was true not only financially but also politically, for the government was seeking a favorable resolution of the territorial dispute.

Accordingly, a large number of Lithuanian officials found themselves abroad in the early months of 1919, representing their country. Dr. S. Rosenbaum and Dominik Semashko, a Belorussian, were sent to the Paris Peace Conference as members of a mission headed by Voldemaras. The participation of a Jew and a Belorussian reinforced the belief, shared by world opinion, that the government truly represented all the constituent peoples of Lithuania.

At the Conference, the delegation worked hard to obtain recognition of Lithuanian independence within territorial boundaries defined by the Lithuanians themselves. The two minority representatives attempted to marshal support for these general Lithuanian demands, especially with regard to the status of Vilna, and the unwavering support of the Lithuanian Jews and the Belorussians was a constant motif in the ensuing negotiations. The minority delegates also repeatedly protested what they described as Polish violations of Jewish and Belorussian national rights in Vilna. Toward this end, Dr. Rosenbaum enlisted the help of the Comite des Delegations Juives (Committee of Jewish Delegations) aupres de la Conference de la Paix and American Jewish organizations.

At home, the promised general election was held on February 16, 1919, and the Taryba elected Antanas Smetona President of Lithuania by unanimous vote on April 4, 1919. Within a few weeks, the Lithuanian government had attained the most stable position it had known to that time. Thanks to the joint efforts of the delegation in Paris and of Lithuanian nationals abroad, coupled with reports from the Allied missions in Kaunas, the Lithuanian national identity, with its minority components, was becoming firmly established throughout the world.

The Jealous Soviet Neighbor

Although the Bolsheviks had settled their war with Germany, revolutionary battles within the Czar's Empire continued without respite. The Bolsheviks had an agenda, to which they were doggedly committed: spread their revolution throughout the Empire, establish their rule, consolidate their power, and only then pacify the country. Conditions in Russia were desperate.

In pursuit of the first of these objectives, Bolshevik forces crossed the Lithuanian border on December 2, 1918, captured Panevezys, and engaged the newly organized Lithuanian army in battle. The Lithuanian command, composed of officers who had served in the Czarist ranks, seethed with hatred of Jews, Poles, and Bolsheviks, in roughly that order. To defeat the Reds, they incited the population against the Jews.

A month later, in January 1919, the Red Army invaded Lithuania in force. Advancing through Vilna, it soon occupied the whole of eastern Lithuania and then captured Siauliai and Telz en route to Kaunas and Alytus. In July, the freshly minted government and administration of Lithuania left Vilna. With the help of remnants of the German army, the Lithuanians succeeded in halting the Reds near Kaunas.

Taking advantage of the ensuing chaos, Lithuanian troops attacked Jews and looted their homes in Panevezys. The commander of the local Lithuanian battalion then offered the Jewish community protection in return for a 3,000-ruble tribute. The government attempted to prevent and stop the atrocities and the extortion, but was powerless. The government was presented with a petition for damages on behalf of the victims, to no effect.

The Bolsheviks reoccupied the Vilna area in December, and might have stayed for the duration had it not been for the turmoil in Russia. The Red forces were rushed home in February 1920, where their intervention was urgently required. Soviet Russia and Lithuania began peace negotiations in

Moscow on May 9, 1920, and concluded a peace treaty on July 12. The treaty granted Lithuania sovereignty over Vilna, Grodno, and their gubernias. The Soviet Union renounced all claims to Lithuanian territory and recognized the independence of the new Republic. Both states undertook not to allow foreign armies to establish bases, or foreign political organizations to operate, within their sovereign territories. As for reparations, Lithuania was absolved of all responsibility for outstanding debts from Czarist times, and Russia promised to make a "contribution" toward the construction of the new Lithuanian state.

Provisions were made for the exchange of prisoners and internees, and Lithuanians in Russia were given the right to choose between Lithuanian and Soviet citizenship. Many Lithuanian Gentiles, Lithuanian Jews, and Russian Jews took advantage of this clause to opt for Lithuanian citizenship. Many of them had actually chosen to emigrate to America, South Africa, or Palestine; for them, Lithuania was merely the first port of call. Others decided to stay in Lithuania.

Jews were highly visible in the formation of this treaty: Simon Rosenbaum, as a leading member of the Lithuanian negotiators, and Maxim Litvinov and subsequently Adolf Yoffe, representing Russia.

The Soviets kept their word.[113] In late August 1920, the Red Army withdrew from Vilna and its outlying districts; the Lithuanian Army once again assumed control of Vilna. The Soviet government, politically isolated, was pleased to pacify one of its borders in a neighborly fashion and to begin developing commercial and cultural relations with Lithuania.

The treaty was also good for the Jews of Lithuania. It more than doubled their numbers and brought large new communities from Belorussia and parts of Poland into the envelope of Jewish national autonomy. Rosenbaum aptly commented: "We have always wanted [Lithuania to be] a country of nations rather than a national country."

The Struggle for the Capital that Never Was: Vilna

Vilnius had always been prominent in the history of the Lithuanians, the Poles, and the Jews. For 200 years, the city had been one of the country's revolving "Jewish capitals" in that the Lithuanian Jewish Council held some of its meetings there.

The various Jewish Charters and privileges throughout the years had aroused the bitter hostility of the Catholic hierarchy, whose anti-Jewish attacks and incitement had made strong inroads in the consciousness of the Polish minority in Vilna. The resulting hatred and bigotry affected relations between Jews and Poles for generations to come.[114] Ironically, it was during the period of Czarist rule, despite the many restrictions and much suffering, that the renown of Vilna among Jewry reached its peak. It became so important a center of Jewish cultural, political, and intellectual activity that it was renowned throughout the Jewish world as the "Jerusalem of Lithuania."

When the Great War erupted in 1914, the Jews of Vilna suffered greatly at the hands of their Russian masters, who, angered and aggravated by their losses and calamities, subjected their Jewish vassals to a vicious crackdown even in terms of the time. Mere existence entailed a desperate struggle. Nevertheless, local Jews helped care for the Russian wounded in both their hospitals and their homes. With the expulsion of Jews from the western provinces of Lithuania, refugees thronged the city and its neighboring townlets; the local community always found ways to house and support them.

The city began to change hands like a faded but nevertheless desirable piece of clothing. The Germans evacuated Vilna in November 1918, turning the historical Lithuanian capital into the center of a bitter territorial contest between Poland and newly reconstituted Lithuania. Rejecting every diplomatic intervention, Poland occupied Vilna in April 1919, and attempted to move further into the country from there. In the city itself, Polish forces treated the Jewish population to spree after spree of random looting, killing, and pogroms. Important as it was to harass the Jews, Poland had other objectives in Lithuania. Its agents armed members of the Polish minority and incited them to overthrow the country's newly established National Council; its armed forces clashed with the Red Army. In June 1920, the Poles were forced to retreat from the Russian front with great losses. Vilna found itself again in the hands of the Russians, who now, for reasons of their own, encouraged the Lithuanians to retake the city and its environs. On October 7, 1920, upon the insistence of the League of Nations, the Poles and Lithuanians signed the Suwalk Treaty, under which Lithuania recovered its historic capital.

After the pogroms they had suffered under the Poles and their mistreatment by the Polish army, the Jews of Vilna regarded this turn of events as a deliverance. In the name of 60,000 Jews, a delegation headed by Dr. Jacob Wygodski met with the Jewish National Council and a representative of the Lithuanian government, Ignas Yoninas, and pledged their willingness to help build the old-new state. The Jews of Suwalki, too, aligned themselves with pro-Lithuanian groups, quite unlike the hostile local Poles and the ambivalent Belorussians.

The ink on the Suwalk Treaty was given two days to dry. On October 9, General Lucien Zeligowski and two Polish rebel divisions marched into Vilnius. The Polish government pleaded ignorance, even though the entire operation had been directed from Warsaw. The Poles named the newly occupied territory "Litwa Srodkowa" (Middle Lithuania).

In view of their declared allegiance, the Jews, Lithuanians, and Belorussians in Vilna expected protection and pressured the Allied missions to provide it. The Lithuanian government, hoping that an alliance with the Jews and Belorussians would create a pro-Lithuanian majority in Vilna, mobilized their army. Jewish units, invited by the National Council to volunteer for military service, joined the national troops. The Council also campaigned to raise money for defense purposes.

On October 13, 1920, the *Times* of London reported the arrival in London of a special delegation chosen by the Lithuanian National Assembly, composed of Dr. M. Soloveitzik, the Minister for Jewish Affairs; Rev. Justin Staugaitis, Vice President of the National Assembly; and Prof. Vincas Chepinskis, a former Lithuanian envoy to Great Britain. The delegation met with the British Home Secretary and the Union of the League of Nations. Their program was to continue to Paris and Rome, where they would ask the Vatican for help, and to other European capitals, where diplomatic and financial support of Lithuanian opposition to the abrogation of the Treaty would be sought.

Members of parliament, recognizing the significance of Jewish support, petitioned Lithuanian and world Jewry with letters in which they repeatedly emphasized the legal rights of the autonomy regime and its future constitutional legitimacy. Lithuanian officials abroad made much of their government's favorable policy toward Jews, as defined in the Paris Declaration, in hopes of tapping international aid.

The Vilna problem, however, continued to fester. For the fledgling state, it was an intolerable burden that threatened relations with more powerful neighbors. For 18 months the Jews of Vilna, together with other minorities and the Lithuanian population of the city, fought a losing battle with Poland, endangering their lives in defense of their homeland.

General Lucien Zeligowski's occupation of Vilnius on October 8, 1920, brought the issue before the International Court of Justice in The Hague. Vilna remained the capital of Lithuania in name only; Kaunas was again designated the provisional seat of government. The Lithuanians, for their part, insisted that the Jews of Vilna continue struggling for the unification of the city with the new Republic.

Poland pressed ahead. In January 1922, its regime held an election to establish a Sejm for the Vilna District. All three non-Polish groups in the district – Jews, Lithuanians, Belorussians – boycotted the poll. The League of Nations appointed a special mission under Colonel Chardigny of France to mediate the dispute. In his report on these elections, Chardigny asserted that the Jewish Lithuanians and most of the Belorussian minority had refused to vote because of their conviction that the elections would be manipulated to misrepresent the population's will. Be this as it may, the newly elected Vilna Sejm took office and concluded a union with Poland, which the Polish Parliament ratified in April, 1922.

The loss of the capital was a severe blow to the Lithuanians, one with which they never came to terms. The now-tiny country was powerless against its much larger and stronger neighbor, and it protested in the only way it could. Lithuania severed all diplomatic and other relations with Poland, and until 1938, when the Soviets returned Vilna to the Lithuanians, the two countries had no official contacts whatsoever. Jewish families were split and unable to visit or even correspond with each other, since postal agreements had been cancelled. A letter from Kovno to Vilna, for example, had to be routed through a third country. Rail and other transport connections between Lithuania and Poland, of course, were out of the question.

Poland responded by treating the Lithuanians of Vilna as second-class citizens. Lithuanian educational and cultural activities were severely restricted, their books and newspapers banned. The Jews in Vilna suffered doubly, both as Jews and as Lithuanians, and pogroms and violence were their regular lot, as they were throughout Poland. For the Lithuanians, the dispute over Vilna fueled an all-consuming hatred of Poland and their own sizable Polish minority, even though both peoples shared the Catholic faith. However, Lithuania did not mistreat its Polish citizens for fear of retaliation by its stronger neighbor.

Lithuania never admitted defeat on the question of Vilna and made numerous international diplomatic appeals to seek its return. Thus in 1927, immediately following the *coup d'etat* that brought Voldemaras to power, the new Lithuanian premier met in Geneva at the League of Nations Council with Marshal Pilsudski, President of Poland, in an attempt to reopen the issue. In response, Poland threatened to go to war over Vilna; Lithuania was forced to yield and, for lack of choice, maintained a disgruntled silence for more than a decade. On March 17, 1938, Poland presented the Lithuanian government with a 48-hour ultimatum demanding irrevocable recognition of Polish sovereignty in the Vilna region, normalization of diplomatic relations between the two countries, and full autonomy in Lithuania for the Polish minority. To reinforce its ultimatum, Poland massed troops on its border. The home front was convulsed with anti-Lithuanian demonstrations, accompanied by attacks and riots against Jews, demanding the occupation of Lithuania in its entirety and the reconstitution of the historic Commonwealth.

Smetona panicked, the Lithuanian Cabinet resigned, and martial law was proclaimed. Unwilling and unable to go to war, the Lithuanian government signed an agreement on March 30, 1938, restoring diplomatic relations with Poland. However, a new constitution that Lithuania adopted less than two months later named Vilna the capital. Thus both Poland and Lithuania included Vilna – variously termed Vilna, Vilnius, and Wilno – in maps representing their respective territories.[115]

Jewish Autonomy in Lithuania, 1919-1926

Minority Rights: A Phenomenon of the Time

Perhaps one of the most favorable outcomes of the Great War was the growing international commitment to protection of the civil rights of ethnic minorities throughout the world. Reflecting the beliefs of Renan, Taine, and Otto Bauer, as well as declarations made during the 1878 Congress of Berlin, international guarantees for equality, cultural integrity, and the legitimacy of minority self-rule or autonomy were now recognized as integral ingredients of lasting peace.

This renascence of political liberalism generated a new-found impetus for the home rule that ethnic minorities have always coveted. The Paris Peace Conference was the site of endless deliberations, promises and compromises.

Foremost among the groups lobbying for autonomy were the Jews, represented by the Comite des Delegations Juives. On May 10, 1919, this committee petitioned conference members to secure adequate constitutional guarantees of civil, religious, and political liberty for Jews in all newly created or enlarged European states, both as individuals and as members of their particular minority group. The delegation also asked the League of Nations to endorse such a policy and urged participating countries to sign and honor the principles expressed in the League's Minority Bill of Rights.

The peace conference concerned itself with autonomy for all ethnic minorities. The Jewish delegation, by contrast, focused on the fate of Jewry in the new states and the Jewish role in the new balance of power. Drawing on the philosophy of Simon Dubnow, the father of this modern movement, the Jewish delegation pushed hard to secure assurances of Jewish rights to participation and representation in the governmental mechanisms that were to be created in the post-war world.

To describe his theory of Jewish nationalism in the Diaspora, Dubnow coined the term "Autonomism." Its aim was to create a future for Jews who, while belonging politically to the states in which they lived, would concurrently exist within a national cultural entity.

There were two principal conditions for this concept of Jewish autonomy: 1) the Jews must have autonomous national institutions, local and regional, which would direct and carry out all tasks serving the Jewish national interest, avoiding, however, the ghettoization and withdrawal from the non-Jewish world that characterized the Jewish situation in the Middle Ages; and 2) Jewish rights must not be restricted to functions peculiar to Jews. Jews must not refrain from active participation in economic life and should remain an active force in national life generally.

Dubnow believed that Jews needed autonomous institutions in every country where they lived. In his view, Autonomism was not a product of political necessity, but, historically speaking, a way to sustain national existence in dispersion. In the fourth of his *Letters on Old and New Judaism*, entitled "Autonomism, the Basis of the National Program," Dubnow stated his credo:

> The Jew says: As a citizen of my country I participate in its civic
> and political life; but as a member of the Jewish nationality I
> have, in addition, my own national needs, and in this sphere I

must be independent to the same degree that any other national minority is autonomous in the state. I have the right to speak my language, to use it in all my social institutions, to make it the language of instruction in all my schools, to order my internal life in my communities and to create institutions serving a variety of national purposes; to join in common activities with my brethren, not only in this country but in all countries of the world, and to participate in all the organizations which serve to further the needs of the Jewish nationality and to defend them everywhere.

Dubnow then formulated the chief axiom of Jewish autonomy as envisioned under his doctrines:

Jews in each and every country who take an active part in civic and political life enjoy all civil rights, not merely as individuals but also as members of their national groups.

Since it was clear that Jews did not live in one clearly demarcated territory even within one state, communities scattered throughout a given state should be given "personal autonomy."

Dubnow placed special emphasis on the importance of Yiddish as an instrument of autonomy. In his essay "Affirmation of the Diaspora," a response to Ahad Ha'am's article on "Negation of the Diaspora," Dubnow wrote:

Among the forces that form the basis of our autonomy in the Diaspora I reserve a place for the powerful force of the folk language used by seven million Jews in Russia and Galicia.... Insofar as we recognize the merit of national existence in the Diaspora, we must also recognize the merit of Yiddish as one of the instruments of autonomy, together with Hebrew and the other factors in our national culture.

While the crux of Dubnow's philosophy rested on the preservation of the national character of the Jewish people, whom he regarded as destined to remain a permanent Yiddish-speaking secular minority in their adopted homelands, he valued religion and religious movements for their role in serving the nation. Thus he favored a full spiritual program in the Diaspora.

Even Jewish groups that could not accept his concept of autonomy respected Dubnow's views. Thus the Zionists, too, lent firm support to the goals expressed within this doctrine. A worldwide cry for Jewish autonomy was on the rise, especially in countries such as Lithuania and Poland where traditions of autonomous institutions were deeply ingrained.

The coalition government of Lithuania did not ignore the call for minority rights as articulated by the Jewish Committee. It did refrain from signing the Minority Bill of Rights. However, in August 1919, after lengthy discussions between the Lithuanian delegation to the Paris conference, headed by Voldemaras, and the Comite des Delegations Juives, the Lithuanian government promised to grant and respect its minorities' special rights and deal directly with their representatives. Through the Voldemaras delegation, it reached a formal agreement with the Comite des Delegations Juives regarding national autonomy for Lithuanian Jewry. This all-important document, which Lithuanian Jews called the "Paris Declaration," reinvigorated the autonomy movement and heralded an unparalleled era of Jewish self-expression and governance in Lithuania. While other newly formed countries in Europe reached autonomy arrangements with respect to their Jewish minorities, those forged in Lithuania were the farthest reaching and the longest lasting.

The Paris Declaration provided a pragmatic framework within which Jewish participation in the new Lithuanian state might be built. It provided for the establishment of a Jewish Ministry to deal with Jewish affairs and proportional representation in the legislative, administrative, and judicial branches of government. Absolute civil rights were guaranteed, including the right to use the Yiddish language in both public and governmental institutions. Autonomy was promised in all internal affairs such as religion, education, social services, and culture.

Aside from representation in the national governing bodies, a superordinate council for the Jewish community and a national council (Natzional Rath) were to be created as the major supervisory institutions for the various agencies of autonomy. These councils, empowered to issue ordinances binding upon both Jews and governmental agencies, would be vehicles for the exercise of Jewish power.

Structure of Autonomous Lithuanian Jewry

Generally speaking, the Jewish community in Lithuania was made up of three main elements: Zionists, Yiddishists (Democrats), and Agudath Israel. In the Zionist rubric were the General Zionist Party, the Mizrachi (the Religious Zionists), and Tse'irey Tsiyon (the Zionist Socialist group, later known as the Zionist Socialists). All of these, with the exception of the Po'aley Tsiyon Smol (Left), were legal and above-board. The main Yiddishist factions were the Bundists, the Communists, and Po'aley Tsiyon Smol. Since all of these were illegal in independent Lithuania, they operated under different names, such as "Workers Faction No. 7" and "Workers Faction No. 5." Agudath Israel represented the ultraorthodox.

Initially, two groups opposed the concept of Jewish national autonomy in Lithuania: the small Jewish Communist group and Agudath Israel. The Communists not only refused to collaborate with bourgeois elements but disavowed Jewish national status altogether. Agudath Israel rejected the possibility that Jewish institutions might be secularized, although it participated actively in the workings of autonomy. Thus, upon the establishment of the Lithuanian state, nearly all nationally conscious and socially effective Jews were receptive to the national autonomy idea.

Of all the new countries, only Lithuania attempted to create Jewish national autonomy in its full form, as opposed, for example, to Latvia and Estonia, where it was confined to education. This was because Lithuanian Jewry was one of the least assimilated Jewish collectives in Europe. Jews in Lithuania displayed an unflinching will for autonomy and a united front in the struggle for cultural identity. As a people, the Jews of Lithuania rejected assimilation as a solution, especially in view of the mounting secular antisemitism and the example of Germany and other countries in Europe.

The Slezevicius government named Dr. Max Soloveitzik to the position of Minister for Jewish Affairs; he assumed his ministerial responsibilities on June 2, 1919. Soloveitzik and the three Jewish representatives in the Seimas, as the parliament was now called, demanded full rights in citizenship, language, and political liberties, plus proportional representation in legislative, executive, and judicial institutions. The need for cultural autonomy was explained, and the system through which local *kehillot* (community councils) would implement this autonomy, under the supervision of the superordinate Community Council, was set forth in detail. Soloveitzik and the parliamentarians also requested implementation of all aspects of the Paris Declaration, including official recognition of the Ministry for Jewish Affairs. (The vagueness of the status of this entity – headed by a minister without portfolio, disregarded by the national leadership – reflects the government's ambivalence toward Jewish autonomy.)

From his first day on the job, the new Minister for Jewish Affairs set about building the basic structure of Jewish national self-rule in every city and townlet, in preparation for democratic elections that the Jewish communities were to hold. On July 6, 1919, the Ministry apprised the Jewish National Council of its new autonomous status; henceforth the Council was empowered to handle all cultural affairs and levy taxes. Although this had not yet been enacted into law, the Jewish faction in the Seimas hoped that the forthcoming nationwide elections for Jewish Community Councils, scheduled for October 3, 1919, would force the government to incorporate this basic right of Jewish self-government, as well as the proportional-representation provisions, into the Constitution.

The election preparations continued. In the cities, the polling was to be proportional, based on candidate lists; in smaller communities (those with fewer than 1,000 Jewish inhabitants), deputies would be elected on an individual basis. The age of suffrage was 20.

In February 1920, Soloveitzik selected a provisional Jewish National Council, which would serve until democratic elections for the first National Council (*Natzional Rath*) could take place. Its functions were to stay in touch with every council's electoral body in the communities and to advise and update him on all Jewish and national issues that came up in the Seimas.

The Coalition Falls

The delicate balance of power that had held the various political factions together under Slezevicius fell apart late that summer. The coalition government resigned on October 2, 1919; a new government headed by Ernestas Galvanauskas, an engineer, took office without the participation of the Social Democrats and the Populists (alternately known as the People's Socialists). The Nationalists received 38 delegates out of a total of 78 in the Seimas, the elected legislature that replaced the unelected Taryba. The two minorities' ministers (Jewish and Belorussian) were invited to join the new government.

On October 3, 1919, coinciding with the Seimas elections, 80 Jewish communities were organized and legalized. Addressing the Taryba on December 6, 1919, in an effort to secure the support of the minorities and the peasants, Galvanauskas said:

> We urge the national minorities, together with all our citizens, to build the new, free Lithuania. We promise to create for them, by law, the conditions they will need for free and full development. But the task of achieving interrelations among our different national groups will be the responsibility of the Constituent Assembly.[116] As for the present, we propose solutions to problems as they arise, as we promised the Jewish minority in the Paris Declaration of August 5, 1919. We are also acting to legalize the institutions created by the Jewish National Autonomy, namely the democratically elected Community Councils, so they may work constructively, and to empower them to levy taxes to meet their needs.

Though Galvanauskas' statement fell considerably short of advocating the incorporation of the autonomy clauses into the Constitution itself, the Jewish communities were pleased, viewing it as an expression of the Premier's intent to honor the Paris Declaration.

On January 6, 1920, by invitation of Soloveitzik, the first Assembly of Jewish Councils convened in Kaunas. Its delegates were chosen under the following rules, set by the Ministry for Jewish Affairs: Each 200 voters were entitled to elect one delegate; a remainder of 101 voters on any list was entitled to an additional delegate; and any community with less than 101 voters could join another community to elect a delegate. In all, 82 Community Councils elected 141 representatives. The returns follow:

Affiliation	Delegates
Zionist parties, including Mizrachi and Tse'irey Tsiyon	61
Achdut (Agudath Israel and Tse'irey Agudath Israel)	54
Folkists and Po'aley Melakha	23
Unaffiliated	3

The Jewish Communist Party did not participate.

The National Assembly thus elected then chose a four-member National Council (*Natzional Rath* or, in Hebrew, *Va'ad ha-arets*), patterned after the ancient Lithuanian Va'ad ha-medina, to serve as its inner executive.

The conference was opened by Dr. M. Soloveitzik. The Prime Minister, E. Galvanauskas, and the Foreign Minister, A. Voldemaras, affirmed their support of Jewish autonomy and wished the Assembly the successful realization of its plans. Voldemaras introduced himself as "a friend of the Jewish people":

> We want to give the Jews not only political but also national
> rights. We understand the need for Jewish national autonomy.
> We want all minorities to live in peace and harmony in
> Lithuania.

Mr. Jouzas Voronka greeted the Assembly on behalf of the Belorussian community; Vytautas Vileishis did so for the Municipality of Kaunas.

Dr. Max Soloveitzik reported to the Assembly on his first nine months as Minister in the pre-Assembly cabinet. He complained of having been excluded from the actual political workings of the government. He did not consider his function limited to that of Secretary of State for Jewish Affairs; he wished to be a full and active cabinet member, involved in all aspects of government. He also accused several fellow ministers, especially representatives of the clerical and Nationalist parties, of having treated him with hostility. These men, he said, regarded Jewish autonomy and his own function as provisional institutions. He then used the dais to demanded that the government base its minorities policy on the principles of human, civil, and national rights.

The main controversy during the debates had to do with the proposed nature of the *kehillot*. R. Joseph S. Kahaneman, dean of the Ponevez Yeshiva and one of the most outstanding personalities in Achdut (the Agudath Israel movement), insisted that the *kehillot* be strictly Orthodox in character and outlook. Dr. Simon Rosenbaum sharply criticized this viewpoint, insisting that Lithuanian Jewry needed *kehillot* in which all Jews, religious and non-religious, might participate and feel at home.

Although the resulting sharp exchanges and conflicting views threatened to shatter the Assembly on several occasions, a schism was avoided thanks largely to Soloveitzik's efforts. Indeed, almost all its resolutions were adopted unanimously.

The 34 elected members of the National Council now formed the highest authority of Jewish autonomy. The function of this council was to mediate between the Community Councils and Assemblies and the Ministry for Jewish Affairs. The Assembly minutes show that political and diplomatic problems were given exclusive consideration during the week of proceedings. Just the same, elections for officers were held: Dr. S. Rosenbaum as Chairman of the National Council, Dr. Nachman Rachmilewitz and Attorney Ozer Finkelstein as Deputy Chairmen, and a ten-member executive committee from the membership at large.

On January 10, 1920, the Lithuanian government finally passed a provisional law with regard to the kehillot, the Jewish National Council (Natzional Rath), and the Ministry for Jewish Affairs.

The law which empowered *kehillot* to tax the Jewish population contained the following seven provisions:

1. All Jews residing in a given area will be members of the local *kehilla*. The *kehillot* will provide for all matters relating to Jewish worship, charity, social welfare, schools and culture. The Jews will have the right to elect committees within the *kehillot*. Note: in such localities where the Jews will not be able to create an independent *kehilla* because of their small numbers, they will join with neighboring communities to form a common committee.

2. The Minister without Portfolio for Jewish Affairs[117] will devise election regulations and confirm and register the committees that are elected according to them.

3. *Kehilla* committees [*va'adey kehilla*] duly approved by the Minister without Portfolio for Jewish Affairs are permitted, to meet the needs set forth in Paragraph 1, to levy special taxes on the Jewish population.

4. Each *kehilla* committee is empowered to devise its own taxation system and set tax rates, and the Minister will approve them.

5. The amount of taxes remitted by any person to the *kehilla* committee should not exceed the total annual government and municipal taxes remitted by that person.

6. The *kehillot* themselves should collect these taxes and deliver them to the State Treasury. Persons who fail to pay their taxes will be treated under the general regulations covering tax collection. If it is necessary to collect taxes from a delinquent's property, the taxes owed by the delinquent to the State will take precedence over those due the *kehilla*.

7. With respect to enforcement, the Minister without Portfolio for Jewish Affairs will, after due discussion with the relevant Ministers, issue a special series of regulations.

(Signed)   Antanas Smetona, President
              Ernestas Galvanauskas, Prime Minister

Kaunas, January 10, 1920.

This provisional law formed the underpinnings of Jewish autonomy and created conditions under which the *kehilla* committees, its most important instruments, might function. It also defined the basic legal rights of the Community Councils and encouraged them to continue their work of building the mechanism of national autonomy. The Jewish Minister and his office were now officially responsible for managing the entire apparatus of Jewish self-government.[118]

The Constituent Assembly and a New Coalition government

General elections for a new 112-member Constituent Assembly were held by direct and secret ballot on April 14-15, 1922. On June 10, the chamber passed legislation establishing a provisional Constitution that was superseded by a permanent Constitution on August 1, 1922. These documents replaced the Taryba with the Steigiamasis-Seimas (Parliament) as the supreme authority of the land and demoted the president, Antanas Smetona, to figurehead status.

The conservative Christian Democrats held a majority in the Constituent Assembly and first Seimas with 59 seats out of the 112. The Populists received 29 seats, the Social Democrats 13, and the minorities 11. The Jewish political parties presented a joint list of candidates, one that excluded several leftist groups such as the Bund-Yiddishists, Po'aley Tsiyon Smol, and the Jewish Communist Party. The general Lithuanian Communist Party boycotted the elections. Six Jews were elected to the Constituent Assembly: two representing the Zionists, Rosenbaum and Soloveitzik; two representing Achdut (Agudath Israel), Dr. N. Rachmilewitz and R. Abraham Popelas; and two representing the Folkists-People's Party, Attorneys Nachman Fridman and Ozer Finkelstein (the latter replaced after his death by Samuel Landau). The six Jewish delegates accounted for 5 percent of the Seimas. The Jewish faction in the Seimas, which participated in all the committees of the Seimas, was chaired by Fridman, who was also appointed to the Seimas Executive.

The national elections brought a new government to power: a coalition (the country's sixth) headed by Dr. Kazys Grinius of the Populist Party. Dr. M. Soloveitzik was appointed to serve as Minister without Portfolio.

On June 23, 1920, in his inaugural speech to the Seimas, Prime Minister Grinius said:

> Together with the most important problems facing Lithuania, there is the question of creating conditions for the national minorities, united with us in the ideal of building the state, so they may develop their own national culture freely. This right, proclaimed upon the establishment of the State, is now being implemented. The government will continue this work and will give sympathetic consideration for the forms of autonomy that are best suited to the minorities' needs.

Although the Jewish community appreciated the speech and its promises, it was greatly disappointed with the election returns, which had brought the conservative Christian parties to power. government was now in the hands of a political bloc not renowned for its tradition of cooperation with minorities. In fact, the Christian Democrats, the Christian Workers, and the Peasants Union had not played an important role in shaping reborn Lithuania at all. This untested majority greatly concerned all minorities, none more than the Jews.

The election results also showed that there were fewer Jews in Lithuania than previously believed. This would seriously mitigate the Jews' political impact in affairs of state.

On May 20, 1920, after long and hectic debates in the cabinet, an ordinance to implement the *kehillot* law was passed. This law was formulated along the lines of the Communities Law. It defined the *kehilla* as a legal entity empowered to impose taxes; issue bylaws in matters of religion, education, and social welfare; and register births, marriages, and divorces. Community Council elections were to be conducted democratically, using the principle of proportional representation. Every citizen registered as a Jew in public documents was deemed a member of the *kehilla*. To dissociate oneself from the Jewish community, one had to undergo religious conversion or prove that the personal documents were inaccurate.

Along with this Communities Law, two statements were gazetted in *Vyriaustybes Zinios* (Government News, N.32) on May 20, 1920. One was a statement by the Prime Minister: the law, he said, marked the first experiment of its kind. It was enacted not because it was in Lithuania's interest but because the Jews themselves had requested it. The law was inviolate, amendable only in accordance with the community's wishes. The second statement, made by the Minister for Jewish Affairs, limited the number of Jewish communities in any given locality to one and designated the Community Council as the legal representative of the local Jewish population. This statement affirmed that the *kehilla* was the historic form of Jewish national life and that its functions and power were consonant with the Paris Declaration. The two statements were followed by instructions, issued on May 1, 1920, ordering all government agencies to turn over their registration ledgers to the Community Council.

On October 1, 1920, the Minister of the Interior, Jouzas Puryzkis, and the Minister for Jewish Affairs, M. Soloveitzik, published a joint circular confirming the Paris Declaration and giving the National Council sole provisional responsibility, until the Constituent Assembly would draft official legislation, for the registration of births, deaths, and marriages, to be recorded in Yiddish and Lithuanian after rabbinical confirmation.

The Tides of Lithuanian Jewish Autonomy

"Instrukzia": The Special Law for the Kehillot

On April 8, 1921, the Lithuanian government, grateful to the Jews for their loyalty and patriotism in Vilna, passed a Special Law establishing the Ministry for Jewish Affairs and equipping it with a budget. The size of the Ministry staff was first set at 24 and shortly upped to 30. A second crucial area of Jewish community function was empowered on April 23, 1921, when the government issued directives forming education commissions within the Jewish Councils to supervise Jewish schools.

The Minister for Jewish Affairs had no special building but was given a suite of offices that he subdivided into departments: general affairs, legal, education, press, social welfare, and so on. The Minister was to be considered a full-fledged member of the government, in no way inferior to any other minister. He was to participate in the government's overall work and also safeguard Jewish interests and rights. To fulfill his obligations to the communities, his office was given central power and influence over them. For Lithuanian Jews, the Ministry was a symbol of hope, the guarantor of their political and civil rights as a minority.

The Minister for Jewish Affairs had two basic areas of responsibility. The first included general participation in all government work and protection of Jewish interests and rights. The second was responsibility for carrying out the provisions of Paragraphs 2, 4, and 7 of the provisional Law of the *Kehillot*. This brought him into constant and close contact with the Natzional Rath and the Jewish community, which considered the very existence of the Ministry an important guarantee of Jewish political and civil security. Although he had no authority over the Jewish school system, the Minister for Jewish Affairs had considerable influence in the Ministry of Education, with which this authority resided. Thus he was able indirectly to help the Jewish schools cope with their legal problems, financial pressure, and special requests pertaining to the schools' character and curriculum. He made every effort to secure government accreditation of as many Jewish primary schools as possible, for only with such accreditation could the schools qualify for full budgetary and legal rights and their teachers for recognition as state employees.

The Jewish autonomous institutions themselves, however, still lacked legal recognition and preoccupied themselves with securing it. In its meeting of September 1921, the Jewish National Council placed this at the top of its priorities. In its two resolutions, it decided to continue fighting for recognition and to convene a second Assembly of Jewish Communities in February 1922.

Although institutional recognition was slow in coming, senior officials spared the Jewish community no praise. At a meeting of the Constituent Assembly on December 17, 1921, Prime Minister Grinius lauded "Lithuanian citizens of the Jewish nation" for their active participation in building the Lithuanian state and asserted their privileges would be second to none. Hoping that their fellow Jews in Eastern Lithuania, i.e., Vilna, would continue to support a united Lithuania, Grinius promised full respect of Jewish culture, religion, and language; pledged government support for their national institutions; and reiterated the government's commitment to full Jewish autonomy.

Some of this was honored with alacrity. On December 20, 1921, the government awarded the *kehillot* all privileges that municipal agencies enjoyed, including free franking. Progress in other respects did not follow. One such case was the absence of Jews in the civil service. When Jewish members of the Seimas complained about this, the government explained that Jews lacked a command of the Lithuanian language. This was true enough, but the Jews were not placated. Many German- or Russian-educated Lithuanian bureaucrats, they noted, had the same drawback and were not penalized.[119] But the government remained intransigent, creating a lasting bone of contention in its relationship with the Jews.

The Second Assembly of the Jewish Communities

With the approach of the Second Assembly of the Communities in February 1922 – roughly two years after the First Assembly – the Natzional Rath held important discussions on the basic principles of the Assembly election procedures. The central question was whether delegates to the Second Assembly should be elected by the *kehilla* committees or by the Jewish population of Lithuania at large. The former position prevailed, and for this purpose all the Jewish communities in Lithuania were divided into 15 areas. Delegates were elected according to candidate lists, on the principle of proportional representation, by members of the *kehilla* committees. Every Jew was eligible for election.

The Second Assembly of the Communities opened on February 14, 1922. Its 130 delegates, including 40 rabbis, represented 185 *kehillot*. The factions were Achdut (Agudath Israel), Mizrachi, General Zionists, Tse'irey Tsiyon (Socialist Zionists), Folkspartei, the Artisans Association, and two left-Socialist groups: the Jewish Communists and Po'aley Tsiyon Smol (Left Socialist Zionists). Since the last two groups were illegal, they ran as "List No. 5" and "List No. 7," respectively. The Zionist factions constituted a small majority of the delegates.

The first item on the agenda, as before, was the quest for official recognition. The Natzional Rath asked the Minister for Jewish Affairs to petition the government for legislation giving the Rath full legal recognition and ensuring political equality for all citizens. Prime Minister Galvanauskas had been presented with a plan to this effect before the Assembly, in hopes that an affirmative reply might be obtained for the Assembly itself. Although this detailed working plan for Jewish autonomy was fashioned primarily on Paragraphs 73 and 74 of the constitution, the Prime Minister rejected it, explaining that the Taryba[120] lacked the power to guarantee its provisions.

The Jewish Council then drew up a second, less ambitious plan, which focused on the immediate needs and legal norms that would anchor the existence of the democratically elected councils of the Jewish communities.

Galvanauskas accepted the second plan with some reservations. However, many Lithuanian members of the Taryba, especially the Christian Democrats, believed it might lay the foundations of a "state within a state"; they opposed any special law pertaining to the Jewish community and council. Another surprising source of resistance was a small faction of Jews who supported the Christian Democratic Party. These delegates objected to compulsory affiliation with the Jewish community and opposed the Natzional Rath's taxation powers.

In March 1922, the government gazetted this plan as a provisional law. This document deserves two remarks: Minister Voldemaras lent it his full support, and its provisional nature was emphasized. Not until the Constituent Assembly could debate and endorse it would it be given permanent status.

It was under these circumstances that the Second Jewish National Assembly of the Communities convened. Prime Minister Galvanauskas greeted the 130 delegates in the name of the government, noting that only Lithuania among European countries had given the Jews full freedom to develop their national culture. The government hoped that the experiment of Jewish autonomy in Lithuania would serve as an example and an inspiration to other nations. Speaker after speaker followed in this optimistic vein: Antanas Jonynas, the Lithuanian envoy to the League of Nations; Vytautas Vileisis, the Mayor of Kaunas; and A. Zwikowitz, representing the Belorussian minority. Dr. Jacob Hellman, a Latvian Jew and a member of the Latvian Parliament, expressed the hope that Latvia would follow Lithuania's example. Leon Motzkin, Chairman of the Comite des Delegations Juives, who had made a special trip from Paris to attend the Assembly, asserted that fifteen million Jews throughout the world were observing the experiment of Lithuanian Jewry in its struggle for national rights. Congratulatory telegrams and messages poured in from Jewish communities and personalities worldwide.

Seventeen sessions were held. The conference chairman, Dr. N. Rachmilewitz, spoke of the future: the community's major priority, he stated, was the drafting of a National Autonomy Law by the Constituent Assembly. He spoke of the hope of reunification with the Jews of Vilna, and of the community's responsibilities toward world Jewry, which was carefully observing the unparalleled autonomy experiment with pride and anxiety. M.

Soloveitzik, the Minister for Jewish Affairs, described Lithuanian Jewry as the fountainhead from which the future form of Diaspora Jewish life would emanate.

As soon as the rhetoric ebbed, the leadership came in for much severe criticism for its internecine quarrels, paucity of positive achievements, excessive bureaucracy, and constant bickering and petty politics within the *kehillot*. The Natzional Rath coalition was reshuffled: 16 members of Achdut (Agudath Israel), four of Mizrachi, seven General Zionists, eleven Zionist Socialists, and two Folkists.

The resolutions of the Assembly's Political Committee, as proposed by Dr. J. Brutzkus, expressed confidence in 1) the Jewish faction in the Seimas, which defended Jewish national interests with dignity; 2) the Natzional Rath, which, in spite of all difficulties, had managed to lay the foundations of Jewish national self-rule in Lithuania; and 3) the Minister for Jewish Affairs, thanks to whom an important post had been created in the struggle for Jewish rights. The resolutions passed by majority vote, with the abstentions of the left-proletarian factions. Then Brutzkus tabled a resolution on minority rights in the constitution. It, too, had three clauses: 1) the minority rights proposed in the constitution made it possible to solve the minorities' national problems legitimately; 2) no firm guarantees for the development of national autonomy had been proffered; the constitution must clearly assign responsibility for implementing all laws concerning a national minority to the minister for that minority; 3) the Assembly wishes to place all religious matters under the jurisdiction of the Natzional Rath. This resolution, too, passed by a majority vote.

The last meetings of the Assembly dealt with problems of education and the school system. When it became obvious that no agreement was possible on the question of curriculae, the Assembly resolved to empower parents to determine the character of their children's schools. Dr. Soloveitzik suggested that the controversy be referred for solution to the Natzional Rath and backed his proposal by threatening to resign. "If we can neither tolerate nor trust each other," he reasoned, "we shall not be able to build autonomy. Let us rather reject it first!" Soloveitzik's proposal was accepted by all factions except the proletarians; the thorny curriculum issue was handed to the national council.

Crisis: The Constitution of 1922 and a Test of Strength

Jewish autonomy tumbled into crisis two months later. In April 1922, Soloveitzik resigned as Minister for Jewish Affairs to protest the failure of the Lithuanian draft constitution to guarantee the existence of the Ministry and other national autonomy institutions. He returned to the Cabinet after entreaties by the government and the Natzional Rath, but resigned for good on August 1, 1922.

The new constitution itself was gazetted on August 6. Instead of incorporating the Autonomy Law, the document contained only a general proscription of mistreatment of any citizen on account of nationality, beliefs, or race. The articles pertaining to national minorities' rights were purely rhetorical and contained no juridical guarantee to ensure the existence of national autonomy. Since Lithuania had just signed a renewed Minorities Declaration and presented the League of Nations with its own version of this document on May 12, 1922, the Jewish leadership regarded the constitutional lacuna as an act of hypocrisy and a breach of government promises to the Jews.

Dr. Soloveitzik, disillusioned and embittered, left Lithuania in late 1922. Although a Zionist, Soloveitzik had reconciled his belief in a Jewish national home in Palestine with his commitment to national autonomy in Lithuania. A fervent democrat, he regarded Lithuania as the most creative source for the building of the future modalities of Jewish life. He envisaged minority rights for Jews as a model for all minorities. Above all, as a democrat, he believed in the constitution and the supremacy of the law. However, having assessed the government's methods and motives in drafting the new constitution, he became increasingly convinced that minority rights would be neither safeguarded nor sustained within this framework. Having lost faith in the promises of the Lithuanian government to the Jews and other minorities, he considered resignation his only option.

Morale in the Jewish parliamentary faction, too, was dashed. The delegates felt that their fight in the parliamentary assemblies of March, April, and May of that year, to obtain, legitimize, and preserve the right to cultural autonomy, had been in vain. Exercising their right to political representation under the electoral laws, they were active in most of the Seimas committees but were powerless to resurrect the spirit and promises of the Paris Declaration.

The government defended its failure to include the Autonomy Law by noting that no other state had reached a similar arrangement with its minority groups. Several weeks later, the Lithuanian Ambassador to Washington stated that the relevant provisions would be modified, but only in accordance with the prerogatives set forth in the League of Nations proclamation, e.g., the right to citizenship and particularistic schools. Thus Lithuania quietly rescinded its offer of full autonomy by adhering to the letter, but certainly not the intent, of the law.

The Jewish faction in the Seimas, climbing out of its trough of disillusionment, faced an immediate test of strength, its first, in demanding that the Lithuanians keep their promises to the minorities. They fought alone on this issue, without the help of any Gentile parties. The Speaker of the Seimas, Aleksandras Stulginskis, who at the time was also the acting Prime Minister and the newly appointed President, took the initiative in seeking a compromise. During its third session (August 1, 1922), the Seimas agreed to amend the new constitution by inserting Paragraphs N-73 and 74 on minority rights. These provisions adhered to the existing model: favorable declaratory principles that failed to provide specific legal guarantees for the institution of national autonomy.

The texts, presented to a special commission of the Assembly on August 1, 1922, read as follows:

> Paragraph 73: Citizens of national minorities, which make up a sizable part of the population, have the right to carry on autonomously the affairs of their own national culture, popular education, and mutual aid, and to elect representative institutions to manage these affairs in a manner provided for in special laws.

> Paragraph 74: The minorities to which reference is made in Paragraph 73 are entitled, within the framework of separate laws, to tax their members for cultural purposes and to receive, from both the government and municipal agencies, their rightful share of the funds assigned for popular education.

In the meantime, however, the minorities faced new problems. In September 1923, for example, the government claimed that the language provisions of the minority declarations did not apply to business signs. Its argument: under

Lithuanian law, these signs were an integral part of business firms, which fell
into the category of "public institutions." Only the Lithuanian language might
be used for this purpose. Thus the freedom of language, an important
component of minority rights, was dealt a stunning blow. The Lithuanian
people dealt the minorities' cause an even more stunning blow on February
4, 1923, by tearing down, vandalizing, and covering up signs in Yiddish, Polish,
and Russian.

The government, for its part, showed little inclination to fulfill its
commitments as outlined in the Minorities Treaties. The legislature took the
matter somewhat more seriously. The Minorities Proclamation, pigeonholed
in the Seimas for a year and a half, was finally introduced in the plenum on
September 18-19, 1923; no objections to it were raised. At a second reading
on October 26, however, the majority Nationalist Party argued that the
Proclamation needed no parliamentary ratification because it was an
"international instrument." Here the outraged minority groups were backed
by the Liberal and Socialist parties, who accused the Nationalists of acting
under material rather than legal considerations. Finally, to please what it
called "world opinion," the Seimas endorsed the Minorities Proclamation,
concluded at a Minorities Convention on December 11, 1923, between the
League of Nations and Lithuania. The government neither gazetted nor
implemented the legislation that the Seimas had passed. Actions speak louder
than words.

*Solidarity Crumbles: Elections to the First and Second (Regular)
Seimas*

It will be recalled that the Jews had presented a joint candidate list for
elections to the Constituent Assembly. Now, with the approach of balloting
for the first regular Seimas in October 1922, the Jews were unable to agree
on a unified slate and instead prepared three separate lists: Zionists, Agudath
Israel, and Folkists. Even though the chamber was reduced from 112 members
to 80, the Jewish electors would have had six mandates if strictly proportional
terms were applied. They were not. The election committee, influenced by the
Christian Democratic and Nationalist Parties, interpreted Paragraph 76 of
the Constitution in such a way as to leave the Jews with only three seats. (The
Polish minority was given similar treatment; it received two seats instead of
the four it had expected.) The Christian Democrats garnered 38 seats, the

Populists 21, the Social Democrats 11, and the newly legalized Communists (now called the Workers Party) five.[121]

The First Seimas convened on November 13, 1922, and remained in session until March 29, 1923. The Jewish delegates were Dr. Joseph Berger and Dr. Julius Brutzkus, Zionists; and Dr. Leib Garfunkel, Zionist-Socialists. Brutzkus replaced Soloveitzik as Minister for Jewish Affairs. This was an unfortunate choice: Brutzkus could hardly speak Lithuanian and had no experience in working with Lithuanian authorities. He resigned shortly after his appointment. Then, against the express wishes of the Jewish deputies, President A. Stulginskis replaced Brutzkus with Bernard Friedman, a Russian-Jewish assimilationist who belonged to no active Jewish group and was anathema to the rank-and-file. The Jewish parties jointly declared a boycott against the new Minister for Jewish Affairs. Then, together with their Polish colleagues, the Jewish deputies walked out of the Seimas in protest against the way the minority laws had been reconstrued.

Their action had two results. First, it deprived them of their parliamentary salaries. Second, it gave the Christian Democrats the parliamentary majority that they lacked, having earned only 38 mandates in the 80-member Seimas. After being entreated by the other opposition parties, the Jewish and Polish delegates reappeared in the Seimas on March 29, 1923, during its 9th Session. When a no-confidence motion called that day ended with a tie, the government dissolved the Seimas and called new elections.

The right-wing press, specifically *Rytas* (Morning) and *Tautos-Valia* (People's Voice), blamed the Jews for the downfall and deplored their alleged ability to decide the fate of Lithuanian governments. Excerpts from important Lithuanian newspapers, published in the *Idishe Shtime* in 1922-1923, are highly interesting and revealing. The writers asserted that the Jews of Lithuania had been "given too much," that the budget had no money left for the minorities, and that the Jews' demands were excessive in view of the country's weakness and poverty. The newspaper *Lietuvos Zinios* urged Lithuania to follow Europe's example and exchange the principle of *Cuius regio eius religio* to *Cuius regio eius nazio* – where the ruler once determined his country's religion, he should now determine his country's national identity. This principle, *Zinios* continued, should also apply to the language of the country, which the Jews, according to the official government paper *Lietuva*, perversely refused to learn. Instead, they maintained their loyalty to Yiddish, a "corrupt Russian-German tongue." The Jews were creating "a state within a state." Jews were guilty of dual loyalty; insofar as they were Zionists, they were "temporary citizens" of Lithuania. After the elections, journalists accused the Poles in "our Seimas" of being under the influence of, and taking orders from, Warsaw, whereas the Jews, opportunists as always, "will join forces with those [parties] from which they can extract the most."

For the elections to the Second Seimas on May 12-13, 1923, the minorities decided that, despite their differences, they would fare better if unified in one bloc embracing Jews, Poles, Germans, Russians, and Belorussians. Two lists were drawn up – a Polish list and a joint list of all the other minorities – with an arrangement for residual votes. The tactic succeeded in the narrow sense. Out of a total of 78 seats, the minority lists gathered 14, a gain of nine over the First Seimas: seven for the Jews, four for the Poles, two for the Germans, and one for the Russians and the Belorussians. The seven Jewish deputies elected were Dr. Simon Rosenbaum, Dr. Jacob Robinson and Meshulam Wolf (Zionists); Abraham Eisik Brudni and Dr. Leib Garfunkel (Zionist Socialists); R. Joseph S. Kahaneman (Achdut – Agudath Israel); and Ozer Finkelstein (Folkists). Brudni's mandate was not ratified, for he was a Russian refugee and therefore ineligible; his seat was taken by Joseph Roginsky. Meshulam Wolf subsequently ceded his place to Dr. Itzchak Raphael Holzberg (Achdut). In 1925, R. Kahaneman gave his seat to Hirsch Abramovitz (Labour). When Dr. Rosenbaum left for Palestine in 1925, Dr. Joseph Berger replaced him.

In the broader sense of accumulation of power, the Jews lost badly. The elections gave the Christian Democrats 40 mandates, the Populists 16, and the Social Democrats eight. The Christian Democrats, thus endowed with a majority of two in the Second Seimas, used their clout to bar Jews from all but two of the parliamentary committees. Jews thus were deprived of the means of bringing their influence to bear on parliament. They had lost the vehicle through which they had planned to further the struggle for autonomy rights.

The tone at the Cabinet level was more favorable. Ernestas Galvanauskas, the Prime Minister and Minister for Foreign Affairs, solemnly informed the Seimas upon presenting his new government that no effort would be spared to implement the laws governing national minority rights, which were now part of the constitution. Galvanauskas then included the Jewish faction and the Populists in his coalition government. Dr. Rosenbaum was appointed as Minister for Jewish Affairs. The Jewish faction in the Second Seimas, under the leadership of Dr. Jacob Robinson, gave the Jewish community its largest, strongest, and best-organized representation ever. It participated in every political decision of the government and, at this particular time – due to respect for Robinson – was active in all matters connected with Lithuania's socioeconomic structure and international relations.

The parliamentary majority, by contrast, was nationalistic and antisemitic, influenced by the clericalism of a powerful Church. Its intention to liquidate the national autonomy was clear. On December 21, 1923, the Seimas deleted from the budget the payroll of the Ministry for Jewish Affairs. It forbade Jewish deputies to deliver speeches in Yiddish and it deprived the minority of basic rights promised in the League of Nations act. An attempt was made to undermine the minorities' school systems by attacking the systems' languages of instruction. Gradually, the participation of minorities deputies was limited to internal and economic affairs. None of the other parties protested this obstruction of democratic procedures in the Seimas.

No Longer a Minorita Gratissima: The Last National Jewish Assembly

The third and last National Jewish Assembly was held in Kovno on November 20-26, 1923. It differed from its two predecessors (late 1919, early 1922) in that its delegates were democratically elected by the Jewish population as a whole, on the basis of proportional representation. Deputies to the previous conferences had been chosen by the kehilla committees alone. Only Achdut (Agudath Israel) boycotted the elections to the Assembly as well as the Assembly meetings. All other parties participated, including the Jewish Communists.

Elected to the Presidium were Dr. Rosenbaum, President; Dr. Berger (General Zionists); Rabbis Israel Nissan Kark and Nathan Natelewitz (Mizrachi); A. E. Brudni (Zionist-Socialists); Dr. Garfunkel (Zionist Socialists / Hitahdut Po'aley Tsiyon); Hirsch Abramovitz (Hantwerker, the Manual Workers party); and Ozer Finkelstein (Folkspartei). The Communists and Po'aley Tsiyon Smol refused to join the Presidium but participated in working committees.

The 80-delegate Assembly was inaugurated by Dr. Rosenbaum, the Minister for Jewish Affairs and the President of the Natzional Rath. Greetings were delivered by the Mayor of Kaunas, representatives of the Lithuanian Polish and German minorities, the Jewish community of Kaunas, and others. Again messages arrived from all over the world. Historian Simon Dubnow sent a moving letter in which he described the National Assembly as the heir to the 300-year-old *Va'ad Lita*, the famous Council of Lithuania. He stressed the deputies' great responsibility in carrying on this tradition with respect and dignity. Greetings arrived, too, from the World Zionist Organization in London, the Zionist Executive in Jerusalem, the American Jewish Congress, the Joint Distribution Committee, and many others. Prime Minister Galvanauskas attended the second session of the Assembly, and in mentioning the principles of the rights of the minorities guaranteed by the constitution, underscored the important function of the Jewish minority in the Lithuanian economy.

The Assembly began with a general discussion of the political situation of Lithuanian Jewry and the state of Jewish autonomy. Dr. Rosenbaum traced developments and progress since the Second Assembly and reported on his activities as Minister for Jewish Affairs. He still regarded the autonomy as "a model for Jews worldwide." The reports and the debate that followed them, however, painted a picture of deterioration in the political circumstances of the Jews of Lithuania. Political reactionism was on the increase; the autonomy was clearly in danger. Thus, it was argued, every effort should be made to give the Natzional Rath legal status in accordance with the constitutional safeguards of minority rights. Following the general debate, the Assembly heard reports on the activities of the individual Natzional Rath departments.

The Assembly debates treated the Jewish school system at great length, with special emphasis on an administrative anomaly that threatened its integrity. The Jewish schools, as noted, were under the supervision of the Ministry of Education, not the Ministry for Jewish Affairs. Existing law did nothing to guarantee the Jewish schools' special ambiance and curriculum. The language of instruction was indeed Hebrew or Yiddish, but this, too, was not anchored by law. Indeed, interference by the Ministry of Education in Jewish education was increasing. The National Assembly resolved that if and when the Natzional Rath obtained legal recognition, it must insist that the government place the schools of the Jewish minority under the responsibility and supervision of the autonomy institutions.

Following a lively discussion, the Assembly resolved by majority vote (only the Communists were opposed) to ask the Executive of the World Zionist Organization for permission to send a representative to the council of the reorganized Jewish Agency for Palestine.

At the end of its deliberations, the Third National Assembly took several resolutions. One expressed confidence in the Minister for Jewish Affairs, Dr.

Simon Rosenbaum, of the Natzional Rath, and the Jewish faction in the Seimas. Another resolution supported the efforts to give the Natzional Rath legal status. The Natzional Rath was given responsibility for all matters relating to religion. The Assembly condemned the increasing attacks against Jews in Lithuania and the government's apparent impotence to counteract them.

In organizational affairs, the Assembly urged all *kehilla* committees to use their right to tax community members for *kehilla* needs. The Assembly also resolved to establish a National Autonomy Fund for the needs of the Natzional Rath and the furtherance of its activities.

With respect to Jewish schools, the Assembly urged the Natzional Rath to take over jurisdiction for the general system as well as direct responsibility for schools not affiliated with networks (Yavneh, Tarbut, Peshore ["Compromise"], Kultur Lige). The religious or secular character of these schools would be decided upon by a majority of students' parents. It was also resolved that all schools that taught in Hebrew should introduce the study of Yiddish, and vice versa.

Finally, the Assembly chose a new 40-member Natzional Rath representing all factions except two: the Communists, who declared themselves unwilling to join the Natzional Rath; and the Achdut, which did not participate on this occasion.

The overriding issue, the threat to the very existence of Jewish autonomy and all the Jews' achievements in national rights, had somehow been eclipsed. Although the reports left no doubt about the danger, the delegates wished to believe that the Lithuanian state would keep the promises and commitments set forth in the year-old State constitution. With this, the Assembly adjourned.

Developments during the rest of the year were strongly inauspicious. The results of a 1923 census showed a total of 153,332 Jews in the country (7.7 percent of the population); conventional wisdom had placed their number at 250,000. (The population of the Vilna area accounts for the difference.) Thus, although still the largest of the minority groups, their political base was not as formidable as they reckoned.

On December 20, 1923, the Minister of Finance, Vytautas Petrulis, delivered an antisemitic speech in the Seimas in which he characterized Jewish businessmen as chronically prone to tax evasion, a practice that existed to some extent in every community. (In 1926, during the tenure of the

Third Seimas, Petrulis – then Minister of Finance, Commerce, and Industry – was convicted of taking bribes and sentenced to one year in prison).

The budget deliberations brought further bad news. Under pressure from the Christian Democratic ministers, the government decided to slash the number of officials in the Ministry for Jewish Affairs from 29 to three. If this were not enough, the Christian Democratic bloc in the Seimas proposed to delete from the 1924 budget every appropriation for two minorities ministries, Jewish Affairs and Belorussians.

In view of this government posture toward the minorities, the Jewish faction decided to vote against the entire draft budget for 1924, thus joining the opposition. On December 22, 1923, Rosenbaum tendered President Stulginskis his resignation as Minister for Jewish Affairs. Stulginskis officially released Dr. Rosenbaum from his duties on February 2, 1924, but invited him to stay on temporarily as Minister without Portfolio for Jewish Affairs. On March 19, the Seimas also abolished this position. A coalition crisis in June led to the formation of a new government under A. Tumenas, in which none of the minority parties was represented.

Rosenbaum's resignation-dismissal spelled the end of efforts to endow the Natzional Rath with legal status. When first appointed minister, he had prepared a proposal that would have accomplished this. The government had accepted the proposal at first, making only slight changes. However, it was brought to the Seimas for approval in the last days of the Galvanauskas regime, when it clashed with an alternative proposal, sponsored by antisemitic elements within the Christian Democratic bloc, to amend the *Kehilla* Law. Under this draft legislation, these public agencies would become private societies. Any number of *kehillot* might be set up in any locality, and Jews would not be obliged to belong to any of them. The *kehillot* would be deprived of their responsibility for religious services and their authority to levy taxes; *kehillot* would be supported only by membership dues and private donations. Population registers would be transferred to the rabbis. *Kehillot* would come under the jurisdiction of the Ministry of the Interior. The Natzional Rath was not mentioned at all.

The Rath plenum called for an emergency meeting on September 17, 1924, to discuss the new situation. A police agent dispersed the gathering as an illegal assembly; the government ordered the Natzional Rath to shut down for functioning without its permission.

On March 24, 1925, the Seimas met to discuss the two conflicting bills, that legalizing the Natzional Rath and that amending the *Kehilla* Law as proposed by the Christian Democratic bloc. The latter, sponsored by the ruling party, passed over the sharp protests of the Jewish faction, which stalked out of the Seimas in protest. The government gazetted the new law on November 26, 1925.

Two additional pieces of legislation, the Festivals Law and the Signs Law, came in on July 15, 1924. These left no doubt about the erosion of the rights of the Jews and other minorities. For the Jews, the Festivals Law was the more onerous by far – a reincarnation of Czarist madness. The new legislation prohibited labor on Sundays and other Christian festivals. Since Jews did not work on Saturday and usually (especially in the winter) worked only half-days on Friday, the new law left them with only four and a half days a week to make a living. The Jewish faction in the Seimas managed to vitiate the impact of the law by keeping the Jewish schools open on Sundays; in villages with less than 3,000 people, Jews were allowed to do business on Sundays from 1 to 4 p.m. Nevertheless, most Lithuanian Jews were deeply affected by the new law. When the Festivals Law became part of the constitution, the Jewish population openly demonstrated their opposition to it in public meetings and prayer gatherings all over the country. The government, unmoved, called in the police to disperse the protesters. Rabbis were accused of incitement but were not brought to court. Jews bombarded the Seimas and the Prime Minister with telegrams. The law was given a second hearing, and, despite vigorous Jewish opposition, was confirmed on September 3, 1924 for its final reading in the Seimas. Father Jonas Vilimas, a cleric who held a seat in the Seimas, explained the purpose of the Festivals Law:

> We must liberate Kaunas from the Jewish bloodsuckers and introduce the Sunday and Festival Laws. Let the Jews hire Christians to work for them in their business on Saturdays and Jewish festivals.[122]

Although it was small consolation to the Jews, the Populist Party organ *Lietuvos Zinios* suggested that the Festivals Law was actually directed more against the Protestants than the Jews, to force them to observe Catholic devotional holidays.

The Festivals Law was attacked from certain quarters as unconstitutional and in contravention of the League of Nations provisions on "equality before the law with special reference to race, language and religion." This stipulation was proffered in two versions: an American phrasing of May 10, 1919, and a variant proffered by the Jewish delegation to the League of Nations:

> Those who observe other than the first day of the week as their Sabbath shall not be prohibited from pursuing their secular affairs on any other day than that which they observe; nor shall they be required to perform any acts on their Sabbath or Holy Days which they shall regard as a desecration thereof (American version).

> Those who observe any other day than Sunday as their Sabbath shall not be required to perform any acts on their Sabbath or Holy Days which by the tenets of their faith are regarded as a desecration, nor shall they be prohibited from pursuing their secular affairs on Sunday or other Holy Days (Jewish delegation version).

Thus the Jewish faction of the Seimas, together with the Association of Jewish Businessmen and the Association of Lithuanian Rabbis (Agudath Harabbonim), summoned the Jews to a mass demonstration on November 18, 1924, against what they termed "an assault on Jewish survival and liquidation of the Natzional Rath and the Autonomy. They desecrate our rights, ruin our existence, insult our language;... [enforced] rest on Sundays and Catholic holidays will bring economic ruin."

The Sign Law was in fact a reconfirmation, on July 15, 1924, of an earlier decree forbidding the display of Yiddish and Hebrew storefronts, nameplates and signs, and prohibiting, subject to a fine of 1,000 lits (approximately $100, then considered a large sum of money), the use of any language other than Lithuanian in business records. This decree was fiercely opposed by the Jewish faction of the Seimas, which accused the government of creating thereby "250,000 dissatisfied, unhappy citizens whose rights are being trampled." Local Jews compared their situation with that of the 800,000 Lithuanians in America, who were free to use their language as they saw fit.

Even before the sign decree was promulgated, Lithuanian extremists had taken to painting over Yiddish signs as an act of patriotism. Official attitudes toward this practice may be judged by the results of a court case in Vilkaviskis, where a Jewish municipal councillor, Bendet Rabinovitz, had been convicted and fined 300 lits for advising Gentile Lithuanians "to learn how to write before defacing signs."

The Lithuanian press strongly criticized the Jews for their opposition to the decree, accusing them of refusing to learn the language of their land of domicile; it prescribed a boycott of all Jewish businesses whose owners did not speak Lithuanian, coupled with the publication of their names. The Trimitas, a Catholic nationalist organization, likened the minorities' languages to those of "savage African tribes."

Nevertheless, several prominent Lithuanian personalities raised their voices in defense of the right of Jews, as well as the other minorities, to use their own language. They included Jonas Basanavicius, a founding father of independent Lithuania; former Prime Minister Slezevicius, and A. Valaitis, an important journalist with *Lietuvos Zinios*.

World Jewish organizations stepped into the fight. On November 28, 1924, the Comite des Delegations Juives in Paris proclaimed its concern for their plight. It accused the Lithuanian government of destroying Jewish national autonomy piecemeal by dismantling its institutions, enacting the Sunday and Festivals laws, and enforcing the sign decree. Lithuania was betraying its promises to the League of Nations to honor freedom of religion and language, they said. The Comite was particularly concerned by the abolition of the Ministry for Jewish Affairs and other Jewish institutions, and promised to call the matter to the attention of the League of Nations. The Comite letter was sent to every Lithuanian member of the Seimas.

The Lithuanian press, ever conscious of world opinion, responded to these actions by accusing local Jewry of having incited overseas agencies to meddle in local affairs, a course of action that they regarded as disloyalty and perfidy. The Jewish faction and the National Assembly Executive denied any previous contact with the Comite. Organized Jewry and the Jewish press in Lithuania, as elsewhere, fought discrimination in the parliament and in state and municipal agencies, but were reluctant to appeal to Geneva as anything but a measure of last resort.

Divide et Impera: The End of Jewish Autonomy

The Minister of the Interior dissolved the elected Jewish Natzional Rath on September 15, 1924. Although the Rath continued to function unofficially until 1926, the Jewish members of the Seimas were the only remaining official representatives of the community.

On January 12, 1925, prominent Jews representing the *kehillot*, political organizations, economic groups, and the press, came together in Kovno under the chairmanship of Joseph Roginsky, Deputy Mayor of the town, per invitation of the Jewish deputies in the Seimas. They had three purposes: to organize their work on behalf of the communities; to attend to the needs of Jewish Lithuanians repatriated from Soviet Russia; and to improve the status of nonresident Jews working in Lithuania. They extended legal help to individual Jews and to communities alike. In February 1927, after assuming the responsibilities of the Natzional Rath, the faction obtained permission to form and register two corporations that might fill the administrative vacuum: Ezra (Self-help) for secular needs; and Adath Israel for communities' religious requirements. These corporations also took possession of the assets of the moribund councils.

In March 1927, the ultraorthodox Achdut (Agudath Israel) group stole a march on everyone by reaching a private understanding with the all-powerful reactionary clerical Christian Democratic Party. One of the Achdut deputies, Dr. Itzchak Raphael Holzberg, seems to have conducted private negotiations with the government and members of the Christian Democratic bloc, behind the backs of the other Jewish faction members, regarding certain provisions of the *Kehilla* Law. In return for several promises, including the establishment of a new entity to be known as the Religious *Kehilla*, Holzberg had agreed to refrain from voting against the government, in direct contrast to faction policy. The rest of the faction also accused Holzberg of actively opposing his Jewish colleagues in the Seimas, in concert with the Christian Democrats, by contributing articles to the *Kovner Tsayt*, a government-sponsored and -financed Yiddish-language newspaper that began to appear in late 1925.

The faction plunged into acute internal conflict; the community split. Achdut (Agudath Israel), although consistently opposed to the secular nature of the cultural autonomy, had thus far collaborated with the other Jewish parties despite its reservations. The leadership of this faction, composed mainly of rabbis and wealthy ultraorthodox laymen, still believed in the efficacy of the *shtadlan* system, i.e., direct personal intercession and pleading with the authorities. The schism within the leadership could no longer be papered over. On March 2, 1926, the Jewish faction expelled Holzberg from its ranks for his breach of faction discipline.

Holzberg denied all the charges vigorously. In fact, he claimed, he had left the faction of his own accord six months before his expulsion. He added that every action he had taken as a Seimas deputy had been in full consultation and agreement with the leaders of the Association of Lithuanian Rabbis (Agudath Harabbonim). Holzberg made special mention of R. Abraham Duber Shapiro, Chief Rabbi of Kovno; R. Joseph Kahaneman of Ponevez, himself a member of the Seimas, whom Holzberg termed his "mentor"; and R. Moshe Mordechai Epstein, head of the Yeshiva of Slobodka (later of Hebron Yeshiva). These luminaries did not feel the need to defend him, nor were they concerned. In any case, they were not part of the Jewish coalition and, indeed, acted on their own when this suited their interests.

In the meantime, a new National *Kehillot* Law in the Holzberg spirit passed its final reading in the Seimas on November 15, 1925. The Minister of the Interior began to make rulings on its basis, which the remaining members of the Jewish faction refused to honor and carry out. In search of a more accommodating and collaborative Jewish leadership outside the faction, the government appointed a new administrator ("Referent") for Jewish affairs in the person of Hayyim Krone. Krone, a 26-year-old student at the Telz yeshiva and a member of Tse'irey Agudath Israel, had been recommended by none other than Dr. Holzberg. All community leaders outside Agudath Israel greeted his appointment with outrage and viewed it as a government attempt to divide and conquer. The Agudath Israel attitude was consistent with its general policy and philosophy of acting alone and collaborating with governments (as in Poland) even at the expense of Jewish unity. Various authorities, aware of this stance, exploited Agudath Israel to divide and rule. The fact that the authorities in this particular case similarly opposed the new National *Kehillot* does not alter the overall policy.

On November 27, the Zionist Organization and the Seimas faction convened in Kovno to deal with the situation. Their achievement was to call Krone names. He was compared to Bernard Friedman, the assimilated Jew who had been appointed Minister for Jewish Affairs after Soloveitzik and Brutzkus had resigned. They also condemned Krone as a tool of the government and a creation of the Christian Democrats.

A more important meeting, a consultative all-party event, was held on December 7 in Kovno to consider the implications of the newly passed National *Kehillot* Law and the community's response to it.

The discussion centered on three differing points of view. Some participants, such as Dr. Joseph Berger (a General Zionist), favored cooperation with the government, arguing that the new National *Kehillot* should be organized to the best possible benefit of the community. Otherwise, other agents, less qualified and not committed to the community's best interests, would step in. Achdut (Agudath Israel) opposed the establishment of the new National *Kehillot*, even though the Referent, Hayyim Krone, was one of their number. These new community institutions, they feared, would be purely secular and would expunge the religious-affairs aspect of the *kehilla* structure. The third view, held by the majority, opposed the creation of the National *Kehillot* because, being under full government control and supervision, they would be politically and financially powerless. Their activity would be confined to such matters as welfare and education. As such, they would revert to the *kehilla* concept of the Middle Ages – a far cry from the autonomy structure that the Jews of Lithuania envisaged and had been promised.

By a vote of 24:3, with the Achdut (Agudath Israel) representatives abstaining, the conference resolved to refuse to organize the new National *Kehillot* as conceived by the law. This refusal did not amount to a breach of the law as interpreted by the Minister of the Interior, Stasys Enzulaitis, who held that the National *Kehillot* were a privilege, not a duty, which the Jews of Lithuania might invoke or reject as they pleased.

The reason for the Achdut (Agudath Israel) abstention became clear later on. On November 19, eight days before the conference and also before the government had published its guidelines regarding the new National *Kehillot*, Achdut (Agudath Israel) had secretly registered a society known as the Religious *Kehilla*. This agency, it would seem, was to become the legal heir to all religious property and institutions. Interior Minister Enzulaitis backed the new entity by abolishing the system of official rabbis, instituted by the Russians in the Pale of Settlement and upheld by independent Lithuania. In its place, he authorized the creation of a nine-rabbi Executive Council, headed by R. Baruch Gurwitz of Alexotas (near Kovno). This board, not the National *Kehillot*, would henceforth be responsible for all religious affairs including registration of births, marriages, and deaths.

Since this move coincided with the aims of the ultraorthodox and meant little to the secular Jewish leadership, it was left to the Mizrachi rabbis to protest. An association of Mizrachi rabbis indeed argued that the newly formed council represented only 30 of the 120 rabbis in Lithuania and therefore had no right to speak and act in the name of the collective. The rift within the religious leadership became irreconcilable on March 18, 1926, when

R. Israel Nissan Kark, Chairman of the Association of Mizrachi Rabbis, urged the Jewish community to boycott the Agudath Israel – Achdut religious *kehilla*. Those affiliated with Mizrachi obeyed; the others did not.

The Third Seimas Elections: The End of Democracy in Lithuania

Even though Jewish autonomy was now officially defunct, the political activity of the Jewish minority continued unabated.

The forecast by the Jewish faction that no one party would be able to govern was proven right. Thus, new elections were called for June 2, 1926. The results decimated the Jewish representation in the Third Seimas, chiefly because of disarray and schisms within the Jewish community. Instead of a strong, unified front, three lists of candidates were put forward: a United Jewish Democratic List (UJD), composed of the Zionist, Mizrachi, Socialist, Folkist, and Labor Parties, together with small merchant groups and the unaffiliated; an Achdut (Agudath Israel) list backed by several large Jewish business concerns; and a slate representing elements within the right-wing propertied class.

An attempt had been made during the election campaign to unite the UJD and Achdut (Agudath Israel) lists, but negotiations broke down when the UJD presented two terms that Achdut (Agudath Israel) refused to accept: 1) Achdut (Agudath Israel) must cease its independent political activity, dissolve its Religious *Kehilla*, and send Hayyim Krone back to his yeshiva; and 2) Achdut (Agudath Israel) members of the Seimas must subordinate themselves to the authority of the joint list and fight together for Jewish national autonomy. As these talks went on, the UJD list reached an agreement with the German and Polish minorities.

Had the UJD-Achdut negotiations been concluded earlier, the outcome of the elections might have been different. As it happened, the Achdut rabbis threatened anyone voting for the UJD list with excommunication, invoking the rarely used epithet *arur* (Heb. "accursed"). The two lists could not even agree on a residual-vote arrangement; the UJD list did come to terms with the Polish and German minorities on the extra votes in a purely technical agreement.

The lack of cooperation deeply undercut Jewish political influence. The UJD list was the only Jewish slate that obtained any seats at all. Three of its candidates – Robinson, Finkelstein, and Garfunkel – were elected, as against seven Jewish delegates in the Second Seimas. Votes cast for the other Jewish lists were lost to the community. One of the 15 seats obtained by the Social Democrats went to a Jew, Lazar Epstein, a former member of the Bund.

In the interim period before a government could be formed, A. Stulginskis, the acting President of the Republic, invited the oldest member of the Seimas to preside over the first two sessions. By chance, the senior parliamentarian was Ozer Finkelstein. Finkelstein took the opportunity to congratulate the new coalition and the country itself for the liberal, democratic government for which it had voted. He was warmly applauded by all but the Christian Democrats, but even they cheered when he made reference to the importance of Vilna.

On May 31, 1926, the Jewish faction in the Seimas formed an advisory subcommittee (*beirath*) representing all political parties and economic associations – including Achdut, despite all the election-campaign recriminations and infighting.

The coalition government formed in June, supported by the Jewish faction and all the minority delegates, was decidedly left-wing. Mykolas Slezevicius was selected as Prime Minister and Dr. Kazys Grinius (Populists) as President. In October 1926, the new government declared an amnesty for most political prisoners, including some Communists. With the approval of the Seimas, the prevailing Defense Regulations that the Christian Democrats had applied to constrain freedoms were abolished. Political offenses previously tried by military courts were now given to the jurisdiction of the civil courts. Unions resumed their activities. The salaries of the clergy were cut from the government budget.

On June 9, 1926, President Grinius made several promises. He would work for the repeal of laws enacted by the Second Seimas that interfered with freedom of the press and public assembly. He would campaign for the principles of full democracy. The government would fully honor its obligations to the minorities as solemnly undertaken to the League of Nations.[123] Just two days later, Jewish deputies were elected to the economic, education, and house committees of the Seimas. In a policy statement on June 23, 1926, the government promised Jews full equality before the law, as guaranteed by Article 10 of the constitution. Minority rights neglected for the past two years would be restored in accordance with Paragraphs 73 and 74 of the constitution.

The situation of the Jewish community began to improve. The new Minister of the Interior, M. Vladas Pozela, abolished the office of the Referent of the National *Kehillot* and dismissed Hayyim Krone. The unpopular, government-sponsored Yiddish newspaper *Kovner Tsayt* was shut down. Plans to repeal the Sunday and Festivals Laws were at hand.

These developments so encouraged the Jewish leadership that it began again to plan for Jewish national autonomy. By early September 1926, Deputy Garfunkel unveiled his national autonomy project. The Seimas first debated it on October 5, and discussions in the legislature, and in all Jewish political groups and the Advisory Subcommittee, continued through the end of November.

Others, however (pro-Communist and other previously banned elements) made use of the new liberalization and democratic freedoms to promote their political programs. The Nationalist Party and the far-right factions, which harped on the dangers of communism, decried this and mobilized their supporters for anti-government demonstrations backed by press campaigns. Capping the ferment were rumors that the government was about to cut the defense budget, which indeed consumed a hefty share of state revenues.

On the night of December 17-18, 1926, a group of army officers carried out a *coup d'etat*, abolished the Seimas, and arrested several legislators. A. Voldemaras of the Nationalist Party, joined by the Christian Democrats and members of the Peasant Party, seized the reins of government and ousted Grinius. They appointed a Seimas of their own choosing, which elected Antanas Smetona as President. In January 1927, they recalled the members of the Third Seimas for several months. When, however, one of the Populist members was illegally arrested, the Socialist delegates including the Jewish faction were instrumental in passing a non-confidence motion on April 12, 1927.

President Smetona immediately dissolved the Seimas and did not, as required by the constitution, call for new elections. This marked the end of democratic Lithuania. With the demise of the parliament, Lithuanian Jewish hopes and aspirations for national autonomy perished as well.

Legacy of the Autonomy Period: The Lithuanian Jewish School System

Meeting Community Needs: A Model for Diaspora Jewry

Even as national autonomy for Lithuanian Jews floundered and failed, quality education, traditionally a prime concern of all Diaspora communities, reached a pinnacle in this small country at precisely that time. The success of Jewish education in Lithuania, which preceded, coincided with, and outlived autonomy, was such that Jews around the world, echoing Napoleon's likening of Vilna to Jerusalem, regarded the country as a second Eretz Israel.

Enrollment rates were stupendous. By 1925, 93 percent of Jewish children in Lithuania attended Jewish elementary schools; 80 percent attended Jewish secondary schools. The languages of instruction were Hebrew, Yiddish, or both. The system was accredited by the Lithuanian Ministry of Education, and elementary school teachers were paid by the state in the same manner as their non-Jewish colleagues. Some expenses, too, were met by municipal authorities.

The government and the intelligentsia fully encouraged Jews to assume responsibility for educating their own, and the government especially favored the establishment of Jewish schools by local communities. Such positive attitudes can be explained not so much by government appreciation of Jewish educational needs as by the absence of a ramified national school network and the poor standard of such schools as existed. In any case, the Lithuanians, immersed in their own difficult struggle against German and Russian assimilationist tendencies, could not hope at this stage to influence others.

As official commitments to autonomy waned, the government took actions that would have led to the demise of the Jewish schools had they not developed organically and independently of political maneuvering. The education system survived the liquidation and collapse of the Jewish autonomous institutions in 1924-25, and continued to flourish even after the Ministry of Education gradually reduced its subsidies in the late 1920s, leaving the communities to bear the funding burden largely by themselves. The reason for their survival was the confidence of the Jewish community in its spiritual traditions and its dedication to education, rooted in Jewish ethics and culture.[124]

The Charter for the Jewish school system was set forth in Paragraphs 5, 6, and 7 of the 1922 League of Nations Minorities Proclamation. These provisions affirmed the inherent right of all minority groups to establish their own education systems with government support. These rights, extended to the high-school and gymnasium level, were reconfirmed in the first and second Lithuanian constitutions.

Constitutional guarantees notwithstanding, government support was inevitably accompanied by restrictions and controls, most of which eventually clashed with the Jewish *weltanschauung*. The Ministry of Education supervised the administrative, financial, curricular, personnel, and admissions aspects of the system. Since all the inspectors were Lithuanians who knew neither Yiddish nor Hebrew, their jurisdiction was limited to the small portion of the curriculum devoted to secular Lithuanian subjects. They had little influence, especially in the early years.

Another source of tension originated within the Jewish community itself, for the polemic over the ratio of secular to exclusively Jewish studies refused to ebb. It reflected not only the Jews' relationship with the Lithuanian authorities but the community's own quest for identity in a changing world. The Lithuanian government, influenced by the Catholic Church, constantly urged the Jewish schools to place greater emphasis on Lithuanian subjects, and subsequently, to allocate more hours for the study of Lithuanian language and culture. Jewish educators sought to keep Lithuanian national influence in their schools to a minimum. However, most Lithuanian Jews, including the Orthodox, were convinced by now that some form of secular Lithuanian education was needed in order to achieve full Jewish participation in national life, a cause universally regarded as being in their own best interest.[125]

However, with the failure of Jewish autonomy and the bitter recriminations that followed, many began to feel that independent Lithuania had too little to offer. Large numbers of Jews then found inspiration in the Zionist ideal and the rebirth of Eretz Israel. This elevated the importance of study of Hebrew language and literature, Zionist ideology, and preparation for life in Eretz Israel. Consequently, the Hebrew education system profited vastly. Just as Lithuanian Jews were pioneers and pacesetters in many fields of Jewish education, they were also key players in the dissemination of Zionist ideals.

The curriculum and ideology of the Jewish schools varied greatly, but many similarities were visible. The most obvious distinctions focused on the language of instruction and the extent of Orthodoxy practiced. The Yavneh schools were firmly Orthodox and maintained a rigid distance from their less

Orthodox counterparts – though not to the extent of eschewing Hebrew as the language of instruction for all subjects. The Kultur Lige schools, influenced by Socialist-Marxist ideas, were noted for secularism and an almost exclusive use of Yiddish in the classroom. In the middle were the *peshore* ("compromise") schools; these adhered to a somewhat traditional orientation and taught all subjects in Hebrew. Appropriately, they were considered offspring of the Zionist movement.

The predominant vehicle of Jewish education in Lithuania was Tarbut ("culture" in Hebrew), a self-contained education system spanning kindergarten to gymnasium. Tarbut schools were neither religious nor anti-religious; their orientation was Zionist-nationalist. Bible and Hebrew language and literature were taught, and students were imbued with love of Eretz Israel. In its 22 years of existence (1918-1940), Tarbut enrolled some 60,000 pupils, 70 percent of Jewish children in the country. The influence of Tarbut transcended its enrollment figures, because it sponsored cultural and educational activities for all segments of the community including adults. Indeed, Tarbut was an all-pervasive element in Jewish Lithuania and a significant force in linking the varying communities with one another.

The community regarded preschool education as the stepping stone to all further Jewish schooling. This thinking was much ahead of its time and clashed frontally with the government program, in which attendance was compulsory for four years only, starting at the age of seven. In practical terms, this meant that various sectors of the community shouldered the burden of financing the preschools. Affluent parents paid tuition (30-50 lits per child per month) themselves, the *kehillot* provided the schools with grants, and overseas bodies such as the World Zionist Organization and the Jewish Agency for Palestine proffered assistance.

The four-year limitation of the government elementary-school program created a special problem for the Jewish schools, which, with their additional Hebrew syllabus, neither hoped nor expected to complete primary education within four years. Jewish schools sought to enroll their pupils for at least eight years, two in kindergarten and six in elementary school. The resulting conflict with the government education authorities was an early manifestation of many disputes that followed.

Jewish education did not end at sixth grade. After completing primary school, most youngsters began a four-year period of study in gymnasium, or, in communities too small or poor to afford a full gymnasium program, in a *progymnasium,* a regional institution of sorts, located in the large cities after the Central European model. Eleven such schools were established throughout Lithuania: three in Kovno and one each in Shavli, Panevezys, Marijampole, Virbalis, Vilkaviskis, Ukmerge (Wilkomir), Rasenai, and Yurbarkas. Students attended for eight years, sometimes entering the gymnasium after four years in the attached elementary school. All were privately maintained, supported in part by parents, local communities, and overseas Jewish organizations. They had the further purpose of enrolling students who, for whatever reason, could not commit themselves to eight years of post-primary education but could do so for four years. The *progymnasium* set high standards of education and achieved impressive results. The syllabus of the Tarbut progymnasium was especially broad, including Bible and Prophets; Mishna; Hebrew language and literature; Lithuanian, German, or English; mathematics; natural sciences; geography; Jewish and general history; arts and crafts; music; and physical education.

A major turnabout took place after World War I in the source of study materials. Before the Great War, most printed materials used in Lithuanian Jewish schools came from Palestine. Many Hebrew books, especially textbooks, were published in Vilna, Warsaw, and Odessa; others were brought in from Bessarabia. The 1920s, however, witnessed an outpouring of Hebrew textbooks from Lithuania to other Diaspora communities. These books focused innovatively on subjects that Hebrew texts had rarely treated previously, e.g., physics, mathematics, and Russian and German literature in translation.

Additional educational resources were culled from the extensive countrywide network of Jewish libraries. By 1930, Lithuania had 110 Hebrew public libraries and another 120 school libraries, all formed after the Great War and funded by *kehillot,* parents, and overseas support groups. The most important and largest of these facilities was the Abraham Mapu Library in Kovno, established in 1919.

Difficulties notwithstanding, the quality of Jewish education in Lithuania was outstanding. Graduates met the entrance criteria of most European universities. The Hebrew language was widely used, not only in the classroom but in the street. Tarbut graduates were prominent among Hebrew teachers throughout the Diaspora.

Several problems arose in the matter of government supervision. The Ministry of Education was not eager to hire Jewish inspectors, and its non-Jewish inspectors were initially handicapped by their inability to understand Hebrew. When matriculation examinations were first given, for example, only the results of papers given in Lithuanian could be judged. In 1928, however, the Ministry sent several inspectors to the Hebrew University in Jerusalem to study Hebrew. Having mastered the language, these government officials became much more influential. For the first time, they were able to evaluate the Hebrew-language curriculum, assess the quality of teachers and teaching, and issue such criticism and recommendations as they saw fit.

In 1927, Tarbut founded its own Hebrew Teachers' Training Seminary, which benefited to some extent from government subsidies. During its years of existence (1927-1933) it turned out 164 teachers, who were duly accredited by the Ministry of Education. The graduates, who accounted for some 60 percent of Hebrew elementary-school teachers in the Tarbut system, were allowed to teach Jewish subjects in the first four grades of the gymnasia. In 1933, the government closed the seminary and opened its own teachers' college at the University of Kaunas, meant to serve as a training center for the entire country. Although no explicit reason for this action was given, the Jews felt that the government was interested in exercising greater control over Jewish education. From this time on, the only recognized Jewish teacher-training program was the Yavneh-sponsored Orthodox college at Telz.

The Yavneh system deserves special emphasis. Until World War I, Jewish religious education in Lithuania followed the traditional path: *heder, Talmud Torah, yeshiva qetana, yeshiva gedola*. A bare minimum of secular subjects was taught in the first two of these; the yeshivot devoted no time whatsoever to secular studies. The language of instruction in all of these prewar institutions was Yiddish.

This changed in 1921, when the Yavneh network, newly formed by the non-political religious organization Tse'irey Israel and directed by Yitzchak Kopelovitz (the only director it would ever know), incorporated the *hadarim* and *Talmudey Torah* into a broadly based school system that would eventually win the full support of all important rabbis in Lithuania. In doing so, Yavneh implemented four significant and far-reaching organizational innovations: elementary education was introduced for girls (*heder* had been for boys only); secondary education was made available for boys and girls; teacher-training programs for male and female educators were established; and the first

Orthodox kindergartens were opened. The curriculum, too, contained several fundamental changes: Hebrew as the language of instruction for all subjects, and study of the Lithuanian language. Just the same, only Orthodox teachers were employed for both religious and secular subjects. With these policies, the Yavneh network was able to meet the community's needs, conform to Ministry of Education requirements, and match the level attained by other Jewish and Lithuanian schools.

At first the government took account of the religious nature of these schools, granting them the coveted right to teach more hours than the nonreligious schools. The system burgeoned. In 1920, Yavneh opened 40 elementary schools throughout Lithuania; the following year it received requests to open another 80 schools. By 1928, one-third of all Jewish schools in Lithuania were affiliated with Yavneh.

In its early stage, Yavneh had much trouble finding qualified local teachers for its secondary schools. Teachers were "imported" from Germany or recruited among the German-Jewish scholars who attended Lithuanian yeshivot. Yitzchak Kopelovitz and other religious educators shared the conviction, later adopted by Tarbut, that only a school system that produced its own teachers could call itself complete. Thus in 1921, Yavneh founded a seminary for male teachers in Kovno. It functioned there for two years; in 1923 it moved to Telz in order to profit from the influence of R. Joseph Leib Bloch, the famed *rosh yeshiva* of the great Talmudic institution in that city. Yavneh established a women teachers' seminary the same year, also located in Telz. Eventually, Yavneh filled its faculty positions with its own alumni and Orthodox graduates of the University of Kaunas. To maintain the quality of its personnel, Yavneh established a Teachers' Association at the end of 1927 and an in-service training center in the village of Kulautuva, near Kovno.

All Yavneh schools and institutions, including the teacher-training programs, were closed in 1940 with the onset of Soviet occupation in Lithuania. Their influence on Jewish education in the Diaspora, however, transcended and outlived them. Today, Jewish communities around the world have Yavneh school systems, modeled after the parent program that flourished briefly in independent Lithuania.

Lithuanian Jewish children who did not attend schools affiliated with Tarbut or Yavneh generally enrolled in Yiddish-speaking schools, the first of which were founded in 1918-1920. This trend, initiated by local Jewish communities, was encouraged and supported by the German military authorities that ruled Lithuania in the early postwar period. These schools' exclusive use of Yiddish as the language of instruction coincided nicely with the broader German plan to annex Lithuania and replace the native tongue with German; Yiddish-speaking Jews were regarded as being "halfway there." Another factor that stimulated the growth of Yiddish schools was a large postwar influx of Jewish children returning to Lithuania after attending similar institutions in Russian refugee centers.

Very few of these first schools were politically aligned; their sole affiliation was with the Kultur Lige ("Culture League"), founded in 1919. The Lige drew its original membership from two main groups: intellectuals whose prime concern was elementary education for the masses; and various Bundist and socialist elements. However, the non-partisan nature of the Yiddish schools changed drastically in 1921, when the Lige was taken over by members of the Jewish Communist Party who had infiltrated its ranks. At their urging, a Lige conference held that year resolved to purge Hebrew language and Bible from the curriculum. The communist influence was further reflected in a resolution to adopt the Yiddish orthography preferred by the Yevsektsia. This had the effect of rendering Yiddish words of Hebrew origin in a manner that would not remind students of Hebrew. To entrench these principles, the conference then banned non-supporters of the Third International from membership in the Lige. The dramatic radicalization purged the Yiddish schools of many of their most important founders, although the noted educator Dr. Helene Chazkelis and a few others were allowed to remain.

Both the Jewish community and the anti-communist Lithuanian authorities came to regard these schools as ideologically leftist, which they were. Relations between the Yiddish schools and the government deteriorated into spates of arrests and harassment of teachers by the secret police. The nadir was reached in 1924, when the government officially banned the Kultur Lige and its associated institutions as part of a crackdown on socialist-left education. The associated institutions suffered greatly; many teachers were arrested, fled the country, or went underground.

The leadership vacuum was filled by a new organization, Hovevey Da'at (Hebrew for "Lovers of Knowledge"). Under its tutelage, Yiddish schools previously affiliated with the Kultur Lige reopened and several secular schools in the provinces, previously closed down for suspected left-wing teachings, were allowed to reopen. Hovevey Da'at functioned until 1939, when the government forced it to close for good as an expression of its growing awareness of the Soviet threat to Lithuania. (Indeed, the Soviets invaded the country one year later.) During its fifteen-year tenure (1924-1939), Hovevey Da'at sponsored 15-20 Yiddish primary schools with a total enrollment of 1,300-1,700. The schools hosted evening classes for youths and adults with enrollment of 1,200-2,000. Several kindergartens were established, and some 300 children, mostly from low-income families, attended.

When the Laudininkai, the Lithuanian Folkist (Populist) Party, came to power in 1926, it recognized a different agency, the Jewish Folkist Society for the Dissemination of Culture, as the authority that would supervise and manage the Yiddish schools. (The Folkists were more firmly associated with certain Lithuanian circles than Hovevey Da'at.) Under the leadership of Dr. Mendel Sudarsky, a well-known physician, the schools succeeded in their struggle to maintain independence.

The Yiddish Reali[126] Gymnasium in Wilkomir (Ukmerge) is perhaps the best case in point. The Gymnasium was founded in 1920 in the face of opposition from radicals, who rejected this type of school altogether as being "for the bourgeois." The first Yiddish high school established in Lithuania, and for six years the only one, the Reali differed from other Yiddish schools in that its curriculum included Hebrew and Bible. It also made every effort to minimize the leftist influence that had proved so prejudicial to the Yiddish elementary schools. In its best years, the Wilkomir Reali Gymnasium had a student body of 250. The economic depression of the 1930s sent it into decline; it was forced to close down in 1933.

The second Yiddish gymnasium was founded in 1926 in Kovno. Named the Yiddish Commercial Gymnasium, it was established by the Jewish Folkists with government permission. Beginning with 35 students, it attained a total enrollment of 400 in 1938. Its curriculum included the sciences, Jewish and general history, religion (which was obligatory), and the business studies for which the school was named. It had an extensive extracurricular program of drama classes and many indoor and outdoor sports. Later renamed the Sholem Aleichem Gymnasium, it was the only Jewish high school that the Soviets allowed to function normally during their occupation of Lithuania. After ordering the Tarbut and Yavneh schools to close their doors, the Soviet authorities reassigned their students to newly organized Yiddish schools that toed the Soviet line.

Importantly, the share of Lithuanian Jewish children who attended Yiddish schools and gymnasia never exceeded 15-20 percent. These

institutions catered mainly to children from the poorer strata of the
community. Several exceptions existed. For example, affluent parents with
far-left ideological commitments made exclusive use of these schools.

"Lithuanization"

As briefly noted, the Jews never succeeded in obtaining the appointment of
even one Jewish inspector for their schools. Even during the brief golden era
of Jewish autonomy, when the Ministry for Jewish Affairs had its own
department of education, the Jewish voice in government was not strong
enough to secure a national role in school administration. The most
influential Jew in education was German-born Dr. Leo Deutschlander, who
served as an advisor to the Ministry of Education in 1919-1924; however, he
was merely a liaison officer between the Ministry and the Jewish Committee
for Education, a subcommittee of the Natzional Rath.

From 1926 onward, a process that may be termed Lithuanization gathered
steam. The government increasingly acted on Christian Democrat
propositions to curtail the development of minority education. It abolished
the Tarbut teachers' college (which, in 1927, had been transformed into the
higher Hebrew Pedagogical Institute and existed in this form until 1933) and
withheld permission for the opening of new schools. Some Jewish elementary
schools were forced to close, and the state subsidies given to others were
reduced. Teachers and students were ordered to spend more time on
Lithuanian studies, and the required language of instruction for some
subjects reverted from Hebrew or Yiddish to Lithuanian, contrary to
Paragraph 9 of the first constitution.[127] Public notices and posters in
languages other than Lithuanian were forbidden. The education inspectors
gradually clamped down on the Jewish schools, in contradiction of Paragraph
9 of the first constitution, which allowed elementary schools the explicit
privilege of teaching in the mother tongue of the minorities.

An upturn in the number of Jewish children attending public elementary
schools had become evident by 1935. In 1937, 45 Jewish schools out of a total
of 365 left the Jewish education system and merged into the public network.
The rest of the impressive system carried on until the Red Army marched into
Lithuania in 1940.

Jews in Lithuanian Economy and Society

Social Structure

The Great War had left Lithuania in shambles: its agriculture backward, its industry ruined, its productivity poor, and its most important export market, Russia, gone.

Lithuanian farmers began to move into the cities, displacing minorities from the high social strata there. By 1923-1924, a Lithuanization of the social infrastructure had begun. Lithuanians occupied 90 percent of the positions in the civil service and administration of both the cities and the country as a whole; their share in the liberal professions was two-thirds. The social rejection of minorities was achieved mainly by peaceful methods, without pickets, protests, or large-scale pogroms.

The Lithuanian leadership was of peasant stock. It lacked an intelligentsia tradition; its concern was with furthering the interests and improving the quality of life of its own class. For this reason, it invested much effort and took much pride in land reform. At first members of this group took very slowly to city life and the liberal professions, but they became more aggressive by the late 1930s. The masses regarded the Lithuanian professional – the professor, the physician, the lawyer – not only as a patriot but also as a folk teacher and leader.

The circumstances of the Jews in Lithuania were very different. The country's largest minority group had long been urbanized. Jews were the skilled white-collar functionaries of Lithuania in the early independence years, holding executive positions in banking, trade, and industry. With their credit facilities and international connections, they were the country's leaders in import-export.[128] In 1923, almost 90 percent of all Lithuanian trade was in Jewish hands.[129] Moreover, professionals were in desperately short supply, especially in the early independence period, and Jews stepped into the breach en masse. Until 1923, interethnic economic and social relations were generally cordial, if only because there had been little integration before.

When the extraordinary peasant migration from the villages to the cities began, the new city dwellers met with educational and general standards of living that they had never encountered. They found the adjustment to urban life difficult. In time, however, they and their children moved into the new middle and professional classes and as such displaced the Jews from their formerly accepted traditional role.

The mid-1920s was a time of general deterioration in interethnic relations, especially where the Jews were concerned. Although there were enough jobs and opportunities for all, the Lithuanians were especially keen to better their own status to the exclusion of all others. This transition was fraught with resentment and friction. The government-owned cooperatives, which employed only Lithuanians, took over a growing share of activity formerly dominated by the private sector, in which Jews had been predominant.

The Lithuanians who moved into the cities supplanted Jewish private initiative and business, and the government provided various kinds of support – subsidies, tax benefits – to Lithuanian private or cooperative undertakings only. Lithuanian social groups were strongly differentiated; they had very little contact with each other and hardly communicated. The cultures they represented never learned to coexist, because the tendency in Lithuania was not to assimilate and absorb but to isolate and reject. The government, for its part, did everything it could to undermine the economic position of the Jewish middle class.[130]

Land Reform and the Jewish Farmer Class

The land reform of 1922 was set in motion in order to create a new middle class that would help obtain important export markets for Lithuanian agricultural products. In this sense, it was a great success. The newly created farms became the backbone of the social, economic and political leadership of the state. In the reform process, the government took title to real property previously owned by the Russian government, banks, church organizations, Russian colonials, and any individually-owned parcel larger than 80 hectares.[131] Most of the individuals affected were Poles. The land was redistributed to the armed forces, army volunteers, landless farmers, and other rural inhabitants with small holdings. It was a massive reform; it affected approximately 60 percent of the country's area and took the entire independence period to implement. However, army volunteers of minority ethnicity were excluded from these benefits. Jews were specifically excluded from the loans and tax relief that the Lithuanian peasants had been given.[132]

The Jewish farmer class, engaged mostly in market gardening and dairy farming, was a veteran player in the economic life of Lithuanian Jewry. According to a Russian census conducted in 1897, 5.5 percent of Jews in the District of Kaunas, 6 percent in the District of Vilna, and 9.2 percent in the Suwalki District worked in agriculture. The actual numbers were much higher; many Jews were afraid to declare agriculture as their occupation and concealed their landholdings by registering them in the names of non-Jewish acquaintances. Most of the land then farmed by Jews was leased, but the incidence of outright Jewish possession increased with the passing of time. By 1922, more than half of the land farmed by Jews was Jewish-owned. Jews owned estates, domestic gardens, and several types of farms: peasant-type, near the city, and near urban markets. Most of the Jewish estates were in Vilkaviskis, Marijampole, and especially Memel, where the Napoleonic Code allowed Jews to purchase and work their own land under conditions more favorable than elsewhere.

Near-urban farming was more suited to the Lithuanian Jewish character than rural farming, which only about 200 Jewish peasant families practiced. Near-urban farming allowed Jews to combine their livelihood with life in a Jewish atmosphere. Such a farmer could put his business talents to better use. Thus many cities with important Jewish communities were surrounded by fields and gardens worked by Jews. Jews were especially expert in the growing and processing of tobacco. Between 1916 and 1940, this industry was almost exclusively in Jewish hands, the most important plantations being in the vicinity of Kalvarija and Verzsbelowa.

Other Jewish farmers, not possessing land of their own, leased large parcels near major cities (Kovno, Kaidan, etc.) for the purpose of intensive market gardening. The Jews of Kaidan became famous throughout Lithuania for their excellent cucumbers. Even urban-dwelling Lithuanian Jews were accustomed to growing their own vegetables and fruit. Many a Jewish family had its own garden patch, which it worked either alone or with hired help. In this fashion, thousands of Jewish families provided their own food, including dairy produce, eggs, and poultry. Many such families, especially those on the outskirts of the big cities, sold food to augment their income.

Thus it is not surprising that approximately 1,000 Jewish families put in claims on the eve of the land reform. As farm laborers, market gardeners, and veterans of the war for Lithuanian independence, they were entitled to do so. The Lithuanian-dominated bureaucracy, however, made the registration process very difficult for them, and the Minister for Jewish Affairs had to intervene (with little success) at the cabinet level. With very few exceptions, land applications submitted by Jews were refused.

Still, in 1922, Shabtiel Deutsch, a writer for the *Idishe Shtime*, urged his fellow Jews to become farmers and market gardeners as a means of integrating into the new society. He also advised them to form their own farming cooperatives, so that the Jews might develop together with the rest of the country. He warned the Jewish community against self-imposed segregation and rejection of general trends. The very presence of so many successful Jewish farmers was cited as evidence of great potential in the new Lithuania for the harmonious and stable integration of Lithuanian Jewry into general society.[133] The secular Jewish intelligentsia, too, regarded work on the land as an ideal. Thus the Jewish poetess Judica Garud wrote that "the city to the village, is as a sick man to a healthy one."

The land reform and the years of economic crisis decimated the large Jewish estates. Some of them were taken over by priests, others by former Lithuanian cabinet ministers. In some cases, the Jewish property owners were bought out; in others, the sale of produce was restricted. The reform eliminated dairy farming by Jews altogether, although the production of so-called "Dutch cheese," which required considerable capital investment and expertise, remained exclusively in Jewish hands.

Jewish domestic vegetable gardening continued. The Lithuanian ORT organization, through its Kovno Agricultural Vocational school and its instructors who were always ready with advice, played a considerable part in its development.

Exclusionary Lithuanian Cooperatives – The "Three Giants"

The cooperative concept was introduced to Lithuania by the Germans in 1915. At that time, this form of activity was small in scale and relatively unimportant to the Lithuanian economy. The cooperative movement became popular after independence was achieved. Between 1923 and 1926, at the behest of the government, the existing cooperatives were reorganized into two centralized, semi-independent organizations: Pieno Centras, a central dairy cooperative that gradually brought almost all the country's dairies under its control; and Maistas, a meat-processing and -marketing cooperative that slowly took over a growing share of the domestic and foreign meat and poultry business, which the private sector had dominated theretofore. In 1934, a third actor of this type came on the scene: Lietukis, which quickly assumed control of all aspects of the flax industry.[134] The three cooperatives formed what became known as the "three giants." The government endorsed their monopolistic practices and subsidized them heavily. Consequently, private initiative in these industries, in which Jews were particularly involved, was stifled. Specifically, Jewish merchants in these fields complained that they received neither credit facilities nor export licenses. (The banking industry, with the exception of small Jewish banks, was government-dominated.) The "three giants" encouraged their own middlemen and educated their own class of private traders.

The new Lithuanian middle class favored this sort of economic development and took pride in its newly formed "giants." Also, convinced by now that Lithuania was too poor a country to countenance a multiethnic society, the non-Jewish middle class fought to oust all members of minority groups, especially Jews, from the mainstream of economic life.

Jewish Cooperative Societies

The Jewish middle class, long aware of this trait of Lithuanian society, worked actively to develop its own people's cooperatives, credit unions, and banks. By 1898, numerous mutual loan associations (*gemilut hasadim kases*) were active throughout the country. In 1911, there were 24 such loan associations in Kovno alone, in addition to five credit cooperatives in Suwalk, with a total of 3,517 members.[135] The Jewish community of independent Lithuania inherited 26 such entities, which were legally registered in 1919 as an Association of Jewish Cooperatives. The Jews also had their own *folksbenk* ("people's banks"), where Yiddish was used in transactions and conferences even though five percent of the clientele was not Jewish. The seed money and the banking experience and know-how required for the establishment of the central *folksbenk* was provided by the American Jewish Joint Distribution Committee. This came about after lengthy discussions between the AJJDC representative in Lithuania and the local community leadership, the latter insisting that it wanted help and assistance, but not charity, which was the usual province of the AJJDC. The rest of the capital came from Jewish merchants who were dissatisfied with the service provided by Lithuanian banks, especially with respect to long-term credit, and by Jewish artisan guilds that instructed members to open saving accounts with the *folksbenk*.

The *folksbenk* performed as well as the general Lithuanian economic situation permitted and were affected by specific Jewish crises and problems. Evidently, they did well.[136] The Jews of Lithuania had such confidence in their banks that the institutions long outlived the autonomy. Only in 1940, when the Soviet Union occupied Lithuania, did they close.

Beginning in 1921, 47 Jewish cooperatives co-founded a bimonthly journal called *Zydu Koperatorius* (Jewish Cooperatives), subsequently the newspaper of the Jewish *folksbenk*. Part of each edition was devoted to studies of the social and economic structure of individual Lithuanian Jewish communities, and reports were published for their mutual benefit and development.

On May 16, 1922, the first All-Lithuanian Cooperative Congress took place with the participation of 188 delegates. Twenty Jewish *folksbenk*, four manufacturing cooperatives, and two agricultural cooperatives took part. Reporting on this Congress, Dr. Abraham Zabarsky, a founder of the *folksbenk* and later president of Bank Hapoalim in Israel, remarked:

> The very fact that Jewish delegates sat with their Lithuanian colleagues to discuss common attitudes toward taxation and other problems was in itself a major achievement. The opportunity to present Lithuanian society with a report on the work and activity of the Jewish cooperative movement was [a matter] of great moral significance, because this particular aspect of Jewish life was unknown to the Lithuanian public, and the Jew was seen only as the shopkeeper and trader with whom they were in daily conflict.[137]

Nevertheless, most of the conference delegates were hostile toward their Jewish colleagues. For example, the representative of the Jewish cooperatives who was elected to the presidium was denied a place on the platform.

Antisemitism in Modern Lithuania

In the country's early years, most Lithuanian national antipathy was directed against Russians and Poles, although it was never expressed in attacks on individuals, even during the heights of anti-Russian and anti-Polish sentiments in 1918-1920. The Jews, however, were the targets of Lithuanians' residual xenophobic inclinations; they were the ideal scapegoats in this sense, and were perfect scapegoats in the mythology of oppression that fueled economic hatred.

Lithuanians habitually felt, correctly or not, that they always received a raw deal in their transactions with Jews; they could not advance in certain businesses because these were "full of Jews." These were not fraternal lodge mutterings. They were openly expressed in the press and in everyday conversation.[138]

Lithuania was a Catholic country in which government, people, and most political parties were influenced by the Church and its agents. The Jews were conspicuous and often held to be ludicrous, with their strange customs and language, their class consciousness, and their continuous struggles: for justice, for recognition as citizens, for their own place in society, for equality under the law.

The rise of the Lithuanian lower-middle class coincided with an organized, active, and dynamic form of economic antisemitism, initiated and led by the Verslininkai. According to this new doctrine, the apportionment of the tiny country's wealth and economic potential would be greater and tidier without the Jews. This philosophy, with assistance from Nazi Germany, was responsible for the ultimate liquidation of the Jewish community of Lithuania.

The Jews as a distinct group were to be tolerated, sometimes even encouraged, as long as they were needed or considered irreplaceable. If the Jewish-Lithuanian harmony was under strain, it was not because the Lithuanians were growing richer but because the Jews were growing poorer and weaker and thus less essential to the national economy.

The antisemitic trend was fueled by an upturn in general political nationalism, a brand of thinking that excluded every minority group.[139] Slogans such as "Lithuania for the Lithuanians" and "No place for others in the economy, schools, or universities," became the platform of the Verslininkai and other fascist and ultranationalist groups. Although these factions were able to recruit and influence large numbers of people, some Lithuanians distanced themselves from the extremist camp. Some did so out of apathy; others vigorously opposed the idea of a totalitarian state – particularly those influenced either by the socialist ideas that Russia had brought to Lithuania or by the ideals of Western democracy. One need not be surprised that Jews flocked to the anti-fascist and anti-nationalist groups. In response, the antisemites concluded that all Jews were Communists...and capitalist oppressors. The masses soon treated antisemitic slogans of these types as gospel truth; they became common currency and were exploited by the Verslininkai to attract popular support.

It took only until 1921 for the blood libel to make its debut in independent Lithuania, when one Aliecha, a postal clerk in Kupishkis, accused "the Jews" of kidnapping a Christian child for ritual purposes. The community was exonerated in a subsequent trial.[140] By the next year, the Lithuanian press complained bitterly of the "many little countries" that the minorities, including the Jews, were aiming to create in Lithuania.

The rhetoric had come to the attention of Jewish communities abroad, but these were not truly concerned or worried about the situation of their Lithuanian coreligionists. Thus Lucien Wolf, a member of the Board of Deputies of British Jews, deemed these early manifestations of antisemitism to be "transitory" and insignificant.[141] Had Lithuania not signed the League of Nations proclamations on human rights and minority rights?

But it continued. Also in 1922, a secret society called Rytas (Morning) demanded the revocation of all special rights and privileges given the Jews under autonomy and prescribed a general expulsion of Jews from the country for "bringing Bolshevism to Lithuania," for which "God would punish them." Rytas was representative of other Lithuanian ultranationalist groupings, and its statement evoked a protest by American Jews outside the residence of Dr. Korneris, the Lithuanian Ambassador to the United States.[142] An important newspaper, also called Rytas, joined the antisemitic camp in 1924, allying itself with a newly organized group of intelligentsia in their fight against the Jewish National Council and Jewish equality before the law. By 1924, the Verslininkai seemed to be a strong, successful organization. Overt antisemitism was no longer a crime. By 1927, Young Lithuania, a fascist movement modelled on the Nazi organization, numbered some 40,000 members.

It is fair to note that some opposed the trend. Commenting on the liquidation of the Natzional Rath, Dr, Simon Rosenbaum, former Minister for Jewish Affairs, mocked the Lithuanian patriots who, in their enthusiasm to erase Jewish signs, had also erased Lithuanian signs. He warned that in its zeal to sunder Jewish rights, the government was in effect sowing the seeds for the destruction of democratic Lithuania. Occasionally, Gentile voices sharing Rosenbaum's beliefs could be heard. Lietuvos Zinios, in an editorial signed by A. Valaitis, called for a struggle to cleanse Lithuania of antisemitism. Valaitis' denunciation of antisemitism was predicated on his belief that this doctrine was a harbinger of ultranationalism, as manifested in the campaign to vandalize foreign-language signs. Valaitis complained that this evil had become widespread among the white-collar classes, the intelligentsia, and throughout the press – sectors of society that had harbored no anti-Jewish feelings before the Great War. He was right: until World War I, most of their hostile sentiments were directed against their Russian oppressors.

In 1927, to counter the attacks, the Jews established a biweekly Lithuanian-language journal called *Musu Zodys* (Our Word). In later years the Association of Lithuanian Jewish Ex-Servicemen took part in much of the anti-defamation activity by organizing meetings and gatherings, attended by Jews and Lithuanians, to further mutual understanding and respect and to bridge the widening chasm between the two societies.

Yet the government of Independent Lithuania, having replaced a backward, quasi-feudal, agrarian system with a more progressive, industrialized and socially mobile one, had fallen far short of its avowed aims. The government's rhetoric tended to hide this fact, not so much from its own citizens as from the rest of the world. It was obvious that in a situation such as this, the government, while proclaiming itself democratic, had to withhold much information from the public, even though freedom of the press and minority rights were written into the constitution.

When Smetona returned to power in 1927, he was faced with a difficult situation. Several groups, throwing caution to the winds, had indulged themselves in open criticism of the government and laid bare all the country's ills, vividly denouncing corruption, mismanagement, and political imprisonment. Jewish groups (except Achdut\Agudath Israel and the illegal Communists) were especially outspoken, pointing to appalling inequalities in opportunity, lack of the authentic representation promised them under autonomy, and other shortcomings. government spokesmen admitted that things were far from perfect and promised reform. But in doing so, they accused the Jews, in the classical European fashion, of having caused most of the country's problems in the first place.[143]

In late 1933, President Smetona, ostensibly and officially a friend of the Jews, surprised the British Consul in Kaunas in a private conversation by describing the Jews of Lithuania as "active Communists" and "dishonest traders." He also referred "not without some relish" to the three million Jews in Poland, "who, with their pro-Moscow tendencies, might shortly be a source of considerable embarrassment to the Polish government."

Dr. Jacob Robinson, a former member of the Seimas, confirmed Smetona's forked tongue years later by relating the following episode. In 1941, after settling in the United States, Smetona delivered himself of some strongly

antisemitic remarks at a press conference. When he later invited Robinson to
a meeting in order to discuss the Lithuanian government-in-Exile, Robinson
confronted him about his remarks. Smetona attempted to placate him by
claiming to have spoken in this fashion "only for the benefit of my own
Lithuanian-American public."[144] This, Smetona claimed, was what they
wanted to hear, for they blamed the Jews for Lithuania's troubles. Robinson
never saw Smetona again.

As antisemitism increased in scale and blatancy, opposition and protest,
even by the few intellectuals who had first been inclined to offer them, became
weaker. The few who dared raise their voice in protest were branded as
left-wing intellectuals whom the "Bolshevik" Jews were exploiting to incite
the workers.[145]

There was no doubt that the Jews had numerous enemies in the new
middle class, in government, and in the right-wing and Catholic sectors of
Lithuanian society. There is also no doubt that the example of Germany
stimulated the antisemitic movement in Lithuania, as it did elsewhere. The
Smetona government, however, could not allow itself to follow the Nazi
pattern to its logical conclusion, nor did it wish to do so. In Lithuania, things
had to be planned and designed so as not to reflect adversely on the
government.[146] The preferred Lithuanian modality was the smear campaign.
Indeed, such activities in their antisemitic context, intended to condition
public opinion and excuse government actions, went on for years. Often, when
Jews were attacked in the streets and savagely beaten, the police stood aside
idly. Sometimes thugs and plainclothes police intermingled indistinguishably
as the assaults went on.

By 1934, the government jettisoned the ballast of moral values in its
anti-Jewish policies. At this stage, antisemitic discrimination turned into
persecution. The Jews tried in vain to explain their special problems, that
they wished only to be allowed to live Jewish lives as Lithuanian citizens in
the free democratic Republic. They were shouted down and accused of selling
the country to Bolshevism. The Nationalists became more extreme, the
Fascists stronger and more numerous. By the late 1930s, the Jews' initial
anger had given way to despair, for the Jewish Question and the fate of
Lithuanian Jewry were about to become part of the most horrific catastrophe
in European and human history.

Summing Up Lithuanian Jewish Autonomy: Vision and Reality

Jewish autonomy in Lithuania was an unprecedented experiment for Jews and Lithuanians alike. The participation of Jews in the overall political activity of the country generated a brief efflorescence of Jewish political and national life, coupled with substantial advances in Jewish self-expression that outlived the autonomy itself. Even after the hopes aroused by Jewish cultural autonomy and the establishment of a Jewish ministry had been dashed, Jews remained optimistic as long as Lithuania remained democratic. In retrospect, one marvels at the degree of wishful thinking that the Jewish community entertained amid entrenched local antisemitic prejudice, the influence of the neighboring countries, and the general Jewish situation in the world. The Lithuanians regarded the Jewish problem something other than theirs, and as something that had never really been solved anywhere in the world. Just the same, Jewish autonomy survived longer in Lithuania than in the other countries where it was tried.

The Seimas, ostensibly empowered to manage the country's affairs including Jewish autonomy, was a remarkable but lamentably short-lived institution. Its decline began almost imperceptibly at the time of the 1926 *coup d'etat*, and progressed until the Soviet invasion in 1940. Ruthless government patronage enabled the one-party system to subdue the enfeebled assemblies with little resistance. It became possible with the stroke of a pen to override the constitution, dismiss the Seimas, banish deputies, and exile undesirables. Even the majority groups were aware of the menace. The minority groups knew full well that the promises made to them on rights and constitutions had not been honored. The Jewish faction in the Seimas continued to function as long as it could but, truth to tell, never accomplished much of significance.

The Seimas retained popular support as long as it was able to hold democratic elections. The people of the new Lithuania, however, lacked the maturity, the will, and the democratic heritage to fight for their democratic parliament. The fact that the Seimas was unable to contest the government's authoritarian leadership indicated that it had never mustered the nation's whole-hearted support. For its part, the Seimas sensed less danger from the masses than from the government, which, instead of promoting debate of public issues, played on public hysteria and diverted public resentment against its policies toward convenient scapegoats. Seats in the Seimas were sought for prestige, money, and power, and were often obtained through ministers' personal recommendations and by nepotism.

The government's de facto dictatorship created fears of a social revolution – first from the Soviet Union and later from Nazi Germany – that would envelop and overrun the country. The actual threat was more prosaic and physical; to some extent, it could have been foreseen.

*Seal of the
Minister for Religious Affairs*

*Seal of the
Jewish National Council*

Chapter 6

DEVASTATION LOOMS

The Baltic Union for Neutrality

In neighboring Germany, the National Socialist Party under Adolf Hitler came to power in March 1933. A time of reckoning for all humankind was imminent. For Lithuanian Jewry, the first steps to annihilation had been taken.

The Lithuanian government and public watched as the new Nazi regime earned a moral boost by signing a Concordat with the Vatican despite its undisguised persecution of German Jews. They noted the lack of world reaction to the introduction of the Nuremberg Racial Laws in 1935. They realized that one might not only hate and persecute Jews but demonize them as well. They then acted on these realizations. Consequently, the share of Lithuanian Jews who perished in the Holocaust, over 90 percent, was among the highest in Europe.[147]

Threatened by both of their totalitarian neighbors, Soviet Russia and Nazi Germany, who considered the Baltics a political arena in which to vie for dominance, the three Baltic states – Lithuania, Latvia, and Estonia – signed an agreement in the fall of 1934 to coordinate their foreign policy and mutual defense in a hopeless attempt to maintain their neutrality. Of all the minorities in Lithuania, the Jews were the strongest supporters of the Baltic Union.[148]

Avenging Lost Vilna: Memel-Klaipeda

Memel, a city-enclave covering an area of a little more than 1,000 square miles, bordered the Russian Empire and belonged to Germany until 1919, when, in the aftermath of the Great War, it was ceded to the Allies under the Treaty of Versailles and administered by the French. In early 1923, the Lithuanians, seeking an outlet to the sea, seized the town in a surprise attack and forced the French garrison to surrender and evacuate. The case was referred to the League of Nations, which concluded the Memel Convention a year later. The Convention gave Lithuania its maritime outlet by declaring the city and its surrounding district an autonomous region under Lithuanian rule, henceforth known by its Lithuanian name, Klaipeda. However, the League limited Lithuanian sovereignty there by providing for the establishment of a local autonomous government with an elected chamber known as the Seimic or Seimelis (small Seimas). The governor was to be appointed by the president of Lithuania.

The League hoped that its action would appease the Lithuanians after the loss of Vilna and were confident that Germany would accept the loss as part of the price of defeat in World War I. It was wrong on both counts. More than half of the 141,000 inhabitants of prewar Memel spoke German as their mother tongue and continued after the annexation to regard Germany as their fatherland. Germany was as disinclined to accept the loss of Memel as Lithuania was to accept the loss of Vilna. Thus Germany and Lithuania now had a juicy bone of contention.

Jews in Memel are first mentioned in a document dated 1567, which refers to an edict dealing with their expulsion from the city. During the eighteenth century, Jews were allowed to visit for business purposes but not to establish permanent residence. They would thus spend weekdays in Memel and the Sabbath elsewhere. It was during this period, the early Enlightenment age, that Memel became a focal point of trade in Hebrew books printed in Germany, which were sold to Jews in Lithuania, Russia, and Poland. Only after the emancipation of the Jews of Prussia in 1812 by Napoleon were they permitted to settle freely in Memel.

It was a hybrid Jewish community, part German and part Eastern European, chiefly Lithuanian. Although German Jews formed the leadership of the *kehilla*, each group had its own synagogue and community institutions. R. Israel Salanter, the founder of the Musar movement, lived and taught in

Memel for 20 years (1860-1880) and built a *beit midrash* there for Lithuanian Jews.

The Lithuanian Jewish community of Memel shared the fate of other Jewries under Russian rule. In 1886, as a reprisal for Russia's expulsion of Germans from Kaunas, Prussia ordered the expulsion of all Russians from Memel. The Eastern European Jewish community of the district was virtually wiped out. By special permission, a group of some 100 wealthy Lithuanian Jewish families whom Prussia valued for their Russian connections were allowed to remain in Memel, although their civil and personal rights were severely restricted. These conditions prevailed until the end of the Great War.

When the French administration occupied Memel and its surroundings after the War, Jews in the Lithuanian border towns began to flood the region. The Lithuanian authorities encouraged this influx because it helped increase the non-German population and influence in the area. Therefore, Lithuania's annexation of the Memel-Klaipeda strip led to a blossoming of Jewish community activities in the area. Powered by the Zionists, who held a decisive majority in the *kehilla*, religious, cultural, and welfare institutions flourished. Klaipeda became the center of an important *hakhshara* (training program) of the Hehaluts movement, which prepared potential immigrants to Palestine for pioneering farm labor on kibbutzim. The community provided Hehaluts with a large parcel of land and a large house for this purpose. Thus thousands of young Lithuanian Jewish idealists passed through Memel-Klaipeda and made use of these facilities on route to Eretz Israel. Hebrew-speaking circles became very popular; Hebrew kindergartens and a Hebrew day school were established as an alternative to the German-language schools that most Jewish children had attended. Politically orientated Zionist groups proliferated there; the newly formed Maccabi and Bar Kokhba sports clubs attracted numerous members. In all, the community numbered about 9,000, accounting for 17 percent of the total population.

Throughout this period, the "western" (German) and "eastern" (predominantly Lithuanian) elements in Jewish Klaipeda continued to maintain their separate identities. However, all members of the community, influenced though many were by German culture and education, considered themselves loyal Lithuanian citizens and were grateful to the new state for the autonomy and equal rights that it had granted them. This explains why Jews did not participate in the region's struggle against the Lithuanian central government. In fact, they overwhelmingly if discretely sympathized with pro-Lithuanian parties. However, the Memel-Klaipeda administration was dominated by pro-German elements. A large majority of members of the judiciary, the civil service, the health and medical services, industry, and the liberal professions were either German-born or -educated. German ethnics also controlled the press, including the Lithuanian newspaper that had the largest circulation in Klaipeda. The Jews, wary of German reprisals, kept their pro-Lithuanian passions to themselves.

In the 1930 elections to the Klaipeda Seimic, the pro-Lithuanians succeeded in obtaining only four of the 29 seats. This dealt a harsh blow to the prestige and authority of the Lithuanian government in the newly semi-acquired district. Pro-German influence on the region increased alarmingly, accompanied by pressure from the growing National Socialist party in Germany itself. The pro-German parties in the legislature took their directives from Berlin, via the German Consul in Klaipeda or through nearby Koenigsberg, and did nothing to conceal this. In 1933, the Lithuanian government protested Germany's interference in the affairs of Klaipeda to the International Court in The Hague. The court ruled in favor of Lithuania, whose authority in the region was thereby strengthened.[149] In the next local elections (1932), the Jewish community actively and openly supported the pro-Lithuanian candidates. With the Jews' assistance, these candidates obtained almost 20 percent of the votes, a considerable improvement on their previous result but of little effect on the supremacy of the pro-German parties.

In June 1933, a National Socialist organization, Sovog (*Sozialitische Volksgemeinschaft*), was formed in Klaipeda under Dr. Ernst Neumann. Sovog opposed the more moderate pro-German groups in Klaipeda and, amid bloody rivalry among the groups, quickly succeeded in gaining a majority in the next round of municipal elections (1932), as well as control of the local economy, schools, and streets. By the end of 1933, some Jews had sold their business and either moved to Lithuania proper or emigrated overseas. Others, though uneasy and frightened, chose to remain despite the growing antisemitism in the region, fomented by pro-German and anti-Lithuanian forces.

In late 1933, with the support of Gauleiter Koch of Eastern Prussia, Neumann became the official representative of the German Nazi Party in Klaipeda and openly demanded the return of the Memel-Klaipeda region to Germany. Shortly thereafter, accused by the Lithuanian government of inciting and financing Nazi sympathizers and organizations in Klaipeda and

Lithuania proper, Neumann was tried and sentenced to 12 years of hard labor; many of his followers received lesser sentences. Hitler was enraged. In 1936, there was a blood libel in Klaipeda, which the local Nazis exploited extensively to foment further antisemitic actions and propaganda.

Between 1936 and 1938, Berlin stepped up its pressure on the district that it called Memelland. Its tactic was patterned on the Sudeten model, i.e., vociferous allegations of Lithuanian mistreatment of the German community in Klaipeda. Trade relations between the two countries were severed and, for all intents and purposes, the frontier was closed by Lithuanian initiative. Lithuania could hardly afford a breach with Nazi Germany, which was one of her most important export markets. Consequently, in late 1936 the Lithuanian government granted full local self-government to the German community of Klaipeda at the expense of local Jews and other pro-Lithuanian groups. All the political prisoners were granted presidential pardons; Neumann returned to Memelland from prison in Lithuania to become the local Nazi *fuhrer*.

By 1938 the Klaipeda administration was almost completely dominated by local Nazis, including the president of the Directory,[150] an ex-prisoner who had been convicted and sentenced with Neumann and who supported the latter in his demand that the 1935 Nuremberg Laws be applied to the area. In the December 1938 elections to the Memelland legislature, the Nazis took 25 of the 29 seats. With this, most of the 8,000 Jews who remained in Memel (and another 13,000 non-Jewish Lithuanians) abandoned their homes and businesses and fled to Lithuania as refugees. The news from Germany was terrible, and Neumann proclaimed Memel as German soil once and forever. Just the same, a significant number of Jews preferred to stay behind in the belief that nothing would happen to them.

Lithuania itself, including most of its Jewish community, shared this confidence. As Nazi Germany consummated its rape of Memel, Lithuania celebrated its twentieth anniversary of independence.

Lithuania and Germany signed a non-aggression pact on January 16, 1939. Just ten weeks later, on March 23, Nazi Germany occupied Memel-Klaipeda without firing a shot and incorporated it into the Reich. Several hours before the new agreement with Lithuania was concluded, Hitler himself arrived in Memel on a battleship and at the head of an impressive fleet of warships to take over Lithuania's only port and the surrounding territory.[151] The few Jews who remained in Memel shared the fate of German Jews in the Holocaust; the majority, who fled to Lithuania, were spared this demise only to share the destiny of Lithuanian Jewry.

Lithuania, Lithuanian Jewry, and the Soviet Occupation

The Molotov-Ribbentrop Pact – the Soviet-Nazi "nonaggression treaty" of August 23, 1939, which astonished an unsuspecting world – secretly partitioned Eastern Europe into Russian and German spheres of influence, with all three Baltic states, Lithuania, Latvia, and Estonia, in the Soviet orbit. When the German invasion of Poland nine days later marked the beginning of World War II, these Baltic states, unaware of the provisions of the Molotov-Ribbentrop Pact, loudly proclaimed their neutrality in hope of avoiding the conflict. On September 18, the Red Army occupied Vilna and its district together with the rest of the Soviet share of Poland, as agreed upon with the Germans.

At the time of the annexation, the Vilna area had a Jewish population of more than 100,000 – some 70,000 in the city itself (of a total population of 200,000) and more than 30,000 in 20 neighboring townlets and villages.

Pact or not, the Soviet Union and Germany discreetly competed for the goodwill of the Baltic states. Baltic representatives were invited to both Moscow and Berlin to discuss trade and other bilateral agreements; each of the two powers attempting to twist their arms as vigorously as possible without appearing to do so.

Events progressed speedily. In early October 1939, the Kremlin ordered Lithuania to sign a mutual assistance agreement allowing the Red Army to station a 50,000-man garrison force on its soil and make use of Lithuanian air bases. An irresistible reward was offered: restoration of Vilna to the Lithuanian map. After desperate attempts to maintain its neutrality, Lithuania signed the agreement with Molotov cynically expressing mock surprise that Germany had not informed the Lithuanian government of the provisions of his pact with Ribbentrop. The treaty was concluded on October 10, 1939. Thus Lithuania reclaimed without bloodshed the ancient capital that it had never renounced and for whose restoration it had yearned for the past 20 years.

Overnight, the Jewish population of Lithuania increased by 100,000 and now totalled over a quarter of a million people, roughly ten percent of all inhabitants of the expanded territory. In Vilnius and Kaunas, anti-Jewish riots erupted as if part of the reunion celebrations. Jews were beaten in the streets of Vilna and their homes looted. Violence was particularly egregious in the university and the seminaries. Unfriendly, provocative articles appeared in the press, denouncing "foreign elements in our midst" and welcoming a German plan to establish a Jewish state in the Polish city of Lublin for all "undesirable elements." The Jewish leadership in Kovno threatened to call the attacks to the attention of the world press if they did not cease immediately. Within a few days, calm was restored. For their part, the Jews of Vilna were happy to be reunited with their Lithuanian coreligionists after the forced 20-year separation, and to be part of still-independent Lithuania instead of wholly occupied Poland.

The tide of Jewish refugees fleeing Poland continued to rise in the ensuing months. In all, some 25,000 Polish and a small number of German Jews found temporary refuge in Lithuania; about 15,000 stayed in Vilna, the rest in Kovno and smaller cities. Some of these refugees eventually succeeded in emigrating from Lithuania with the help of the AJJDC and the Jewish community; the remainder shared the fate of the Lithuanian Jews, first under the Russians and then at the hands of the Germans.[152]

The Russia forces dug in, establishing bases throughout Lithuania – in Kaunas, Vilnius, Siauliai, and Panevezys – but especially along the German frontier. The Red Army soldiers behaved correctly toward the local population, took children for rides in their vehicles, and sang in the streets, attracting crowds of admiring passersby. The military insisted on paying for all locally requisitioned supplies, and their purchasing power helped boost the Lithuanian economy. The troops claimed that they lacked nothing back home...but their one-track buying habit – snap up everything in sight – attested to the opposite.

As 1939 drew to a close, the economic situation in Lithuania continued to improve. Business was good. The Red Army garrisons and their families, combined with the thousands of refugees, caused trade and commerce to thrive. Farm exports, especially to the country's two behemoth neighbors, increased. Fear of possible involvement in the war was never far from anyone's thoughts.

For the Jews of Lithuania, and for the Jewish and non-Jewish refugees, Nazi Germany represented the greater threat. However little they sympathized with the Bolsheviks, the presence of Soviet garrisons on

Lithuanian soil gave them a sense of security. For their part, the Lithuanians in general disliked the Russians and, after the initial enthusiasm, did not conceal their hostility toward the Soviet troops and their families. Reporting to the State Department, J. C. Norrem, United States Minister to Lithuania, commented as follows: "The Red Army in Lithuania was greeted only by a foreign race [meaning the Jews] but not by the Lithuanian people."[153]

The Kremlin lodged repeated official protests with the Lithuanian government against what it termed hostile acts: kidnapping of Red Army soldiers (who had actually deserted), spying to obtain military secrets, and a very unfriendly press. In turn, the Lithuanians desperately sought to placate the Soviet Union. In the meantime, despite its non-aggression pact with the Soviet Union, Nazi Germany did what it could to aggravate the turmoil in Lithuania. Members of an important Catholic youth movement took to parading in the streets in uniforms similar to those of the Hitler Jugend. The influx of a suspiciously large number of German tourists brought warnings, even in the Catholic press, of the danger of a fifth column. Vast sums of money were transferred to Lithuania in support of local Fascist groups, especially the Activistu Frontas and former members of Voldemaras' Iron Wolf organization. With the money came anti-Jewish and anti-Soviet printed propaganda, as well as arms. Throughout all this, trade with Germany flourished, from which Jews had long been excluded under a boycott arranged collaboratively by Germany and Lithuania.

Soviet impatience with its balky vassal came to a head on June 15, 1940, when Moscow presented Lithuania with an eight-hour ultimatum demanding the appointment of a new, friendly government which would honor all the provisions of the Mutual Assistance Treaty and allow Red Army reinforcements to enter Lithuania without restriction – in order, the Kremlin said, to ensure the safety of the Soviet troops already stationed there.

The Lithuanian Cabinet rushed into session and found itself split on whether to accept or reject the ultimatum. President Smetona and several of his closest ministers favored rejection. They were outvoted, the majority reasoning that in view of the war, regardless of its present dilemma, Lithuania would be unable to maintain its neutrality or even, perhaps, its independence. Thus, it was in the country's best interest to face reality and agree to become to all intents and purposes a Soviet protectorate.

In protest, Smetona left Lithuania that very day. Crossing into Germany, he stayed briefly in Koenigsberg and entertained hopes for Lithuanian autonomy under German patronage. The German authorities allowed him to fly the Lithuanian flag over his residence but made it clear that Lithuanian autonomy was not on their agenda. Despairing of new hope, Smetona moved on to Switzerland and then Brazil. He finally settled in the United States of America, where in 1944 he perished in a fire in Cleveland, Ohio.

Massive Red Army forces crossed the Lithuanian border on June 15, 1940. Within two days, some 300,000 Soviet troops occupied the principal strategic positions in the country. They encountered no resistance and the population remained calm.[154] The borders with German-occupied Poland were closed, and the escape route through which thousands of Polish Jews had found – and additional countless thousands sought – refuge in Lithuania was blocked.[155]

On June 15, 1940, the day that Paris fell to the Germans, the Soviet Union began its occupation of Lithuania and installed a new "peoples' Provisional government" that included two Jews: Dr. Leon Kagan, Minister of Health; and Hersh Alperovitz, Minister of Commerce. The Communist Party, outlawed until the Soviet occupation, was officially legalized. Political prisoners, most of whom were communists, were freed. All active non-Communist forces in the government were isolated – some by imprisonment, others by removal from public life. The army, police, and civil administration were purged of unfriendly elements, and Party members and sympathizers were appointed in their place.

It was under such circumstances that "free elections" to a People's Seimas were held on July 15, 1940. The voter turnout was an eyepopping 95.1, and all the listed candidates were elected. More than half of the 85 delegates to the new People's Seimas were recently released political prisoners, and only four of the deputies represented the Lithuanian Jewish minority, even though Jews now constituted about 10 percent of the population.[156] Hardly a week passed before the new Seimas formally asked the Supreme Soviet to admit Lithuania to the USSR as the 16th Soviet Socialist Republic. A special delegation rushed to Moscow to present a petition to this effect; none of its members was Jewish. The request was granted on August 3, 1940, and the Provisional government was replaced by a Soviet of People's Commissars – Kremlin jargon for a council of ministers that wielded dictatorial powers.

Moscow now embarked on a sweeping Sovietization of Lithuania, directed on-site by the Soviet legation in Kaunas. First, all institutions were repatterned on the Soviet model.[157] All societies and organizations not affiliated with the Communists, both general and Jewish, were closed down. Only the Communist press was allowed to appear. All workers were enlisted in the official Communist trade union, and Party emissaries were appointed to oversee all institutions. Many Soviet officials moved into Lithuania and the notorious NKVD – the "state security service," i.e., the secret police and the forerunner agency of the equally notorious KGB – was placed in charge of state security.

The country was renamed the Lithuanian Soviet Socialist Republic, the LSSR. Of the 50 members of the Central Committee that ran the new government, two, Isaac Meskup (Adomas) and Samuel Yomyn, were Jewish. Of the 20 commissars and 40 assistant commissars, only Chaim Alperovitch was Jewish. Of the many thousands of senior government and municipal officials, fewer than 30 were Jewish. These men were appointed not necessarily for their allegiance to the Communist Party but rather because the new regime needed their experience and skills. These proportions suggest that Jewish involvement in the new leadership of the LSSR was very small. They are highly significant in view of subsequent allegations by Lithuanian antisemites that Lithuanian collaboration with the Nazis in the murder of Jews during the Holocaust had been provoked by massive Jewish support of and identification with the hated Communists during the Soviet occupation.

Circumstantial evidence reinforces this refutation of the antisemites' charges. The Sovietization process included confiscation of large landholdings, which were declared state property and promised to landless peasants – pledges on which the regime later reneged. All banks, cooperatives, industrial plants, businesses, and large apartment houses were nationalized. More than 80 percent of all the nationalized businesses, almost 60 percent of the nationalized industrial plants, and an unknown percentage of the large apartment houses were owned by Jews. Moreover, Jews were particularly hard hit by the subsequent nationalization of bank accounts and safe deposits.

As former capitalists now evicted from their factories and businesses, and as shopkeepers and members of the despised "bourgeoisie," Jews were among the first victims of the Soviet rule. Many were arrested as "enemies of the people." Jews found themselves in a precarious and extremely vulnerable situation. Portrayed by the Communists as having collaborated with former President Smetona and Lithuanian capitalists to oppress the Lithuanian worker and peasant, they were also accused by the anti-Communist nationalist underground of having brought Communism to Lithuania and having prepared the way for the Soviet invasion. It did not matter that, because of the fear of an impending Nazi invasion, members of the Polish and Belorussian minorities in Lithuania had also welcomed the Red Army as the lesser of the two evils; the Jews alone were perceived as having played a major role in the annexation of the country and the loss of its national independence. The Church and Lithuanian leaders, including those in the growing underground movement, did nothing to dispel this untruth, for which Lithuanian Jewry would pay dearly.[158]

The next stage of Sovietization entailed the proletarization of the entire Lithuanian population. This forced Jews to turn to trades and light industries in which they had no prior experience. Desperate for work of any kind, former businessmen, bankers, and property owners worked as glaziers, carpenters, and tinsmiths. Jews turned out steel, textiles, knits, and picturesque painted scarves for peasant women. Rabbis, former yeshiva students, and Orthodox Jews in general became experts in cooperative industries such as bootmaking and weaving, at which they were more likely to find a way to observe the Sabbath and Jewish festivals.

Generally speaking, Jews felt that the establishment of a Soviet government eliminated the immediate Nazi threat. Just the same, the community was far from reconciled to its new situation. The new regime ordered the dissolution of all Jewish organizations, parties, and youth movements. Many synagogues and all yeshivot, and other religious institutions were shut down, all army chaplains were dismissed, and religious instruction was forbidden. After all, Marxist gospel proscribed religion as the "opium of the masses."

The Zionist groups were the first to fashion organized underground movements for the purpose of maintaining and continuing Jewish educational, cultural, and religious activities. One such enterprise was Irgun Brit Zion (IBZ), which opened clandestine classes in Hebrew language, Bible, and Jewish history; for the Orthodox, Talmud and Torah studies were included. The movement assumed the responsibility of preserving and storing Jewish community archives and Hebrew and Yiddish books that the authorities had banned. Illegal news bulletins and publications, some handwritten, were secretly prepared and distributed. They included *Nitsots* (the Spark), the Hebrew organ of the IBZ underground. The IBZ and other underground organizations also became involved in rescue work. Through the network of secret cells, hideouts, and lines of communication that they had established throughout Lithuania, they helped Jews who feared arrest to escape abroad. It equipped these Jews with forged documents that identified them as refugees, thus enabling them to apply for emigration visas – a privilege denied Lithuanian Jews.

Although they attempted to adjust to their new circumstances as best they could, an overwhelming majority of the Jewish masses were unreceptive to the ceaseless drumbeat of Communist propaganda and unenthusiastic about the new social and economic order in Lithuania. The underrepresentation of Jewish Communists in the administration did nothing to alleviate their plight; neither were their Soviet Communist Jewish colleagues of much use. Both of these groups, driven by a compulsion to demonstrate their dedication to Bolshevism, were totally unsympathetic to Jewish needs and concerns. Relentlessly they enforced the new rules and regulations in an effort to eradicate, as speedily as possible, every vestige of organized religious, Zionist, Bundist, and Folkist activity.

Reluctantly Jews submitted to the radical changes necessitated by the new system. Some of the accommodations were relatively painless. The introduction of the Russian language as a vehicle of Sovietization, for example, presented no great difficulty to most Lithuanian Jews; many of them had attended Russian schools before the Revolution or spoke Russian at home as a first or second language. However, enforcement of Communist education methods caused Lithuanian Jews great hardship and suffering, since the Soviet methods ruled out the teaching of the Hebrew language and any form of religious study or Jewish national culture. This was a terrible blow to a community that had been justly renowned for its religious educational institutions and its strong attachment to and support of Zionism. When the education authorities began to require school attendance on the Sabbath and Jewish festivals, Sabbath observance became exceedingly difficult. Another enormous problem was the unavailability of kosher food. Jews who persisted in their former ways and refused to adjust to the new order were not only barred from public life but were constantly harassed. Eventually, most of them were arrested if not exiled. A number of the younger Jews accepted the message of the newly secularized education system, adapted to the country's changing conditions, and became estranged from their families. Local Jewish institutions and local organizations that received funds from abroad, including welfare agencies, were taken over by the government and placed under the control of Jewish Communist officials. On January 1, 1941, the authorities ordered the AJJDC offices in Vilna and Kovno to close.

At the beginning of the Soviet occupation, the authorities replaced Lithuanian bureaucrats who had fled the country or joined the anti-communist underground with Jews, who almost by definition could not be suspected of pro-German sentiments. On the whole, however, Lithuanian Jews loathed the Jewish Communists who took part in government work, even as low-ranking employees. The Jewish Communists, for their part, made no effort to hide their hatred of Jewish "clericals" (as all religious Jews were termed) and Zionists. The Hebrew language was anathema to them; they construed the conflict between Yiddish and Hebrew as part of the class struggle. They maintained that Yiddish, the language of the masses, needed to be purged of its Hebraic features. Hence the "Soviet" Yiddish spelling, a phonetic orthography that obfuscated the Hebrew origins of many Yiddish words.

The Jewish Communists had their own perspective on "the Jewish problem." Only Soviet socialism could solve it, they maintained; any deviation from this policy, even within their own socialist camp, must be uprooted. This explains their harsh treatment of Bundists and other Jewish socialists, many of whom were sent to Siberia, some of whom were executed.

The struggle between the Jewish Communists, acting on behalf of their Soviet masters, and the Jews of Lithuania, was a confrontation between a well organized, nationally oriented community, deeply rooted in Jewish tradition and culture, and a powerful contradictory ideological bureaucracy that resembled the Yevsektsia, the Jewish section of the Soviet Communist Party that was active between 1918 and 1930. In their view, which the ruling Lithuanian Communists shared, there was no place in the new Lithuanian order for rabbis or priests. Zionists, Bundists, and Jewish socialists who did not conform with the official party line were harmful to the masses, since these groups drove a wedge between the Jews and the general public. The Jewish Communists maintained that Jews had to discard their separatism and join hands with the progressive Lithuanian forces for the good of the new Lithuania.

Although all the private schools had been closed, several Jewish schools were allowed to reopen under government control. Yiddish, in its Soviet form, became the language of instruction in these schools; the teaching of Hebrew was forbidden. The government-mandated curriculum placed heavy emphasis on Marxist theory and politics and reduced the instruction of Jewish cultural subjects to a bare minimum. Consequently, some Orthodox Jews preferred to enroll their children in non-Jewish schools; others kept their children at home.

Most of the 350 teachers of Hebrew and Jewish subjects who had worked in Lithuanian Jewish schools before the Soviet occupation were dismissed. Most sought to earn their living in a different trade or profession. A few, however, made their peace with the new system and its demands. Some of them eventually became the most virulent anti-religious critics of the old, traditional way of Jewish life. They ridiculed Jewish customs, especially observance of the Sabbath and festivals, and penalized students who continued to abide by them. Orthodox students who refused to write on the Sabbath were warned by their teachers, some of whom were yeshiva graduates, that the new Lithuanian society would have no room for their ilk and that, unless they changed their ways, they would be sent to prison or Siberian exile. In several cities, thousands of parents signed petitions that they sent to the Communist Jewish authorities responsible for the schools, protesting the abolition of Hebrew and the compulsory studies on the Sabbath and festivals. The petitions were rejected out of hand, and leaders of former religious and Zionist parties, now banned, were accused of inciting the parents.

Eventually, the Jewish primary and secondary schools were closed and their students distributed throughout the general school system. All students were required to fill out a questionnaire with family details including history, names of relatives abroad, party affiliation, and family business and holdings. Students of a bourgeois background were classified separately, as were their parents, and were treated as second-class citizens. The new Jewish student elite was composed of the offspring of working-class families, whose parents were informed that the new society of Lithuania promised their children a secure future in which no Jewish education would be needed.

A number of young Jews took advantage of the new circumstances and immersed themselves in the general cultural life of the country. The Lithuanian universities abolished the *numerus clausus* and admitted gifted Jewish students of working-class origins and others who would previously have been excluded. The general school systems hired Jewish teachers, Jewish actors with satisfactory political credentials were permitted to work in the

Lithuanian theater, and several Jewish journalists were allowed to write for the general press.[159]

The head of the Lithuanian Minorities Office was a Jew, Dr. Henrik Zimanas, whose main function was to deal with anti-Communist Jews. A former assistant lecturer in the sciences at the University of Kaunas, Zimanas had abandoned his profession for politics and secretly joined the illegal Lithuanian Communist Party. In view of his command of the Lithuanian language, he was placed in charge of all Party publications, political writings, and translations. Unaware of Zimanas's political affiliations, both Jewish and Lithuanian intellectual circles had warmly welcomed and accepted him, impressed by his general erudition and his knowledge of Lithuanian language and culture. In 1938, his Communist affiliations still generally unknown, Zimanas had been appointed editor of the newspaper *Folksblat*, the organ of the Yiddish Folkists, a left-wing but non-Communist organization. When he ultimately came out of the closet, Zimanas proved to be a harsh, vengeful, uncompromising Communist fanatic, determined to change and reeducate Jews to the realities of adjusting themselves to the new economic and social order. During the Soviet occupation, when thousands of Lithuanian Jews were imprisoned or expelled to Siberia, many former friends and colleagues sought his help. Zimanas mercilessly rejected their entreaties, maintaining that because of their opposition to Communism, Lithuanian Jews, especially the Zionists among them, were a potential fifth column that would bedevil the new Lithuanian government in times of trouble. In this respect, Zimanas represented the thinking of the small but powerful group of Jewish Communists who, although connected with the community by nothing other than lineage, controlled the lives and destinies of the Jewish masses at this time.[160]

By August, all Jewish libraries were closed and their collections distributed among the general libraries. Most Jewish newspapers had ceased publication, although the most widely read of all, *Idishe Shtime* (Jewish Voice) of Kovno, continued to appear as of November 1940, under a new name, *Der Emes* (The Truth). A similar "Truth," the *Vilner Emes*, was published in Vilna, under the editorship of the famous Yiddish writer and poet, Chaim Grade.

To facilitate the observance of the Sabbath and Jewish festivals, Orthodox Jews organized their own workers' cooperatives, which were allowed to choose their own day of rest. Such cooperatives existed for the production of heating stoves, food, and textiles; several small grocery shops also formed their own cooperative. The phenomenon was commented upon and widely discussed in *Der Emes*, but the cooperatives were acting within their legal rights and their members were thus entitled to enjoy their Sabbath rest without hindrance.

Official approval of such practices was not forthcoming. The government resorted to all available means – public lectures, the press, the theater, and every literary forum – to deride, ridicule, and mock the primitiveness and fanaticism of Jewish religious practices and customs. It declared war on rabbis and all former religious functionaries for whom, it maintained, there was no place in Lithuania's new society. Nevertheless, throughout the year of the Soviet occupation, Orthodox Jews continued to maintain and defend their way of life. Kosher food, although expensive, was available, as were *hallot* (braided loaves) for the Sabbath and festivals and *matsa* (unleavened bread) for Passover. The largest kosher meat and delicatessen concern in pre-occupation Kovno, Rozmarinn, became a cooperative and displayed signs which read "Kosher, like before." Although Jewish community offices were officially closed, rabbis quietly continued to meet all religious needs for very modest private remuneration. A few synagogues still functioned, although most had been closed or converted into social clubs or cultural centers. Even though the yeshivot had been dispersed, small groups of yeshiva students continued to study together, often moving from one town to another to escape detection. Other study circles met secretly in private homes; if the authorities were aware of these clandestine activities, they took no action to prevent them.

Between June 14 and June 22, 1941, Lithuanian President Justin Paleckis, following a familiar Soviet pattern of arrests, terror tactics, and show trials, authorized a mass deportation to the Soviet Union of over 30,000 Lithuanians whom the government had branded "enemies of the State." The exiles included many thousands of Jews, who, by no coincidence, comprised the community's political, cultural, and organizational leadership. One of the deportees was a future Prime Minister of Israel, Menachem Begin, then a Polish-Jewish refugee in Vilna. The deportations were orchestrated by Ivan Serov, the Deputy Peoples Commissar for State Security; the NKVD; the head of the Lithuanian Police, Antanas Snieckus; Soviet Commissar Victor G. Dekanozov; and Antanas Guzevitcius. The purpose was to purge Lithuania of "socially dangerous elements," i.e., potential security risks on account of suspected disloyalty or surmised ties with Nazi Germany.

Informed that they were to be sent to an unknown destination in the Soviet Union, each family was allowed to take no more than 100 kilograms of baggage. A member of the Fishl family of Slobodka, a suburb of Kovno, described his experience:

> The police came at night and pointed their revolver at us. They spoke in Russian and Lithuanian and were accompanied by a young Jewish lad, a member of the Komsomol [the Communist Youth Movement]. They ordered us to leave within half an hour. We were driven in a van to the railway station and put into a guarded carriage. They separated the heads of the families, who were sent to a special prison carriage. The carriages were shut and bolted. At every station where the train stopped, we were given about a kilo of bread and a bowl of hot watery soup once a day. The sanitary conditions and overcrowding were terrible, especially for the elderly, the small children, and the babies.

The deportees were sent to various remote parts of the Soviet Union – heads of household to gulags in Siberia, others to Central Asia. Many traveled for more than a month before arriving at their final destination. On the way, they heard that war had broken out between the Soviet Union and Nazi Germany. They worked hard for pitiful remuneration and endured hunger, sickness, and many other hardships. Those sent to Siberia endured extreme cold, insofar as they could. Not allowed to travel or to change their assigned place of residence, the healthy supported the sick and elderly, selling whatever possessions they had brought in order to supplement their meager earnings. Those consigned to the gulags were exposed to starvation, freezing cold, and hard labor. Transcending all of these was the cruelty of their guards, who considered them criminals and traitors. False confessions, often extracted by means of torture following days of relentless interrogation, resulted in sentences of five to ten years of penal servitude; their principal crime was capitalism. Attempts to escape the brutal gulag regime by volunteering to serve in the Red Army were rejected.

When exiled to locations outside the gulag, Lithuanian Jews established strong personal ties, supporting and encouraging each other to overcome their common plight. In several gulag localities they organized Hebrew and Yiddish classes, continued to cultivate Jewish values, and maintained their religious practices under the most difficult of circumstances. Those who insisted on refusing to work on the Sabbath and festivals arranged to make up the lost time on alternate days. There were especially vigorous efforts to ensure burial rites in accordance with religious custom.

Lithuanian Jewry was left very much to its own devices during these years. Most importantly, the community and non-Jewish Lithuania parted ways. Between 1939 and 1941, some 40,000 Lithuanians, mostly members of the intelligentsia, left Lithuania for Germany – ostensibly as *folksdeutsche* (ethnic Germans) – only to return with the German forces that invaded the country in June 1941. Jews had dreaded the coming war; Lithuanians awaited and hoped for it as the solution to their suffering under the Soviet regime.

During the Soviet occupation, Lithuanian underground propaganda incited the population not only against the occupation forces but also against Lithuanian Jews, who were depicted and vilified as a monolithic bloc of Communists and collaborators with the hated invader. Recurrent antisemitic writings and speeches by respected Lithuanian secular and religious leaders fomented an atmosphere of even greater animosity and violence, which was to result in terrible massacres of Jews by Lithuanians after the Red Army retreated under the German onslaught.[161]

Lithuanian leaders attempted – some still attempt – to explain these massacres as the consequences of total Jewish identification with Communism and the Soviet forces that had destroyed Lithuania's short-lived independence. The allegations are patently untrue. Commenting on similar accusations against Polish Jewry, Josef Cardinal Glemp of Warsaw, head of the Catholic Church in Poland, wrote in a pastoral letter to Polish churches:

> We are aware that many of our compatriots still remember the injustices and injuries committed by the Communist authorities, in which people of Jewish origin also took part. We must acknowledge, however, that the source of inspiration of their activity was clearly neither their origin nor their religion but the Communist ideology from which the Jews themselves in fact suffered many injustices.

Developments after Barbarossa underscored the irremediable split. The Sikorski-Stalin agreement, signed in London and Moscow on July 30 and December 4, 1941, ended the state of war between Poland and Russia and enabled General Wladyslaw Anders to form a six-division Polish army. In March and August of 1942, 75,000 Poles who had enlisted in the new force were allowed to leave for the Middle East. Many of them were Jews, and they helped their Lithuanian coreligionists reestablish contact with family members abroad, including some in Palestine.

The Jewish exiles attempted at this time to establish contact with their exiled Christian compatriots in the hope of returning together to a free Lithuania at the war's end. With very few exceptions, the Christian Lithuanians rejected these advances. The conflict between the two groups was fundamental and unbridgeable. Whereas the Lithuanian exiles looked upon the Soviet Union as the hated enemy and considered Nazi Germany their future liberator, the Jewish exiles, in spite of their suffering under the Soviets, sided with Moscow against the Nazis without reservation. This explains why most members of the Lithuanian brigade attached to the Red Army were Jews. The Soviet Union, for its part, never viewed Lithuanian Jews as real or potential sympathizers. Even after the end of the war, the Soviets still considered the Lithuanian Jewish exiles Zionist agents. Some of these individuals remained in exile for 12 years, others for 18. Still others were never allowed to return to Lithuania or to emigrate.

The conflict between the Jewish and Lithuanian exiles to the Soviet Union reflected the opposing attitudes of the two groups to the Soviet occupation of Lithuania in general. Caught up in the great-power politics of their totalitarian neighbors, Lithuanians as a collective clearly preferred Nazi Germany to the Soviet Union; Lithuanian Jews had no choice but to accept the Soviet Union and the Red Army as their protectors against the Nazis.

Just before the Nazi invasion in June 1941, Deputy Commissar Serov gave orders to shoot some political prisoners who could not be moved. A new and lengthy list of deportations was drawn up. In 1969, Lithuanian historian Albertas Gerutis described the Soviet deportations as "the most tragic episode that the Lithuanian nation experienced." He must not have had Lithuanian Jews in mind. For them, the Soviet deportations were humane, merciful, even civilized, in comparison to the German treatment of Lithuanian Jewry – with Lithuanian Gentile collaboration.

Chapter 7

THE BLOODBATH

On June 22, 1941, Nazi Germany launched Operation Barbarossa, its surprise attack on the Soviet Union, with which it had concluded a non-aggression pact in 1939. Lithuania, now a Soviet Socialist Republic that abutted the German front, took the brunt of the assault in its very first days.

The Red Army broke and ran. At first, members of the government, Communist Party officials, and local residents who had collaborated with the Soviet authorities joined the retreating units and fled to safe haven in the Russian interior. Few Jews managed to escape in this manner. In the meantime, the Germans advanced but, for the moment, skirted the cities of Lithuania.

The general Jewish population was paralyzed in its choice of fight or flight. Fear and premonitions of doom pervaded the community. Some Jews who were offered transport by the Soviet authorities refused to leave because their children were away at "Pioneer" (Party-sponsored) summer camps; others were not allowed to bring parents along and remained behind for this reason. Some moved from the major cities to smaller provincial towns, believing that this would enhance their safety; others moved in the opposite direction under the same rationale. Some Jews attempted to follow the Red Army and reach Russia on their own. These, more often than not, encountered bands of armed Lithuanians who slaughtered them without mercy. Entire families, panic-stricken, packed a few valuables and crowded aboard the few trains that still headed for the Russian border. The Germans bombed the trains and railway tracks. Many were killed or wounded; survivors continued toward the border by any means available, often by foot. Nevertheless, some 15,000 Jews succeeded in reaching the Russian border and escaping to the interior. Others, reaching the border, found that it had been closed to the fleeing refugees or had become the front line. When these unfortunates attempted to circumvent the battle zone and to return to their homes, they were captured by armed pro-German Lithuanians who arrested any Jew on sight. The few Jews who did manage to return to their places of residence found that their houses and apartments had been requisitioned by Lithuanians and Poles, who refused to leave. Without recourse to the law, these Jews either moved in with relatives or friends or sought other solutions. It soon became apparent that the whole country – cities, towns, villages, roads – was now under the control of mobs of armed Lithuanian hooligans. For the Jews, all avenues of escape were cut off.

Generally speaking, the German Army enjoyed the full support of the Lithuanian population. Hatred of the Communist regime that had destroyed Lithuanian independence, and the belief that a victorious Nazi Germany would restore this independence within the projected new order in Europe, motivated large groups of Lithuanian nationalists and right-wing extremists to organize an armed underground movement, pro-German and anti-Soviet, well in advance of Barbarossa. Armed and bankrolled by the Germans, driven by ideological antisemitism, these partisan groups were ready and eager to collaborate with the German army when it moved into Lithuania on June 22, 1941.

Under Nazi tutelage and guidance, the Lithuanian nationalist leadership had concentrated its activities in the two areas around Kovno and Vilna. A key figure in these clandestine operations was the Lithuanian Ambassador to Berlin, Colonel Kazys Skirpa, a former cabinet minister and a well-known admirer of Hitler, who coordinated operations from his seat in Germany. These cells of Lithuanian fascists, Nazi sympathizers, and Lithuanian nationalists were important constituents of the LAF, Lietuvos Aktyvistu Frontas (Lithuanian Activist Front), the largest and best organized of the nationalist groups. But there were many other factions, such as the Iron Wolf, the Lithuanian Freedom Army, the Falcons, and the Lithuanian Restoration Front. They penetrated the universities, the civil service, the professions, even the high schools. According to Lithuanian sources, the number of members in these clandestine groups and anti-Soviet units reached 100,000.

On March 24, 1941, three months before the German invasion, the Lithuanian underground published its "Directives for the Liberation of Lithuania." Skirpa and his colleagues were in constant contact with the Gestapo and the Eastern Command of the Wehrmacht, and served as a liaison between the Germans and the Lithuanian anti-Soviet underground. On June 19, three days before the outbreak of hostilities, Skirpa and his collaborators, claiming to speak for all Lithuanians worldwide, presented the German government with a memorandum requesting German support for a new independent state of Lithuania.

Leaflet No. 37, issued in Berlin by the Lithuanian Activist Front and distributed throughout Lithuania just before Barbarossa, included the following statements:

> The crucial day of reckoning has come for the Jews at last. Lithuania must be liberated not only from Asiatic Bolshevik slavery but also from the long-standing Jewish yoke.

> In the name of the Lithuanian people, we solemnly declare that the ancient right of sanctuary granted to the Jews in Lithuania by Vytautas the Great is abolished forever and without reservation.

> Jews who are guilty of persecuting Lithuanians will be brought to trial. Those who manage to escape will be found. It is the duty of all honest Lithuanians to take measures by their own initiative to stop such Jews and, if necessary, to punish them.

> The new Lithuanian State will be rebuilt by Lithuanians only. All Jews are excluded from Lithuania forever. . . . Let the Jews know the irrevocable sentence passed upon them; not a single Jew shall have citizenship rights.

> The errors of the past and the evils perpetrated by the Jews will be set aright, and a firm foundation for a happy future and the creative work of our Aryan nation will be laid. Let us prepare for the liberation of Lithuania and the purification of the nation.[162]

In the meantime, the Red Army had been taken by surprise and was unprepared for battle. Its poorly coordinated units were unable to put up any effective resistance and were forced into a disorderly retreat. As they fled, they were constantly harassed and attacked in Kaunas and elsewhere by members of the Lithuanian national army, the "Shauliai" (marksmen) and partisan groups under Jurgis Bobelis, former head of the Lithuanian Army officer corps. It is estimated that the Red Army killed 4,000 Lithuanians and wounded 12,000 in these clashes.[163]

The Missing *Vox Humana*

Red Army units, however, were not the sole or even the principal targets of the armed Lithuanian bands. In the chaos, these roving gangs carried out an unprecedented murderous pogrom against the entire Jewish community of Lithuania. Within days of the German invasion, Jewish men, women and children were hunted down and butchered savagely in every city and townlet where they were found. Synagogues were torched, Torah scrolls befouled. In one stroke, a millennium of relatively peaceful coexistence between Jews and Lithuanians came to a tragic end.

On June 23, to the sound of church bells pealing in praise of the Nazi victory over Soviet forces in Lithuania, partisan forces took over the Kaunas radio station, captured several ammunition depots, and seized the police stations. With this, they released all political and criminal prisoners.

The LAF set up a provisional government that, as its first act, proclaimed a new independent State of Lithuania. The new government dismantled the institutions of the Lithuanian SSR, disarmed the LSSR militia, and arrested commissars and Communist Party leaders who had failed to escape. Colonel Bobelis was named Commandant of the new security forces in the Kaunas area, and it was he and one of his lieutenants, Jonas Klimaitis, who were responsible for the killings in the Fourth, Seventh, and Ninth Forts near Kaunas, of which much will be said below.

Colonel Kazys Skirpa, still at his post in Berlin, was named Prime Minister of the provisional government. His cabinet included representatives of the major nationalist and fascist groups. Pro-Nazi literary historian Jouzas Ambrazevicius (who changed his name to Brazaitis when he moved to the United States) became acting Prime Minister and Minister of Education, while

Rapolas Skipitis, a man with many German connections and friends in high places, was handed the Foreign Affairs portfolio. The well known German collaborator and admirer of Hitler, General Stasys Rastikis, former commander of the Lithuanian Army, became Minister of Defense. This crew restored capitalism and private property rights — for everyone but Jews, whose disposition began with elimination of civil rights and confiscation of property.[164]

The Wehrmacht began to dig in. On June 24, two days after the invasion, German forces entered Kovno and Vilna. Within a week of the first crossing of the frontier, the occupation of Lithuania was complete. In certain areas, Lithuanians used the interval to stage pogroms and kill Jews at random. German forces under General Friedrich Wilhelm von Kuchel, who marched and drove into Kovno in an orderly parade, were greeted by cheering, flag-waving crowds, who showered them with flowers and gifts. The Lithuanians' relief, enthusiasm, and joy were unconcealed. Prominent personalities including the Metropolitan of Kaunas, Archbishop Juozapas Skvireckas, prelate of the Papal palace, broadcast greetings to "the brave German soldiers and their leader, Adolf Hitler," and offered up prayers for their wellbeing. (When asked to intercede with the provincial government on behalf of the pogrom-bloodied Jewish population, Skvireckas refused.)[165]

On June 25, Lithuanian partisans who defined themselves as freedom fighters began a three-day killing rampage against Jews in smaller towns and villages, during which the entire populations of over 150 Jewish communities perished. Some Jews were driven from their homes and burned alive, after having been savagely beaten and herded into synagogues, schools and other public places that were then torched. In other instances, entire Jewish families were driven to nearby forests or riverbeds where pits or trenches had been prepared, and then shot. In several localities, such as Reiniai and Geruliai in the Telsiai area, in Meretz (Merkine), Plungian (Plunge), Sakiai (Shaki), and Kelm (Kelme), Jews were forced to dig their own graves. Virtually all the Jews in Ukmerge were herded into the synagogue and burned alive. In Seirijai, Jews were dragged naked throughout the streets and then brutally murdered in the presence of a cheering crowd. In Panevezys, Jews including several young women who had been raped were hurled into burning lime.

In Kovno alone, Lithuanian partisans murdered almost 4,000 Jews during the two days that elapsed between the invasion and the arrival of German forces in the city. A particular brutal atrocity took place later in the downtown

Kovno garage of the Lietukis cooperative. Some 60 Jewish men, chosen at random in the streets by the partisans, were taken to the garage and savagely beaten and tortured as a large crowd stood by and observed. As the Jews lay wounded and moaning on the ground, their torturers continued for the amusement of the crowd to beat them mercilessly until they died. Another group of Jews was dragged in to clean the garage and haul the victims away for burial.

In Slobodka (Wilijampole), partisans went from house to house searching for Jews. Their victims were thrown into the River Vilija: those who did not drown were shot to death as they swam. Jewish houses were set afire and their occupants burned alive as partisans blocked the path of approaching firefighters. Hooligans who called themselves freedom fighters slaughtered Jews indiscriminately. In many instances, limbs were torn off bodies and scattered hither and yon.

On June 25, partisans decapitated the Chief Rabbi of Slobodka, Zalman Ossovsky, and displayed his severed head in the front window of his house. His headless body was discovered in another room, seated near an open volume of Talmud that he had been studying.

Most of these 150 localities became *Judenrein* (Jew-free) 24 hours before the German occupation forces arrived. This gave the local population a brief opportunity to pounce upon the homes and businesses of their former Jewish neighbors in a frenzy of pillage and plunder. Many of the killings and lootings were carried out in broad daylight amid acquiescent, often cheering witnesses. When they attended mass in church, the partisans were praised by the priests for their courage and patriotism. The Nazis were blessed and lauded as the liberators of Lithuania, worthy of the eternal gratitude of the country and the Church. What, then, of the Jews? They had it coming for having "collaborated" with the atheist Bolsheviks.[166]

There were a small number of clergymen who did not condone their countrymen's deeds; a handful of clerics even dared to condemn them and express their shame and pain upon the realization that Lithuanians had carried out these atrocities. However, no leading Lithuanian religious or secular authority attempted to admonish the murderers, let alone stop them. The provisional government stood by with benign neglect.

In addition to the general mob looting that accompanied the killings, there existed a refined form of pillage carried out by more educated partisans — their officers — who issued "receipts" for the valuables (cameras, watches, radios, etc.) and moneys that they appropriated from helpless Jewish families. These "receipts" entitled the victims to reclaim their property "after the war." College and high-school students participated in the pogroms alongside the partisans and the hooligans, using every available means – rifles, guns, knives, axes, bare hands – to kill and maim any Jew unfortunate enough to fall into their hands.

The Kovno atrocities spanned both periods of time, that preceding and that following the Nazis' arrival. The victims in this city were stripped of their clothes and valuables, and their mutilated bodies were buried in a mass grave dug by a group of young Jews whom the partisans had rounded up for this purpose. When this macabre burial society had discharged its duties, several of its number were shot and the others were sent to the central prison, where they joined other Jews who had been detained, tortured, and abused by partisans and Shauliai (Marksmen). These unfortunates were held incommunicado, without food, water, or toilet facilities, pending transfer to the Seventh Fort.

The Seventh Fort, a short distance from Kovno, was one of nine such fortifications built by the Russian Army before World War I. It was enclosed by a high, thick stone wall, surrounded by barbed wire, and punctuated by several observation towers. Its underground barracks, originally intended as sleeping quarters for Russian troops, were used by the Lithuanian authorities mainly as storage space. Nearby were several apartment buildings that the Lithuanian and the Soviets had erected to ease the housing shortage in Kovno.

More than 10,000 Jews were brought to the Seventh Fort in the early days of the Nazi occupation. Women and children were separated from the men and incarcerated in the underground barracks; the men remained in the open, exposed to searing heat by day and bitter cold by night.

During the nights, the Lithuanian guards searched the women for valuables and beat those who had nothing to offer. Young, attractive women and girls were dragged from their underground prison and raped, their screams and the subsequent gunshots clearly heard by everyone in the fort and the nearby apartment buildings. During the day, the guards amused themselves and approving crowds in the neighboring buildings by ripping and cutting off the beards of elderly Jews, and by beating them and shooting at them, often more to wound than to kill. On one occasion, a successful Lithuanian basketball team was brought to the Seventh Fort and allowed, as a special reward for its victories, to shoot into the mass of Jews that filled the open area of the fort. The dead were left to rot until the partisans began to fear the possibility of epidemic, whereupon their fellow Jews were allowed to bury them in mass graves.

On July 14, 1941, the surviving women and children were evacuated from the Seventh Fort and marched to the Ninth Fort, where they were released. Most of the women returned home with sunken eyes, infested with lice, ill, and aged beyond recognition, their hair prematurely gray. The same day, after the women and children had been removed, a senior Lithuanian official arrived at the Seventh Fort in search of Jewish ex-servicemen who had fought in the Lithuanian Army during its struggle for independence in 1918-1920. He found approximately 100 men who met this criterion and transferred them from the Seventh Fort to the Central Prison of Kovno, where they were set free after their stories had been verified. The following Sunday, July 20, 1941, some 7,000 Jewish males were executed in the Seventh Fort and buried there in mass graves in full view of Lithuanian civilians both inside and outside the fort.

Even though the German occupation authorities found it difficult to coordinate their activities with the provisional government, which aimed to establish an independent Lithuania, there was no disagreement between them on the Jewish question. As early as June 30, Colonel Bobelis had reported to the cabinet on his plan to turn the Seventh Fort near Kovno into a concentration camp for Jews. The plan was aborted; the Fort was used instead as a killing ground.[167]

On August 1, 1941, the provisional government disfranchised the Jews of Lithuania, subjected them to the restrictions of the Nuremberg Laws, and added several new edicts of its own:

> Jews who had fled with the Soviet forces forfeited the right to reoccupy their homes. If they ever returned to Lithuania, they would be punished. Any person who offered them shelter would be punished together with them.

> Jews were forbidden to walk on sidewalks; they were to walk in single file near the gutter. Jews were forbidden to sit on benches in public parks and gardens and were barred from public transport. Every public vehicle was required to post a sign reading "Non-Jews only." Jews were forbidden to own radios or sell their property.

The edicts were signed by acting Prime Minister Ambrazevicius and Jonas Slepetys, the Minister of the Interior. They were published in the official gazette of the provisional government, *Laikinosios Lietuvos Vyriausybes*.

In its Circular No. 7 of August 1941, the Provisional government issued directives regarding non-Jewish Soviet citizens who had been left behind after the retreat of the Red Army:

> Families of former Bolshevik soldiers and other persons from various locations in the USSR remain in some parts of Lithuania. These foreigners should be put to hard physical labor. If they exist in large concentrations, they should all be sent to labor camps.

These Soviet non-Jews, like the Jews, were tortured and killed wherever encountered in Lithuania.

The Lithuanians had always held Germany and German culture in great esteem, and the advent of Hitler and National Socialism did nothing to diminish it. It was thus inevitable that Lithuania should choose to side with Nazi Germany against the Soviet Union and to place its aspirations for restored independence on the expectation of a Nazi victory. Lithuanian nationalism, as the country's dominant political force, was inextricably wed to the fate of Nazi Germany. It took only until July 17, 1941, however, for the Lithuanian leadership to realize that the Germans had neither Lithuanian sovereignty nor even a semblance thereof in mind. It was on that day that Berlin informed the provisional government that Hitler himself had decided to deny political independence to Lithuania and all the other occupied countries in Eastern Europe.[168]

The Germans emphasized their intentions by first emasculating the provisional government and then, on August 5, forcing it to suspend its activities. The LAF was outlawed at this time; some of its leaders were arrested.[169] Even an offer by the provisional government to mobilize all its resources in the service of the German war machine, including the dispatch of 100,000-150,000 Lithuanian troops to the Russian front, did not help.

The Nazis seized control of Lithuania, renamed it General Betzirk Litauen (General District of Lithuania), and declared it part of Ostland, a complex military and civil administration that embraced the three Baltic countries and Belorussia. In Ostland, the Gestapo and the SD security service vied with the Wehrmacht for authority. Lithuania itself was divided into four autonomous districts: Vilnius, Kaunas, Panevezys, and Siauliai.

On July 17, Hinrich (alternate references: Heinrich) Lohse, Gauleiter of Schleswig-Holstein and a high-ranking Nazi, was appointed Reichskommissar for Ostland; he chose to establish his headquarters in Riga, capital of Latvia. Theodore Adrian von Renteln, a Russian-born ethnic German, was appointed general commissar for Lithuania. Lohse and Renteln were both members of a secret group, directed by the highest Nazi authorities in Berlin, that had been instructed to prepare plans for the Final Solution of the Jewish problem.[170]

Reichskommissar Lohse established his Kaunas office on July 25. Three days later, this office announced that Germany had annexed Lithuania from the Soviet Union and would henceforth exercise all legal rights vis-a-vis the country, its population, and its resources. Frustrated and embittered by Germany's refusal to acknowledge the Lithuanian claim to independence, the deposed members of the provisional government joined forces with the LAF leadership to organize an underground movement that circulated its own clandestine newspapers and literature. As before, antisemitism was not a bone of contention between these circles and Hitler's Germany. The underground publications followed the former provisional government's antisemitic policies and continued to disseminate anti-Jewish propaganda. The underground movements enjoyed great prestige throughout the country and had strong influence on the local population, which generally obeyed its directives.

The German civil administration took control of every aspect of the Lithuanian economy. It seized all the properties, industrial plants, farmland, and commercial enterprises that the Soviets had expropriated and nationalized, rejecting out of hand the possibility of restoring them to their former Lithuanian owners.[171] The contours of the German plan – the eventual colonization of most of Lithuania – began to emerge by May 1942, when the first 20,000 German farmers arrived. The Nazis classified Lithuanian nationals as racially inferior to Scandinavians but somewhat superior to the despised Poles and the hated Slavs. To impress the locals with their new status, government offices made sure to treat Lithuanians with pronounced disrespect.

Nevertheless, many Lithuanians, including several who had held portfolios in the former provisional government, collaborated with and loyally served their German masters in a General Council (*General-Rat*) that the new regime appointed to help administer the country and implement the new rules and regulations. The Council was chaired by General Petras Kubiliunas, a former supporter of Voldemaras, who had served a prison sentence for an attempt to assassinate Smetona in 1935.[172] In 1942-43, the Germans gave the Council one year to mobilize 100,000 men and women aged 17-45 for transport to Germany, where they would be put to work in the war industries. Persons who failed to register for this mobilization were liable to three months' imprisonment and a fine of 1,000 marks. Sanctions or not, the Council was only able to provide 5,000 workers,[173] although they found it less difficult to recruit Lithuanians for police and military units.[174]

This was the first indication of anti-German sentiments in Lithuania. The resentment began to grow as the Lithuanians realized that they had become second-class citizens in their own country. By October 1943, it had become general knowledge that Lithuanian nationals received half the rations of German nationals, whose numbers were steadily increasing in accordance with the Nazis' intent to Germanize the Baltic countries. Resentment mounted. However, it neither vitiated the Lithuanians' visceral hatred of the Jews nor translated into any sympathy for the Germans' principal victims.

Lithuanian Jewry in the Nazi Chokehold

Non-Jewish Lithuanians' attitudes and sentiments toward the Jews fell into three general categories: 1) the extremists, who wished to rid Lithuania of its Jews forever by killing them; 2) the "moderates," who objected to the murder of innocents but believed that Jews should be severely punished for "the suffering they had caused Lithuania," especially during the period of the Soviet rule, and favored a quarantining of the community under Pale or ghetto conditions ("There is no power on earth that can force us to live with you Jews in the same place" [Jonas Matulionis, Finance Minister in the Provisional government][175]); and 3) those who passively accepted everything taking place. In general, public opinion was almost totally anti-Jewish, and in such an environment the implementation of the Final Solution encountered no opposition.[176]

The German civil administration, together with Lithuanian volunteers and mobilized personnel, was instrumental in the nearly total extermination of Lithuanian Jewry and the mass murder of Jews from other European communities who were taken to Lithuanian soil for murder. In addition to Lohse and Renteln, the German officials most responsible for the killings throughout Lithuania included Franz Walter Stahlecker, Karl Jaeger, Wilhelm Goecke, Wilhelm Kittel, Franz Murer, Helmut Rauca, 1st Lieut. Hamman, Fritz Jordan, Hans Kramer, and Christian Hingst. The killings themselves were carried out by special task forces, the Einsatzgruppen, who had trained for this very arduous assignment by murdering mentally ill and handicapped Germans. Transferred to the Nazi-occupied territories for special missions, these commandos were considered elite Nazi troops and were given special privileges, including triple pay, extra home leave, and exemption from service on the Eastern front.

Their methods of killing were diverse and, in many senses, pioneering. Legally subordinate to the Wehrmacht, the Einsatzgruppen took their orders from SS Reichsfuhrer Reinhard Heydrich. Each Einsatzkommando, a subunit composed of 100-150 men, was attached to an army unit that it followed closely. Locally recruited militiamen were used as support troops; without their help, the mass killings could not have been accomplished. Six Einsatzkommando units were combined into mobile formations called Rollkommandos. Their ostensible function, described as "special political police duties," had to do with suppressing any elements behind the lines that were hostile to the Reich. They received their orders directly from SS Reichsfuhrer Reinhard Heydrich.[177]

Heydrich's basic instructions to the Einsatzgruppen, issued on July 2, 1941, included the following:

> Do nothing to interfere with any purges or spontaneous pogroms that may be initiated by local anti-Communist or anti-Jewish elements in the newly occupied territories. On the contrary, they are to be secretly encouraged.[178]

Einsatzgruppe A, responsible for the Baltic countries and Belorussia, was headed by Brigadefuhrer Franz Walter Stahlecker, a former seminary student who was thought to be somewhat of an intellectual. His most notorious assistant was the epileptic and deranged Dr. Juris Eduard Strauch. They chose the Czarist forts, huge fuel storage depots, and tank pits and trenches prepared by the Russian Army as the sites of massacres of exceptional cruelty and brutality. Their victims included not only Jews but also Lithuanian Communists and Russian civilians.

The first Jews to fall into this dragnet were 4,000 refugees and deportees from other occupied European countries. They were taken to the Ninth Fort in early December 1941, ostensibly for labor in German-occupied Russia. On December 10, after being told that they required inoculation, they were taken away in groups of one hundred and shot. Another 3,000 Jews who arrived shortly thereafter suffered a similar fate. By the end of the month, the number of non-Lithuanian Jews massacred at the Ninth Fort reached 22,000. Their belongings were searched and looted, first by the Germans and then by the Lithuanian volunteer militia, Tautinio Darbo Apsauga (National Workers' Guards). The latter were so proficient in this macabre role that the Nazis formed them into five battalions and dispatched them to Lublin, Treblinka, and Maidanek for similar duty.

In their desperation, Lithuanian Jews turned to General Oswald Pohl, the local commander of the Wehrmacht, in the hope that he would protect them from both the SS murder squads and the Lithuanians. Pohl refused to receive them, explaining that Jews were not under his jurisdiction. In fact, German soldiers participated in the beatings and lootings and occasionally assisted Stahlecker's Einsatzkommandos. Stahlecker was pleased with the Wehrmacht's cooperative role, which had been defined by guidelines to the troops, issued by Field Marshal Walter von Reichnau on October 11, 1941, stressing the importance of this assistance:

> The soldier in the Eastern Territories is not merely a fighter according to the rules of the art of war, but also the bearer of a ruthless national ideology. Therefore the soldier must understand the necessity of a severe but just revenge on subhuman Jewry.[179]

The Germans had a further stipulation: Lithuanians were not to benefit from the looting of Jewish possessions. At the beginning of the occupation, the German authorities posted signs and issued radio announcements promising severe punishment to anyone found looting - "Jewish assets belong to Germans only." It is true that some Lithuanians had utilized the chaotic first days of the occupation to couple murder with pillage, but the Germans soon expelled them from the Jewish dwellings that they had occupied and requisitioned these and other former Jewish assets for themselves. When the

Germans moved in, Lithuanians had also peremptorily expelled their Jewish partners, without remuneration, from the cooperatives that they had established together under Soviet rule, forcing them to relinquish all machinery, raw materials, and even their tools. When informed of these actions, usually by other Lithuanians, the Germans confiscated these assets as well. A Lithuania that collaborated with Nazi Germany in the genocide of its Jewish citizens surely had no objection to German theft of Jewish property.

At this early stage, few Lithuanian Jews perceived their suffering as anything more than another round of pogroms. Many rationalized the Germans' forced-labor mobilizations as evidence that they would be allowed to survive; after all, Germany needed workers for its war machine and economy.

Lohse, the Reichskommissar, and Renteln, the general commissar for Lithuania, knew better. They were privy to all plans connected with the Final Solution, including the fateful decisions to be taken later at the Wannsee Conference on January 20, 1942. On August 20, 1941, Lohse gave his commissioners secret provisional orders on the treatment of Jews in the newly occupied Soviet territories. Included among the Jews were persons of mixed parentage, as defined in the Nuremburg Laws, and Jewish converts to Christianity. For the first time, mention was made of the use of gas chambers and the need to research new methods of mass killing.[180]

The new instructions stipulated that all Jews be registered by categories (converts, half-Jews, etc.) and places of residence. Jews must wear two yellow stars: one on their chests, another on their backs. Jews were no longer permitted to employ Christians. Jewish children were barred from schools. Jews were forbidden to function as lawyers, notaries, bank officials, or real-estate agents. Jewish physicians might treat other Jews only. Jews were allowed to shop only after regular business hours and, when leaving their homes, to choose specially designated destinations only. Jews were forbidden to possess property, pharmacies, motor vehicles, money, and a catch-all rubric called "valuables." Anything in any of these categories was subject to confiscation. Jews must salute any German they encounter. (A Jewish doctor in Kovno failed to salute a German on the first day of the occupation of Kovno, and was shot on the spot.[181])

These were the Germans' last direct communications with individual Lithuanian Jews. To prevent further defilement of the *Ubermentschen*, all major Jewish communities were instructed to appoint several members to councils that would henceforth receive German orders and decrees affecting the Jewish population.

Ghettoization – The Storm in the Eye of the Storm

The first important message communicated through mediation of the Judenrat (Jewish Council) was the order to move into ghettos, given on August 4, 1941. This transfer, the Gestapo promised, would protect the Jews from further excesses. In Kovno, Karl Jaeger of the Gestapo attempted to convince the Jews to make the move peacefully by offering the following rationale:

> The Lithuanian population refuses to accept you in its midst. For your own protection, you should be pleased to part ways with them and live on your own. In the ghetto you'll have self-rule, your own little state, and your own police force. The cities and townlets are too dangerous for you.

The procedures for relocation into the Lithuanian ghettos were different in each of the major centers. In Vilna, the Jews were given one day's notice to make the move. Those in Shavli were given two weeks; those in Kovno had roughly one month. Each of these cities actually had two ghettos, adjoined either by a wooden bridge or by a special path along a main street. For a brief period of time there were several smaller ghettos, the largest of which was in Swentzionys near Vilna. Most of these, however, were liquidated by the end of the first year of German occupation, their former inhabitants buried in nearby mass graves.

Reichskommissar Lohse considered the ghettos a short-term plan, to be used only until more intensive measures for the Final Solution might be put into effect. His instructions to his subordinates regarding the provision of food for the ghettos were explicit: Jews in the ghettos would receive only such food as the rest of the population could do without, and not more than was necessary and sufficient to maintain life. The official and unofficial Lithuanian press (the former Nazi-controlled, the latter in the underground) fully supported these German policies, and its anti-Jewish articles were an important factor in helping to influence otherwise indifferent Lithuanians and in inciting and further stimulating the dedicated collaborators.

After having told the Jews that their ghettoization, being for their own protection, would last only for the duration of the war, the Germans explained their forces' random shootings and ruthless terror as aberrations committed by a few "bad apples." As for deportations to extermination and concentration camps, the Germans explained that the deportees were being sent on "special military labor assignments" and would return as soon as their job was done. Their new locations, the Germans assured them, would offer much better housing and other conditions than the ghettos could provide. Long after the deportees had been murdered, Lithuanian railway personnel who had been involved in their transport approached the victims' relatives and offered, for a fee, to send the victims money, parcels, and letters. In a number of instances, Lithuanians offered to smuggle Jews out of Lithuania into Sweden in exchange for money or valuables. No one who attempted to accept this perilous invitation ever reached his or her destination.

The relocation of Jews into the areas designated as ghettos required an exchange of dwellings with Lithuanian Christians who lived there. The site chosen for the Kovno ghetto – into which almost 35,000 Jews, including refugees from outlying provinces, were ordered to move – included part of Slobodka, a Kovno suburb separated from the city proper by the River Neris-Vilija. A bridge connected the two towns. The southern sector of Slobodka was all-Jewish; its northeastern sector was almost entirely Christian. In the Christian district, some 4,500 Lithuanians lived in huts and dilapidated apartments. Many of the huts lacked indoor toilets and running water; inhabitants sank wells in the middle of small vegetable gardens. Most of the apartments, some not yet completed, were built by the government of the LSSR for employees of factories in Slobodka.

The Lithuanian authorities were displeased with the proposed ghetto boundaries, which included some of their own properties. On August 3, 1941, they protested to the German authorities that the projected ghetto boundaries were too generous; surely a smaller area would suffice for the housing needs of 35,000 Jews. The Germans acceded to the Lithuanian request and readjusted the borders of the ghetto, reducing the original size of the ghetto by about one-third before the Jews moved in. Paneriu Gatve Street ran between the two sequestered areas, creating "large" and "small" ghettos in Slobodka, linked by a bridge over the street.

Desperate to find homes for their families, the Jews of Kovno rushed in panic to meet the Germans' August 15 deadline for resettlement. The few

Lithuanians who had to relocate had a large selection of well-appointed houses and apartments to choose from; the Jews were at a tremendous disadvantage due to lack of time and a limited supply of available housing. With their backs to the wall, Jews offered Lithuanians furniture, well-equipped kitchens, pianos, silver, and other valuables as part of the exchange. Abuses were rife. Many Lithuanians asked for a signed agreement showing a prewar date of sale in order to keep the Germans from requisitioning these homes for their own families. Others, by threatening to denounce Jewish homeowners as Communists, blackmailed Jews into signing contracts transferring their homes intact. Lithuanian movers exploited the tense situation by charging exorbitant prices for hauling Jewish belongings to the ghettos; many poorer Jews had no choice but to carry their remaining possessions on their backs. The move to the ghettos was a heartbreaking sight that entailed many hours of arduous toil. Many Jews, unable to bear the agony, simply abandoned some of their parcels and crates. The streets of Kovno were strewn with abandoned Jewish belongings, which Lithuanians happily and hastily collected before the Germans could do so. Upon reaching the ghettos, the Jews found the housing supply utterly insufficient; some of them crowded into schools, synagogues, and abandoned factories.[182]

With this, the ghetto gates were slammed shut. The cities of Lithuania were free of Jews. Shut off from the rest of the world by barbed wire, Lithuanian Jewry had become a captive of the German authorities. There were many overlords by now: the SS, the SA, and the German civil administration, assisted by Lithuanian civilians and *wachmanner*. The frantic scramble for space in the ghettos, and the panic and anxiety at being forced to abandon family homes, were but preludes to the collective shock that the Jews experienced when the high barbed-wire fences of the ghettos closed in upon them. They contemplated the congested quarters that would henceforth be their homes: five to seven families in one small house or apartment, sharing one kitchen and an outhouse toilet. Anxious concern for missing relatives and fear of an unknown future merely compounded their misery.

Life became a succession of routine humiliations. No Jew was allowed to venture on the streets of Kovno or any other ghetto without wearing the infamous Yellow Star. Jews were not allowed to talk to each other on the streets while walking to and from work. No Jew was allowed to address an Aryan in any fashion.

Despite all this, however, the newly ghettoized Jews imagined at first that their confinement might enhance their chances of survival. Some of them simply did not know better. They believed the Germans' lies, including accounts of the "rest villages" to which children, the ill, and the elderly were being sent. However, there was evidence to support the "for your protection" argument. By the time the ghetto system was introduced, an estimated 25,000 Jews in Vilna had been murdered at Ponar,[183] more than 10,000 Jews from Kovno had been slaughtered at the Fourth, Seventh, and Ninth Forts, and over 5,000 Jews from Shavli and its surrounding villages had been massacred in forests and at river banks in Kuzki, Geruliai and other locations. In July and August 1941, entire communities in more than 180 locations throughout Lithuania were decimated.[184]

On August 4, 1941, by order of the German authorities, the executive board of the Kovno *kehilla* met for the last time to reconstitute itself as the Judische Altestenrat Kauen-Wilijampole (the Jewish Council of Elders of Kovno-Slobodka) and to elect a Judenalteste (the "Jewish elder" or chairman). As there were no volunteers for this post, it was only upon the urging of the Chief Rabbi of Kovno, Abraham Duber (Dov Ber) Shapiro, and R. Moshe Yaakov Shmukler of Shantz, that Dr. Elhanan Elkes eventually agreed to accept the position.

Dr. Elkes was profoundly respected by the Jews of Kovno as an excellent physician, a cultured, unpretentious and caring human being, a dedicated Zionist, and a man of strong character. Thus he accepted the challenge of the tragic role thrust upon him, and represented his community with dignity during the ensuing three years of encounters and dealings with the Gestapo and other German authorities. The Kovno Altestenrat, under Elhanan Elkes, acted out of a sense of duty and responsibility for the Jewish community of this city. Its members fully understood the dangers that they and their fellow Jews in the ghetto faced. They were helpless and unable to change the conditions in the ghetto, and the Germans considered them hostages who could easily be brought to their knees. Nevertheless, neither Elkes nor the Altestenrat members were ever subjected to the criticism or condemnations that were sometimes leveled against other Judenraten.

Now that the Jews had been expelled from general Lithuanian society to enclosed ghettos, the creation of a Jewish administration was vitally important to the Jews and coincided with German interests and policy. Since the Jews of Kovno regarded the Altestenrat as a reincarnation of the old *kehilla* tradition, they allowed the council to assume many responsibilities on its own initiative. The Nazis, in turn, regarded the Judenrat as a mechanism that would administer the ghettos and implement their orders. Hence the Germans kept the activities of the Jewish councils under close supervision. Most Judenraten in the ghettos of Lithuania cooperated with the German authorities when forced to do so, but they never willingly collaborated with the Nazis or the Gestapo.

The Judische Altestenrat of Kovno-Slobodka functioned until July, 1944. At this time, faced with the approach of the Red Army, the Germans liquidated the ghetto and sent all survivors to concentration camps in Germany. Dr. Elhanan Elkes died in the Landsberg concentration camp in October 1944.

Ghetto Life

As noted, the Germans had two expectations of their Jewish councils: to obey their orders scrupulously and to expedite their plans. The Judenraten were to register the ghetto inmates and keep accurate lists. They were responsible for the collection of goods and valuables belonging to Jews, including gold and silver jewelry, books, electrical appliances, new shoes, and miscellaneous items. The councils were required to establish administrative departments that would keep the ghetto running smoothly, overseeing such things as food distribution, health and sanitation, labor, and police. On their own initiative, the councils planned social, cultural, and educational activities; organized libraries, scheduled theatrical performances and concerts; and met the inhabitants' religious needs. The German authorities were aware of some of these unauthorized activities but rarely intervened. The underground movements used these gatherings for various purposes including the coalescence of organized resistance to the German war effort.

The Nazis tried very hard to foist candidates of their own choosing on the Jewish councils in the ghettos. They bullied and threatened members who refused to carry out their directives or, as often occurred, failed to implement them in full. It is clear that, at least during the first years of the councils' existence, the members of the Lithuanian ghetto councils not only risked their lives to defend the rank-and-file but also made every effort to improve their constituents' health and welfare and alleviate the ubiquitous suffering and deprivation as best they could. Secretly and at great personal risk, they helped the resistance movements and assisted those who sought to escape from the ghettos. In later years, the composition of the council memberships changed. Some leaders had been arrested; others had resigned in frustration or depression. Some of their successors lacked the altruism and sterling qualities of character that the original council members had displayed.

Of all the functions that were entrusted to the Jewish councils, the Jewish ghetto police (*Ordnungsdienst*) had the most important duties and became perhaps the most dominant and powerful agency within the ghetto confines. Their uniforms consisted of a special hat, an armband, and a cudgel. Their ranks were filled first by volunteers and later by conscripts who were rewarded with larger rations and other privileges (see below); all regarded their duties as a service to the community. The police were responsible for the enforcement of labor conscription, tax collection, and confiscations. More crucially for the occupiers, the ghetto police were supposed to fight smugglers, round up deportees when ordered to do so by the Germans, and hunt for wanted persons.

Most of the Jewish police complied with these orders perfunctorily at best. Smuggling was widespread; its perpetrators, many of whom were children, acted as a lifeline for the ghettos by augmenting the meager food rations supplied by the Germans. The smugglers were well paid for their services and admired for the great risks they took. As for manhunts, the *Ordnungsdienst* often helped intended victims to escape by informing them that they were being sought. In many instances the police refused to help the Nazis set their dragnets. In several ghettos, especially that of Kovno, many Jewish policemen were active members of the resistance movement. There is no denying, however, that the behavior of some Jewish policemen in many of the ghettos was comparable to that of the Jewish kapos in the labor and extermination camps. Some invoked their power to abuse and mistreat fellow Jews, besmirching the good names of many others who performed their duties as caring human beings. Those in the latter category did everything they could, up to the sacrifice of their own welfare, to alleviate their coreligionists' sufferings. Members of the *Ordnungsdienst* had certain privileges and compensations: slightly larger food rations, exemption from forced labor. They were also the last to be transferred from the ghettos – but transferred they were, like all other Jews.

Helpless in the face of their all-powerful enemies, the Jews in the ghettos, tortured by hunger, insecurity and fear, teetered between despair and hope.

Death from starvation, cold, and disease, was an everyday occurrence, and the death toll rose with each passing day. Deprived of all human rights, ignored by private and international relief organizations, and cut off from all sources of general or local news, the ghetto Jews were prone to rumors, true and false, that circulated among them. Despite their personal agony, they endeavored to retain a semblance of dignity and to help each other as best they could. They were still convinced, and so remained throughout the ghetto period, that they would be spared as long as the Germans put them to gainful labor. Consequently, they were puzzled when every so often, despite critical manpower shortages in the armaments industries in which they were employed, numbers of Jews were taken out of their work places, never to return. To the very end, they were unaware that the Final Solution was at hand and could not fathom the Reich's priorities.

The Nazis constantly changed their tactics in their treatment of the ghetto Jews, who never knew what their German masters had in store for them. Physical resistance by the ghetto inhabitants was out of the question. The Jews were too poorly organized and equipped to contend with the efficient, ruthless, and heavily armed forces that faced them. Most Jews in the ghettos, who had no way of reaching the forests or the Jewish partisan groups, opposed direct resistance to the Germans for fear of mass reprisals. Nevertheless, the underground movements were active in the ghettos. They prepared young people, singles and families alike, to join the pro-Soviet partisans in the forests or to form their own camps. They taught ghetto inhabitants how, upon escape, to avoid Lithuanians in the cities and anti-German Lithuanian partisans in the forests, who were not so anti-German as to allow Jews to further their cause. As a condition for admission to friendly partisan groups, these youngsters had to provide their own weapons, which they might acquire only with the greatest danger. The few who escaped to the forests during the ghetto period found themselves in hostile territory. Lithuanian civilians not only withheld food and supplies but often denounced them to the Gestapo. Nevertheless, the Jewish partisans proved to be dedicated, reliable resistance fighters who acquitted themselves well against the enemy.

Unable to offer physical resistance in the ghetto, the masses of trapped Jews chose spiritual resistance. Their slogan was 'Bleybn a mentsh' – stay human, do not surrender to the Germans' dehumanization mechanisms. Those who won this inner struggle despite the terrible conditions were able to preserve their moral and intellectual standards which they used to reaffirm their identity as Jews; this reaffirmation, in turn, gave them the strength to go on living. The songs and poetry composed in the ghettos, and later in the camps, were only one manifestation of Jewish despair and longing. They also articulated their authors' protest against the indifference of the world to their fate.

The Nazi pattern in Kovno, as in all the ghettos, began with an attempt to liquidate the community's intelligentsia in order to diminish the likelihood of effective leadership and opposition. Thus the first order to the Judische Altestenrat, issued on August 18, 1941, was to organize a contingent of 500 volunteers associated with the community intelligentsia – physicians, lawyers, architects, teachers, and other university graduates – for labor in the municipal archives. When the number of volunteers fell short of the quota, Lithuanian partisans rushed into the ghetto and recruited the needed increment by force. These 500 highly qualified Jews marched out of the ghetto and were never seen or heard from again. A short time later, Lithuanian acquaintances on the "outside" disclosed that they had been shot by the Lithuanian Third Operational Group (a militia formation) in the Fourth Fort at Panemune.[185]

One week after the ghettos were sealed, German and Lithuanian troops searched every Jewish house for valuables and anything that might take their fancy. The spoils in this larceny included wedding rings pried off their victims' fingers. Then the predators, convinced that some valuables had been concealed, shot a few Jews at random, beat many others, and gave the community two days to "voluntarily" surrender all remaining cash, gold articles, jewelry, silver tableware, silver- and gold-plated cutlery, and other items. Should even one forbidden specimen be discovered in subsequent searches, the ghetto was informed, 100 Jews living in the culprit's vicinity would be shot. The Germans designated several collection centers and retreated to wait.

During the next two days, Jews could be seen carting their valuables to the collection points. In random searches carried out soon afterward on several ghetto streets, the Germans were unable to uncover any remaining articles of value. Every Jew was allowed to retain 100 Soviet rubles or ten German marks. The Germans' take in Slobodka alone exceeded 50 million marks' worth of gold and jewelry.[186] The Jews of Kovno ghetto had endured their first Nazi *aktion*.

On September 15, 1941, SS Sturmfuhrer Fritz Jordan issued distinctive passes (which the Jews called *Jordanscheinen* – "Jordanpasses") to some 5,000 artisans and specialists and their families. The distribution of these permits caused panic in the ghetto, for it was assumed that only passholders would be allowed to remain and all others would soon be hauled away to destinations unknown. Eleven days later, on the pretext that German guards had been fired at, German and Lithuanian guards (members of the local militia and police) surrounded a section of the ghetto and drove large numbers of their corralled captives into an open plaza, where they conducted a selection. Jews found holding "Jordanpasses" were sent to one side, and those without passes, approximately 1,000 in number, were taken to the Ninth Fort and shot that very day.

Lithuanians who had previously lived in the area of the small ghetto insisted upon returning to their former homes. Thus the next *aktion* was the liquidation of the small ghetto. On October 4, the Lithuanian militiamen and police marched in again, this time to the small ghetto. Again the "Jordanpass" method was used to select Jews for death in the Ninth Fort. The community orphanage and old-age home, located in the small ghetto, were liquidated at this time. Children and their teachers, the elderly and their caregivers, were loaded onto vans and driven to the Ninth Fort, where some 2,000 Jews were murdered that day. One Jewish institution remained in the small ghetto: the hospital. This building was set afire after all its doors had been sealed to prevent escape; it burned to the ground together with patients, doctors, nurses, and everyone else trapped within. The fortunate but now-homeless "Jordanpass" holders, and others who had lived in the small ghetto, were herded across the wooden bridge that led to the large ghetto, where they had to fend for themselves in finding accommodation within its suffocating congestion.

At this point, posters appeared in the ghetto announcing that a census would be held on October 28. Members of (slave) labor brigades, together with their families and the elderly and the ill, were to assemble in Democratu Square near the offices of the Jewish Council, where an *appel*, a roll call, would take place. All dwellings were to remain open for inspection; anyone found hiding would be shot.

Nearly 30,000 Jews crowded into Democratu Square that chilly autumn morning. As they gathered, a large group of drunken Lithuanian militiamen and police along with sober German police, headed by Helmut Rauca (who was extradited many years later from Canada to West Germany) and other high-ranking officials of the security police surrounded the plaza. The census proved to be a selection, directed by Rauca himself. As the work brigades and their families passed before him, he unhesitatingly separated families, sending to the left the ill, the elderly, families with small children, and anyone whom he deemed unfit for hard labor. "Jordanpasses" did not matter this time. Lithuanian police then chased the Jews who had been chosen, 10,000-12,000 in number, into the still-empty small ghetto, whence they were marched to the Ninth Fort. All others were ordered to return to their homes. Dr. Elhanan Elkes, chairman of the Jewish Council, interceded with the Germans and was allowed to enter the small ghetto and bring back a small number of trained artisans and specialists – but suffered a severe head injury when beaten by a Lithuanian policemen.

The fate of those who were paraded to the Ninth Fort might have remained forever unverified had it not been for two youngsters who managed to survive and return to the ghetto. According to their eyewitness report to the Jewish Council, the selected Jews were separated into groups of 100, ordered to undress, and gunned down by Lithuanian units supervised by a few German soldiers. The slaughter took a day and a night to achieve. The victims' clothes were collected by the Germans for repair, cleaning, and shipment to Germany; the killers divided the valuables among themselves.

At this time, the members of the Jewish Council were reluctant to disclose the gruesome details of what later became known as *"di groyse aktsie"* (the big aktion), but Lithuanian Jews all over the world chose October 28 as the date on which to commemorate the destruction of Lithuanian Jewry.

"Di groyse aktsie" apprised the ghetto Jews of the true state of their vulnerability. It helped shatter the myth that they would be spared as long as their labor was needed. Rauca himself assured the Jewish Council that there would be no more *aktionnen*, but no one believed him. Jews understood with resignation that every day that they spent under German rule would bring new threats to their survival. Nevertheless, life had to continue even in the ghetto; as long as they were alive, Jews needed food and a warm place to return to after a day of backbreaking forced labor. The Germans, too, noticed that the Lithuanian winter, which had hardly begun, was very cold. Consequently, they organized a "fur *aktion*," confiscating for their own use, and for the use of Germans in other occupied countries, thousands of fur and sheepskin coats, shawls, and other articles of warm clothing.

Final Solution or not, the Germans appreciated the potential sources of qualified manpower that existed in the ghettos. To exploit this resource, they established workshops that would utilize the skills of Jewish tailors, shoemakers, carpenters, tinsmiths, locksmiths, toymakers, and other craftsmen. Officially, the articles produced in these workshops were meant for the use of the German Army, but private German and Lithuanian enterprises employed these artisans for their personal gain or for the manufacture of gifts that they sent to chosen recipients – relatives and acquaintances in Germany, girlfriends in Lithuania, and so on.

By the end of 1941, the Nazis cited the need for manpower in Lithuania as a pretext for the transport of many Jews from Germany and other German-occupied countries to this country. These unfortunates never reached the ghettos; they were murdered in the forts of Kaunas, where many inscribed their names and hometowns on the prison walls while waiting their turn to be killed. The murder squad was Einsatzkommando 3, commanded by Karl Jaeger. Jaeger's secret reports from Kaunas, dated November 25 and December 1, 1941, summarize the activities of Einsatzkommando 3:

> I can state today that the goal of solving the Jewish problem in Lithuania has been attained by Einsatzkommando 3. There are no Jews in Lithuania anymore, except those needed for work and their families. Their numbers are 15,000 in Vilnius, 15,000 in Kaunas, and 4,500 in Siauliai. I intend to kill off these working Jews too, but the civil administration [the office of the Reichskommissar] and the Wehrmacht need them and their families for the war effort. The goal of ridding Lithuania of Jews could not have been achieved without the cooperation of the Lithuanian partisans and the respective civil offices. Only proper timing helped us to carry out five *aktionnen* per week and to do the current job in Kaunas and elsewhere. The *aktionnen* in Kaunas itself, where a sufficient number of trained partisans was available, may be described as shooting at ducks in an arcade, especially if compared with *aktionnen* elsewhere in the country. In certain *aktionnen* we used only eight to twelve German troops to direct the Lithuanians. We can now report a total of 133,346 Jews killed to date. (...)

Alongside the Jewish *aktionnen*, the chief task of the Einsatzkommando 3 was to clear the overcrowded prisons in various localities [i.e., by killing the prisoners]. Before the Einsatzkommandos took over their security duties, it was primarily the Lithuanian partisans who killed the Jews.[187]

By February 7, 1942, the newspaper *Deutsche Zeitung in Ostland* was able to report: "Regarding the future destiny of Eastern European Jewry there is no problem; the plan is prepared and already in action."

Even as non-Lithuanian Jews were transported to Lithuania for death under the pretext of labor, the German war machine conscripted ghetto Jews for real slave labor in armaments factories and construction of airports and other military facilities. Germany also placed Jews in private industrial and manufacturing concerns, some, as noted, located within the ghettos and camps themselves. Lithuanians, too, occasionally obtained special permission from the Nazis to put Jews to work on their farms and in their businesses. This unpaid labor created fortunes for its exploiters.[188]

On January 3, 1942, Franz Stahlecker, reporting to his superior, SS Reichsfuhrer Reinhard Heydrich, had the following to say:

> Among my other complaints against the Lithuanian militia is their laziness and their unbridled greed for plunder. The only way to motivate them is to give them *schnapps* [brandy]. They perform better when they are drunk. Two hundred twenty-nine thousand and fifty-two Jews have been liquidated to date.

Stahlecker, with fewer than 500 German troops under his command at the time, illustrated his report with a map on which he marked his killing areas with little coffins.

The surviving inhabitants of the ghettos were unaware of these reports and were repeatedly assured that *aktionnen* were aberrations and the deportations meant solely to resettle them under improved conditions. Selections were held in town squares or in open markets in the ghettos. Those selected were herded into waiting cattle trains or other available transport and driven to nearby woods, moors, ravines, or the edges of huge trenches, where they were mown down by machine-gun fire. The dead and the wounded were hurled together into mass graves and covered with lime and earth.

Gradually, the Jews in the ghettos began to suspect the truth although they found it inconceivable that the Germans were capable of such atrocities.

Seven months into their occupation of the Baltic countries, the Germans discovered that, after having liquidated so large a number of Jewish communities, they were running short of slave labor in Latvia and Estonia. Thus they ordered the Kovno-Slobodka Jewish Council to provide 500 Jews for work in Riga. The ghetto population had stopped believing that this was the Germans' intention, so no volunteers stepped forward. When the Jewish police proved unable to meet the quota, German and Lithuanian troops marched into the ghetto and selected 400 Jews at random, who were indeed sent to Riga.

However, *aktionnen* of various kinds continued unceasingly. On February 27, 1942, for example, there was a "book *aktion*" throughout Lithuania; entire libraries and private collections containing rare manuscripts and volumes were confiscated and shipped to Germany.[189] In all, more than 100,000 books in many languages were removed from Kovno alone, including the religious library of the Yeshiva of Slobodka. After sorting, many of the captured books were sent to the Petrashun paper factory to be reduced to pulp.[190]

The war was beginning to go badly for the Wehrmacht; Allied forces had landed in North Africa and the Soviets had taken the offensive at Stalingrad. Jews heard snippets of this and other news while working outside the ghettos; some risked their lives to bring newspapers home. The reports, however filtered, kindled a flicker of hope that Jews liberation might not be too far off. However, they were careful to give their captors no indication that they knew what was happening on the front. Indeed, each piece of bad news or word of a German reversal merely whet the guards' lust for cruelty and violence.

Vilna Jewry, the largest community in Lithuania, was confined in two terribly overcrowded ghettos in the Straschun and Ludska sections of the city. Before the occupation, the Jews of Vilna had been apprised of German atrocities by the many refugees from Poland who had flooded the city. Thus they were more realistic and less illusion-prone than their counterparts in Kovno about the fate that awaited them. When the German invasion began, the Vilna Jewish leadership – that which had survived the Soviet abuse – gave highest priority to self-defense plans.

The Vilna ghettos – "large" and "small," as in Kovno – were established on September 6, 1941, after some 25,000 Jews had been murdered in the forests of Ponary, ten miles out of town. The victims of this bloodbath, perpetrated by Lithuanians and Germans, included Jewish elder Saul Trotsky and most of the members of a Judenrat that had been elected only a few weeks earlier.[191] The population of these ghettos, the large and the small, was 30,000 and 11,000, respectively.

On September 7, the Germans appointed Jewish councils in each of the two ghettos, headed by Anatole Fried and Isaac Leibovitz. Jacob Gens was appointed by the Germans as chief of the Jewish police and was later chosen by the Germans to serve as Judenalteste, the head of the ghetto. Gens was a controversial figure. The husband of a non-Jewish Lithuanian wife, he could easily have gone into hiding with his wife's family. Instead, he chose to enter the ghetto and volunteer his services to the German authorities in the belief that he could help save Jews. Although some considered him a German collaborator, he was later shot by the Gestapo for allegedly having helped the Jewish underground.

The new Judenrat, following the prescribed ghetto pattern, was responsible for law and order by means of the Jewish police and established departments for labor, health, supply and distribution, housing and social welfare, and culture. Religious life continued to function surreptitiously. With the help of refugee writers, public figures, and poets, a cultural program of concerts, folk music, and lectures was offered.

On October 21, following a series of aktionnen, including one on Yom Kippur (October 1), the small ghetto was liquidated and most of its inhabitants taken to Ponar, where they were massacred. By the end of 1941, the registered population of the Vilna ghetto had dwindled to 12,000; another 8,000 "illegals" resided there in hiding.

Between the beginning of 1942 and the spring of 1943, the Vilna ghetto experienced a period of relative calm. There were almost no aktionnen; most Jews were at work either outside the ghetto or in workshops established within the ghetto. The policy of the Judenrat was based on the premise that as long as Jews were productively engaged in essential work for the Germans, it was in the German interest to allow them a respite, perhaps even to survive. Cultural activity flourished so strongly during this period that a theater was established in the ghetto. A Yiddish-language wall newssheet called, *Geto Yedies* (Ghetto News), was published, offering information, announcements, and regulations issued by the Judenrat.

In early 1942, the various political parties in the ghetto joined forces to establish an organization that they called the FPO (Fareinigte Partizaner

Organizatsie, Unified Partisan Organization). The FPO's principal founders and leaders, termed commanders, were Yitzhak Wittemberg, Abba Kovner, and Joseph Glazman. Wittemberg, the first commander of the FPO, came from a working-class family and had been a member of the Communist Party from his early youth. He had gained some prominence as a Communist activist during the brief Soviet occupation of Lithuania, and became the leader of the Communist underground in the ghetto when the Germans occupied the area and established the Jewish enclaves. He was one of the sponsors of the FPO idea, and his willingness to collaborate in the underground with Zionists of all kinds (including Revisionists, members of the right-wing Zionist movement), in spite of grave ideological differences, attested to his Jewish consciousness and his desire to share his fellow Jews' destiny.

Abba Kovner, born in southern Russia, had studied at the Hebrew Gymnasium in Vilna. As a teenager, he had joined Ha-shomer ha-Tsa'ir, a left-wing Zionist movement, and had been active in the Zionist underground during the Soviet occupation of Vilna. When the Germans moved in, Abba Kovner became convinced of the need to organize a Jewish resistance movement. On December 31, 1941, at a meeting of the Hehaluts Zionist youth movement in Vilna, the following proclamation by Kovner was read to those in attendance:

> It is Hitler's intention to destroy the whole of European Jewry. The Jews of Lithuania are destined to be the first in line. Let us not go as sheep to the slaughter! It is true that we are weak and defenseless, but the only reply to the enemy is resistance!

After the death of Wittemberg in July 1943 (discussed below), Kovner stepped in as commander of the FPO.

Joseph Glazman was born in Alyta, where he was active in Betar, the youth movement of the Revisionist Party. In 1937 he became the leader of the Revisionists in all of Lithuania. During the Soviet occupation, he was active in the Revisionist underground. When the Vilna ghetto was created, he organized the Revisionist underground cell there and joined the Jewish police to facilitate his activity. In late November 1941, he was named Deputy Chief of Police in the ghetto. After helping found the FPO, Glazman became its deputy commander and chief of intelligence. He was also prominent in the educational and cultural programs of the ghetto.

During the period of comparative calm in the ghetto, relations between the Judenrat and the FPO were correct; both sides strove to avoid unnecessary confrontations. In the spring of 1943, however, when conditions in the ghetto deteriorated and the leaders of the FPO believed that the Germans were about to liquidate the ghetto, tensions between the two groups increased.

Jacob Gens, the former police chief whom the Germans had named to head the ghetto in place of Anatole Fried, was convinced that the FPO was menacing the lives of every inhabitant by smuggling weapons into the ghetto and maintaining contacts with partisans in the forests. He therefore tried in June 1943, to undermine the power of the FPO by exiling its leaders, including Glazman, to labor camps outside Vilna. This resulted in a violent clash between FPO units and the ghetto police; several weeks later, Gens allowed Glazman to return to the ghetto.

A particularly traumatic incident was the arrest of FPO commander Wittenberg, in early July 1943. As he was being taken out of the ghetto, armed FPO units attacked the Lithuanian guards, freed him, and spirited him into hiding. The Germans issued an ultimatum threatening to level the ghetto if Wittemberg was not surrendered to them by morning. Jacob Gens, chief of the Jewish police, urged the FPO to turn Wittemberg in for the sake of the common weal. After much soul-searching, Wittemberg reasoned that the time for a general uprising in the ghetto had not yet arrived. He surrendered to the Germans and was murdered by the Gestapo.

However, the denouement of the ghettos was at hand. On June 21, 1943, Heinrich Himmler ordered the liquidation of all the ghettos in Ostland. Jews fit for labor were to be sent to concentration camps; the rest were to be murdered. This ultimate *aktion* began on August 4. By September 4, more than 7,000 able-bodied men and women had been transported to concentration camps in Estonia.[192]

When German units entered the Vilna ghetto on September 1, 1943, members of the underground engaged them in an armed clash in which Yehiel Sheinbaum, leader of an underground group that had joined the FPO, and other fighters were killed. The underground attack succeeded in killing or wounding several guards. Police chief Gens stepped in again. Fearing that further hostilities between the underground and the German troops would lead to the immediate destruction of the ghetto, Gens negotiated a withdrawal of German soldiers by promising to meet the required quota of workers for the Estonian and Latvian camps. Ensuing deportations to Estonia and Latvia reduced the ghetto population to a mere 12,000. On September 14, Gens was summoned to the Gestapo and summarily shot.

The ghetto of Vilna was liquidated on September 23-24, 1943. Some 4,000 men and women were sent to Estonia and Latvia, and an equal number of women, children and elderly were deported to the extermination camps of Sobibor. Several hundred women and old people were taken to Ponar and murdered there. The FPO succeeded in evacuating the last of its fighters through the sewers. Some 3,000 Jews were left behind. They were put to work for the Wehrmacht in Kailis, at a Lithuanian fur factory, and for HKP (Heeres Kraftfahrpark), an army vehicle park. On July 3, 1944, these Jewish workers were taken to Ponar and murdered. The Red Army liberated Vilna ten days later.

Although there are no exact figures, an estimated 100,000 Jews in Vilna and its surrounding areas perished during the Holocaust. No more than 2,000-3,000 Jews survived the German occupation. One-third of these had done so by escaping to the forests. The remainder had either survived the Estonian and German concentration camps or managed to obtain Aryan documents.

When the war erupted, Shavli had hosted the third largest Jewish community in Lithuania. Here, too, two ghettos were formed: one in the Kaukas area of the city, the other in Traku. The Judenalteste of Shavli was Mendel Leibowitz, a former businessman of impeccable character and integrity. A long-time community stalwart, Leibowitz was trusted and respected by his fellow Jews in the ghettos throughout his years of service as chairman of the Jewish Council. The Germans, following the Kovno model, allowed Leibowitz to choose the members of his Judenrat; these proved to be as dedicated as he in striving to improve the conditions and welfare of the Jews in the ghettos.

The agonies of the Holocaust in Shavli are rather thoroughly documented, owing largely to the ghetto diary kept by Dr. Eliezer Yerushalmi, a well-known educator. In 1946, at the trials of major Nazi war criminals in Nuremberg, the Soviet government presented sections of Dr. Yerushalmi's diary as documentary evidence. However, the Soviets prevented the full publication of the diary because of its incriminating evidence against the Lithuanians, who in the meantime had become part of the Soviet Union.

Relations between a Jewish Council of integrity and a Nazi apparatus could only be fraught with tension. The first dispute arose on July 20, 1941, when the Council pressed the authorities to relieve the unbearably crowded conditions in the ghettos. The non-Jewish Lithuanians urged the Germans to deny the Jews any such relief, demanding instead that all the Jews in Shavli be expelled to Zagarai, a small outlying town.

The Jews in the Shavli ghetto survived as long as they did because of their skilled labor in the Todt Organization (the Wehrmacht engineering corps), the Frankel tanneries, and the former Bata shoe factories, which provided essential services and goods for the German war machine.

On November 4, 1943, as in all other ghettos, the Germans committed an atrocity in Shavli that came to be known as the *kinderaktion* – the children's *aktion*. The ghetto population in this city, unlike that of Kovno and Vilna, had some advance knowledge of what was coming because of Lithuanian contacts. Thus, as the fated day approached, parents of small children took desperate action to smuggle their offspring out of the ghettos. Children were drugged and placed in sacks or rubbish bins that were routinely removed from the ghettos; non-Jewish Lithuanians were given huge bribes to rescue and look after them. These parents, although inconsolable, hoped against hope that their small children would survive in this fashion. Other parents simply hurled their children over the ghetto fences into the waiting arms of Lithuanians with whom they had reached terms. Older children dressed as adults and tried to slip out the ghettos with labor brigades.

During the *kinderaktion*, large empty trucks crept through the ghettos, loudspeakers booming orders that all children were to be placed aboard at once. These orders alternated with the sound of loud music to drown out the screams of children who were being torn from their parents' arms. Mothers pleaded to be allowed to accompany their offspring, only to be brutally driven off by heavy blows. Babies were seized by their limbs and their heads smashed against stone walls or the fenders of the waiting trucks. Dogs were brought in to sniff for hidden children, who when discovered were torn to pieces. Amid the bloodthirsty cacophony of blaring music, wailing parents, and barking dogs, dwelling walls were torn down and floors ripped apart in an effort to find every last child.

The chief of the Jewish police in the Shavli ghettos was Ephraim Gens, brother of Jacob Gens, who held this position in Vilna. A former Lithuanian army officer and a university graduate, he, like his brother, believed in the German military code of honor and trusted the Lithuanians with whom he had grown up and whose culture he had internalized. Convinced that the

Germans and Lithuanians would never harm innocent children, he was the first to surrender his own small daughter so that others might follow his example and avoid the problems that resistance would cause.

The experience of Shavli provides ample evidence of Lithuanians' willingness to collaborate in the implementation of this plan. Lithuanian squads roamed outside the ghetto fences and walls in search of any Jew who managed to escape the killing fields. The Lithuanian guards who surrounded the ghetto enforced every minor detail of the many restrictions imposed upon the inhabitants.

Ghetto inhabitants who still possessed money or valuables bartered them for food, at great personal risk, with Lithuanians eager to profiteer on the black market. To some extent, these transactions helped alleviate food shortages in the ghettos. The Lithuanian players in this activity were also exposed to danger and punishment if caught. For fear of jeopardizing this meager lifeline to his ghetto a Shavli Jew, Bezalel Mazovetski, refused to divulge the name of his Lithuanian contact and was hanged in the ghetto square, preferring to die than to reveal his supplier's identity.[193]

The brutality of the Lithuanian guards in Shavli was such that the Jews occasionally turned to the Germans for help. Such was the case when, in February 1943, Lithuanian ghetto guards began beating Jews who were cutting down trees in a nearby forest. The rabbi of Posbol, a townlet in the vicinity, wrote to the Shavli Jewish Council that after Lithuanian partisans had liquidated the small Jewish communities in Birz, Salat, New Radvilishki, and other localities, the few survivors had asked the Germans to save them from their Lithuanian tormentors.

The basic weekly food ration in the ghettos was comprised of 700 grams of black bread, 113 grams of flour, 100 grams of legumes, and 125 grains of horse meat. This was barely sufficient to sustain life. Orthodox Jews would consume horse flesh only when faced with starvation and ordered to do so by their rabbis, and sometimes not even then. Distribution of food supplies was entrusted to Lithuanians. Occasionally the German authorities would order them to augment the rations of especially hardworking brigades; the Lithuanians often refused, whereupon the Jews complained to the German official in charge of the supplies.

Late in 1942, the Germans deprived the Lithuanians of their right to abuse the ghetto Jews; henceforth their duties were limited to guarding the ghetto gates and helping the Einsatzkommandos.

It is important to note that there were Lithuanians, albeit too few, who helped Jews survive by concealing them and caring for them at great personal risk. Prominent among these was Jonas Gylys of Varena (in the vicinity of Shavli), a parish priest, whose sermons regularly attacked the Lithuanian functionaries and termed them butchers and vandals. On September 14, 1941, Jonas Kvaraciejus, in charge of the police station in Varena, sent a secret report to the head of the Gestapo in the Alytus District:

> Father Gylys called at my office and asked to be allowed to speak to the detained Jews. Although permission was refused, he went to the synagogue where they were being held and spoke to them, trying to pacify them and telling them to be brave. But at this stage he was stopped and ordered out of the synagogue.

The synagogue was set afire a short time later; everyone inside perished.

By early 1943, some 50,000 uniformed Lithuanian volunteers had joined the ranks of the Wehrmacht.[194] However, continued reports of German reversals on the eastern front began to mitigate the enthusiasm of the Lithuanian leadership and people for the German war efforts. This new trend gathered momentum after the surrender of the Wehrmacht at Stalingrad in February 1943.

At this stage of the war, the Germans counted on mobilizing another 250,000 Lithuanian workers for essential war labor in Germany. In fact, they succeeded in recruiting only some 7,000 laborers. An anti-German underground movement had begun to operate in Lithuania, and its ranks of sympathizers and its acts of sabotage (derailment of military trains and so on) mounted steadily. Anti-German partisan groups proliferated in the Lithuanian and Belorussian forests, but these, like the nationalistic Lithuanian resistance, never welcomed young Jews who escaped from the ghettos. At best, such units accepted Jews reluctantly especially when a Russian officer was in charge.

In the autumn of 1943, Obersturmbannfuhrer (Lt. Col.) Wilhelm Goecke introduced a radically new system of internal administration in the ghettos: the so-called *Kasernierung* or "barracks system." The ghetto inhabitants were divided into small working camps and allocated to nearby barracks, in effect converting the ghettos into concentration camps. The SS replaced the German civil authorities as the agency in charge of these camps, and the Jewish Councils were renamed the Lageralteste and given different functions.

Men were separated from wives and children and all were issued prisoner's garb in place of their civilian clothes. Each Jew became responsible for the others in his block. Block leaders were appointed, who were required to conduct a headcount every morning and evening to make sure nobody had escaped. If even one Jew was missing, the block chief was shot. As bad as sanitary conditions and toilet facilities had been in the ghettos, they were even cruder under the new system.

At the time of the *Kasernierung*, there were 15,000 Jews in the ghetto of Kovno-Slobodka, 3,000 in Vilna, and more than 5,000 in Shavli, where the Judenalteste was a convert from Memel named Georg Pariser, who lived in the ghetto with his Aryan wife and children. His predecessor, Mendel Leibowitz, had been killed on July 18, 1944, by a bomb that a Red Army aircraft had dropped on Shavli, damaging parts of the ghetto.[195]

In spite of the *Kinderaktionnen*, a few children managed to survive in the ghettos until this time. With the liquidation of the ghettos, it became virtually impossible to continue hiding them. In their desperation, parents now pursued contacts with former acquaintances, churches, Lithuanian children's homes, and Christian orphanages in an attempt to find foster homes for their doomed offspring. Few of the people or institutions they approached agreed to take these children; those who reluctantly consented to do so demanded exorbitant sums of money or valuables. Very few were willing, even for payment, to accept male children, whose Jewish identity was much more difficult to conceal.

Although some of these children survived the war, most were handed over to the Gestapo or even killed by their guardians when their parents were no longer able to meet the payments to which they had agreed. In some cases Lithuanians agreed to accept children for the sole purpose of converting them.

Several Christian clergymen were prominent among those who tried to help save Jewish children. One was Lapin or Lapinunis, a priest from Shavli, whose superiors reprimanded him for his efforts. Bishop Vincent Brizgys, initially indifferent to the fate of Jews in his diocese, began to support efforts to conceal Jewish children some time after the summer of 1943. Clandestine groups were organized for the purpose of rescuing Jews, principally by anti-fascist elements but also by small cells affiliated with the national church. Bronius Paukstys, a priest in Kovno, rescued 100 Jewish children by baptizing them. After the war, however, this cleric expressed his satisfaction that at least 30 of these children would remain Christian forever, since their parents and all their relatives had perished.[196]

It was clear by the end of 1943 that almost 90 percent of Lithuanian Jews had either died or moved on to slave-labor camps in Estonia, Latvia, and (at a later date) Germany. At this very late stage, several leading Lithuanian personalities protested the crime. General Vitkauskas, former commander-in-chief of the Lithuanian armed forces, urged Lithuanian collaborators "to cleanse yourselves of the innocent Jewish blood on your hands" before the expected Soviet victory.

Three organized Lithuanian groups were trying to help such Jews as still remained. The largest of them was the anti-Fascist left. Another was the VLIK (Vyriausias Lietuvos Islaisvinimo Komitetas, the Committee for Lithuanian Independence); the third was a national church cell. *Tevynes Frontas* (Homeland Front), the organ of Lietuvos Islaisvinimo Sajunto (the Independence Fighters), published a warning in early 1944 against "helping the Germans to kill innocent Jews and others, since the Lithuanians themselves will be the next in line to be killed. Any Lithuanian guilty of such crimes will be considered a common murderer." This belated outcry was signed by Prof. Kazys Grinius, Prof. Jonas Aleksa, and Bishop Mykolas Krupavicius. Dr. Ipolitas Zhilinskis, the head of the Lithuanian Red Cross, refused to affix his signature or offer his help.

By early 1943, the events in Lithuania became known internationally when the Swedish press reported that 170,000 Lithuanian Jews had already perished at the hands of the Nazis.[197] The news prompted the Pittsburgh Conference of Lithuanian Catholic communities in America to reaffirm its historic friendship with the Jews of Lithuania, express its anxiety for their destiny, and urge the American government to save their Lithuanian Jewish compatriots.

In bloodsoaked Lithuania and elsewhere, the Nazi leadership began to take steps to eradicate all traces of their crimes against the Jews. For this purpose they used young Jews from the Kovno ghetto and Jewish Red Army prisoners-of-war. The Nazis' mass graves, each containing 3,000-4,000 Jewish corpses, were located in ditches west of the Ninth Fort. The graves were now opened and the bodies searched for valuables and gold teeth. Then the bodies were stacked on layers of wood, drenched with gasoline, and set ablaze. The ashes were scattered to the winds. To keep these gruesome operations secret, the Nazis murdered the firestokers when they were no longer needed. On New

Year's Eve of 1944, however, 64 Jewish firestokers succeeded in fleeing from the Ninth Fort. Some of them returned to the ghettos, where they disclosed the story of their macabre assignment. A similar account was told by 20 of the 80 Vilna Jews who had been drafted into a corpse-burning detail at Ponar. After these incidents, the FPO succeeded in freeing several hundred Jews from the Kailis concentration camp in Vilna; they fled to the forests and joined the partisans.

Even though its forces were retreating rapidly on all fronts, the Third Reich continued its war against the Jews without abatement, as if this were indeed its principal war aim. Deportation of Jews by rail was given higher priority than the Wehrmacht's most urgent transport needs. Units of young, healthy SS troops were used to guard, transfer, and kill Jews rather than serve on the eastern front, where their presence was desperately required.

Aware by now that the Red Army was advancing on Lithuania, the Jewish remnants in the ghettos and camps built *malinas* (places of concealment) in hope of holding out until the liberators arrived. Every possible space – under apartment floorboards, cellars, lofts, and gardens – was converted into a *malina*. The Nazis, no less aware that their stranglehold on the Jews was about to end, spared no efforts in locating these concealed bunkers and demolishing them, usually by means of explosives. The forces committed to this action, which was often the last step committed before retreat, were SS units helped by Lithuanian and Ukrainian collaborators.[198] Thus many Jews who had managed to survive in the ghettos and camps, overcoming constant danger and difficulties, met their death just days – sometimes hours – before the Soviet troops arrived.

In July 1944, shortly after the great Russian offensive at Vitebsk, Goecke informed Dr. Elhanan Elkes, leader of the Slobodka ghetto and the camps nearby, that all Jews in Lithuania were to be deported to Germany. The remnant of the Shavli ghetto camps had in fact been evacuated a month earlier, together with Russian prisoners of war and wounded German soldiers. Most of the Jews were sent to the concentration camps of Stutthoff and Dachau-Kaufering. By the time these camps were liberated by American, British, and Russian forces, very few of these unfortunates remained alive.

On July 13, 1944, Red Army formations under General Ivan Chernyakhovsky marched into Lithuania. The surviving remnants of a once proud, exemplary community emerged from the few *malinas* and the forests to return to their homes. Lithuania had begun the war with more than 200,000

Jews, and ended it with about 1,700 – 800 in Vilna, 700 in Kovno, and 200 in Shavli. They were joined later by Jews returning from exile in Russia with the 16th Lithuanian Division of the Red Army, which itself included many Lithuanian Jews, and others who chose to return from Germany after the camps there were liberated in 1945.

These survivors met with undisguised hostility on the part of their former Lithuanian neighbors, who had taken possession of Jewish property and goods in the belief and expectation that their legal owners had perished. These Lithuanians were disappointed to see that some Jews had in fact survived. They refused to vacate the homes they had "inherited" or to return the valuables that their former Jewish neighbors or friends had left with them for safekeeping.

This overt antagonism and the Jews' inability to recover their possessions induced many of the survivors and returnees, who had initially planned to rebuild their lives in Lithuania, to emigrate. Returnees who decided to stay found it vastly difficult to obtain the bread rations that the Red Army had arranged for the civilian population; the Lithuanians in charge refused to register Jews[199]. A newly organized Jewish Committee had to petition the highest authorities in the land to rectify the anomaly. Another important task of the Committee was to arrange for proper burial of the Jewish corpses or parts of bodies left unburied after the bunkers were detonated. Searchers at the Ninth Fort found piles of bones amid mountains of ashes – remains of the bodies that the Germans had exhumed from the mass graves and set afire in an attempt to eradicate all traces of their crimes. These bones, too, were buried in the mass graves that the Jewish Committee organized.[200]

Heartrending scenes took place when relatives of parents who had perished arrived to claim Jewish children who had been left in private Lithuanian homes or in the care of Church and secular institutions. Many of these children had been baptized by their foster parents and refused to accompany uncles or aunts whom they no longer recognized. The religious institutions were especially reluctant to surrender children for whom they had cared and to whom they had become attached. Bishop Adamovicius, expressing official Church policy, rejected all pleas to help locate these children or to release them when they were found and identified. Thus most of the several hundred Jewish children in Lithuania who managed to survive the Holocaust were lost to the Jewish people.

Chapter 8

POSTSCRIPT: "*LIETUVA TEVYNE MUSU*"

For centuries, Jews had lived peacefully in Lithuania and considered it their homeland. They enjoyed its beautiful scenery, its mountains and forests, its rivers and lakes. Lithuanian Jews, together with Lithuanian non-Jews, respectfully sang the anthem of the newly created independent state that was established after World War I, "*Lietuva Tevyne Musu*" (Lithuania Is Our Fatherland), and regarded themselves as equal partners in the rebuilding of modern Lithuania. The emergence of political freedom for all gave Lithuanian Jews an opportunity to participate fully in government and every walk of life. Jews were represented in the Seimas and, for a brief period of time, in the cabinet. They enjoyed a period of Jewish autonomy, during which all forms of Jewish life flourished. For this, too, they were grateful.

As early as the mid-1930s, however, Jews were given sufficient reason to understand that they had no future in Lithuania. Jewish autonomy had long since withered. Jews were being eliminated from the economic life of the country; anti-Jewish manifestations increased. General Lithuanian public opinion responded favorably to the rise to power of Hitler, and many Lithuanian nationalist parties lauded the National Socialism and official anti-Jewish policies of neighboring Germany. When Nazi Germany invaded the Soviet Union, Lithuania clearly cast its sympathies with the former; after the Soviet occupation, Lithuanians fervently hoped for a German victory that would liberate them from the hated Communists.

Lithuanian Jewry was trapped between the warring powers, each of which had its own specific anti-Jewish policy and agenda. However, whereas the Soviets systematically destroyed Jewish religious and national institutions and forced Lithuanian Jews to adapt to a new economic order, the Germans committed unspeakable atrocities, caused endless pain and suffering to innocent men, women, and children, and systematically murdered all but 6,000-8,000 of Lithuania's Jews. Countless Lithuanians played an all too willing part in this orgy of savagery.

It is difficult to understand the reason for the extreme violence that so many Lithuanians perpetrated against their Jewish neighbors, with whom they had lived in comparative peace for so long. The very low proportion of Jews who were saved or concealed in comparison with other German-occupied countries is equally hard to comprehend. Lithuanian Jews had rarely suffered the indignities of the pogroms that were so common in Poland and Russia. Yet in 1941, as soon as the Red Army pulled out of Lithuania, even before the German forces arrived, pogroms that claimed thousands of Jewish lives erupted throughout the country. From the time the Nazis arrived until the moment they left, Lithuanians helped them implement the Final Solution in the ghettos, the forts, and the labor camps. They proved so effective in their work that they were organized into special Lithuanian battalions that were dispatched to other areas on the eastern front for similar killing operations.

Some Lithuanian apologists have attempted to explain this phenomenon by blaming the atrocities on criminal Lithuanian elements whom the Nazis had incorporated into their forces. These individuals, the apologists say, should be tried in criminal courts. However, these "criminal elements," most of whom succeeded in escaping to the United States, Great Britain, Australia, Canada, and other countries in the free world, were shielded and socially accepted by their countrymen. Other Lithuanian apologists have repeated the calumny that the Jews had brought these troubles upon themselves by collaborating with the Red Army and the Soviet occupation in destroying Lithuania's hard-won independence.

The attitude of postwar Lithuanians to the account of their participation in the Holocaust is mirrored in their public posture of silence and denial. Historian I. F. Stone attempts to describe this syndrome in his book *The War Years 1939-45*:[201]

> The essence of tragedy is not the doing of evil by evil men, but
> the doing of evil by good men out of weakness, indecision, sloth
> and inability to act in accordance with what they know to be
> right.

While not all Lithuanians actively supported Hitlerism, public opinion applauded Hitler's anti-Jewish policies. There were exceptions; a small number of Lithuanians, mainly peasants, risked their lives to save Jews.[202] The figures speak for themselves; only 6 percent of Lithuania's Jews survived the Nazi occupation. The deeds of the humane few cannot atone for the crimes of the many. The return of the Red Army to Lithuania in 1944 spared the remnant of Lithuania's Jews from certain death. Many Lithuanian collaborators and war criminals fled the country frantically to avoid punishment for their actions. For the expatriate Lithuanian communities abroad, the reestablishment of the Lithuanian Soviet Socialist Republic was a trauma with which they found it most difficult to come to terms.

More than one million Lithuanians live in the United States today. The Lithuanian-American Council, representing them, has constantly tried to belittle Lithuanian participation in the Holocaust. In 1987, the council's Chicago-based director of public relations, Father Dr. Juozas Prunskis, demanded that the Israeli Association of Lithuanian Jews publish a statement acknowledging that "only a few Lithuanians were among the murderers of Jews; the rest were innocent bystanders." Should the Association refuse to issue such a statement, Prunskis threatened to "expose Jewish deeds under the Soviets." The Israeli group disregarded both Prunskis' demand and his threat.

The slanderous insinuation that Jewish collaboration with the Soviets was a principal reason for the Lithuanians' violent assault on Jews after the Soviet retreat, although still prevalent, was modified if not refuted in 1977 by Bishop V. Brizgys:[203]

> It cannot be said that the Lithuanian Jews were
> pro-Communists, although they were happy with the Soviet
> protection in 1940 against the Nazis. The great majority of
> Lithuanian Jews, like the Lithuanians, preferred to live in
> freedom and not in a Soviet-dominated Lithuania. Many Jews,
> like Lithuanians, were arrested by the NKVD [the Soviet secret
> police], whose head, Gladkov, was presumed to be a Jew, and

were later imprisoned without trial. Some of the Jews and Lithuanians were deported and perhaps even executed in Russia. Both Lithuanians and Jews gave their support to the Bolsheviks but the Jews were extremely few in number.

In 1982, Dr. Stasys Sereika, a member of a new generation of Lithuanian scholars in America, urged his compatriots to "recognize the severity of their crimes against the Jews." Eight years later, on May 8, 1990, the Supreme Council of the newly independent Republic of Lithuania issued the following official declaration, signed by its president, Vytautas Landsbergis, on the role of Lithuanian antisemites in the Holocaust:

> The Council, in the name of the Lithuanian nation, condemns the genocide committed against the Jewish nation during the Nazi occupation in Lithuania, and notes with sorrow that Lithuanian citizens were among the executioners who served the occupiers. For the crime committed against the Jewish nation in Lithuania and outside its borders, there is not and cannot be any justification or any statute of limitations on criminal prosecution. The Republic of Lithuania will not tolerate any display of antisemitism.

The Holocaust was nothing if not Nazi Germany's denial of the right of the Jewish people to exist. Holocaust-era Lithuania, too, denied its Jews the right to exist. The legacy of the victims of the Holocaust demands that the world know the truth, so that what happened to them will never recur. This, and not a call for vengeance, was the wish of those who survived – and those who did not.

The following is a list of townlets and localities where Lithuanian Jews lived. Some of these localities did not belong to Lithuania at various periods of time, but are Lithuanian in culture and in their treatment during the German denouement. Most were rendered *Judenrein* during the Holocaust period, and remain so today. Some of their Jewish inhabitants perished or were killed in the localities themselves; others were taken to ghettos. Of a prewar Jewish population of 250,000, only 6,000-7,000 are believed to have survived.

In view of the shifting borders and sovereignties in this area (Polish, Belarus, German, Russian), many localities acquired numerous names. Those presented here are Lithuanian; their Jewish names are given in parentheses.

Name	District or Nearest City
Akmene (Ukmian)	Mazeikiai
Alexandrovol	Rokiskis
Alunta	Utena
Alsedziai (Alsad)	Telsiai
Alytus	
Antaliepte	Zarasai
Anyksciai (Aniksht)	Utena
Anyskai (Anishok)	Trakai
Ariogala	Kedainai

Asmena (Oshmian)	Vilnius
Augustavas	Suvalkai
Aukstadvaris (Visokidvor)	Trakai
Babtai (Bobt)	Kaunas
Bacivniai	Siauliai
Backinikl	Vilnius
Bagailoviskis (Bogoslavisok)	Ukmerge (Vilkomir)
Balbiriskis (Balbirishok)	Marijampole
Balninkai (Bolnik)	Ukmerge-Vilkomir
Barstyciai	Mazekiai
Batakai (Batok)	Taurage (Tavrik)
Bazilionai (Bazilian)	Siauliai
Beisogola	Kedainai
Betigala (Batigole)	Raseniai
Birstonas (Birstan)	Alytus
Birzai (Birz)	
Boidai (Boid)	Kaunas
Burtimonys (Burtimants)	Alytus
Cekiske (Tsaikishok	Kaunas
Dainjenai (Daujen)	Birzai
Darbenai (Darbian)	Kretinga
Darsuniskis (Darsunisok)	Trakai
Daugai (Doig)	Alytus
Debeikiai (Dveik)	Utena
Dotnuva	Kedainai
Druskininkai	Trakai
Dubingai (Dubinik)	Ukmerge-Vilkomir
Dukst	Utena
Dusetos (Dusiat)	Zarasai
Eisiskes (Eishishok)	Vilnius
Erzvilkas (Erzvilki)	Taurage-Tavrik
Gargzdai (Gorzd)	Kretinga
Garliava (Gudleve))	Kaunas
Gaure (Gavre)	Taurage (Tavrik)
Gelvonai (Galvan)	Ukmerge-Vilkomir
Giedraiciai (Gedrovitz)	Ukmerge-Vilkomir
Girkalnis (Girtigola)	Raseiniai

Grinkiskis (Grinkisok)	Kedainai
Griskalbudis (Griskalbud)	Sakiai
Gruzdziai (Gruzd)	Siauliai
Gudzuinai	Kedainai
Ilakiai (Jalok)	Mazeikiai
Inturike (Riterde)	Utena
Jasinnar	Vilnius
Juzintai (Juzint)	Rokiskis
Jieznas (Yezne)	Alytus
Jonava (Janeve)	Kaunas
Joniskis (Janisok)	Siauliai
Josvainiai (Josvian)	Kedainai
Jurbarkas	
Kaisiadorys (Kosidar)	Trakai
Kaltinenai (Kaltinan)	Taurage
Kalvarija	Marijampole
Kamajai (Kamai)	Rokiskis
Kapciamiestis (Kopceve)	Alytus
Karlu-Ruda (Kazlove-Rude)	Kaunas
Kaunas (Kovno)	
Kedainai (Keidan)	
Kedainiai	
Kelme	
Klovainiai (Klobian)	Siauliai
Klykolai (Klikol)	Mazeikiai
Kovarskas	Ukmerge-Vilkomir
Krakes (Krok)	Kedainai
Kraziai (Kroz)	Raseiniai
Krekenava (Krakinova)	Panevezys
Kretinga	
Krincinas (Kritzian)	Birzai
Krivkai (Kruk)	Birzai
Kriukiai (Kruki)	Sakiai
Kruonis (Kron)	Kaunas
Kudirkos-Naumiestis (Naishtot-Shaki)	Sakiai
Kuktiskes (Koktiske)	Utena
Kulautuva (Kalatove)	Kaunas

Kuliai (Kul)	Kretinga
Kupiskis (Kupishok)	Panevezys
Kurkliai (Korkli)	Ukmerge-Vilkomir
Kursenai (Kursan)	Siauliai
Kurtuvenai (Kurtuvian)	Siauliai
Kvedarna (Chveidan)	Taurage
Kybartai	Vilkaviskis
Labanor	Svencionys
Landvarova	Vilnius
Latzkova	Telsiai
Laukuva (Loikeve)	Taurage (Tavrik)
Lazdijai	Suvalkai
Leckava (Lackeve)	Mazeikiai
Leipalingis (Liepun)	Alytus
Letvaris	Vilnius
Ligumai (Ligum)	Siauliai
Linkuva	Siauliai
Lingmian	Svencionys
Liudvinava	Marijampole
Luksiai (Lukshi)	Sakiai
Luokove (Luknik)	Telsiai
Lyduveniai (Liduvian)	Raseiniai
Marijampole	
Miroslav	Alytus
Mavrotz	Kaunas
Mazeikiai	
Medingenai (Medingian)	Telsiai
Meisigola	Vilnius
Merkine (Meretz)	Alytus
Meskuciai (Maskotz)	Marijampole
Mikaliskis	Vilnius
Miligan	Vilnius
Moletai (Malat)	Utena
Molocino	Vilnius
Mosedis (Misiad)	Kretinga
Musninkai (Mosnik)	Ukmerge-Vilkomir
Naumiestis (Naishtot-Ponevez)	Panevezys

Nemaksciai (Nemoksht)	Raseiniai
Nemunaitis	Alytus
Nemunelis-Radviliskis	Birzai
Nevarenai (Naveran)	Telsiai
Obeliai (Abel)	Rakiskis
Oniskis (Onishok)	Rokiskis
Oran	Trakai
Osmany	Vilnius
Pabirze	Birzai
Pagegiai	Taurage
Pagiriai	Keidainai
Pajuris (Pajure)	Taurage
Pakruojus (Pokroy)	Siauliai
Pakuonis (Pekun)	Kaunas
Palanga	Kretinga
Pandelis (Ponedel)	Rokiskis
Panemunelis (Panemunek)	Rokiskis
Panevezys (Ponevez)	
Panosiskes (Panoshishok)	Trakai
Papile (Popilian)	Siauliai
Pasvalys (Posval)	Birzai
Pasvitinys (Posvitin)	Siauliai
Pikeliai (Pikeln)	Mazeikiai
Pilviskiai (Pilvishok)	Vilkaviskis
Piniava	Panevezys
Plateliai (Plotl)	Kretinga
Plunge (Plungian)	Telsiai
Posvitin	Birzai
Pravieniskis (Provinishok)	Kaunas
Prienai	Marijampole
Pumpenai (Pumpian)	Panevezys
Punia (Pun)	Alytus
Pusalotas (Pushalat)	Panevezys
Radeikiai (Radeik)	Utena
Radviliskis (Radvilishok)	Siauliai
Raguva (Rogove)	Panevezys
Ramygala (Ramigole)	Panevezys

Raseiniai	
Raudone	Yurbarkas
Raudondvaris (Roiterhoif)	Kaunas
Rekyva	Siauliai
Rietavas (Riteve)	Telsiai
Rokiskis (Rokishok)	
Rozalimas (Rozalia)	Panevezys
Rudamine (Rodamin)	Lazdijai
Rumsiskes (Runshishok)	Kaunas
Sakiai (Shaki)	
Siauliai	
Salakas (Salok)	Zarasai
Salantai (Salant)	Kretinga
Salociai (Salat)	Birzai
Salos (Sol)	Vilnius
Sanciai	Kaunas
Saukenai (Sukian)	Siauliai
Savlaniai	Panevezys
Sazineliai	Panevezys
Seda (Siad)	Mazeikiai
Seduva (Sadove)	Panevezys
Seinai	Suvalkai
Semiliskes (Semilisok)	Trakai
Seredzius (Serednik)	Kaunas
Sesuoliai (Sesvil)	Ukmerge-Vilkomir
Seta (Shat)	Kedainai
Siauliai (Shavli)	
Siaudine	Telsiai
Siaudine	Sakiai
Seirijai (Serei)	Alytus
Siesikai (Shesik)	Ukmerge-Vilkomir
Silale (Silel)	Taurage
Silute	Klaipeda-Memel
Siluva (Sidlova)	Raseiniai
Simkaiciai (Shumkaitz)	Raseiniai
Simnas (Simne)	Alytus
Sirvintai (Shirvint)	Ukmerge-Vilkomir

Skapiskis (Skopisok)	Rokiskis
Skaudvile (Shkudvil)	Taurage
Skiemonys (Skumian)	Utena
Skuodas (Shkud)	Kretinga
Smargon	Vilnius
Smilgai	Panevezys
Stakliskes (Stoklisok)	Alytus
Stakliskes (Stoklisok)	Kaunas
Subacius (Suboch)	Panevezys
Suginet	Utena
Suvainiskis	Rokiskis
Suvalkai	
Svedasai (Sviadosh)	Utena
Sveksna	Taurage
Sulviniski	Panevezys
Svieriai (Svir)	Vilnius
Svencionys	Vilnius
Taujenai (Tavian)	Ukmerge-Vilkomir
Taurage (Tavrik)	
Tauragnai (Toragin)	Utena
Telsiai (Telsh)	
Tirksliai (Tirksle)	Mazeikiai
Trakai (Trok)	Vilnius
Troskunai (Trashkun)	Panevezys
Tryskiai (Trishk)	Siauliai
Turgeliai	Vilnius
Turmantas	Zarasai
Tverai (Tver)	Telsiai
Tytuvenai (Zitoviani)	Raseniai
Ukmerge (Ukmerge-Vilkomir)	
Ulkeniki	Vilnius
Ulsan	Vilnius
Upyna	Alytus
Utena (Utian)	
Uzpaliai (Ushpal)	Utena
Uzventis (Uzvent)	Siauliai
Vabalninkas (Vabolnik)	Birzai

Vaiguva	Siauliai
Vainutas	Taurage
Vandziogala (Venzegole)	Kaunas
Varena (Oran)	Alytus
Varniai (Vorne)	Telsiai
Vaskiai (Vashki)	Birzai
Vegeriai	Mazeikiai
Veisiejai (Visei)	Alytus
Veiveriai (Veiver)	Kaunas
Veivirzenai (Vevirzan)	Kretinga
Veliuona (Vilun)	Kaunas
Vidiskiai (Vidisok)	Ukmerge-Vilkomir
Vidukle	Raseniai
Vieksniai (Vekshne)	Mazekiai
Viesintai	Panevezys
Vievis (Vievje)	Trakai
Vilkaviskis	
Vilkija (Vilki)	Kaunas
Vilnius (Vilna)	
Virbalis (Verzbelove)	Vilkaviskis
Visniava	Vilnius
Vistytis (Vistinitz)	Vilkaviskis
Visoki-Ruda	Kaunas
Volozin	Vilnius
Vizuoniai (Vizun)	Utena
Zagare (Zager)	Siauliai
Zapiskis (Zapishok)	Kaunas
Zarasai (Ezereni)	Utena
Zarenai (Zaran)	Telsiai
Zasliai (Zosli)	Trakai
Zeimelis (Zeiml)	Siauliai
Zeimiai (Zeim)	Kedainai
Zelva (Podzelva)	Ukmerge-Vilkomir
Zemaiciu Naumiestis (Neishtot Tavrik)	Taurage
Zidikai (Zidik)	Mazeikiai
Ziezmariai	Trakai

NOTES

Notes to Chapter 1

1. Basanavicias, Jonas, *On Ancient Lithuania*, Vilnius, 1921.
2. Cf. B. D. Dwight, *Modern Philology*.
3. Tacitus, *Chronicles*: "De Situ, Moribu et populis Germanicus."
4. Nalkovsky, Waclow, *The Commonwealth of Poland and Lithuania*, London, 1911. Ibrahim ben Jacob, a merchant travelling on business, gives us the first insight into Jewish life in Lithuania. According to this source, the first Jewish community in Gardinas (Grodno) dates from 1128, and that in Kaunas (Kovno) from 1280. Nalkovsky describes the Lithuanian people, their customs, organization, and pagan religion, as well as their friendliness to strangers.
5. The term magnate denotes a member of a large, powerful family noted for its regular involvement in politics.
6. Benjamin of Tudela and rabbinic sources of the thirteenth and fourteenth centuries speak of Jews who live east of the River Elbe, terming them "Jews of Canaan." Many of them spoke a Slavonic language. Since the word "slav" is a cognate of slave – Heb. 'eved – Tudela associated the Slavonic lands with the Biblical slave-nations and termed them the lands of Canaan. Some of the Jews in these countries moved to Lithuania proper in search of better conditions.
7. Yanulaitis Augustine, *The Jews of Lithuania*, Kaunas, 1923.

8. The crusades of 1095, 1195, 1202, 1203, and others. The blood libel was invoked in Fulda, Kuzingen, Tauringen, Otrberg, Orenschtat, Koblentz, Munchen, Baden, Elsas, and many other localities in the early thirteenth century.

9. The Jewish city names – Kovno for Kaunas, Vilna for Vilnius, Shavli for Siauliai, Grodno for Gardinas, and so on – are used in this chronicle when the object of reference is Jewish; otherwise, the Gentile names are used. Variants are provided in parentheses at times to avoid confusion.

10. Yadviga, daughter of King Luis of Buda, became Queen of Poland at the age of eleven. At the age of 12 she was married to Jagiello, aged 36, the King of Lithuania, who paid Prince Wilhelm of Austria 200,000 florins for the betrothal. She was escorted to Poland by a large retinue of priests, advisers, and servants, all fervent Catholics.

11. The rulers of Lithuania were wont to change capitals, perhaps in order to choose new allies from the nobility.

12. Some sources believe he died in 1433 after three years of illness.

13. Some of the differences are extreme. For example, Karaites observe the Sabbath in the dark and refrain from cutting bread or any other food on the holy day.

14. See Bershadsky, Sergei *King Vytauta's Charter*.

15. By the end of the fifteenth century, approximately 6,000 Jews in Lithuania came under the jurisdiction of the royal government, represented by the Voivode in the cities and the Starosta in the provinces, safeguarding their statutary rights, privileges, and obligations.

16. After the expulsion of the Jews of Spain, Lithuania was the only European country in which Jews managed estates in *arenda* and practiced a wide range of trades, crafts and skills, becoming indispensable craftsmen in the economy of the villages and townlets.

17. Poland and Lithuania in the sixteenth and seventeenth centuries were considered paradise for nobles, heaven for the Jews, and hell for the serfs.

18. King Casimir's six sons, the so-called princes of the Renaissance, attended schools in Holland, Italy, and France.

19. Olesnicky, although no friend of the Jews, encouraged Joseph Yazowia, chaplain of the widowed Queen Sofia, to consult Jewish scholars in order to translate the Bible into Polish.

20. In 1440, Grand Duke Casimir allowed the Jews to build the first synagogue in the country. Until then, the Jews had gathered in quorums *(minyan)* in rooms or private houses *(shtiblakh)*.

21. A letter written in 1490 by the plenipotentiary of Moscow to the court of Casimir, the Grand Duke of Lithuania, complained that his Jewish tax-lessee,

Michael Danilov, was imposing heavy taxes on merchants crossing Vilna en route to Moscow.

22. See discussion of the unique *Liberum veto*, below.

23. According to a Jewish legend, after the death of his Queen, Casimir took a Jewish mistress named Esterka, whom he would have married had she agreed to convert to Christianity. Casimir built her a castle, and she began to settle Jewish families in its vicinity. This, the legend says, was the origin of the town of Carzimiez near Cracow, where a large Jewish community flourished for some time.

24. Generally speaking, the Jews enjoyed religious and economic tolerance during Alexander Jagiello's reign because they were able to provide much needed services. The economic struggle between the burghers and the Jews forced the former to create the municipal economic and credit system that subjugated the town and preserved the burghers' interests and privileges under the Magdeburg Laws, which gave them several liberties and exemptions. The legal and the social status of the Jews was defined as *incolat*; this was the term used in official documents. The burghers occasionally demanded similar privileges for themselves, which they called *incolatum*, and struggled within the law to delimit the Jews' privileges. The burghers protested the lack of coinage and boycotted enterprises that could not undertake to deal solely in cash. Gradually, the Jews came under discriminatory legislation that further restricted their economic activities. They were also at a disadvantage in combating the municipal economic system; unable to control production, they could not fix the price of goods. Thus, the few wealthy Jews preferred to maximize their profits by serving the state and the nobles as the agents of feudal lords. As the beneficiaries of royal protection, they were also able to mobilize funds for the nobles' local and foreign expenditures.

25. In fact, a sizable group of prominent Jews in the Commonwealth chose to convert: Josephowitz, Hlebickis, Abramowitz of Vorniany (a Calvinist center in Lithuania), and Jelensky Franciszek, later a district treasurer for the Grand Duchy, who married into the nobility, the *schlachta*. Several of these converts became well- known public figures by marrying into high society.

The Lithuanian Statute of 1588, confirmed in the Constitution of 1601, explicitly ennobled converts in perpetuity. Converts were given these and other privileges because of a combination of Catholic missionary expansion, the prevailing Renaissance atmosphere of humanism, and a benevolent attitude toward converts. Their names were entered into the records of the Grand Duchy's ruling class.

26. The Lithuanian Statutes of 1529, 1566, 1588, and 1601 set forth the privileges, freedom, and special laws given to the Jews. The Constitution of 1539, enforced with special vigor in privately owned towns, were of fundamental importance to the Jews, making them the only group that enjoyed the right to appeal the decisions of lower instances to the Royal Court. According to the Polish-Jewish historian Balaban, the massive influx of Jews into magnate-controlled towns actually magnified the nobles' power when the Jews were ousted from the Royal towns. It also gave the *schlachta* greater dominion over their villages and therefore limited the privileges of the Jews there. From 1539 to 1764 the Jewish Council of Lithuania (the *Va'ad ha-Medina*) advised individual communities to negotiate privileges in addition to those given the Jews by the Royal Court in order to secure their own regional, community, and individual needs. The old Jewish charters and laws were regularly updated to reflect changing circumstances, but there was no uniform pattern throughout the country and its Commonwealth. Jewish auspices negotiated individual contracts with the nobles, the *schlachta*, starosta, voivodes, burghers, magistrates, officers of the law, artisan guilds, the clergy, monasteries, churches, and other minorities such as the Germans, Ukrainians, and Belorussians.

27. In 1513, Bernard of Lublin published the first Polish-language typeset book, called *Souls of Paradise*, in Lithuania. The privilege to print and sell Hebrew books was awarded in 1560.

28. Bitzunas, a Lithuanian historian, describes the tax-farming budget in his *Pisari Poboravije*.

29. The *shok*, one of several currencies used in fifteenth-century Lithuania, was equivalent to 12.5 lits in independent Lithuania.

30. A Polish translation of the Bible and other religious texts, dedicated to Sigismund Augustus, was printed at the Radvilas printing press in Brasta (Bresk-Litvosk). The center of Lithuanian Calvinism at the time was Ukmerge (Vilkomir). John Laski, one of the most important leaders of the Polish Lithuanian Reformation, interrelated and corresponded with Erasmus of Rotterdam and Calvin of Basel.

31. In a letter to his superior in Rome, the cardinal legate in Poland, Giovanni Commendone, admiringly described the Jews of Lithuania as "devoting time to study of Hebrew books, sciences, astronomy and medicine."

32. Sigismund Augustus's interest in reforming the Commonwealth government derived from Peter Tomicki's diplomatic and private correspondence with the king, coupled with the influence of John Zamoyski and other members of his court.

33. An agreement limiting royal power, invoked by the magnates in their struggle with the king.

34. The Roman Catholic prelates never accepted the new denomination as an equal, and their elitism is widely blamed for the evolution of the Uniate Church into a "peasant religion" which, in turn, formed the social nucleus of anti-Polish and, especially, anti-Jewish Ukrainian nationalism.

35. Jews benefited politically from the wars between Sigismund Vasa and his uncle Charles IX by acquiring new privileges for the community and individual-family levels. In 1601, in the city of Slutzk (home of Januz Radziwill), Mendel Joselowitz of Brest-Litovsk obtained permission to allow additional Jews to settle in Slutzk and to extend his diverse business interests. The king also insisted that the Jews' rights and privileges, once granted, be honored throughout the Commonwealth. In return, the Jews helped him increase his war chest. His Irish physician, Bernard O'Conner, noted in his diary that "the Jews in the Commonwealth continually enjoy religious and other privileges."

36. The *schlachta* demanded the right not only to serve the markets but to establish a sales depot and to have a say in the disbursement of the revenue resulting from the accumulation of increased taxes. Small Jewish businessmen, peddlers, and craftsmen were excluded from the favorable rules, regulations, and privileges. Indeed, they were the casualties of most of the restrictions and all the additional taxes.

37. The *schlachta* made it clear to the king that he was *electio viritum*, i.e., elected by them and therefore subject to their restrictions.

38. From 1630 on, Jews were subjected to increasingly heavy taxation that undermined and overwhelmed the community's fiscal system. As the king's military needs grew, so did the levies on the Jewish communities.

39. Joseph Shlomo del Megido of Kandia (1591-1655), Prince Radziwill's personal physician and, on occasion, Sigismund Vasa's medical adviser, wrote an interesting letter describing the Jewish and Karaite communities that he encountered as he crisscrossed Lithuania for the purpose of propagating and spreading Jewish scholarship in that country. He found established communities in Zamut, Suwalk, Troky, Panevezys, Pasual, Salant, Pushelat, Birz, Shat, Krany, Shantz (Kaunas vicinity), Rasein, Vizun, Meretz and Yurburg.

      One of Del Megido's correspondents was the Karaite *hakham* Zerach bar Nathan of Troki, whom he found to be most knowledgeable in the study of Torah. At this time, Jews and Karaites frequently shared and exchanged interpretations of the Torah.

40. In Italy, however, the Christian moneylending houses of Lombardy found a way to circumvent this proscription, thus establishing the rationale for all future Christian banking enterprises.

41. Crisis and hard times in the history of the Commonwealth (wars, epidemics, economic setbacks) were invariably accompanied by threats to the Jewish communities. Judeophobia was based not only on theological speculation but also, and chiefly, on economic and moral decline, for which pogroms and violence were merely external manifestations.

42. Jewish religious law proscribes the consumption of this commodity but allows its sale to Gentiles.

43. Polish Catholic intolerance toward the Orthodox population of the Ukraine took a turn for the worse at precisely this time. Catholic actions, including attempts to effect forced conversion to the Uniate Church, exacerbated the Cossacks' religious, racial, and social enmity vis-a-vis the Poles. The Jews, again, absorbed the major blow.

44. In 1643, Commonwealth law categorized merchants as Poles, foreigners, or Jews. The Cossacks, being a class of their own, were classified not as merchants but as fighters. Cossack is Tartar for "wanderer."

45. After the upheaval of 1648, the king introduced several protective measures meant to tide a few wealthy Polish and Jewish victims over the ravages of the wars and pogroms. Some of these affluent Jews, who returned from the Ukraine to Poland and Lithuania, integrated into general society by converting; other Jewish converts left the Ukraine and settled in Lithuania as members of the gentry.

46. Moses ben Naphtali Hirsch Rivkes, *Be'er ha-Gola*, Amsterdam, 1661.

47. The general economic and social situation in the Commonwealth mitigated and vitiated the royal powers. The king acknowledged this by accepting the Constitution of 1667 and, in 1669, the *pacta convecta* that enabled the Sejm to dictate his every move.

48. The Vasa rule and the problems it caused inspired the Jewish communities to consolidate and reorganize. The merchant sector became more dominant in the community and seized control of the *kahal*. The *shtadlan* represented the community vis-a-vis dignitaries and legislators. Whereas his role diminished and expired in Western Europe after the French Revolution, it remained vastly important in Eastern Europe and, especially, in Russia, until the second half of the nineteenth century.

49. One never knows. In 1950, a hand-written letter by Shabbetai Zevi was discovered in a Salonika prayerbook that had once belonged to Shabbetaeans. In the letter, he requests that a mahzor (prayerbook for Rosh Hashana and Yom Kippur) be sent to him. The name by which he signed this

letter – Yehuda Shabbetai Mohammed Zevi – suggests that the missive was written after his conversion.

50. In 1679, King Sobieski struck a deal with a large group of Tartar horsemen, inviting them to settle and take permanent possession of prime pasture and farm land in eastern Poland, abutting the border with Tartar Russia. Their main center became the townlet of Krusz and the area they occupied was known as Kruszyniany Poland. In return, they functioned as a buffer against the warring, looting, murderous Tartar hordes who had been infiltrating the Commonwealth borders relentlessly. Sobieski's wise decision brought an end to the Tartar troubles in Poland and Lithuania.

51. The large number of the Jewish Frankists who converted to Christianity was a cause of grave concern to the Jews, the Lithuanians, and the Poles. In response, the nobility forced the Diet of 1764 to revoke the clause in the Lithuanian Statute of 1588 granting converts full gentry rights. However, the *ex gente judeorum*, as they were called, fought back and demanded that their rights be ratified. Thus fifty-eight former Jewish families were ennobled in 1764-1765 by special decree of the king and the Diet, and several more were ennobled in 1768-1790. Most of these converts or their children assumed public office, became wealthy, and married into old noble families. In 1782, following the first partition of Poland and Lithuania, an ukase (decree) of Czarina Catherine II forced them to provide the Russian and Austrian governments with proof of their nobility.

52. When first steps were taken in the seventeenth century to decentralize the state economy, a small tribunal met in Vilna to adjudicate tax disputes.

53. These imports, largely from Asia, included carpets, tapestries, and other luxuries such as embroidered coats and belts. So successful were the importers that local industry declined and the poor, under pressure to begin with, suffered more.

54. The expression is attributed to Napoleon, who invoked it while stationed in the Lithuanian capital.

55. After his coronation, he brought Jewish advisers from Germany and reconfirmed the Jewish charters, which, however, he was powerless to enforce.

56. Under the Royal Court and the Sejm, the Commonwealth failed to develop modern political institutions and an effective centralized state bureaucracy. This made governmental reform difficult to achieve. In Commonwealth history, the Sejm of 1719 is known as the "Dumb Diet" because of its inability to make decisions.

57. Girls were generally barred from schools at this time, although some were privately educated.

Notes to Chapter 2

58. The nature and formation of the Karaite community are described in Chapter 1, under *Vytautas the Great*.

59. Official documents used the word "synagogue" to denote the Jewish community as such, and not merely a place of prayer; cf. "church."

60. The continuous need of governments and kings to reconfirm the Jewish charters was brought before a special commission in the form of an *arenga* – a preamble meant to explain the necessity and urgency of these documents. The special commissions' decisions to reconfirm the charters were also accepted by the *Komisye Boni Ordinis* (commissions of public order).

61. Karaite recourse to the "Rabbanite" system did not extend to emergency fundraising. The Jews of Lithuania sought assistance from coreligionists in Germany and Holland; the Karaites sent emissaries to their brethren in the Crimea.

62. The government did prosecute some of these offenders. At this time, too, it neither aided nor abetted the Church institutions in their anti-Jewish actions.

63. Famous publications in Lithuania at that time included *Be'er Avraham* (Well of Abraham) by R. Avraham Lisker, *Mey Be'er* (Water of the well) by R. Judah Zundel of Keidan, and *Aspaqlaria ha-Meira* (Illuminating mirror) by R. Zvi Hirsh Halevi Horowitz.

64. Insofar as this chronicle concerns itself with the Jewish community, the "Jewish names" for Kaunas, Vilnius, and other Lithuanian towns will be used.

65. Vilna had only one prayerhouse worthy of this title; smaller and less formal facilities – *shtiblakh* – abounded.

66. Gonta and his Haidamacks were the most feared names of the time.

67. Larger cities such as Vilnius, Kaunas, Gardinas, and Minsk retained their earlier status.

68. In 1787, Poniatowski proposed a military alliance with Russia to help Muscovy cope with a two-front (Turkish-Swedish) war. The Sejm of 1788, convening in Warsaw, rejected the idea. An indication of the strength of general Russian influence was the habit of private citizens to travel to St. Petersburg to seek intervention of the Russian Court in matters of personal advancement in the government administration.

69. The Dutch currency was one of many that were used in Lithuania at the time.

70. An application of the famed Jewish value of *pidyon shevui'im*.

71. Since Jews were barred from Polish and Lithuanian universities, those wishing to enter the professions had to study abroad. A favored destination was the University of Padua in Italy.

72. As Solomon Maimon describes in his autobiography.

73. All community members received these documents, which were authorized by the Russian Empire to which Lithuania now belonged.

Notes to Chapter 3

74. The sobriquet *gaon* (denoting eminence or genius) was first applied to the spiritual leaders of the post-Talmudic (sixth through the eleventh centuries) leaders of the Jewish communities of Babylonia; it was also a collective title for some post-Talmudic sages in Palestine. An honor very sparingly bestowed, it was conferred on R. Elijah for his undisputed authority in matters of religious law among all Jewish communities in Eastern and Central Europe.

75. Indeed, the yeshiva world uses the expression "learning Torah" to denote all such study, irrespective of its connection to the Pentateuch.

76. The institution of the *maggid* is discussed in Chapter 3.

77. It is true that the Christian Lithuanian affluent class attempted to imitate their Polish peers, who took interest in Enlightenment but pursued a life of luxury and pleasure, explaining that "work was unworthy of a gentleman." Little of this mentality rubbed off on the Jews.

78. "Reb" sometimes, but not always, denotes a lesser rank of erudition than "rabbi"; it is also a term of endearment.

79. This is the English rendition of the title as presented in *Encyclopaedia Judaica*. Figuratively, the Hebrew expression denotes a trifling thing.

80. See above re *Hamelitz*.

81. During Israel's War of Independence in 1948, Arab Legion forces occupied the area and reduced it to rubble again; the only restoration done since the resumption of Jewish control of the Old City in 1967 has been one representative arch.

82. Some time later, approximately 40 delegates who favored the Uganda scheme, led by well-known Anglo-Jewish author Israel Zangwill, broke away from the Zionist movement and formed the Jewish Territorialist Organization, devoted to establishing Jewish autonomy "in any territory in which the predominant majority of the population shall be Jewish."

83. The Zionist political parties followed the same paradigm when founded in Lithuania and for decades thereafter.

84. The Bund's leadership was influenced by the Narodniki, the Populists (who absorbed the ideas of the Decembrists, Alexander Herzen, Belinsky, and Proudhon), and, above all, the writings of Nicholas Gavrilewitz Chernishevsky, who shared the ideas of the Western democrats of the Industrial Revolution. The Russian poor were considered the poorest and most miserable in Europe. The great utopian dream, shared by all revolutionaries in Russia, was to provide this working class with its basic necessities: food, clothing, health, education, and security. The Bund addressed itself to the special needs of the new Jewish proletariat in the cities and the poor in the townlets, who lived under conditions of horrendous poverty.

Notes to Chapter 4

85. Lithuania was as determined to resist Russification as it had Polonization. In this sense, Lithuanian Jews and Gentiles fought shoulder-to-shoulder. At the very end of the Czarist period, the Lithuanian delegation to the Third Duma, including Jewish advocates Fridman and Niesselowitz, succeeded in obtaining permission to reintroduce the study of the Lithuanian language and culture in the Baltic country.
86. Jews could buy their way out of the Pale by paying a bribe, a doubling of their regular taxes, from which artisans, manufacturers, merchants, and city dwellers were exempt.
87. The Lithuanian famine of 1870, and official indifference to the suffering it caused, led many Lithuanian Jews and Gentiles to seek emigration.
88. The gentry was especially unhappy; it had placed great hopes on Napoleon's promises for the resurrection of a free Lithuanian and Polish Republic or, at least, Lithuanian semi-autonomy under the French.
89. Disillusioned by the failure of his wavering policy of liberalism, Alexander I also declared war on political and quasi-political movements of all kinds, some exogenous (e.g., the Freemasons) and others indigenous (the Constitutionalists, the Republicans, the Revolutionaries, the Decembrists, and so on). Some of these groups, originally reformist, began to preach revolution in view of the regime's reactionism.
90. The blood libel had been officially outlawed by Czar Alexander in 1817. However, this form of antisemitic defamation, originally invoked by the Romans against the Christians, simply refused to disappear. "The absurdity of the blood libel," said Ahad Ha'am, "at least offers us the consolation of knowing that indeed the whole world can be wrong and the Jew right."

Between 1880 and 1911 alone, Russian Jews faced more than 100 accusations of ritual murder. The last ritual murder charge in the Empire was brought against Mendel Beilis of Kiev in 1911, who was allowed to languish in prison for two years without trial. The Beilis trial evoked protests and demonstrations in Russia and around the world. Unprecedented defense tactics were invoked, and Beilis was acquitted – all of which did nothing to improve the immediate condition of Russian Jewry.

The Russian masses, goaded by their Church, firmly believed in the truth of the libel. Whenever a court of law exonerated a Jew accused of ritual murder, antisemites treated the acquittal as proof that a Jew had once again managed to escape justice.

91. Derives from *cantonment*, the barracks in which the conscripted children were housed.

92. Gitelman, Zvi, *A Century of Ambivalence*, 6.

93. Some progress could not be stopped. The Imperial economy was in very bad shape and desperately needed modernization. The government, reluctantly at first, began to promote the formation of private credit institutions. Some of the seed money for such ventures originated abroad, and Jews were involved on both ends. In 1860, for example, Rabbi Dr. Isaac Ruelf, a German Jew, sent 630,000 marks, a large sum in those days, to help the Jews of the Kovno District establish industrial credit facilities and to support Lithuanian Jewry in general.

94. Coverage of government brutality and the terrible conditions of the masses remained strictly censored.

95. Joseph Jacob described the pogroms in a review that was smuggled out of Russia via the office of Rabbi Isaac Elchanan Spektor, the Chief Rabbi of Kovno, and published in *The Times* of London on January 11, 1882. Diplomatic reports with eyewitness accounts were dispatched by John W. Foster, the American Ambassador to St. Petersburg. Additional reports were presented by the Lord Mayor of London, Lucien Wolf, S. S. Cox, the Austrian Envoy to Moscow, Von Kalnoky, Henry Edward Cardinal Manning, and others.

96. The Russo-Japanese war erupted despite Count Witte's objections. It was triggered by the Czar's indifference to the strong objections of Japanese Prince Hirobutu Ito to a Russian infringement of Japanese sovereignty. The Czar's confidant, A. M. Bezobrazov, made great profits for himself, the Czar's circle, and family members including his minister, Von Plehve, in the timber business by means of his Eastern Asiatic Industrial Company, which sold stocks and bonds for the Yalu river project. After protesting to the Russian government with no effect, the Japanese concluded an alliance with England

against the Russian occupation of Manchuria. The Russian response to this move was war.

97. Prince Mirsky proposed that the Czar accept the 1904 Manifesto for a democratic Duma. The tyrant turned him down categorically; the only assembly he would accept was "a consultative Duma composed of 43 percent peasants, 34 percent landowners, and 23 percent burghers."

98. Russian industrialization had placed 10 percent of the country's Jewish population in the proletariat; in Lithuania, according to Dr. Brutzkus, 54 percent of employed Jews worked in factories.

Notes to Chapter 5

99. The Russian census in 1897 reported that 13 percent of the total Lithuanian population of 2,200,000 was Jewish. In 1916, the German Verwaltungsgebiet Oberost accepted these findings.

     In Latvia, Jews accounted for 5 percent of the population (79,644 out of 1,350,000); in Estonia, they were a mere 0.4 percent (4,666 out of 970,000). In 1991, by comparison, the three Baltic countries had a combined population of 6,944,000 of which 0.35 percent were Jews.

100. The tribunals were established in the early nineteenth century; the government kept their powers under tight rein.

101. In his memoirs, Advocate Gruzenberg writes that the expulsion of 2,500 Jewish soldiers from the Kaunas district, together with a false accusation by the Russian government against Jewish doctors, came a few days before the Germans captured the city of Kaunas.

102. In the West, by contrast, the expulsion of Lithuanian Jewry caused general outrage; Russia encountered difficulties in obtaining foreign loans. Hence the official elimination of restrictions on Jewish residence may have been a conciliatory attempt to reverse negative public opinion; it also triggered an influx of Polish and Lithuanian refugees into the Russian interior.

103. Diary of Boris Smoliar, an American journalist who witnessed the proceedings and published his reports in the Yiddish-language newspaper *Zukunft*.

104. In June and July of 1941, Kuzhi served as a center for the liquidation of Jews in the area.

105. In 1941, by comparison, the going rate for a day of slave labor was 80 pfennig per Jew. German and Lithuanian organizations that used Jewish labor received and, as a rule, pocketed these moneys. They also falsified the numbers of Jewish laborers in order to boost their profits.

106. *Jewish Chronicle*, January 22, 1917.

107. *Pinkos far der geshikhte fun Vilna in di yoren fun milkhomo un okupatsie*, Ed. Zalman Reisen, Vilna, 1922.

108. *Jewish Chronicle*, June 8, 1919.

109. As a humanist and democrat, Prime Minister Slezevicius believed that the Communists in Lithuania should be treated no differently from any other party and refused to regard them as agents of a foreign power. The press and the Nationalists assailed this conviction; the Lithuanian masses waited until Slezevicius' death in 1939 to demonstrate their respect and love for this man.

110. *Jewish Chronicle*, January 10, 1919.

111. On December 29, 1918, the first Bulletin of the provisional government, gazetted in *Lietuvos Aidas* (Lithuanian official news), included the names of the deputies of the new Taryba. The bulletin was also published in Yiddish.

112. Until that time, some in Europe had doubted the legitimacy of Lithuania as a state. For example, one Johannet asserted ("Le principe des nationalités," *Le Temps*, February 1, 1919) that "Lithuanian separatism had been artificially created by the Germans, invented in Berlin in 1916."

113. Moscow's ostensible magnanimity may be explained by its interest in ending the civil war then raging in central Russia – a brutal conflict in which Poles tussled both with the Red Army and with Lithuanians who had been expelled from their homeland in 1915.

114. For their part, the Poles had been unpopular and unwelcome in Lithuania since the days of Vytautas the Great. Considered outsiders who had been imposed by force upon the Lithuanians, many had in time assumed control of large estates, where they installed numerous Polish workers and peasants. Lithuanians perceived them as colonists.

115. Stephen Graham, correspondent for *The Times* of London, commented in a report from Kaunas on September 12, 1924, that "Maps in this part of the world provide a unique amusement. Maps of Lithuania show her in possession of a handsome portion of White Russia, half of East Prussia with Memel-Klaipeda, and of course the Vilna county. A map of Europe that shows the Poles' pretensions includes all of Lithuania and three quarters of the whole of central Europe. The historical mind of Poland is likely to prove an important factor in the political life of the border states." In fact, the problems with Poland, as well as the Poles' mistreatment of their minorities, did affect Lithuania.

116. A short-lived interim electoral body that chose the members of the Seimas.

117. As contradictory as the Minister's title sounds, this is the phrasing used in all official documents, including those of the British Public Records office.

118. Lithuanian Jewry was rather well organized for community action. In its issue of May 27, 1920, *The Times* of London carried the following report from Kaunas: "The Jews of Lithuania made a remarkable demonstration in front of the British Consulate this afternoon as an expression of gratitude to Britain for her work in the emancipation for Palestine. Probably 20,000 were present, with several bands. The Consul, Colonel Ward, received a deputation and delivered a speech. There were scenes of wonderful enthusiasm with the bands playing British and Jewish hymns." The much smaller Jewish communities in the two other Baltic countries were less well organized.

119. Pocius, Yonas, *Present Day Lithuania in Figures*, Vilnius, 1971. All told, there were 181,000 illiterates and 223,000 semiliterates in Lithuania during the 1919-1927 period. Isidor Lazar (*Idishe Shtime*, N.573, June 10, 1921) asserted that only one-third of the members of the Seimas were able to speak Lithuanian.

120. The Provisional Lithuanian Government, not to be confused with the 20-member provisional council that summoned the Constituent Assembly.

121. In strict numerical terms, the minorities and the left could have commanded a majority and formed a coalition. In practice, their interests and priorities precluded this.

122. *Idishe Shtime*, September 16, 1924.

123. Interview with the *Idishe Shtime*, June 9, 1926.

124. Israel Cohen ("A Visit to Kovno," *Jewish Chronicle*, April 16, 1926) writes: "The extent ... to which Hebrew is spoken, not only in the school but also in the street, at home, in sports societies, and at public meetings, is most impressive. Its prevalence may be the natural outcome of the tradition created by Abraham Mapu (born and died in Kovno), father of the modern Hebrew novel. But it possesses much greater significance as a testimony to the seriousness with which the great majority of Lithuanian Jews consider it their destiny to live in Eretz Israel."

125. The establishment of 64 Polish primary schools, with the endorsement of the Social Democrats' Minister of the Interior, triggered public demonstrations said to be organized by the Christian Democrats, and the introduction of an interpellation into the Seimas by the same party, in conjunction with the Nationalists, against the "Polonization" of the country. It subsequently became the basis of one of the popular slogans in support of the *coup d'etat* on December 17, 1926, i.e., that the Social-Democrat government was selling out Lithuania to "non-national" elements. (British Foreign Office document 12548-5888, London, 1926).

126. A *reali* school is one with a scientific orientation.

127. Arthur Barker (*The Times* of London, November, 23, 1927): "The difficulty of obtaining public servants with a sufficient Lithuanian educational background extends throughout every branch of state employment. The 'great patriots' come home from their offices to speak Russian or Polish to their wives and children. University lectures are written in German or Russian, translated into Lithuanian by an assistant, checked by another, looked over by the professor, and then recited from the manuscript. Technical terms have to be Lithuanized, but Lithuanian scholars differ as to how to do this." Nevertheless, the Jews of Lithuania were constantly accused of disinterest in the country's language and culture.

128. A representative example of (unsuccessful) government pressure and interference was its treatment of the Frankel leather works. This enterprise, established by the Frankel family of Siauliai before the Great War, had been one of Lithuanian's largest private concerns, with a headcount of approximately 1,000 manufacturing leather products, such as shoes.

   The Frankels returned to Lithuania in 1920 with £150,000 in capital and succeeded in rebuilding their empire. In the 1930s, the Lithuanian government approached the Frankels and protested that fully 50 percent of the company's work force was Jewish. Since Jews represented only some 7.6 percent of the population, officials argued, the proportion of Jewish employees in the Frankel enterprises should be no greater. The Frankels ignored the request; the government took no further action. In 1940, the New Lithuanian Communist government nationalized the factory along with all other private businesses.

129. Confidential British Foreign Office Report No. 371 9252, by Mr. Vaughan, dated January 30, 1923. See also Jacob Leschinsky, *The Economic Situation of the Jews of Lithuania*, 1919-1939 (Yiddish).

130. Consider the Frankel case (n. 5 above).

131. The limit was increased to 150 hectares in 1929.

132. In one sense, the reform failed: the government could not stanch the exodus from rural to urban areas. Thus the unskilled-labor market was soon flooded with former peasants who competed for jobs with the more highly paid Jewish and Polish workers. In the name of patriotism, the Lithuanian workers were given preference in government institutions.

133. Until the late nineteenth century, entire villages, chiefly in the Suwalki vicinity, had been populated by Jewish farmers, and many other villages had sizable Jewish populations. They were indistinguishable from non-Jewish Lithuanians in manner of life, attire, housing conditions, and love of the land, which they farmed from dawn to dusk.

By the turn of the century, however, very few such villages remained, nearly all the rural Jews having migrated to towns and cities. By the outbreak of the Second World War, only several hundred Jewish peasant families survived in various locations in Lithuania.

These properties were confiscated at the beginning of World War II. For example, the Kinderishki estate, belonging to the Goldberg family, and the Vesulava estate, belonging to the Dimenstein family (Kaunas vicinity) were expropriated by a priest named Volokurtis; the Frank estate, known as Naruikishki, was taken over by a minister named Karvialis.

134. Lithuania was the world's leading flax producer in the 1924-1939 period, during which time flax represented almost 30 percent of total agricultural exports.

135. *Zydu Koperatorius* (the Jewish cooperative journal).

136. Zvi Porat, "The Jewish Credit Cooperation in Lithuania," *Lita*, Vol. 2 (Hebrew).

137. Interview with Dr. Zabarsky in Tel Aviv, July 15, 1975. Zabarsky also told the author that he had published a report on this congress in *Zydu Koperatorius*, No. 7, June 16, 1922.

138. In the nineteenth century, well known antisemitic Lithuanian writers made several attempts to incite the population against the Jews. One such writer was Vincas Kudirka, editor of the newspaper *Varpas* and an admired and respected figure in Lithuanian society.

139. The British expressed this more delicately, insisting that the minorities "should recognize that they are a part of the State in which they live; they should cooperate fully with the State's requirements."

140. Reported in the daily newspaper *Idishe Shtime*.

141. Report of the British Board of Deputies, 1922.

142. *Idishe Shtime*, May 15, 1922.

143. In 1933, we find Prime Minister Jouzas Tubelis, President Smetonas' brother-in-law, supporting a resolution, at an official meeting of the Tautininkai (Nationalist Party), that would prohibit Jewish ownership, possession, purchase, and cultivation of land.

At one time, Chamberlain approved of population exchange agreements as a possible method of resolving the problems of the minorities. This was hardly an appropriate solution for Lithuania and its Jews, because Jews had lived in that country for centuries and had no country to which they might be "exchanged." (One possible destination, Palestine, was ruled out by the British themselves in their infamous White Paper.) Neither did the Lithuanian Jews wish to assimilate.

144. Smetona felt at that time that the Lithuanian leadership in the United States was prejudiced against and unfriendly towards Jews. He hoped to exercise a favorable influence on them.

145. Two Jews chosen by the Municipality of Kaunas – Reuben Rubinstein, editor of *Idishe Shtime*, and Jacob Goldberg, chairman of the Union of Jewish Voluntary Soldiers – ran for office but were not elected to the Seimas. Neither was any other minority delegate.

146. Although Siauliai had a Jewish deputy-mayor for twelve years (1924-1936), there were no Jews among the 150 municipal workers except for five doctors and engineers. Of 800 state employees who worked in the city, only eleven were Jews; six of these belonged to the 100-strong staff of the Department of Justice. In Vilkaviskis, where Jews accounted for 50 percent of the population, only one of the 110 government employees was Jewish. Of 19 municipal employees, however, seven were Jews.

   In 1936, the government carried 55,000 people on its payroll, of whom 33,000 worked in Kaunas alone. Of 800 persons employed by the Municipality of Kaunas, only nine were Jewish. None of the 25 employees of the government Bank in Panevezys was Jewish. Neither were Jews to be found among the 21 State judges and Justice Department officials.

   Three years after their graduation, 30 certified Jewish lawyers from Kaunas and the provinces protested to the Seimas that they had not succeeded in finding employment.

Notes to Chapter 6

147. Yad Vashem documents and statistics.

148. By then, the Hitler-Pilsudski pact of January 1934, had posed an additional threat to Lithuania and sowed fear among Polish Jews.

   Polish-Lithuanian relations were aggravated by the "postcard problem." A simple postcard, printed in Poland and circulated in the Polish, Lithuanian, French, and English languages, depicted Lithuania and part of eastern Prussia as belonging to the Republic of Poland. Acting Foreign Minister Bizauskas complained that this postcard was causing the government and people of Lithuania great apprehension and anxiety. Poland, for its part, asserted that the postcard had been printed by Germany in order to foment greater tension between the two countries, thus enabling it to expand its influence in both.

Latvia and Estonia took exception to the Baltic Union because of Lithuania's problems with Poland concerning Vilnius and with the Germans concerning Memel-Klaipeda.

Dr. Jacob Robinson represented the Lithuanian minorities at the Nationalities Congress in Geneva and was a member of the Geneva commission of the Treaty of Baltic Entente and Cooperation, fashioned by the individual countries' foreign ministers. Although Lithuania was Catholic and Latvia and Estonia Protestant, from 1934 on the three Baltic states considered the Union a shield against their powerful neighbors. After having concluded the treaty, they looked for salvation to the Western powers, especially Great Britain.

149. The British interest in Lithuania was both economic and political. Great Britain had been interested in the Baltic peoples and territories since the Crimean War of 1854-1856. A British colonel, Rowan Robinson, advised the new Lithuanian government on the borders and the neutral zone between Lithuania and Germany; the British were also the first to take steps toward recognition of the Lithuanian state. Another British colonel, B. B. Ward, had advised the Lithuanian government on the creation and organization of its army and its communication system.

The British had serious doubts about the possibility of securing complete and lasting independence for the Baltic states. For example, they rejected a proposal by the Baltic states that they join the British Empire.

150. An autonomous body established by the League of Nations in May 1927, to manage the affairs of Memel as an autonomous entity under Lithuanian sovereignty. The president of the Directory was appointed by the representative of the Lithuanian government in Memel-Klaipeda, who was alternately known as the governor of the district.

151. In the 1938-1940 period, the British and Americans differed in their assessments of the situation in Lithuania. British Ambassador Thomas Preston maintained that apart from the Jews, "the people in Eastern Europe prefer Berlin to Moscow, Hitler to Stalin, admittedly as the lesser of the two evils." Mr. Davis, the American Ambassador to the Soviet Union, visited Lithuania in December 1938, and reported "the general mood of the country to be pro-Soviet, in the belief that only the Soviet Union could help them against Poland and Germany."

152. On November 10, 1938, Lithuania was confronted by the problem of Jewish refugees who had been forced, under the most tragic circumstances, to cross the Lithuanian-German frontier near Augustowo after Kristallnacht. The British Consulate informed London that Lithuania had promptly accepted this first group of refugees for humanitarian reasons. However, the

Lithuanian authorities refused to give the refugees from Klaipeda trading licenses, even when they had obtained concessions from British agencies. Narkaitis, the minister of commerce, explained that "The Jews control too much of [our] trade as it is."

The British had, in fact, "dropped a hint" to the Lithuanian government on the evils of antisemitism. The Consulate reported "a definite movement, aided and abetted by the government, to oust the Jews from the import trade (the export trade is already practically state controlled) and to replace them by Lithuanians."

The Germans, on the other hand, used only Lithuanians or Germans as agents. In such a situation, with at least fifty percent of the agents of British exporters being mostly old established Jewish firms, there was little need to "emphasize the disadvantages, by comparison with the agents of German firms, with which these people [the Jews] will meet in future" in their efforts to sell British goods.

Thomas Preston, the British Ambassador to Lithuania, reported to London that "Since antisemitism was likely to grow rather than to diminish in a government with very strong Christian-Democratic influence, this state of affairs was likely, in the near future, to have a disastrous effect on British trade interests". When war broke out, Jewish refugees continued to flood into Lithuania – mostly from Poland but also from Germany, Austria, Bohemia, Moravia, and other German-occupied territories – until their numbers approached 100,000. This made Lithuania the center of the Eastern European relief program.

In November 1940, there were 3,000 refugee rabbis and students in Lithuania, including the entire student body and staff of several of Poland's most renowned yeshivot, such as Mir, Keltz, Kamenetz, and Radom. The Soviets classified all yeshiva students as "clergy" and "anti-Communists." This subjected them to strict supervision including period disclosure of their sources of income. For the time being, they were tolerated, in the hope that they would change their manner of life or leave.

153. Reporting to the British Foreign Office, Ambassador Preston wrote: "What I am gravely concerned about is the political dangers arising from misunderstanding between the Great Powers over the Jewish question, for instance resulting in Germany and Great Britain finding themselves in the ring with the Jew in the booking office."

The Foreign Office reacted strongly to this report and directed Preston to persuade "his Lithuanian friends" to be less unreasonable than they appeared to be about Jewish support of Bolshevism. "Reasonable Lithuanians must know that this is nonsense and it is not a valid reason for selling themselves and their country to Hitler, and if you can convince them of this, you will have earned our gratitude as well as theirs – for, as you say, this question is bound to affect Anglo-Lithuanian relations one way or the other. As our attitude cannot change fundamentally, we must do what we can to keep theirs in harmony with it. Nor can I agree that the Jews, as you suggested, have nothing to lose by a war which might Sovietize all Europe. The Jews as a whole are far too fond of making money to be pro-Bolshevik and want nothing but the survival of the democratic regimes, under which they can pursue this end unmolested."

154. Ambassador Preston described the conduct of the Red army in Lithuania of which he was a witness, as "exemplary."

155. During the Soviet occupation, Sugihara Sempo, the Japanese Consul in Kaunas, issued a great number of transit visas to Jewish refugees, even after his government had instructed him to stop doing so. He was finally recalled, but his efforts enabled many Jews to flee to Shanghai and Kobi. Yad Vashem recognized S. Sugihara as a Righteous Gentile, the only Japanese citizen to be so honored. On November 28, 1993, in his home town of Yaotsu, near Nagoya, the Japanese government and the municipality dedicated a park in his honor. It is named the Hill of Humanity, the Sugihara Memorial Museum.

The British Consulate in Lithuania also helped Jewish refugees from Austria, Czechoslovakia, and Memelland in their quest for refuge – provided that the destination they sought was not Palestine.

After much pleading and with great difficulty, R. Isaac Halevi Herzog, Chief Rabbi of Palestine, obtained a considerable number of immigration certificates from the British High Commissioner and reserved them for the heads and students of Lithuanian and Polish yeshivot. This offer, forwarded to a rabbinical luminary in Vilna, was politely rejected so as not to expose the yeshiva students to the potentially detrimental influence of the predominantly secular Jewish society and leadership in Palestine.

156. On July 25, 1940, the Soviets installed a People's government, including an 85-member assembly (21 representatives of the workers, 25 of the peasants, 29 of the intellectuals, 7 of the "handworkers" [skilled labor], and three of the military.) Seventy-seven of the assembly members were men; eight were women. Forty-nine, all Communists, had just been released from prison. By nationality, there were 73 Lithuanians, five Jews, three Poles, two Belorussians, one Russian, and one Lett. The Jews were Didzulis-Grosman of Kaunas, Demba Isaac of Panevezys, Friedman-Latvis Berelis of Vilnius, Hatzkelewitz Noach of Alytus, and Vinitzkis Jankel of Kedainai and Kaunas.

157. The Jews of Lithuania received no special privileges during these confiscations. All Jewish-owned land passed into non-Jewish hands. When

the government reallocated farmland later in 1940, Jews were not among the recipients.

158. The hard core of the Lithuanian Jewish Communist Party embraced no more than 0.4 percent of the total Jewish population of Lithuania.

159. Young Jews took advantage of the new opportunities but did not join the Party. Many expressed their aversion to Communism.

160. Zimanas, a controversial figure, became the famous Commander Jurgis during the Second World War. Parachuted into the Lithuanian forests, he organized the most important forest partisan groups in Lithuania and Belorussia. His activities were always shrouded in secrecy and mystery. Defending his attitude and behavior towards Jews after the war, he explained to a friend: "I was accused of not enlisting Jewish families in the fighting ranks of the partisans. I returned to Lithuania to fight the Germans. This was my duty and my responsibility. I was sent to do a job. I took in Jews who were ready to do battle as well as Lithuanians, Poles, or White Russians. It made no difference to me. I came to fight the Germans, not to save Jews. By fighting the Nazis, we saved everybody."

161. Father Prunski based his account and interpretation of the war period in Lithuania, written in 1979 in Chicago, on anti-Jewish Nazi publications and propaganda dating from 1942-1943, emphasizing Jewish involvement in the deportation of Lithuanians to Siberia by the Soviets. Prunski "omitted to mention that as a proportion of the general population, more Jews were deported than non-Jews: 3 as against 1 percent."

Notes to Chapter 7

162. *Documents Accuse*, pp. 27-43, 55-59, and 124-125.

163. Chase, Thomas George, *The Story of Lithuania*, 304.

164. The Germans, including the Nazis, were very eager to take part in activities related to Jews. This not only kept them away from the Eastern front, but also gave them an opportunity to loot, murder Jews, and satisfy their perverse needs and urges.

165. Interview with Dr. Leib Garfunkel, Tel Aviv, July 4, 1975.

166. In July and August of 1941, Jews in some fifty villages and townlets displayed individual acts of resistance. Many perished, but some survived and escaped to the larger Jewish centers.

167. The provisional government approved and authorized Bobelis's plan for the construction of a concentration camp. The following officials affixed their signatures: Antanas Svilpa, Deputy Minister for the Municipal Economy;

acting Prime Minister Abrazevicius-Brazaitis; and Jonas Svelnikas, Manager of Cabinet Affairs. The provisional government used its six-week tenure to rage against its Jewish citizens in the press and radio that it now controlled. This created the atmosphere and provided the license for the Lithuanian populace to take the law into its own hands and punish the Jews as they saw fit. Suddenly the Jews in Lithuania were more afraid of their Lithuanian neighbors than of the advancing Wehrmacht.

168. Many Latvians had enlisted in the Waffen SS, and units of Latvian Siaulai called *Aizsargai*, as did smaller numbers of Estonians, in units named Hiwis or Hilfswillige, i.e., volunteer groups, as well as the extreme nationalists.

169. The Germans had a plan for postwar Lithuania: 85 percent of Lithuanians were to be exiled to make room for German settlers. According to the Lithuanian underground press, Germans from the bombed-out cities of Cologne, Bremen, and from other areas, were being brought en masse to settle in Lithuania.

170. Law Reports of Trials of War Criminals, London, 1948.

171. In accordance with a secret plan of which the Lithuanians knew nothing, the Germans were stripping Lithuania of its resources and sending to Germany whatever they needed for their own use, thereby destroying the country's agriculture, industry, and forests. In addition, peasants were required to "donate" 15 days each month for the benefit of the German authorities. Lithuanian economists estimated that the economic damage caused by the Germans during their three years of rule would take more than ten years to repair.

172. Three ministers in the provisional government joined Kubiliunas' council, which appointed eight councilors as department heads (economy, agriculture, finance, education, justice, communication, labor, and social security). These officials included Jouzas Matulionis and Vitkus-Balys.

173. The Germans met their needs by other means, initially refraining from use of force against a "fellow Aryan-Christian country."

174. "It must be added that the Lithuanians did not consider all cooperation with the Germans as infamous or treasonable; a minimum cooperation with the Germans was even regarded by the strong nationalistic Lithuanian as useful for the purpose of keeping and supporting the German armies fighting Soviet Russia. Thus, neither the insurrectionists of 1941, the local administration officials during the German occupation, nor Lithuanian soldiers in German uniform were regarded as collaborationist" (historian Vytautas Vardys, in *Litaunus* a quarterly journal, issue of November 24, 1954). On April 5, 1943, the Germans called a national conference to enlist Lithuanian support for the mobilization of volunteers. Among the many Lithuanian leaders invited

were some 20 priests and bishops. At the end of this conference, after some differences of opinion, a proclamation was issued urging the Lithuanian people to support the Germans at their time of need. Prof. Mykolas Birziska, rector of the University of Vilnius, was especially influential. Mykolas later claimed that the Germans had threatened to kill all the Lithuanian intelligentsia should they not sign. No documentation in support of this claim has been found.

175. Jacob Goldberg, his former comrade-in-arms in the Lithuanian army, quoted in *Lita*, Vol. 4. Matulionis was described as being a very devout Catholic.

176. The extent to which the Lithuanian people obeyed the instructions and advice of the underground press, and of their priests in every village and city, is remarkable.

177. Report by Karl Jaeger in *Nuremberger Nachrichten*, February, 1950.

178. German documents discovered in Riga, No. 354.

179. International Military Tribunal, *Proceedings of the Nuremberg Trials*, Vol. IV.

180. International Military Tribunal, *Proceedings of the Nuremberg Trials*, Trials of Major War Criminals, 1138.

181. Garfunkel, Leib, *Lita*, Vol. IV.

182. Eventually the non-Jewish population also began to feel the iron fist of the Germans. Some Gentile Lithuanians, including clergymen who were subjected to German persecution, were deported to slave labor camps for allegedly helping the anti-German partisans. An entire village, Pirciupiai, was burned to the ground together with most of its population.

   As the tide of battle turned against Germany on the eastern, European, and North African fronts, the Germans sought additional workers as well as military manpower from the supposedly friendly Baltic peoples. Thus, Alfred Rosenberg, Reich Minister for the occupied territories, issued a flurry of favorable decrees and new promises for the future. In general, the Lithuanians spurned these enticements. Many fled to the forests to join the partisans; others sought refuge with relatives in outlying areas. Just the same, General Urbonas Paul Plechavicius managed to form 13 battalions of 750 men each, and organized 1,800 noncommissioned officers and 1,200 cadets in the military school at Marijampole. By early 1944, he had gathered 30,000 volunteers, and "some [others] had to be turned away." (T. G. Chase, *The Story of Lithuania*, 317).

183. The Jewish name for the location known as Ponary in Lithuanian.

184. Ehrenburg, Ilya, *Black Book*.

185. The Germans cloaked their operations in euphemistic terminology that, at first only the Nazis and their collaborators understood. Thus *"aktion"* referred to a mass killing or selection for slave labor. *Arbeit macht frei* – Labor Liberates – was the obscenity that greeted those deported to Auschwitz on their way to the gas chambers. The Nazi term for ghetto life was *"Geltlose wirtschaft"* – a moneyless economy.

186. As estimated by the ghetto Jewish committee.

187. Cited during the trials at the Nuremberg International Military Tribunal of 1945-46, and the Trial of Major German War Criminals. Jaeger's reports mentioned small numbers of non-Jewish victims of the executions and shootings at the Forts: Lithuanian Communists, Soviet citizens, Poles, and even a few Germans. The Lithuanian mercenaries, he remarked, seemed to have adapted themselves well to the Einsatzkommando work.

188. Lieutenant Zukas, Military Commander of the Rokishkis District, articulated the regime's attitude in his Order No. 5: "I wish to announce that all persons who refuse to use the Jews for labor, or who create favorable conditions for them, under which they may loaf and avoid work, will be punished as saboteurs of the state with full severity of the law, and will be recorded as supporters of Jews. The implementation of this Order will be supervised by the police, the auxiliary police, town and parish councils, state employees, and persons so instructed".

189. A favored repository of this loot was Alfred Rosenberg's "Institute for Research of the Jewish Problem" in Frankfurt am-Main.

190. As Jews were being transported from the ghettos to concentration camps for slave labor, many Lithuanians waited nearby with wheelbarrows and sacks to gather the last of the Jewish possessions left behind, which were then peddled openly in Lithuanian public markets.

191. One of those responsible for the killings in Ponary, including the murder of the Judenrat members, was Christian Hingst, District Commissioner for Vilnius, who was in close contact with the Einsatzkommando 9. The Germans chose Vilnius, as the capital of Lithuania and a city renowned for its culture, as the location of their Research Institute on Judaism and Bolshevism. The Institute was headed by a Lithuanian, Zankus Zabitis, and was supported by Mayor Dabulewitzius. In 1941, this institute published "reports" purporting to describe Jewish involvement in the Soviet Lithuanian government.

192. Dvorzecki, Dr. Meir, *Yerushalayim de-lita ba-meri u-va-sho'a* (Hebrew).

193. There were adult smugglers in the ghettos, including some who engaged in black marketeering and ran illegal restaurants that the Germans sometimes frequented. They were largely reponsible for the demoralization that

reversed collective efforts of the Jews of the ghettos to withstand their ordeal.

194. One of their duties was to scour the ghettos after their liquidation, because it was rumored that the Jews had buried valuables in the ghettos before transport. Thus, Lithuanians swarmed into the empty ghettos and probed the bloodstained soil for days, leaving unburied any human remains they encountered.

195. At this time, 6,000 Jews (including some from Kovno, Riga, Vienna, Hungary, Czechoslovakia, and Germany) remained in the Shavli ghetto. With the final liquidation, they were transferred to small concentration camps in Lithuania. There were also a number of converts and half-Jews, including the famous Professor Weil of Vienna, the son of a Jewish convert to Catholicism, who as a Catholic chose to commune with the Jews in order "to repent for Christian sins against Jews". During his stay in the ghetto, he coordinated cultural activities there.

196. Nishmi, Sara, *Hatsala be-Lita bi-shenot ha-kibush.*

197. Taagepera, Rein, *Lithuania, Latvia, and Estonia,* 1940-1980.

198. The Germans established military units composed of former Soviet Ukrainian prisoners who agreed to fight against the Red Army. These collaborators, known as *perekulshtzikii* – turncoats – served under their own or German officers. By the end of the war, nearly one million Slavs fought on the Germans' side, led by General Vlasov.

199. After the liberation, Petraitis, director of social assistance, refused to issue the few Jewish returnees with bread ration cards, arguing that since they had not registered before they left, it was against the law to register them now. That they had "left" in the course of Nazi expulsions was of no consequence to him.

200. In late 1944, a special commission was set up in Lithuania under Antanas Snieckus, Merchys Gedvila, Nicolas Bartasunas, Professor Antanas Purenas, and Engineer Jurginis, to investigate crimes committed on Lithuanian soil by Germans and Lithuanians. On the basis of the commission's findings, some of the victims' bodies were exhumed and reports were written on the murder and devastation committed during the German occupation. After the war, Attorney Jacob Robinson wrote: "Lithuanian Jews do not blame a whole people collectively for the guilt of many individuals. They and they alone are responsible for the crimes they committed. But the question remains: why so many, and why the attempts by others to defend and cover up these crimes?" In 1940, Jews accounted for 10 percent of the population of Lithuanian. In 1991, 0.16 percent of the country's population of 3,690,000 were Jewish – and not all of them were of Lithuanian origin.

Notes to Chapter 8

201. Stone, I.E. p. 9.

202. Few Lithuanians were prepared to offer their Jewish compatriots comfort and support. The names of several of these Righteous Gentiles are worthy of grateful recognition. They include:

    * Jouzas Pranas, a man who worked all his life among Jews, spoke Yiddish, greatly admired the rabbis and Talmudic scholars of his native Kaunas, and, with the help of a few friends, smuggled 30 kilos of flour into the ghetto so the Jews might bake *matsa* for their first Passover in the ghetto.

    * Bronius Gotautas, a monk who risked his life to help Jews and was ashamed of the crimes committed by his Lithuanian faithful. It was his wish to inform the world that there were decent Lithuanians, too.

    * Jouzas Striaipis of Sarneliai, who, together with his familiy and friends, were instrumental in concealing and caring for nearly 40 Jews, among them women and children, all of whom survived.

    * Dr. Helena Kutergienie, whose son Victoras and family assisted Jews, denounced the Lithuanian intelligentsia, and condemned the blind rage and hatred displayed by her countrymen against the Jews after having been incited to satisfy their lowest instincts.

    * The most famous of these Lithuanian Righteous Gentiles was Onna Shumaite, librarian at the University of Vilna. She not only risked her own life but insisted that her family, friends and professors at the University support her clandestine activity. From those who were afraid to play an active role in her efforts, she demanded money to finance her humanitarian cause.

    * Sophia Binkienie, wife of poet and writer Kazys Binkis, and family, who took great risks to help Jews. She published a book of documents called *Ir be ginklo kariai* (Soldiers without Arms) on the Righteous Gentiles in Lithuania. It is a thin volume containing few names, for there were not many to be found.

203. Brizgys, Bishop V., *The Catholic Church in Lithuania*, Chicago, 1977.

BIBLIOGRAPHY

Alekna, Antanas. *Lietuvos Istorija.* Kaunas, 1931.

Anderson, Edward. *Towards the Baltic Union 1927-1934.* London, 1967.

Augustinas, Vytautas. *Our Country Lithuania.* New York, 1951.

Barnett, Clifford R. *Poland.* New Haven, 1958.

Baron, Salo. *Russian Jews under the Tsars.* New York, 1964.

Basanavicius, Jonas, *Declaration of Independence.* Vilna, 1926.

Belinsky, Michael. *The History of Lithuania.* Wilno, 1912.

Berger, Joseph. *The National Autonomy in Lithuania 1919-1939.* New York, 1951

Bershadsky, Sergei. *King Vytautas' Charter.* St. Petersburg, 1882.

_____. *Litovsky Yevrei.* Moscow, 1888.

Bilmanis, Alfred. *The Baltic.* Washington, 1945.

Block, Eliyahu Meir Rabbi. *Agudath Israel.* Tel Aviv, 1952.

Brutzkus, Julius. *Litauen.* Berlin, 1932.

Bublys, Vladas. *Agricultural Production Cooperatives in Independent Lithuania* London, 1974.

Budrys, Jonas. *The Klaipeda Problem.* Chicago, 1960.

Butenas, Julius. *The Life and Work of Mycolas Slezevicius.* Chicago, 1954.

Byalistotzky, Samuel Dr. *The Torah Center.* Tel Aviv, 1952.

Carlebach, Alexander. *A German Rabbi Goes East.* London, 1961.

Carr, Edward Hallet. *The Twenty-Year Crisis 1919-1939.* London, 1968.

Cassells, H. M. *Economy and Industrial Conditions in Lithuania*. London, 1924.

Cecil, Robert Viscount. *A Great Experiment*. London, 1941.

Chase, Thomas. *The History of Lithuania*. New York, 1946.

Chambron, H. *Lithuania at the Peace Conference*. Paris, 1931.

Cohen, Israel. *Vilna*. Philadelphia, 1943.

Dallin, Alexander. *German Rule in Russia 1941-1945*. New York, London, 1960.

Dinnur, Ben Zion. *Be-'olam she-shaqa*, 1884-1914. Jerusalem, 1958.

Documents Accuse, (Ed.) Rozauskas. Vilnius, 1970.

Documents of the British Public Record Office on the Baltic and Lithuania 1919-1940s. London, 1985.

Documents on German Foreign Policy, 1918-1945. Washington, D.C., 1937-1948.

Dubnow, Simon. *Pinqas ha-medina*. Berlin, 1925.

_____. History of the Jews of Poland and Lithuania. St. Petersburg, 1908.

Dworzecki, Meir. *Jerusalem of Lithuania in the Holocaust*. Tel Aviv, 1951.

Encyclopaedia Judaica. Jerusalem, New York, 1972.

Finkelstein, Louis. *The Jews, Their History, Culture and Religion*. New York, 1949.

Flecher, James. *The History of Poland*. New York, 1985.

Frumkin, Joseph. *Pages of History of Russian Jewry, Recollections and Documentary Material*. London, 1966.

Garfunkel, Leib, *The Jewish National Autonomy*. Kaunas, 1920.

_____. *The Jews in the Lithuanian Seimas*. Tel Aviv, 1952.

_____. *The Destruction of Jewish Kovno*. Jerusalem, 1959.

Gerutis, Alberto (ed). *700 Years Lithuania*. New York, 1969.

Gildenweiser, Alexis. *The Legal Status of the Jews in Russia*. London, 1966.

Goldberg, Hillel. *The Living Message of the Mussar Movement*. Brooklyn, 1989.

Gringaus, Samuel. *The Lithuanian Jews 1919-1926*. New York, 1969.

Grinius, Kazys, *Memories and Thoughts*. Germany, 1947.

Gustainis, Valentine. *Lithuania, The First Twenty Years*. Chicago, 1939.

Halecki, Oskar. *The History of the Jagiellonian Union*. Warsaw, 1920.

_____. *History of Poland*. London, 1968.

Harrison, Ernest John. *Lithuania Past and Present*. New York, 1952.

Hatton, Reginal Marie. *The Vasas of Sweden*. London, 1974.

Hertzberg, Arthur (ed.). *The Zionist Idea*. New York, 1960.

Hilberg, Raul. *The Destruction of European Jews*. Chicago, 1961.

Holzberg, Isaac Rafael. *The Yavne Stream.* Tel Aviv, 1952.

_____. *The Controversy in the Seimas Jewish Faction.* Jerusalem, 1979.

Huxley, James. *Race in Europe.* Oxford, 1939.

ICA Records. *Social Studies 1904-1913 in St. Petersburg.* New York, 1949.

Idishe Shtime. Kaunas, 1921-1940.

Ivinskis, Zenonas. *Geshichte Des Bauerstandes in Litauen.* Germany, 1933.

_____. *Lithuania During the War.* New York, 1984.

Janulaitis, Augustinas. *Zydai Lietuvoje.* Kaunas, 1928.

Jerushalmi, Abraham. *Source Material for Jewish Education in Lithuania.* Kaunas, 1932.

Jerushalmi, Eliezer. *The Shavli Ghetto Diary, 1941-1944.* Jerusalem, 1958.

Jewish Chronicle, 1920-1940. London, 1970.

Jewish Coopertives in Lithuania, Zydu Koperatorius. Kaunas, 1921-1936.

Jungtino, Ishdalinimo Komitetu. *J.D.C. Papers. Refugees in Lithuania 1900-1940.* New York, 1987.

Jurgela, Constantine. *History of the Lithuanian Nation.* Washington, D.C., 1948.

Kairys St., *"Victoras": Freedom* (Lithuanian Socialist Democratic Party). Kaunas, 1931.

Kapsukas, Victoras. *Burzuazine Lietuva.* Vilnius, 1961.

Kazenelenboigen, Uriah. *Etnografishe un historishe grenetzen fun Lite.* Tel Aviv, 1952.

Kazlauskas, B. *L'Entente Baltique.* Paris, 1939.

Kieval, Hillel. *The Modern Manifestation of the Blood Libel.* New York, 1989.

Klausner, Israel. *The History of the Jews of Lithuania.* Tel Aviv, 1959.

Klausner, Joseph. *The Haskalah Movement in Lithuania.* Jerusalem, 1959.

_____. *Hibat tsiyon be-Lita.* Jerusalem, 1958.

Klimas, Petras. *Medieval Lithuania.* New York, 1945.

Laserson, Max. *The Minority Rights in the Baltic Countries.* Latvia, 1931.

Leschinsky, Jacob. *Di ekonomishe lage fun di idn in Lite.* New York, 1951.

_____. *Di katastrofishe lage fun idn in mizrakh und mitl Eyropa.* New York, 1957.

Levin, Dov. *They Fought Back: Lithuanian's Jewry Armed Resistance 1941-1945.* Jerusalem, 1974.

_____. *Articles and Papers on the Soviet Rule in Lithuania.* Jerusalem, 1975.

_____. *The Sovietization of Lithuania.* Jerusalem, 1991.

Levenstein, Lazar. *Jews in the Lithuanian Municipalities.* New York, 1952.

Lietuvos, Aidas. Government News. Kaunas, 1924-1934.

Lietuvos, Statistikos Metrastis. Kaunas, 1923-1939.

_____. *Enciklopedija: "Genocidas."* Vol. VII. Boston, 1968.

_____. *The Jews of Lithuania.* Vol. XXXV. Boston, 1968.

Linde, G. *Die Deutsche Politic im Ersten Weltkrieg.* Wiesbaden, 1965.

Lipetz, Dov. *The Hebrew Movement and Education in Independent Lithuania.* Tel Aviv, 1972.

Lipman, David. *Lita-Zamut 1400-1915.* New York, 1934.

_____. *The History of the Jews of Kovno and Slobodka.* New York, 1934.

Lita. (Ed.) Mendel Sudarsky. New York, 1951.

_____. Chaim Leikowitz. Tel Aviv, 1965.

Lubovsky, B. *The Life of Casimir Jagiello,* Moscow, 1911.

Ludendorff, Erich. *Ludendorff's Own Story.* New York, 1919.

Macartney, C. A., *National States and National Minorities.* London, 1934.

Macovsky, Abraham. *Di idishe fraktsie in zveytn litvish seym.* Kaunas, 1928.

Marcus, Jacob R. *The Jew in the Medieval World.* Cincinnati, 1938.

Margulies, M. *Die Judische Minderheiten.* Munchen, 1928.

Mark, Yudl. *The Yiddish Movement and Education in Independent Lithuania.* Tel Aviv, 1959.

Merkelis, Alexander. *Antanas Sometona.* New York, 1964.

Misiunas, Romuald J. *Fascist Tendencies in Lithuania.* New York London, 1972.

_____. *The Baltic States 1940-1980.* London, 1983.

Narbutas, Theodore. *The Ancient History of the Lithuanian People.* Wilno, 1881.

Niessel, A. *L'Evacuation des Pays Baltiques par les Alemands.* Paris, 1935.

Nishmit, Sara. *Rescue Activities During the Nazi Occupation of Lithuania: 1941-1944.* Jerusalem, 1974.

Norem, Owen J. *Timeless Lithuania.* Cleveland, Ohio, 1944.

Okinshewitch, L. B. *The Law of the Grand Duchy of Lithuania.* New York, 1953.

Pinson, Koppel (ed.) *Nationalism and History,* subtitled *S. Dubnow Letters on Old and New Judaism.* Philadelphia, 1961.

Plieg, Ernest Albrecht. *Das Memelland 1922-1938.* Wurzburg, 1962.

Pocius, Jonas. *Education, Science and Culture.* Vilnius, 1971.

Preston, Thomas. *Before the Curtain.* London, 1950.

Prochaska, A. *The Life of Vitold*. Warsaw 1965.

Rand, V. *The Smaller Nations in the World Economic Life*. London, 1944.

Rauch, Von George. *History of the Baltic States*. London, 1974.

Reddaway, William F. *History of Poland*. Cambridge, 1950.

Reisen, Joseph. *Jews in Lithuanian Agriculture*. Kaunas, 1939.

Reisen, Zalman. *Records of the History of Vilna in the Years of War*. Vilna, 1922.

Robinson, Jacob. *Were the Minorities Treaties a Failure?* New York, 1942.

_____. *Di idishe fraksie (Lite)*. New York, 1952.

Rosenbaum, Simon. *The Question of the Jews in Lithuania*. Kaunas, 1929.

Rubinstein, Benzion. *Di idn in altn litvishen kenigreykh*. New York, 1913.

Saboliunas, Leonas. *Lithuania in Crisis: Nationalism to Communism 1939-1941*. London, 1972.

Schram, Stuart. *The Emergence of Nationalism in the Baltic States*. New York, 1952.

Senn, Alfred E. *The Emergence of Modern Lithuania*. New York, 1959.

Shatzki, Isaac. *Kultur geshikhte fun der haskala in Lite*. Buenos Aires, 1951.

Sliupas, Jonas. *The Role of the Lower Gentry in Lithuania, 1569-1795*. Chicago, 1969.

Sokolov, Nachum. *History of Zionism*. Philadelphia, 1959.

Spekke, A. *The Ancient Amber Routes*. Stockholm, 1957.

Stein, Luis. *The Expulsion of the Jews in the Great War*. Baltimore, 1944.

_____. *The Balfour Declaration*. New York, 1961.

Stromas, Alexander. *Political and Legal Aspects of the Soviet Occupation*. Salford, 1983.

Sudarsky, Mendel. *Idn in der umophengiker Lite*. New York, 1952.

Taagepera, Rein. *Lithuania, Latvia, Estonia 1940-1980 – Similarities and Differences*. Irvine, 1983.

Tarulis, Albert. *Soviet Policy toward the Baltic States 1918-1940*. Indiana, 1959.

Tevynu Balsas. *Kaunas*, 1926-1939.

The Times. London, 1920-1939.

Thomson, Margaret Regina. *The Jews and the Minority Treaties*. Washington, D.C., 1966.

Trevor-Roper, H. R. *The Last Days of Hitler*. London, 1947.

Trotsky, Ilya. *Jewish Institutions of Social Welfare and Mutual Assistance*. New York, 1966.

Valstybes, Zinios and Vyriaustybes, Zinos, *Government News*. Kaunas, 1919-1926.

Vardys, Stanley. *Portrait of a Nation 1940-1965*. New York, 1965.

Vileisis, Petras, *Lithuanian Civilization and Views*. Chicago, 1961.

Wiskerman, Elizabeth. *Undeclared War*. London, 1946.

Woodward and Bulter, *British Foreign Policy First Series*. London, 1919-1939.

Yahadut Lita, 4 Volumes, Tel Aviv, 1967. (The editors include Zvi Barak, Leib Garfunkel, Joseph Gar, Meir Jelin, David Israeli, Joseph Lavi, Dov Levin, Mordechai Karnovsky, and Jacob Robinson.)

YIVO, Records of the Late Middle Ages in Lithuania. New York, 1980.

Zechlin, Egmont. *Die Deutsche Politik und die Juden in Ersten Weltkrieg*. Göttingen, 1969.

INDEX

*Stylized version of the Lithuanian crest "Vytis" (The Chase),
found on coins of the Vytautas period*

Made in United States
North Haven, CT
29 August 2024

56702127R00228